MY LIFE AS A SPY

INVESTIGATIONS IN A SECRET POLICE FILE

Katherine Verdery

Duke University Press · Durham and London · 2018

Library of Congress Cataloging-in-Publication Data
Names: Verdery, Katherine, [date] author.
Title: My life as a spy : investigations in a secret police file /
Katherine Verdery.
Description: Durham : Duke University Press, 2018. | Includes
bibliographical references and index.
Identifiers: LCCN 2017047454 (print)
LCCN 2017052453 (ebook)
ISBN 9780822371908 (ebook)
ISBN 9780822370666 (hardcover : alk. paper)
ISBN 9780822370819 (pbk. : alk. paper)
Subjects: LCSH: Verdery, Katherine, [date] | Cold War—Personal
narratives. | Romania. Securitatea—History—Sources. | Secret
service—Romania—History—20th century—Sources. | Romania—
Politics and government—20th century—Sources.
Classification: LCC HV8241.8.A45 (ebook) |
LCC HV8241.8.A45 V47 2018 (print) |
DDC 949.803092 [B]—dc23
LC record available at https://lccn.loc.gov/2017047454

Frontispiece: The anthropologist in the field, 1993. Author's photo.
Cover art: Surveillance photo of "VERA" in her hotel room, 1985.
Courtesy of the Archive of the Consiliul Naţional pentru Studierea
Arhivelor Securităţii, Fond Informativ.

In memory of four beloved friends
and great anthropologists:

Gloria Jean Davis
Ernestine Friedl
Sidney W. Mintz
G. William Skinner

In recent years, Iași has received ever more frequent visits by certain American grantees and doctoral students, for the purpose of specialization and documentation. Under this cover they had the goal of collecting information and data not intended for publicity, or of a secret character, from the socio-political domains of the Romanian S[ocialist] R[epublic]. In their activities they were supported directly by cadres and agents of the U.S. Embassy in Bucharest who function in R.S. Romania under diplomatic cover.

—ROMANIAN SECRET POLICE FILE ON U.S. RESEARCHERS

Unimaginable! I knew that I was followed on the street, that the telephone was bugged, correspondence opened, any word in public recorded by someone or other, but I did not realize the extent, diversity, complexity, the number of officers, of informers, of technical means, and the gigantic amount of work performed by this unseen army that worked for 28 years in the underground of conspiracy. Only the hand of a Dostoevsky could describe these subterranean people . . . moles, hidden in our houses, whom we could hear gnawing on our tranquility but could not see.

—WRITER BUJOR NEDELCOVICI ON READING
HIS SECRET POLICE FILE

CONTENTS

PREFACE

There's nothing like reading your secret police file to make you wonder who you really are. Page after page, all your activities, all your motives, are subjected to a reading from an alien position embodied in a logic different from anything you recognize. Events you remember as significant might appear without comment, while others you thought unimportant burgeon into grounds for your expulsion from the country.

Although questions of identity may trouble any researcher doing fieldwork, they are unavoidable for those working under surveillance. This is especially true in the Cold War context, and most especially when a change in that context releases the surveillance files into their targets' hands. I had gone to Romania's Transylvanian region in 1973, during the rule of communist dictator Nicolae Ceauşescu, to conduct anthropological research on village life; I returned for further study several times in the 1970s and 1980s, totaling over three years. Then, several decades later, I discovered that Romania's secret police, the Securitate, had kept an enormous surveillance file on me: 2,781 pages. Reading it, I learned that I was "actually" a spy, a CIA agent, a Hungarian agitator, a friend of dissidents: in short, an enemy of Romania. As I read evidence of Securitate officers' view of me, I came to question my work, my intentions, and my very identity. I found in those pages a whole invisible world of events, relations, plans, and interpretations of which I had been largely unaware. They made me reconsider that entire period of my life, along with the many "selves" that emerged from it. Furthermore, the file made me contemplate what it means to be suspected of spying and to what extent ethnography, the research practice of anthropologists, necessarily makes one a kind of spy.

Discovering what it has meant to live under a rule of secrecy when one had thought oneself transparent can be disorienting and upsetting. This is the story I tell here. The book aims to create a feeling for what it was like to live as a guest in one of the most repressive countries of the Eastern bloc, as well as to show how the global superpower conflict was refracted in the experiences of a young woman trying to learn about life there. I use field notes, journal entries, and secret police reports to tell about being a researcher in Romania during the Cold War, with reference to the invisible secret police. Organized by the chronology of the research (which extended to conversations with police and informers up to 2016), this volume foregrounds the voices and work practices of the Securitate officers who were my constant hidden companions and of the informers who assisted them.

The book is a story of the effects of being under surveillance, an experience becoming familiar, albeit in different forms, to everyone. We are all under surveillance now, but most of us have scarcely any idea what that really means. What does it feel like to be spied upon, on the suspicion that you yourself are some kind of spy or traitor? What is it to be enveloped in secrets you find out about long after the fact—secrets that include the names of friends who reported on you to the secret police and the actions those police took to interfere in your life? What is the effect of this experience, once its extent becomes known, on your identity and the relationships of trust that you thought you had built? It is my hope that this book will render visible a certain set of surveillance practices and their effects, in a world in which new forms of surveillance proliferate every day.

A NOTE ON FONTS, PSEUDONYMS, AND PRONUNCIATION

This is a polyphonic work, incorporating the voices of Securitate officers and their informers, my field notes and field index written at the time of my various research stays in Romania, letters I wrote home, people I interviewed for this book after 2008, and my ruminations on this material as I read it in the present. To assist the reader, I have reduced the many voices to three different fonts for the main categories of participants:

1. my narrative voice in the present;

2. *letters sent from the field as well as my field index or field notes written at the time of my research trips to Romania, 1973–2016;*

3. the reports and notes of Securitate officers from the file located in the archive at CNSAS.

In addition, I adopt the following conventions concerning names. In the files, the names or pseudonyms of the persons being followed, and often of those they interact with, usually appear in quotation marks and often in capital letters (e.g., "VERA," "VANESSA"), and I will follow that practice. Likewise, officers invariably put the pseudonyms of informers in quotation marks (e.g., "Ovidiu"). This is so even when it is in fact the person's real name that is used, as sometimes happened. Although officers sometimes also write informers' names in capitals, I do not do so here. When I have interviewed someone who appears in the file as an informer, in an effort to protect these people I create my own pseudonym rather than using that of the officers. I also use pseudonyms (or in some cases simple initials) for some of my interviewees, indicated by an asterisk before the first use of the name. Names that do not appear in capitals, with quotation marks, or with an asterisk are the real names of the persons in question (e.g., David Prodan); those still alive have agreed to this. I have not distinguished my own redactions from those of the archive. Finally, when I am reporting a conversation with someone, I often put my own questions in parentheses.

In my translations from the Securitate file, I have attempted to preserve something of the linguistic character of the originals, with formulaic phrases, an eccentric "lofty" style, use of passive constructions, and inversion of names (often using all names rather than just first or last—VERDERY KATHERINE MAUREEN instead of Katherine Verdery). I have also preserved spelling errors. When fidelity to the original creates excessive awkwardness in English—especially in the use of passives and noun clusters—I have preferred clarity. I rarely include underlining that was added by officers other than the one who drew up the document (usually his superior officers or the archivist). Sometimes I provide the notes of the officers, labeled "N.O." for "Note of the [Case] Officer" and "N.S." for "Note of the Superior Officer." Finally, I use the Romanian (European) style for dates (day, month, year) rather than the U.S. style. Hence, September 23, 1979, is 23.09.79. These documents contain many more markings than I have reproduced (registration number of the document, the number of copies, the typist's initials, etc.). To protect both my own privacy and that of others mentioned in the files, I do not indicate the file numbers in the CNSAS archive from which quotations come, although qualified researchers can discover them.

Except for the vowels â, ă, and î, Romanian is generally pronounced like Italian. Front vowels soften c and g (to č and dj); hard c or g before front vowels is spelled ch or gh; ş is sh, ţ is ts. To make the text more accessible, here are phonetic equivalents of some frequently used personal and place names:

Cluj=Kloozh
Cugir=Koo JEER
Geoagiu=jo AH joo
Hunedoara=hoo neh DWA ra
Iaşi=Yahsh
Moaşa=MWA sha
Moşu=MO shu
Orăştie=aw rush TEE yeh
Securitate=seh koo ree TAH tay
Vlaicu=VLY koo (vly—rhymes with fly)

ACKNOWLEDGMENTS

This book emerged gradually from hundreds of conversations; I can acknowledge only some of them here. First of all, Phyllis Mack read the manuscript multiple times and put up with interminable discussions about it over the six years of its gestation. Heartfelt thanks for her advice, forbearance, and encouragement. Janet Carsten, Silvia Colfescu, Elizabeth Dunn, Gillian Feeley-Harnik, Saygun Gökarıksel, Bruce Grant, William Kelly, Gail Kligman, Douglas Rogers, Anikó Szűcs, and Cristina Vatulescu did me the great favor of reading the entire manuscript in one or another of its many drafts and offering comments, objections, and reassurance. Patrick Alexander, Alvia Golden, Timothy Little, Victoria Mack, Ioana Macrea-Toma, and Lisa Rimbach likewise provided helpful comments on parts of it. For stimulating conversation I also thank Gabriel Andreescu, Sorin Antohi, Liviu Chelcea, Vincent Crapanzano, Irina Grudzinska-Gross, Puiu Lățea, Leith Mullings, Chris Myers, Maya Nadkarni, Alec Niculescu, Andrei Pleșu, Aurel Rădușiu, Zoltán Rostás, Martha Sandweiss, and Liviu Ursuțiu, as well as audiences at Grinnell College, New York University Department of Music, Swarthmore College, and the University of Michigan (Department of Anthropology and the Center for Russian, East European, and Eurasian Research).

Dr. Florica Dobre of the National Council for the Study of the Securitate Archives (CNSAS) in Bucharest, Romania, is the book's midwife. It was she who urged me to petition for access to my Securitate file; in addition, she gave me a great deal of help with the documents in it and recommended additional sources that proved very useful. Other colleagues at the CNSAS also provided extensive assistance, most especially Virgiliu Țârău and Cristina Anisescu, along with Liviu Burlacu, Silviu Moldovan, and the ever-obliging staff of the reading room, as well as CNSAS directors Gheorghe Onişoru, Claudiu Secaşiu, and Dragoş Petrescu. My thanks to them all.

Fellowships at the Davis Center for Historical Studies, Princeton University (2010), and the Bogliasco Foundation Ligurian Study Center, Bogliasco, Italy (2015), provided collegial environments for my research and writing, and funds from the National Council for Eurasian and East European Research (2012–13) and the CUNY Graduate Center enabled me to travel to Romania. The customary disclaimers apply.

At Duke University Press, I am grateful for the warm encouragement of Ken Wissoker and the editorial work of Elizabeth Ault, Barbie Halaby, and Liz Smith, among many others.

Finally and most important of all are the Romanians whose willingness to trust me, despite the ambient atmosphere of suspicion, enabled my research from 1973 to 1989 and, in changed circumstances, to 2016. Just as officer "Blidaru" had hoped, I came to love Romania and its people and to find it an infinitely fascinating place, where I was able to live a life of intense work and pleasure time after time. I offer especially profound thanks to Meri and her family in Vlaicu, to "Beniamin" and Mariana, to Silvia Colfescu, and to the friends I call Ralf and Ana Bierman. To these people, as well as others mentioned throughout this book, I am bound for life.

Prologue

25 SEPTEMBER 1973: a lovely fall afternoon in Hunedoara County, in the Transylvanian region of Romania. Long hair flying out behind me, I am riding my new Mobra motorbike south from the capital, Deva, toward the mountainous commune of Lunca Cernei in the westernmost branch of the Southern Carpathian Alps. From the highway, the scenery is spectacular and will become more so once I head up into the hills on smaller roads, beginning at the village of Toplița. Light plays on the water that flows into the river Cerna, sparkling in the sun; flocks of sheep and goats forage on the stony hillsides. I have an unwarranted sense of well-being as I enjoy the air rushing past me. Well, not "rushing," exactly: at its fastest, the bike goes about fifty-five miles an hour, and I'm taking too much pleasure in my surroundings to push it.

Twenty-five years old and knowing practically nothing about Romania, I have come here from Stanford University to do research for my doctoral thesis in anthropology. The motorbike tour through the county is designed to help me choose a field site. I am to visit some thirty villages in this mountainous region and have so far been having a wonderful time, meeting and talking with people in my still-rudimentary Romanian. They are patient and try to help me express myself.

I've had the Mobra only a couple of weeks and am not used to it yet—nor to the trucks, belching foul exhaust, that repeatedly slow me down. Now the afternoon sky opens into dusk; I'm riding straight into the setting sun and find it hard to see. That is the only explanation I can offer for why I am unexpectedly stopped by a policeman for riding my Mobra into a restricted area, marked (he said) by a sign—I completely missed it—that prohibited entry to foreigners. My brilliant-red license plates brand me as precisely that.

Here is how one of the earliest documents in my Romanian secret police file reported the incident.

Military unit No. 01942 of Timisoara Region   TOP SECRET
Counterintelligence bureau   Copy 2
No. 0016102 of 03 October 1973

Report for the Record

On 29.09.1973 military expert USCATU GHEORGHE, officer on duty at Military Unit 01736 Hunedoara, discussing with some citizens from Lunca Cernei commune, learned from them that on 25 and 26 September 1973 there was an American citizen in the respective commune who was interested in their customs . . .

We specify that in the vicinity of Lunca Cernei commune is found Military Unit 01736 with a special profile. The access roads to the unit are marked with the indication "Entry prohibited to foreigners" . . . which the said VERGERY KATERYNE ignored.

"Special profile": in a word, I had ridden straight into a military base. Marginal comments confirmed that the report had gone from the military unit to the head of the county branch of the secret police, the Securitate, raising suspicion. Other documents revealed its upward path to headquarters in Bucharest.[1] I have been in the county barely four days and already it seems I am not who I think I am.

How had this happened, and what would be its consequences? The causes included the ignorance of a young woman hoping to learn something about life in a distant place, for which neither her training nor the atmosphere in which she was raised—those years we have labeled the "Cold War," with its associated conceptual blinders—had even remotely prepared her. Now here

I was, sitting bewildered and scared in a faraway police station up in the mountains of a communist country, while the policeman telephoned his boss for instructions. Why had my contacts in Deva given me an itinerary going right through a military base? Maybe that was what one of them was signaling with his cryptic advice to be careful when I got to Toplița. Or maybe even they themselves didn't know where the military bases were. How would I get out of this fix, with my barely adequate command of the language? Was my entire dissertation project already hopelessly compromised? (Would anyone care if it were?)

My field notes continue on from officer Uscatu's report:

Field notes, 24 Sept. 1973
The cop eventually put me in the hall, called his superiors in Deva, and asked what to do with me (he spoke so loudly I could hear every word). Suddenly—it seemed almost in mid-sentence—he shouted, "My respects!" and hung up. He now began to encourage me actively to go on, though I was disposed to give up the whole venture. He told me how interesting it was from an ethnographic point of view, while I continued to talk about whether I should stay or go home.

When the policeman returned with the happy news that I could continue my trip, I objected that this made no sense: How could I, a U.S. citizen, do research right on the edge of a military base in a Soviet satellite country? Since selecting a research site was the whole point of my tour through the county, I should simply go back down the mountain and look elsewhere. But now, more baffling still, the policeman became insistent, anxiously urging me to go on: it was beautiful up there, with very interesting folklore; the people were nice, they were expecting me; I should stick to my assigned program. . . . Unluckily, I let myself be persuaded   and as a result, military officer Uscatu heard of my visit to Lunca Cernei and wrote his report. It provided the wording a Securitate officer would later use in launching my surveillance file.

And so began my life as a spy. It contains several different threads, weaving together my experience of surveillance, the attempt to do anthropology in a communist setting permeated with secrets and fabrications, the work of Securitate officers and their informers, and lastly, serendipity, as officer Uscatu's memo blew up to take over my dissertation research because I had made a stupid mistake. It would not be the last time.

The Doppelganger

June 2008. I am perusing my secret police file in Bucharest and come upon the following document.

Ministry of the Interior   TOP SECRET

Cluj County Inspectorate   [5].xii.1984

Service III [counterespionage]

Report with proposals for finalizing the case of "VERA."

VERDERY KATHERINE, 36 years old, professor in the Department of Anthropology of "JOHN HOPKINS" University in Baltimore, U.S.A., benefiting from an I.R.E.X. grant, came to the Romanian S.R. in August 1984, settling in Cluj-Napoca.

From the complex informative-operative surveillance measures undertaken concerning her, it has resulted that her proposed research is merely a cover for unfolding an intense activity of collecting socio-political information that has no connection whatever with her research properly speaking. . . .

From photocopies [of her field notes] it results that the information obtained by "VERA" has a hostile character toward our country, as she constantly seeks to bring out the dissatisfactions and resistant attitudes toward the politics of our Party and state on the part of those she exploits for informative purposes. . . .

Bearing in mind that her presence in our country is aimed at collecting tendentious information of a socio-political character and is at the same time of a nature to stimulate the activity of hostile elements, we consider it necessary to put a stop to this activity and in this sense we propose . . . that her stay in this country be interrupted.

[signed by the heads of the Cluj County Inspectorate, Securitate, and Service 3 (counterespionage), and the heads of the counterespionage division for Bucharest and for all of Romania]

Reading this makes it suddenly clear: I have a secret double, a doppelganger—a being from folklore given this name in the late eighteenth century and often seen as an evil twin or challenger of the self's equilibrium. You can see her traces in this report. She is a schemer who seeks to destabilize the regime. Her name is "VERA," which means "true" in Latin; hence, she competes for reality status with me, KATHERINE VERDERY (KV). Actually, my double is multiple; each "self" has a different name, but they are held together by a single alleged occupation: spying on Romania for the United States. Different names accompany the different time periods and the kinds of spy the Securitate—the creators of my doppelganger—believe me to be. For instance, I am "FOLCLORISTA" ("The Folklorist"), spying for the military (1973–74); I am "VERA," living in Cluj to spy for the Hungarian diaspora in the United States (1984–86); I am "VANESSA," spied on at home in Baltimore for associating with Romanian dissidents (1987–88).[2] Evidently, spying meant several different things, which it is my job to sort out. For the first offense the Securitate drew up a plan for my arrest, for the second I was to be expelled from the country, and for the third they were preparing a penal action against me.

To my family, friends, and colleagues, these possibilities may seem surprising. The Securitate, however, perceives my doppelganger (to them, my "real" self) differently—more daring, more secretive, more deceitful—from the self known to my associates at home. I strain to glimpse myself in her, somewhat embarrassed if I succeed. Because my life as "VERA" occupies more pages than my life as the other nine pseudonyms in this file, for simplicity I will refer to my doppelganger as "VERA"—the capitals and quotation marks indicating a pseudonym, in the Securitate's practice.

The acquisition of a double—of a new identity—will prove to be a central feature of what it's like to be under surveillance.[3] The customary Western self-concept would tell us that we have unique identities (though I will have reason to doubt that), which the states we live in stabilize and meticulously verify on paper. States we visit often do the same. In this light, "VERA" is nearly as real as KV: KV's entire published oeuvre in 2017 is just slightly larger than her file. At the time of our actual paper rivalry, however, "VERA" was much better documented than KV and hence even more real, from state-makers' point of view.

Was "VERA" a spy? I didn't think so—indeed, I initially had the word "spy" in quotation marks in this book's title but decided to leave things more fluid. When I first went to Romania in late July 1973, I imagined myself a nascent ethnographer, whose aim was to write about other societies and peoples—in this case, Romania. I was to spend seventeen months on a scholarly exchange grant from the International Research and Exchanges Board (IREX), gathering data for my thesis.[4] In the proposal that the Romanian side had approved, I had presented a project I fully intended to do. That is, I did not

"Target 'VERA.'"
Surveillance photo,
1984. Courtesy of
the Archive of the
Consiliul Naţional
pentru Studierea
Arhivelor Securităţii,
Fond Informativ
(ACNSAS-FI).

misrepresent my plans, although it would later seem I had, for my project would turn out to be undoable and would have to be changed. Having always considered myself a person of integrity, I felt I had nothing to hide; I believed that if I worked aboveboard, I would have no problems. Thus, in 2008, when I read my Securitate file, I was shocked to discover that they believed otherwise, having uncovered various secret doubles who definitely intended harm to Romania and should be thrown out.

I borrow this image of the doppelganger from others who have written about their Securitate files. I first encountered it in a 2009 interview with Nobel Prize–winning writer Herta Müller, who was born in Romania but eventually emigrated to Germany when the Securitate pressure on her family became unbearable. Here is how she describes being doubled:

> In my file I am two different people. One is called "Cristina," who is being fought as an enemy of the state. To compromise this "Cristina" the falsification workshop of Branch "D" (disinformation) fabricated a doppelganger from all those ingredients that would harm me the most [in her new home in West Germany]—party-faithful communist, unscrupulous secret agent.

Wherever I went, I had to live with this doppelganger. It was not only sent after me wherever I went, it also hurried ahead. . . . It has taken on a life of its own.[5]

Our situations differ considerably, of course. Unlike me, Herta Müller is a world-renowned writer who was the direct target of Securitate harassment and persecution, meeting regularly with her oppressors face to face, as I did not. What joins us, however, is the experience of having been multiplied, turned into something we do not recognize as ourselves. We have been crafted, in a peculiar way, by an organization working presciently on the postmodern assumption that people's identities are unstable and do not unify us, but also on the modernist one that surface appearances are deceiving and reality must be sought beneath them. This combination gives the officers a number of powerful tools as they analyze the behavior of a target (their name for the people they follow) for signs of a hidden truth.

Another Securitate target, Romanian philosopher Gabriel Liiceanu, also has a doppelganger, an "evil twin." Asking himself why he should be so upset at finding in his file a copy of his life, he answers,

This cheap misrepresentation wasn't just bad and ugly. It was also dangerous, because—in the role of "target" that I had been assigned—it had been at the same time aimed *against* my life. It was my *Doppelgänger*, my double, ready to eliminate me. It was I, indeed, but an "I" that was negative, an "I-enemy," which in the end would *have to be* eliminated. . . . This Clone from the File recorded and reproduced the cells of the original, but commandeered them according to its own logic.[6]

In short, the clone worked much like a virus. Because the replica would resemble him, the Securitate could readily substitute its fabrication for his "real" self and change his destiny, making him appear guilty of things that might send him to languish in a Romanian labor camp.

My own reaction is less trenchant than Liiceanu's. Discovering that I have a doppelganger has left me befuddled. When I read their descriptions of myself as a spy, I begin to wonder whether I really *was* one. How much of the practice of anthropologists resembles spying? Then I ask myself whether the unattractive portrait they paint of me might actually be true, or at least have something to it. On the plus side, I find in the indomitable "VERA" some characteristics I would do well to incorporate into what I experience as my current, rather depressed and crotchety self; a bit of Lacanian "mirroring" of the more striking "VERA" could do wonders for me. But, you see, the doppel-ganger is already having an effect: I had to rewrite that last sentence, adding "what I experience as." Far from being intriguing additions to my repertoire, my doubles have unmoored my self-perception.

The unmooring commenced in 2008—shortly after I first began to skim through my file—because of the way it is organized. The documents in each of its eleven volumes follow no chronological order at all, and sometimes the dates on successive pages go backward rather than forward. Whole clusters of types of documents appear together without respect to date—multiple reports of my being shadowed on various days, sheaves of transcriptions of my telephone conversations or translations of my correspondence, groups of "informative notes" by friends and acquaintances who reported on me, and sets of reports from case officers or their superiors on up the hierarchy. It was chaotic, mystifying.

As I read the file more closely, my head began to spin. I was encounter-ing something not written to be read by its subject (like many anthropology books, for that matter) and under no requirement to be intelligible to her. I could make no sense of the mishmash of times and places, the perplexing organization of the documents that made them usable to officers but impen-etrable to anyone else. Because I felt I could not work as I intended with the file that way, I copied it and reorganized the copy in chronological order—as have others who have published their files.[7] This helped to position me in time and space so I could better find myself and recognize my experience. Such self-assertion violated the Securitate's way of rendering me, of course, and may have had the salutary effect of giving me some distance from this alarming mountain of paper. Its organization made clear, though, that the file represented not a personal biography but, at best, an incitement to one.

How, after all, had I come into possession of my secret police file? This is not a normal feature of an anthropologist's research.[8] The answer has two parts and must be contextualized within the scrupulous and bafflingly prolific file-production characteristic of twentieth-century authoritarianisms. First, in 1999, a decade after the revolution that had executed communist dictator Nicolae Ceaușescu, who had ruled the country as a reluctant Soviet ally since 1965, the Romanian Parliament passed a law—as some other Eastern European countries had done earlier—granting people access to their surveillance files and providing for public identification of Securitate officers and informers who appeared there. After numerous and ongoing legal challenges, the law eventually began to be used in a process known throughout the region as "lustration" (purification), for vetting would-be politicians: their files would be checked for evidence of collaboration with the Securitate, in a startling parallel with the exposure rituals of the communist period. That process aimed to prevent beneficiaries of the communist system from holding power in the new one. Many countries chose not to open their secret police files in this way; some did so earlier, others later, others later still.[9] My ability to write this book comes partly from having worked in Romania (which allows full access to one's file), rather than elsewhere. The files have participated in lengthy attempts to revise the country's past and consolidate an anticommunist hegemony, a subject I unfortunately cannot further explore here.[10]

Lustration was only one of the uses to which the secret police files could be put. Anyone who simply wanted to know what had been going on around them during the communist period, and especially the names of those who had informed on them, could request their file. In addition, accredited researchers like me could request any number of files for scholarly purposes. I therefore approached my file already bearing two identities: I was a "victim" (the term Romanians use) of Securitate surveillance, and I was researching the surveillance of foreign scholars during the Cold War, using my own case as an example of how it worked.

The second answer to how I got my file is that shortly after the Securitate archive was opened, I had begun using it for a research project with UCLA sociologist Gail Kligman on how the communists had created Romania's collective farms. The research produced our book *Peasants under Siege*. We worked with the institution set up to administer public access to the archive, the National Council for the Study of the Securitate Archives, widely referred to by its Romanian acronym CNSAS (cheh neh SASS). Because Gail and I found that the CNSAS archive held a lot of useful material, we spent two weeks or so there every summer for several years, getting to know the employees and copying documents for our book. During my 2006 visit, the by-now-familiar supervisor of the reading room asked me why I hadn't petitioned to see my own file. Since I had had no idea that non-Romanians could do so, it had never occurred to me to ask for it; now I learned that the law permitted file access to citizens of any NATO country. When I told her that I wasn't at all sure I wanted to know

Files in the CNSAS archive. Courtesy of Cristina Anisescu.

what was in it, she replied that if I requested it I might never get it, or finding it might take a long time. If it finally came, I could decide whether I wanted to read it or not.

So with some trepidation I applied for the file, and in late fall of 2007 (after, I assume, a close reading and possible culling of its contents) I was told that it was ready for me. The next May, I arrived in the reading room to see on a table three huge stacks of yellowing dossiers plus a fourth small one. There were eleven volumes in all. Each stack contained multiple volumes of 300–400 pages apiece, covered in cardboard and bound with string. I began to read, spending several hours going through them and completely forgetting about lunch. When I finally came up for air, I looked at the people around me and found myself thinking they were all secret police informers rather than objects of surveillance reading their files, like me. How seductive is this secret world of the file! How it sucks you in, quietly insinuating its categories into your thoughts! (A colleague told me then that she had stopped her research in the archive for a while because she was feeling poisoned.) Having seen enough of the file to be both intrigued and appalled, I ordered a copy of the whole thing—and had to buy an extra suitcase to take home its 2,781 pages, which filled my new brown carry-on entirely.

For the next two years the file sat menacingly in a box in the corner of my study while I finished another book. Then I dithered for some time about whether I really wanted to know what was in that box. Finally I read the file with care in the autumn of 2010. That reading aroused very complex feelings: outrage at seeing photos that a hidden camera had taken of me in my under-wear; despair and anger at learning of people whom I had considered close friends yet who had given nasty informers' reports on me; terrible remorse at learning how I myself had delivered friends to the Securitate by being care-less; amusement at how officers had garbled important facts; indignation at the ugly picture of me that surfaces in these pages (cold as ice, manipulative, scheming); and above all, like other readers of their files, astonishment at the remarkable extent of the surveillance—the sixteen- and eighteen-hour days of following me around, the intercepted correspondence, the eavesdrop-ping and wiretaps. . . . My surveillance engaged the visual and the auditory almost equally, enriched by their interplay with the text and with my own sense-making efforts. I found the variety and force of the conflicting emo-tions all these aroused—along with the sensation that the Securitate knew absolutely *everything*, down to my most intimate thoughts—quite exhausting.

These emotions form one of the challenges to my telling this story of sur-veillance. I must try to sort them out, learn something from them, domesti-cate them, domesticate the file itself. I must move from rage and depression at what the officers did to fascination with how they did it. Another challenge concerns how much of my private life to reveal—a scruple my officers did not observe, as they festooned their pages about me with nearly-nude photo-graphs, the names of lovers, and other intimate details, sending some upward for the delectation of their bosses. If the Securitate had no concept of privacy, what hope have I of retrieving any now? Yet other obstacles lie in whether to reveal the names of people who figure in my file, or rather to protect them in exchange for their willingness to speak with me about it (I chose this path), and whether to "correct" things in the file that are outright misrepresenta-tions from my point of view (I mostly decided not to). These are all complex challenges.

> > >

Responding to my file engages me in a complexly layered chain of research. First, I conducted my fieldwork—participating, observing, and talking with people—and stored the results in field notes. These form the first layer of

My Securitate file. Courtesy of CNSAS staff.

the research chain. Alongside this, the Securitate conducted research on me conducting research, using their conversations with Romanian informers, my movements, my phone calls and correspondence, and my own field notes and intimate journals; they stored the results in dossiers of officers' and informers' reports. That is the second layer. Now I conduct research on their research on me conducting research; I use their notes and some conversations with their informers and even, as we will see, with some officers themselves. This is the third layer. And I have plenty of reason to think the successor organization to the Securitate, the SRI (Romanian Information Service), is laying down a fourth layer of research, as my writing offers them new "data" in the form of publications (such as my 2014 book *Secrets and Truths*),[11] as well as through talks and interviews in Romania that show them what I am up to. This time, however, I do not have access to their "research notes": my file access stops at 1989.

Characteristics of the Files

Between July 1973 and November 1988 I conducted forty months of research in Romania, staying for greater or lesser amounts of time in four places and thus posing problems of coordination for the Securitate. I spent the most

Map of Romania with locations mentioned.

time, during the 1970s, in the village of Aurel Vlaicu in the Transylvanian county of Hunedoara. Next were the cities of Cluj in Transylvania's northwest and, briefly, Iaşi, in Moldavia, in the northeast—both in the 1980s. Throughout these two decades I periodically went for my mail to Bucharest, in the south. Although there are some things I would have expected to find in the file and do not, on the whole it represents my life in Romania well, both spatially and temporally. Whether or not it has been "cleaned up," as some would claim, I cannot say.

Because the problems of particular concern to the top Securitate generals in Bucharest varied significantly by region and time period, the language and the issues addressed in the file vary as well. Each of its eleven volumes bears one of four identifying numbers and represents one or another of the places where I lived. The files for Cluj (the largest file by far) and for Vlaicu each have different numbers. A third number contains some duplicates from those two and also material from Bucharest and Iaşi. The fourth small volume (ninety-four pages) covers only 1987–89; it was created by the Foreign Intelligence Service (CIE)—Romania's CIA—rather than the domestic branch, source of the other volumes.

My CNSAS colleague Virgiliu gave me the following account of the archive and its files: "The CNSAS archive is not like a library, and the life of a dossier is not the same as that of a book between covers. It's constantly shifting; things are thrown out by the case officer or the person who puts it together, so no file has in it now everything that was ever destined for it. The officer has his own exigencies, related to justifying or legitimating himself and his activity, but he is also subject to other pressures from above." This means that reading one's file is a bit like an archeological excavation. One knows one will get only fragments of what was there and will have few clues concerning what is not. Moreover, files are shaped differently according to the officers who compiled them and the archivists who periodically culled them. A person's file, then, has considerable individuality—not just because it deals with an individual but because each of the several officers contributes differently to each case.

One of the oddest features of the file is its proliferation of pseudonyms. This is a function of something all intelligence organizations do: compartmentalize their different tasks and services by walling off each sector of activity from the others, so as to protect their secrets. The people who shadow me use one pseudonym for me; the people censoring my correspondence use another—and different ones for the different places where I lived; the people eavesdropping on phone calls or conversations in restaurants may use yet another; and the various case officers who receive all these reports use still others. (Targets do sometimes appear in documents with their own names, especially in the early stages of an investigation.) Officers create a target's pseudonym based on something specific to the person (such as the occupation "Folklorist") or, very commonly, by taking a letter or syllable of their first or last name and creating a new name from it. Hence, I am "VERA," based on "VERdery" with an added *a*. I am also "VIKY," "VALY," "KORA," "KITTY," "KATY," or (for the Foreign Intelligence Service) "VANESSA," "VADU," or "VERONA": ten different characters. In Romania a person who baptizes another becomes their "godparent"; therefore, I am multiply blessed by having so many godparents to watch over me.

The people who informed on me, with a few exceptions, had pseudonyms as well, and so did many of the places in which they met their officers. Informers' pseudonyms are generally created in the same way as the target's. An informer who is employed only on occasion for a specific problem, however, without being recruited and signing an oath of confidentiality that could entail more extensive reporting, might receive no pseudonym; rather, the officer would use the person's name (perhaps enclosing it in quotation marks, to indicate informer status). In general, the only people in a given set of files who do not have pseudonyms are the Securitate officers themselves (known popularly as *Secus* [SEH kooz] or *securiști* [seh koo REESHT, singular *seh koo REEST*]—terms I will use interchangeably). The files therefore create a world of their own, in which the officers are "natives" and thus require no new names, while everyone else has to be re-baptized.

Typical of this world is the use of an idiosyncratic language, including terms like "element" and "target" or "objective" (*obiectiv*) in the sense of a military objective—their words for the people they follow. Once a target becomes sufficiently suspect to have a full investigation, a specific kind of file is opened: a DUI (*dosar de urmărire informativă*) or "dossier of informative pursual." Eight of my eleven volumes form two DUIs, one each from Hunedoara County and the city of Cluj. Two more volumes fall into a different kind of file: those set up around certain "problems." The "problem" might be religious sects, or Romania's German or Hungarian minorities, or foreign students and researchers, by country. The "problem" file for "Lecturers, doctoral researchers, and students from the USA" consists of twenty-six weighty volumes including pretty much every U.S. scholar who ever went to communist Romania, sometimes with a few pages only, sometimes with several hundred. I occupy two enormous volumes of those twenty-six—more than any other U.S. scholar by far. We will see a number of reasons for this, among them the number of forms of spying of which I was suspected and the variety of places in which I spent time.

When I first read my huge file I felt very important, but I was chastened when I looked through that twenty-six-volume file. Nothing in my graduate school training had prepared me for this. Virtually every one of the scholars was assumed to be a spy; I was unique only in the number of pages I commanded. Many had been declared *personae non grata*, refused reentry, and/or tossed out of the country, as was recommended in my case too.[12] A former Secu officer explained it to me in 2014: "There were a lot of foreigners around in those years. We had to see what you were up to. It was, after all, the Cold War!" In these texts, I and other Americans are regularly referred to as "CIA agents." Therefore, in the Securitate's view, "spy" was the default identity for Western scholars.

For officers to assume that "VERA," my spy doppelganger, was my "true" self was, indeed, not far-fetched. Many embassy personnel, particularly the political attachés, likely had intelligence connections, which some of the scholars going to the Soviet bloc might have had as well (one of the Fulbright lecturers himself told me that he did). Recent research shows that numerous U.S. organizations, especially cultural ones, were CIA fronts. Most of the people involved in their activities had no idea that the CIA was their backer—that CIA funds supported work by USAID, and that the CIA regularly approached scholars preparing to go on the exchanges.[13] Although individual scholars protested this treatment, there was nothing like the backlash that arose in the early years of the twenty-first century, with the attempted integration of anthropologists into the Human Terrain System in Afghanistan, for instance. David Price discusses numerous anthropologists accused of being spies, as well as examples of intelligence officers using anthropological cover for their work.[14] These sorts of CIA connections were precisely what the communist secret police suspected. They noted time after time in the files relating to U.S. researchers something like, "We have data showing that Americans in the exchange programs are under the patronage of the CIA, and their research themes are part of a general plan to collect information about our country."

We should not be surprised by this: after all, our own intelligence services made exactly the same assumption about scholars coming from the Soviet bloc. In 1983, a Romanian returning from a trip to the United States informed his handler about an interview given by William Casey, then head of the CIA, in which (in the words of this informer)

---

he called the public's attention to the danger represented by the scientific and technical specialists from socialist countries in programs of cultural and scientific exchange in universities, research institutes, and other American institutions. In the CIA's opinion the great majority of these specialists have technological and scientific espionage as their mission. Especially dangerous are the Fulbright grantees, who almost without exception have such missions. On behalf of the CIA, Dr. Casey . . . recommended avoiding close personal contacts with these specialists from socialist countries.[15]

Tit for tat. Indeed, the exchange-grant agency IREX, my sponsor, had itself been formed by scholars who wished to prevent the chairman of its precursor from using it to promote spying rather than scholarship.

> > >

Reasons for my appearing to be a spy—that is, for my doppelganger to be not a double but my true self—are all over this file. To begin with, I came to Romania in 1973 claiming to be an ethnographer interested in folklore, a discipline familiar to any Romanian having a university degree (and most securişi hired after 1970 had one). For decades prior to the communist regime and to some degree after it began as well, Romanian ethnographers had done first-rate research in rural areas. They tended to do it in a particular way, however, which distinguished them from U.S. anthropologists: a team of scholars would descend on a village for a couple of weeks, each asking about specific things (customs, dress, folktales, rituals, dialect) and each usually concentrating on a small number of village "experts." After that they would pool their results and write them up, often collectively. No one came alone and settled in a single village for over a year, as I did. No one talked with many if not most people in the village, or asked all kinds of questions about everything, from village history under the Habsburg Empire to the way Germans and Romanians raised pigs and cows in the 1930s to intermarriage in the 1970s. The fact that I did so meant I must be going beyond the bounds of the project I had come with, and that made it even more likely that I was lying and spying rather than doing ethnography. In any case, what I was doing bore scant resemblance to anything securişti would have recognized as such. More pertinent, according to Romanian sociologist Nicolae Gheorghe, they didn't really see the difference between ethnography and espionage, something he spent countless hours trying unsuccessfully to explain to his Securitate handler.[16]

Second, the way I carried myself was suspect. At least, so it seemed to my friend Emilia, who told me that when she met me in 1990 she immediately thought I might be a spy: "You were dressed very modestly, you didn't hold yourself above us. Your style was to reduce the difference between yourself and Romanians, under-communicating it." In short, my manner of dress was a form of hiding. Eventually she came to see it as my way of trying to form good relations with villagers, but her first thought was, "Maybe she's a spy. Instead of seeming like someone from a totally different world, you seemed to be one of us"—that is, she thought I had been specifically trained to fit in.

I hid in other ways, too. Often when I took the train, I would not reveal my U.S. identity up front but would participate in the conversation as long as possible until someone would finally ask, "But where are you from *really?*" This sometimes enabled me to avoid tedious talk about life in America and to see what people had to say when my foreignness was not the focus of the conversation. Such hiding and listening, I now realize, made me a lot like a *securist*. Indeed, as we will see, the officers draw a parallel between my ethnographic practices and those of intelligence work. They recognize me as a spy because I do some of the things they do—I use code names and write of "informants," for instance, and both of us collect "socio-political information" of all kinds rather than just focusing on a specific issue. So what *are* the similarities and differences between these two different modalities of information gathering: spying and ethnography? When I read in the file that I "exploit people for informative purposes," can I deny that anthropologists often do just that, as Securitate officers do? Isn't this part of the critique of my discipline that likens it to a colonial practice?

In fact, as I read I begin to feel my doppelganger taking over: I find myself becoming a spy, or at least I see the reasons for the Securitate's pursuing me as one. Our aims and methods differ, of course. But reading the file does make me begin to wonder: Was I a spy, and in what ways? Can I get close enough to the Securitate now to find out?

> > >

What benefit is there to reading one's file? It is a painful process, one that has ruined friendships and even marriages. Consonant with my initial hesitation, I asked for mine without having a specific agenda for it. I'd had a vague idea of writing something from it but no clear sense of what that would be. Once I started to read it, the numerous reactions that washed over me gradually coagulated into the idea of using the file as a way to understand both the communist regime and the experience of surveillance in it. My file would help me recapture my history in Romania; through that, I could approach these larger themes.

To describe being spied upon would also permit me to explore how surveillance affects the process of trying to learn about another way of life—of doing ethnography—in the face of efforts to prevent it. The question my file raises is, what does the presence and intervention of the secret police do to that process? How does one negotiate a relation with "another" in a Cold War climate? Even though I did not fully realize it at the time, constant surveillance substantially shifted the terrain of field research, which relies on that fragile relationship, trust. Although ethnography is possible in its absence, our best work rests upon it. In a context of surveillance, a constant current of mistrust and doubt eats away at trusting relations. Every conversation with someone becomes anchored by the presence of a third, often hidden—a third of whom I was at first largely unaware and with whom I could develop no relationship: the Securitate officer. That third affected all relationships, maintaining a continual drag on the growth of new ones, pulling each of them off center, just as an illicit affair decenters a person's marriage. Sometimes that hidden third was actually involved with my respondents; sometimes he (rarely she) was just a hidden possibility they might fear. He might be undermining the relations I could negotiate with others by spreading rumors that would affect people's vision of me or their sense of safety, and he did so under a regime of secrecy that I could not combat. By emphasizing this, I can use my file to bring global power relations into the intimacy of the field encounter, complicating a certain style of anthropology that focuses mainly on interpersonal negotiation and dialogue.[17]

Secrecy and States

Trying to grasp another way of life is always challenging, but especially so under conditions of secrecy. What is fieldwork like when done in the context of secrets and lies? How did the culture and apparatus of secrecy affect me, my research, my writing, my relationships?[18] In the United States, the concept of transparency has a fundamental place in ideas about personal behavior, as well as in notions of democratic practice (though not, unfortunately, in the practice itself). This made living in a forest of secrets especially fraught for someone like me, at the time an unreflective believer in "telling it like it is."

Secrecy was the essential medium of Securitate practices. It was also pervasive in all spheres of 1980s Romania, under the "wise guidance" of the Communist Party led by Nicolae Ceauşescu, whose rule had by then become an ugly dictatorship. Legislation governing the "state secret" prohibited revealing that secret but said almost nothing about its content. By making it an abstraction, in the words of philosopher István Király, the law "opened the way for a proliferation of the category of the secret unimaginable in other conditions."[19] In the Securitate specifically, both the identity and the work of many officers were secret except to those whom they recruited to inform— and those people were ordered not to reveal what they knew. Because the

Surveillance photo of "VERA" loaded down with sacks, 1985. Courtesy of ACNSAS-FI.

officers assumed that my true purposes were hidden, to discern my intentions they themselves must be hidden as well. They were obsessed with other hidden things too: for instance, my shadowers always mentioned in their reports the bags or sacks I was carrying, in which something could be hidden. They were dying to know what it was. In addition, they were distressed not to be able to get into my locked suitcase to discover its secret contents.

The fact of surveillance itself was not a secret: it was known to all, at least in theory. Cristina Vatulescu observes that secrecy in the Soviet Union became a spectacle, as the NKVD/KGB carefully orchestrated a public cult for itself. During show trials, one could see huge piles of police dossiers on the table, visibly representing the secrets buried within them.[20] Most of the documents in my file are classified TOP SECRET (STRICT SECRET) in the upper right-hand corner (the more lowly designation SECRET appears very seldom). Does this

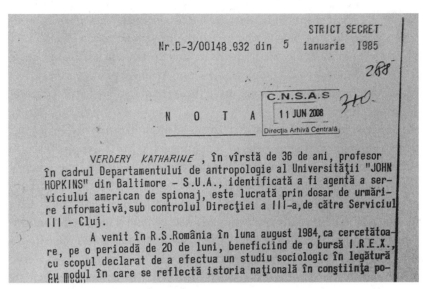

"TOP SECRET" document recommending my expulsion, 1985. Courtesy of ACNSAS-FI.

represent the actual presence of a secret, or is it rather the spectacle of one? Or was putting it there like applying a stamp with the place and date, a routine symbol of their work?

The secrecy I will describe here permeated Romanian society, but it was rooted in a specific social location: that of the state apparatus, occupied by the Romanian Communist Party. To invoke "the state" is to enter a conceptual minefield, which I will not attempt to clear; I merely lay out some of my working assumptions. The term "state" refers to something that has organizational, territorial, and ideological aspects. On the one hand, it has a very material existence in buildings, in institutions such as legislatures, and in bureaucratic practices, all linked to specific territories. On the other, extensive ideological work by groups within it goes into creating the impression that a state is a real actor, which "does" things. A more useful approach would see it as a fiction, an imaginary, which presents the appearance of unitary action. Sociologist Pierre Bourdieu defines states first by their possessing a monopoly on legitimate physical and symbolic violence, then as "a principle of orthodoxy, of consensus on the meaning of the world," "a collective fiction and well-founded illusion," one of whose basic functions is "to produce and canonize social classifications." People, he suggests, are coded by the state, which produces legitimate identities.[21] Sociologist Philip Abrams pursues a similar line, following Foucault, seeing the state as "an ideological power," "an imaginative construction." Because it does not exist, "our efforts to study it as a thing can only be contributing to the persistence of an illusion. . . . The state is not the reality which stands behind the mask of political practice. It is itself the mask which prevents our seeing political practice as it is."[22] If readers find themselves resisting these ideas, that testifies to the power of statist ideology.

Secrecy (which I have explored at greater length in *Secrets and Truths*) has been a fundamental ingredient of those masking processes. Its place in state practices has proliferated in Western countries with the appearance of security states and comprehensive electronic surveillance of citizens. Ethnographies of security in both historical and comparative dimensions have blossomed, joining earlier discussions of secrecy and a flourishing anthropology of the state, which began in the 1980s.[23] Abrams states the connection concisely: "The real official secret . . . is the secret of the non-existence of the state."[24] Secrecy therefore serves "the state" by helping to create its illusion. This aptly describes the Securitate's job, which thrived on masking the actual situation. The Securitate, while committed to assessing objective threats, often produced instead "highly speculative visions of covert dangers" that turned inconsequential persons into "powerful agents of global intrigue," both necessitating and empowering the existence of a secret police.[25]

If *secrecy* is easily made visible, it nonetheless works in tandem with the hiding of *secrets*, which often requires that those who work with secrets be invisible. The Securitate's job was to contain enemies, including us foreigners, by discovering our secrets but not being seen to do so. Toward this aim, they recruited informers, who might help them discover the target's basic secret: whether he or she was an "enemy" and how that enemy was doing his or her evil work. In practice, though, they *assumed* that foreign researchers were enemies, so it was no secret. For me, by contrast, followed by legions of informers and the multiple officers who handled my case, the paramount secret is the rudimentary one of my pursuers' identities—*Who were they?*—and, in the case of officers, their actual physical presence. What did they look like? How did they sound? Which of my friends might be reporting to the Securitate on my activities? Which of the people who sought me out did so from simple curiosity or liking, and which were tasked with doing so by their officer? During my fieldwork, especially in the 1970s, I tended to think about this rather seldom, for three reasons. First, constantly wondering who was trustworthy would make it impossible to work; second, I had a wholly inadequate concept of the magnitude of my surveillance; and third, I thought I would win the Securitate's confidence by being transparent and aboveboard. What remarkable naiveté!—and what ethnocentrism, to imagine that "transparency" would be a value for a communist intelligence service! How little I knew.

I worked, then, surrounded by secrets, many of them contained in my file. The fate of the secret differs, however, in how one approaches it. Some people think secrets exist below the surface, to be unearthed through a dialectic of secrecy and revelation. These people will read the file—and this book—to uncover secrets and their content. For others, by contrast, there is no secret truth to be revealed under the surface, only a collection of fragments too disparate to be read for such a secret. Do I have a secret to reveal or merely the succession of small fragments in which (reflecting the composition of my file) I have composed this book?

Identities

Anthropologists in the field play a variant of the role of "foreign visitor." We go to some place, usually different from our home place, and hang out with the people we meet, trying to learn something of how they see and act in the world. In the process, we present them with the challenge of how to account for our presence, how to understand who we are and what we are doing. There is much room here for reciprocal identity-creation. Sometimes we are seen as missionaries trying to convert the locals, sometimes as poachers on their sacred knowledge. In many places, we have been viewed as spies and kept under surveillance for that reason.[26]

If my file indicates multiple identities, with "spy" among them, the Securitate is not their only source. Romanians I met created them for me as well. For example, one day I went to the university library in Bucharest to do some reading. The librarian filed a report indicating what I had checked out and in addition told the reporting officer that I am "from a family of Hungarian Jews" (surprising, to someone from a family of French and British Protestants). In a positive vein, whereas the Securitate elaborated my qualities as an enemy, many Romanians in the villages and towns where I lived came to regard me as a friend—or at least as someone who was relatively harmless, if not indeed a likable sort of person who might become a friend eventually. Some sought to make me a resource in local quarrels or perhaps saw me as a kind of trader, a possible source of foreign goods (high-quality coffee, blue jeans, Kent cigarettes, maybe even dollars). After I finished my PhD, still others saw me as simply "Mrs. Professor," holder of a respected title that made me seem out of reach. And a few offered to accept me as a kind of kin, the most precious identity of all—the one that keeps me going back to Aurel Vlaicu even now, just to see "my family" there.

In a sense, we are *all* multiplied by those we meet, who create versions of us that may not much resemble our own versions. Although this process is universal, it is particularly intense when major cultural boundaries are crossed: when a person from one cultural tradition enters into a very different one—the common situation of anthropologists—and especially when those boundaries are significant politically. Why, then, am I making so much of my presumed identity as a spy?

The difference—and it was huge—between most anthropologists and those of us working behind the Iron Curtain between the 1960s and 1989 is the towering importance of the Cold War. The Cold War environment virtually required that people from the United States be anticommunist and be seen as such; it shaped the identities that anthropologists doing such work could try to assume; it plunked us down in the heart of the great superpower stand-off; and it made our possible spying a virtual certainty, from the viewpoint of intelligence services on both sides. The meaning of any behavior in this setting was not subject to the usual ways of interpreting behavior but became something quite different. Talal Asad has argued that because national security politics makes the entire range of social conduct potentially suspicious, all behavior becomes a possible sign. Thus, "ordinary life becomes the domain of a search for hidden meaning that then points to hidden danger."[27] I believe this was not true—or was less true—of anthropologists working in other places during the Cold War.

As a result, doing fieldwork in a communist country inserted the researcher directly into a global context, giving things a significance they might not have had elsewhere. An anthropologist in the field "behind the Iron Curtain" was a point at which global political forces intersected; anything she did could be interpreted in that light. To take a trivial example, in 1988 an officer in Bucharest, learning that I had made a phone call to the city of Cluj, assumed that it was to a woman named Doina Cornea, who was then among Romania's handful of well-known dissidents. For that officer, an American suspected of being a CIA agent would naturally want to make contact with Doina Cornea (whom I have never met), though I'd actually called a historian colleague for a chat. But the officer's assumption turned my friendly phone call into a politically suspicious act.

Aside from the Cold War context, there is another important difference between the kinds of identity accrued by the anthropologist working in Soviet bloc countries and those working elsewhere: the communist secret police themselves specialized in just such identity-creation to an unusual extent. The doppelgangers they fabricated acquired a consistency and a degree of elaboration, the product of intense labor, far greater than the identities created elsewhere for the researcher suspected of being a missionary or other sort of person. Thus, although all anthropologists are "produced" to some degree by the environments in which we work, those of us who worked in the Soviet bloc during those years were "produced" much more thoroughly than most.

> > >

When a U.S. editor approached Freud about publishing his autobiography, Freud reportedly answered, "What makes all autobiographies worthless is, after all, their mendacity." Deceitfulness is definitely a trait of this book (though perhaps not entirely in the way Freud meant), for it is based on my file—a fiction generated by the Securitate. My challenge here is to create something partway between fiction and fact. One form of "mendacity" is that I often use quotation marks for people's speech that I did not in fact record (many people had bad feelings about being taped in that society of hyper-surveillance), so the version I provide is actually approximate, rather than exact.

A second form is that I have chosen not to reveal the identities of most of the people I write about—some at their express request, others because I think that is what they would want or because my professional ethics indicate it. Therefore, just like the Securitate, I am compelled to use pseudonyms for my friends, informers, and the officers I interviewed, and to disguise their biographies—particularly those of the people who informed on me. But if I am not to use their real names, I have the problem of making up pseudonyms for them. I cannot simply use the pseudonyms that are in my files, which are recognizable to at least some researchers and former officers. So I must create new ones. When I am dealing with informers or Secus themselves, my pseudonyms take the form used by the officers—surrounded by quotation marks. In other cases I indicate that it is a pseudonym by placing an asterisk before the name at its first use. With some of my friends, I use their own names without special punctuation, and I have their permission to do so. Then there are the names of people who are mentioned in documents, for whom I make up initials. In a few cases my fabrications extend to facts of people's lives, making me every bit the demiurge my *securişti* were. I find this troubling but necessary.

> > >

Identity enters into this story in another way as well, having to do with what field research is like. It often entails a kind of regression to childhood, especially at the beginning. Anthropologists going to an unknown place find themselves in the position of children who are learning to live in society: they may have imperfect command of speech, their control of the language of symbols is at best rudimentary, they don't know the rules of proper behavior or the important social players, and they have yet to establish the system of social alliances that will carry them through. This quasi-infantilization of adult anthropologists can make us vulnerable to forms of regression— certainly it did in my case—that shift "who we are."

Perhaps connected with that: although fieldwork was often difficult, I generally found it exhilarating, in part because I felt less constrained by my personality than I normally do. Not only was being in a different place exciting, but also, like so many other foreigners away from home, I did and felt things that I normally wouldn't. I could approach people with a child's heart, developing continuous crushes in a pattern of even weaker emotional boundaries than was usual for me. I developed a kind of "inner Romanian" (my very own doppelganger?) who enjoyed transgressing in ways I usually forbade myself. Something in the field situation made me more receptive to people than usual—as some of them apparently were to me. This partly reflected our reciprocal interests: each of us wanted things from the other (such as information, Western goods, connections), and liking one another would facilitate that.

The theme of multiple forms of identity, then, engaging me along with Securitate officers and other Romanians I encounter in a constant stream of refashioning, is an apt one. It continues in the form of my writing, as I double myself by sometimes separating a narrative voice in the present from the "Kathy" of my earlier research (usually when "she" is doing something "I" don't like). This profusion of characters suits the fiction of my file, in which officers use bits and pieces of evidence to put together a form of consciousness that they attribute to me as their character. Will there be a "Pygmalion" moment when their creation meets them face to face?

If the identities created by the Securitate predominate in this story, that is because they affected many of my other identities, and because the Securitate left far richer evidence of theirs. Besides, it was their archive that challenged me to reconsider my entire history in Romania, and they gave me the basis for doing so: with a weak memory and no field diary, I have only this file, my field notes (which mainly tell whom I interviewed and what I read), and some correspondence to remind me of what I did in Romania and who I was. My file—and, thus, the angle of vision of the Securitate officers who compiled it—significantly grounds my recollections now. This is not really "my" book, then; it is *ours*. At times I even write about myself in the third person, so as to privilege the officers' angle of vision and their quality as "coauthor." In consequence, this is a many-voiced work that implicitly challenges both the notion of authorship and the idea of a memoir.

If identity is one theme, secrecy is another. It is the premise of the whole endeavor. Without secrecy there would be no file, no doppelgangers, no possibilities for betrayal, no prospect of revelations. What secrets govern this writing, and how will they be uncovered? Do they have to do with why I was not expelled, as several documents proposed I should be? With the reasons I was considered dangerous? With uncovering hidden *securişti*? Or with what unexpected things I find, when I finally get into the ethnography of my fieldwork experience?

Among the U.S. researchers I know who have worked in Romania, nearly all have gotten their files—and are susceptible to jocular comparisons about size. Having a file confirms our sense of our own importance. But once the joking is over, we begin to contemplate the new and different selves that this file creates and with which we have to come to terms. Timothy Garton Ash, reading his East German secret police (Stasi) file, wonders whether he could really be that person they called "Romeo," with his fumblings, clumsiness, pretentiousness, and snobbery.[28] Having these data from the Securitate is a bit like entering into social media: the data swirl around me like a cloud, shaping images of me that have little to do with what I think of myself.

One task the file imposes on me is to understand better the person that reading it has made me, to befriend my doppelganger somehow, so it does not remain an evil twin. Another task is to use my encounter with the file to reveal more about the workings of the Securitate, about which we have had a fairly monochrome view, and of communism more generally. That goal, too, bends the genre of memoir. To be honest, I don't actually know what this book is. Being about parts of my life, it is a kind of memoir, but one that also contains the results of research—some of which is aimed at me myself, as I apply an ethnographer's methods to my own experience. Although this would make it a kind of "autoethnography," much of the research is also about other people, such as secret police officers and informers.[29] Because it tries to bring together two goals usually handled separately—an analysis of surveillance under socialism and a life story of the target of that surveillance—it is a hybrid sort of work. It approaches the secret police differently from my previous book, *Secrets and Truths*, with its extensive scholarly apparatus. This one is more experiential, though it too makes some claims to truth.

In the pages that follow, then, I go about my business as a researcher under surveillance, a process that fragments me into a series of doubles—some created by the secret police, some by my respondents and myself. At the time, I was not particularly aware of this: the last thing on my mind was "my identity" in relation to those I worked with. It was not customary in 1970s anthropology to think too much about that, and in any case, my scholarly sensibilities ran more to politics and the economy than to the fact that everyone was watching everyone else and creating hypotheses about who they were. I knew that in theory the Securitate was interested in me as well as in other people, but I initially had few clues as to the pervasiveness of the secrecy that was in fact my medium. Wedded as I was to the very American value of transparency, only gradually did I realize that my most vigorous efforts to be transparent were seen as hiding something.

The result is an account of how an untested young scholar first experienced communist Romania and attempted to do research in a place permeated with secrets and fabrications; how largely unbeknownst to her, her initial entanglement with the culture and apparatus of secrecy shaped the course of her work over the next sixteen years and beyond; and how her realization of that after the fact altered her sense of what she had accomplished and her assessment of her relations with people. She came to see herself not as a lone researcher but as always accompanied by a secret presence working in parallel with her, seeking to obstruct relations of trust she might try to build and striving to uncover her secrets, just as she herself strove to uncover the secrets of life in communism.

At the same time, this is a story about how Securitate officers—the arm of the Romanian state charged with policing the line between inside and outside, between "friend" and "enemy"—both did their job and imagined the enemy they were policing. In the process of doing so, they carried out that state's work of creating human beings—of "making up people," as Ian Hacking puts it[30]—including people who are its enemies. The officers' imaginings are multiple; the organization does not work with a single master narrative but is itself fragmented across territory and time periods, as well as by its own practices of compartmentalization. Exploring these files helps to decompose the monolithic "totalitarian" identity of the Securitate and in the process to bring together the fragments that constitute my own.

PART I

RESEARCH UNDER SURVEILLANCE

The 1970s
"The Folklorist" as Military Spy

Certain death with a cobra,
But more certain with a Mobra.
—Romanian jingle concerning
the Mobra motorbike

In keeping with the file's casual attitude toward chronology, mentioned earlier, the document indicating when I crossed the border into Romania for the first time is numbered page 234. It says I arrived on a tourist visa on 22 July 1973 and would stay for a month with Mrs. Jana Cionila (the mother of my Romanian tutor at Stanford). During that time I would receive my research visa for the year. Then I would settle on a field site, return to Bucharest for further preparation, and finally establish myself in some village by November. But although there would be plenty of Securitate activity around me during that time, I did not officially acquire a surveillance file until March 1974, eight months after my arrival. My ill-starred adventure with the motorbike would contribute to that.

Arrivals and Misadventures
Arrival in Bucharest

I had headed for Romania by train via Greece and Bulgaria, stopping in Sofia, where I would have to wait several hours for a connection to Bucharest. I spent that time walking around town with a cheerful Libyan fellow who had shared my compartment in the train. We also sat in a park and watched grandmothers babysitting their grandchildren while the parents were at work. Darkness fell. As we stood waiting on the platform, I noticed all at once a sleek locomotive that had slipped almost silently into the station, pulling a long train behind it. Written on a placard on the engine in large Cyrillic letters was "МОСКВА"—"MOSCOW." I felt a sudden shiver of fear, having not realized until then that I would be on a train heading into the heart of the Soviet empire. I still remember that feeling, a visceral sign of the Cold War environment in which I had grown up.

It is worth reiterating my ignorance of the country I was coming to—partly an effect of that same Cold War. There was no literature on Romania in English in my field; virtually no Anglophone anthropologist had worked there yet. I had read the few volumes in French, based on work in the 1930s (which helped me little, four decades later), and a handful of articles in French and English by Romanian sociologist Mihail Cernea, but my Romanian at the time of my departure had not been up to reading works in that language. I was virtually a *tabula rasa*.

Bearing a large bouquet, Jana Cionila met my train and took me to her tiny apartment (a single large room stuffed with furniture and tchotchkes). She chattered constantly in rapid-fire Romanian I could barely make out. A diminutive round woman with short white hair, she had a gold tooth that flashed when she smiled. I tried to be as amusing as possible so I could see it often. Without her warm welcome I would have felt even more desperate than I already did at entering this frightening new country where I knew not a single soul.

It didn't take me long to begin experimenting with who I was, creating my own double even before the Securitate did so. In Bucharest, at Jana's suggestion and seconded by a couple of other people, I decided I would have an easier time in Romania if I were married. This would help me fend off unwanted attentions (which had already begun with the ticket collector on the train). It would also ease prospective visits from my companion at the time, anthropologist Bill Skinner ("Wm," below), if I presented him as my husband. Jana had a few wedding rings—her "savings plan"—and was happy to lend me one, which I would then wear home and give to her daughter at Stanford. I was gradually to discover that Romanians in general and Romanian men in particular had completely different attitudes to young unmarried women and young married ones. It seemed that being married conveyed greater importance and gravitas than being a young single woman, and I found I liked the contrast quite a lot. If only my too-large wedding ring hadn't been constantly falling off, giving me away.

Sitting at dinner I suddenly realized that—perhaps through this ruse of being married—I find I'm considering myself more a woman than a girl, and that's a switch of massive proportions in self-conception. Something to do with not being condescended to, being taken seriously as someone with a task to accomplish, however incomprehensible it is to most of these people. But more to do with my self-perception than with any objective behavior directed at me (after all, I believe I'm taken seriously in the US too). I feel myself a status equal, in opposition to men especially, rather than being a step below.[1]

If being in Romania was to involve "becoming" a spy in the Securitate's eyes, then my identity was already in a state of flux.

One other thing contributed to my new self-perception: height. At the time, I was five foot four, slightly on the short side for women my age in the States. In Romania, the average for both sexes was much shorter than at home (partly, no doubt, from malnutrition during and after World War II). Now I was relatively tall, and it made a difference in how I felt in my relations with people. I could look more people in the eye, or even down at them, giving me an advantage in some social interactions. I felt that somehow I'd gained authority, become more of a "grown-up" (always a struggle for me). When I went home, I was sad to become short again.

> > >

Officer's Note on Informer's Report, 1974: Aspects concerning her connection with the U.S. Embassy awaken special operative interest. Instructions to informer: inform about her doings, especially concerning the support of the Embassy.

My IREX grant was partly administered through the U.S. Embassy in Bucharest, which entailed certain privileges (most importantly, ordering from a duty-free shop and use of the diplomatic pouch for mail) but also connected us with embassy personnel, especially the cultural and political attachés. Fulbright fellows were even more tied to the embassy than were IREXers. Like the other grantees, I accepted this arrangement without questioning it. Unsurprisingly, however, I would learn from my file that these connections aroused the

Securitate's suspicions. Why hadn't I anticipated that, you ask? Because, first, I wasn't really thinking that much about how things would look to the Securitate, and second, I probably thought they knew about our arrangements, since our grants had been approved through Romanian government organizations. (Indeed, my case officer for 1974 mentions them in one of his reports.)

My Cluj Secus would find very suspicious my occasional meetings with the embassy personnel who came through town (and who would take my field notes back to Bucharest for mailing, saving me two full days of traveling for that purpose every month or so). One of the cultural attachés, Merrie Blocker, was a college classmate of mine, and another, Kiki Munshi, a marvelous woman with whom I still correspond; I was happy for these connections, which often proved not just pleasurable but very helpful. Although it puzzles me now to recall how little I questioned the arrangement then as I see its consequences in my surveillance, the relationship with the embassy was on balance beneficial, and I took it for granted as a condition of my fellowship.

Another reason for my not giving more thought to these arrangements—and to my inevitable relations with the Securitate—was, I suspect, a shortcoming of my graduate education, whether of my training or of my absorption of it. As early as his 1919 letter to *The Nation* entitled "Scientists as Spies," famous anthropologist Franz Boas raised a prescient warning about the linkage of anthropology to state power. He wrote: "A person . . . who uses science as a cover for political spying, who demeans himself to pose before a foreign government as an investigator and asks for assistance in his alleged researches in order to carry on, under this cloak, his political machinations, . . . forfeits the right to be classed as a scientist."[2] Although his warning fell on hostile ears, the discipline's later history included several broader critiques of anthropology's political connections, such as the 1960s furor about anthropologists working in Southeast Asia.[3] I remember reading about that but dismissing it as irrelevant because I did not intend to work for the CIA, as some of them did. With the exception of Bill Skinner, my faculty advisors knew too little about conditions for fieldwork in Romania to caution me, and the main lesson I took away from Skinner's experience of having all his field notes confiscated in Mao's China was to be sure I had multiple copies of my notes in different locations and to send them out regularly through the diplomatic pouch. But I remained vulnerable to surveillance, whether through innocence or conceit.

> > >

Although my filter in these pages will be how the Securitate, its apparatus, and its culture of secrecy shaped me and my work, I should first introduce some of the friends who made life in Romania so often delightful. Most will also have some connection with my surveillance, even if only for their response to my thinking about this book. I begin with Silvia and Marina.

At the end of my first week in the country, Angela, the embassy employee in charge of IREX grantees, invited me to go to the Black Sea with her and a number of other friends. One of their group had just dropped out and they had an extra space (which they needed someone to pay for). There were seven people plus me. Two of them, Silvia and Marina, remain my friends to this day. We enjoyed a number of adventures at the Black Sea, including the fun of trying to slip me unnoticed past the hotel reception desk every day, since if they asked for my identification papers and saw my passport, I would have to pay much more for my room. This launched my occasional habit of hiding my identity, trying to "pass" as a Romanian.

A style maven to the hilt who was always well turned out and always on the lookout for Paris fashion magazines, Marina was a very talented seamstress (her regular job was teaching art) and made me several wonderful dresses during that year. After she fled to the United States in 1990, this talent helped her move up from sewing clothes in Milwaukee's garment district to becoming a top buyer for Saks Fifth Avenue. My friendship with Silvia—also an art teacher—began to blossom more fully after Marina's departure, as Silvia and her husband put me up whenever I came to town and she ceased to be just a casual friend. Moreover, she has given me many a valuable reality check in my writing and will appear in that guise in these pages. A truly gifted storyteller with a pixie face and a mordant wit, she has delighted me for twenty-five years with stories, such as those in her wonderful book *Marvelous Aunts* (*Mătuşi minunate*) about the fates of the old privileged classes from which she hails, as they learned to paint radiators for communist enterprises after they got out of prison.

From these friends I learned how Romanians sought to protect themselves from the Securitate and the consequences of being in contact with foreigners, something that was technically against the law unless reported to the police (though few Romanians I knew then obeyed that law). During the 1970s, whenever I came to Bucharest from the countryside, Marina would invite me to dinner with the others on Saturday, asking me to get out of my cab or other transportation a few blocks from her house, then walk the rest (the Secus were not fooled). I was never to call from my hotel room in Bucharest

Silvia, happy to have found toilet paper to buy, ca. 1980. Courtesy of Silvia Colfescu.

but only from pay phones—which, I was to discover from my file, were just as closely monitored. When we were all assembled, they would turn on the TV or phonograph very loud, making it impossible for any eavesdropping Securitate officers to understand what we were saying. My documents show that this strategy was successful, though unfortunately, it at first prevented me, with my barely functional Romanian, from understanding anything either. But the message was clear: my new friends routinely behaved as if an unseen and unwelcome presence was part of our gathering.

With this training, I am surprised to recall how dismissive I was—along with most of the other grantees—of the orientation the embassy personnel provided, which informed us of the multiple sources of surveillance to which we would be subject. We regarded them as paranoid, stuck in an old Cold Warrior mind-set that saw conspiracies and surveillance everywhere. Quite full of myself, I dismissed it all as a Red Scare exaggeration. Although my project was not about "communism," I and some of the other grantees were nonetheless sure that our work might change the way the communist system was understood at home, creating a more "realistic" and less "paranoid" view. Reading my file many years later, though, I discover, to paraphrase Lily Tomlin, that no matter how paranoid we became, it was never enough to keep up.[4]

Professor Mihai Pop

I returned from the Black Sea to meet the person who would be my research supervisor, Professor Mihai Pop. A robust, imposing man, very handsome with wavy white hair, heavy black glasses, and a near-perpetual smile, he was Romania's most eminent specialist in ethnography and folklore. He had agreed to take me on as a personal favor to the head of IREX, Allen Kassof, for although IREX had ranked my proposal first on the U.S. side, the Romanian side had trouble finding an institution to assign me to, for Western-style anthropology did not exist there. The sociologists said I was too much a folklorist, the folklorists said I was too sociological. As a result, my application was rejected. Only Kassof's intervention got me in: he knew Professor Pop well from the early years of the exchanges and simply asked him to take me into the institute he headed, the Institute of Ethnography and Folklore. Professor Pop agreed. He was used to protecting assorted scholarly misfits in his institute and had the political skills and connections to do so.

I was extraordinarily fortunate, for Professor Pop was a remarkable mentor. He regularly invited me to his office and his home, where he would tell me all kinds of fascinating things about social organization and social processes in the countryside. He made the study of contemporary Romanian life sing, without much mention of the impact of the Communist Party. He introduced me to people he thought I would find interesting, took me on a couple of trips to folklore festivals in the most beautiful parts of Romania, and when I got into trouble, went all the way to my proposed field site (an eight-hour train ride) to try to set things right. I cannot say I have done the same for my own students. In addition, he provided a wonderful example of someone who loved life, enjoyed himself and his work, and knew how to play the system to the benefit of those in his circle. A sign of his political adroitness is that he appears in my Securitate file in only one place, with a lengthy summary of my dissertation. We remained good friends until his death in 2000, at age ninety-three, and I am still in touch with his family.

Shortly after I met Professor Pop, I wrote the following appreciation to my partner at home:

> Had lunch with Pop. What I really like is his talking about doing all he does in his life as if each thing were a game, with its own rules and rewards but ultimately to be taken as a form of enjoyment rather than a deadly serious business. He claims that's the route that allows him freedom in Romania, where many people don't find

Professor Mihai
Pop, ca. 1970.
Courtesy of Zoltán
Rostás.

freedom possible. It's not that he doesn't take serious interest in his work—he loves it—but the element of geniality is never lost.

"The Folklorist" Heads Off on Her Motorbike

After reading my research proposal and talking with me at length, Professor Pop decided that the best place for me to go was the county of Hunedoara, especially its southern part. There I would find the conditions my project required: a number of different ethnographic microzones (small areas distinguished from one another by differences in their costume, rituals, dialects, traditions—that is, their "folklore"). My project was to try to explain the distribution of these zones and why they differed in so small a space; my assumption was that it had something to do with patterns of movement, perhaps based on economic behavior. Therefore, I would be working not just in one place but in numerous villages in a region. I would be a nightmare for anyone attempting to keep me under surveillance. Pop suggested that I take a trip out to Hunedoara County for some reconnaissance. Since local transportation was unreliable, I proposed to visit these villages on my new Mobra motorbike. It sported license plates with bright-red numbers—T.C. 2964 (T.C. is "consular transport," used by embassy personnel)—that would help the authorities keep me in their sights.

My Mobra was a very special machine, worth a moment's digression, for as we already know, it was to be the instrument of my first adventure as a "spy." I had bought it in Bucharest from the Comturist ("dollar") shop in what surely qualifies as the most grueling yet hilarious purchasing experience of my entire life. It involved over three days of my being shunted from one office to another, endless waiting, and deepening affection for several other hapless buyers immobilized in the same offices, as well as for many kind people in far-flung storage depots and auto-service shops who finally got me mobile by the end of the third day. At each step I would be told the next step, but no one would divulge the entire process, enabling me to plan. (Precisely the point?) Most important, to the intense mirth of any Romanian who found this out, I had bought the bike with precious hard currency. The Mobra was renowned as a lemon—the subject of a jingle, "Certain death with a cobra, / But more certain with a Mobra"[5]—and I had paid for it *with dollars!* When they learned that, the men who gathered around me as I finally took possession of it roared with laughter and shook their heads in disbelief at the same time.

Before loading it onto the train for Hunedoara I bought a fancy helmet at the duty-free shop, bright blue with sparkles and a snappy plastic visor that clicked sharply into place. For the next sixteen months I was besieged by would-be buyers—of the helmet, not the bike. Wearing it along with my yellow rubberized raincoat (for protection and visibility) and my long hair streaming out behind, I cut quite a memorable figure, one that some villagers remember with amusement even now—and one that made me easy to recognize for the police, as well. I became very fond of my Mobra, even though its fifty-five-mph maximum speed could only be achieved downhill with a tailwind. But like my wedding ring and my newfound height, it gave me a different feeling about myself: I could defy the erratic public transportation system by simply getting on my bike whenever I wanted to go to town. It gave me a sense of mastery, especially once I figured out how to drive it.

Professor Pop had given me the names of two former students who worked in Hunedoara County's education department, S. and C.; he phoned them before I left. When I arrived in the capital city, Deva, I learned from S. that C. had been demoted. The person who greeted me frostily in his place, R., bore the pseudonym "Slimy" in my subsequent field notes. Aside from being a bit creepy, he was walleyed, which hampered connecting with him. Working behind the scenes, S. and C. came up with an itinerary for me that included villages out to the western border of the county, then doubled back to a number of villages in the south and west; there were thirty villages in all, and the tour was scheduled for a bit more than two weeks. My comrades gave me the names of people I could stay with in each village and called ahead to notify them.

Having barely arrived in Hunedoara, I was already being watched.

Source "Iulia"   13.09.1973

Informative Note

. . . In room 120 [of hotel Sarmis, Deva] was housed the said Verdery KAHTERINE MAUREEN from the U. S. A. who is currently a student at the university of Bucharest, possessing study pass no. 159 of this aforementioned university. She has come to town and to our county for problems of folklore, being under the guidance of the Center for Popular Creation and Folklore in the city. The length of her stay will be approximately a month.

Passing over the misinformation in this account, let's go to the Officer's Note ("N.O.") at the end, where he gives "Iulia" (a hotel receptionist) her assignment:

To establish the activity and behavior of the American student MAURICEN KATERINE in the period of her stay in the hotel, noting in particular:
  —the times when she comes and goes from the hotel
  —by whom she is accompanied
  —whether anyone asks for her at the hotel
  —whether she creates relations in the complex of the "Sarmis" hotel with
    its personnel or with persons from outside (Romanian citizens)
  —discussions she carries on.

["Iulia"] was told to seek to get close to the student on the pretext of wanting to speak English and in this way to establish more data with respect to her. Measures will be taken through means for eavesdropping. . . .

Maj. Lung Vasile

Other hotel receptionists enrolled in keeping track of me during that period found potentially suspicious patterns:

Source: Plopeanu
Date: 21.09.73
Source informs you [concerning] the American citizen Katherine Verdery . . .

In the time that has passed so far, absences from the hotel were noted at late hours (22:00–23:00), the room key remaining at the reception, and her motorbike was not parked in front of the hotel as usual. Source does not know at the moment where she might be at that hour.

In addition, Securitate officers minutely informed police in each settlement I was to visit, to find out the following about what I discussed with people I met. It was an extensive list.

Ministry of the Interior   TOP SECRET
Hunedoara County Inspectorate, Service III   [24.ix.73]

NOTE

In the informative supervision of the American citizen Verdery Katherine, we request that the following aspects be kept in mind:
    —concretely what data interest her in the localities she visits;
    —with whom she makes contact and how she leads the discussions;
    —how she intends to use the material collected;
    —what she says about the localities visited, how she assesses the material and the persons with whom she spoke;
    —where she has been besides Hunedoara County and her opinions;
    —what she says about her familial, material, and professional situation;

—with what persons in the country she has relations and with whom she proposes to correspond;

—how and with whom she spends her free time in Deva.

These aspects are to be obtained from the heads of local police from discussions with the persons with whom V.K. has made contact, as well as from the [informer] network.

Informers are to be placed in the localities she has not yet visited.

Maj. Andreşescu Cornel

There followed detailed reports by the local police from each of the villages I visited, which provided a comprehensive view of what I was up to. I was wholly unaware of all this activity.

My "Spying" Commences

Most U.S. scholars came to Romania either to teach as Fulbright lecturers or to do research in libraries, meaning that they generally lived in large cities where they would not have much chance to discover military or other secret installations and to engage in espionage in them. Not this anthropologist. If they thought I was a spy, they had good reason. The adventure I recounted in my opening pages and fill out now is an excellent example of how ignorance blossoms into folly (or so I see it), with consequences that affected my research for many years thereafter.

My tour of Hunedoara circled around a mountainous mass in the west, taking me up some of its valleys. I would soon learn that in recommending this area, Professor Pop had not considered the importance of its *massif*, the farthest mountainous area toward neighboring Hungary and Yugoslavia, both of which were Romania's enemies at one time or another after World War II. That these mountains might hold military bases would have been a reasonable guess. My letters and field notes of the time reveal my progress toward that discovery.

Letter to Wm, 28 Sept. 73 [Mailed through the Romanian mail]
Have for the moment brought to a close my 2½ week madcap run through western Hunedoara, closed two days early by rain. Motorbike has been an utter godsend; I raced through 30 villages, eventually not even going back to Deva but staying in people's houses overnight. Although I particularly liked the Cerna valley, I may not be able to work there because despite my having been programmed from Deva to go there, I was stopped by a cop in the town of Topliţa and told that there's a sign at the

entrance to the valley saying "Entry Prohibited to Foreigners." I swear there was no sign. But I had to sit there while he called Deva and made a full report, "arrested in a prohibited zone while driving with foreign license plates," and eventually they told him to let me through. TopSecMilbase in the most critical settlement for the project.

(You might ask yourself: What the hell was she thinking, sending all this through the regular mail? Clearly I was oblivious of the likelihood that my letter might be intercepted. How could that not cross my mind? Hadn't I been briefed by the embassy about the Securitate's practices? I had, but I'd blown it off.)

A few days later I mailed Wm (this time through the diplomatic pouch) further evidence of how badly I had botched my meetings in Deva:

> Made a possibly fatal error at the beginning. . . . Pop had told me to put a question to his main friend, C., regarding Gurasada, one of the villages I was interested in going to [and possibly in a restricted zone]. So in the course of planning my trip around the county, I put the question, but to "Slimy," rather than C., asking point blank whether there was some sort of military installation in that village. The electricity in the room in that instant was blinding; then he smiled a sinister smile, and he and S. replied, "We don't know." At this point the phone rang, and the sinister guy went out for it; S. meanwhile put his finger on that village on my map and said, "Keep away from there, your question was right." . . . I made a great effort to be good after that, but getting stopped for going into the prohibited zone a week later no doubt did not help. My friend Bear [sociologist Mihail Cernea, who gave me significant help with my research] says I should expect to be under closer watch than I might be in other circumstances.

That was certainly an understatement.

Here was my innocent belief in transparency at its most damaging. Evidently I imagined that by clarifying the status of Gurasada, we could make an efficient choice of what village to settle me in: let's get the military bases out of the way, then we'll talk about the rest. But I asked it of a distrustful apparatchik completely uninterested in an efficient solution toward scholarly ends. This episode erased all doubt that I was completely clueless about politics in communist Romania. It also reveals how convinced I was of my own rectitude and that others would value it as I did.

But there was more, as in the follow-up to that meeting:

> Field notes, 13 Sept. 73
> S. came to my room very tipsy, justified his unexpected visit by saying he works on instinct and sense of smell about people at first sight. He wants to help me. Said I had

created a certain situation, not entirely favorable to future progress, since "Slimy" was now suspicious as all hell. So I sure blew it wide open with that question about Gurasada. . . . Then giving me advice: make sure all my questions are exceedingly clear, in intent and form. Be especially careful at Toplița because many people there work in Hunedoara, which is a very important city in national development.

I remember being confused about what he meant, but I would soon find out, when that truck bearing the Toplița cop pulled me over. This was the incident reported by officer Uscatu of Military Unit 01736, with which I opened: my accidental motorbike ride toward a military base and my ersatz spying.

Arrival in Aurel Vlaicu Village

Following this debacle, how was I to continue to work in Hunedoara? A letter to Wm tells how I was eventually settled there, after Professor Pop took the lengthy train ride out to Deva with me to arrange it:

Letter to Wm, 21 Nov. 73
Pop spoke for some two hours with a couple of county officials in Deva and came out to tell me where they'd decided to send me—after I'd spent 10 hours on the train beating my brains out, writing down questions to ask in order to clarify and better choose . . . all to no avail. Thus I am to go to Geoagiu commune, near Orăștie. Its two ethnographic zones spill over into Alba County, about which I had read absolutely nothing in preparation, and it bears no relationship whatsoever to the project design I came here with.

This location would guarantee abandoning my original project, whose requirements it did not fit, though it did not occur to me that I needed to tell anyone but my PhD committee members and Professor Pop about that. The Securitate, however, would notice the discrepancy, observing that I kept asking questions beyond the purview of my officially approved project.

The person given the task of settling me in a village in her commune was Mrs. M., a functionary in Geoagiu, who was in Deva that day. A talkative, energetic woman in her midforties, well dressed and with coiffed black hair, she accepted this assignment with great trepidation (she told me many years later), fearful of its possible consequences for her job and family. She led Professor Pop and me to a decrepit green van that labored from Deva toward Geoagiu, some thirty kilometers distant. I peered furtively at the 1966 census of Hunedoara County that a colleague in Bucharest had given me (these figures were considered top secret but he hadn't seemed to care), which showed the total population of each village and its ethnic composition. Geoagiu, the

The village of Aurel Vlaicu, 2000. Photo by Karin Steinbrueck.

administrative center of the commune, had some 2,500 people and contained ten other villages. Only four were collectivized, and that seemed essential to me: Why come to a communist country and then avoid one of its most distinctive features, collective farms? Although it later emerged that county officials had assumed without telling Mrs. M. that she would settle me in the commune center, I did not want that: Geoagiu was too big, and it shared its collective farm with another village. I was hoping for something a bit smaller and more self-contained. Of the two remaining collectivized villages, one was tiny and somewhat inaccessible. The last one, Aurel Vlaicu, seemed just right: 915 inhabitants, 20 percent of whom were of Romania's German minority.[6] So much the more interesting, I thought. Mrs. M. was surprised by my choice and opposed it vigorously but failed to talk me out of it, giving in with the words, "All right, we have relatives there you could stay with. They're very nice."

In fact, I was fated to choose this village, which had already been foreshadowed for me right after I arrived in Romania. One Sunday, my hostess Jana had taken me to some friends, with whom we watched TV. Among the programs was one about a Romanian named Aurel Vlaicu. Thus, even before I got to Hunedoara County, I knew who Vlaicu was. One of Romania's two geniuses in the field of aviation and the inventor of Romania's first airplane, Vlaicu was born in 1882 in this village to which his name would be given some years after he died in a plane crash in 1913. Like most villagers, I use the short form "Vlaicu" to refer to the village and "Vlaiceni" [vly CHENi, sing. "Vlaicean"] for its inhabitants.

My choice of Vlaicu was to have some unfortunate repercussions, however, for it lies twenty-four kilometers from the town of Cugir, site of several factories including some in the business of making armaments. Even as I left Deva, the politicos there had told Professor Pop to warn me never to head down the road toward Cugir, which sported that same sort of sign I had already missed once: "Entry Prohibited to Foreigners." A large number of Vlaicu's residents commuted daily to work there. The anxiety this aroused for the Securitate is evident in a group of documents from my file. They contain four undated lists from 1973, the first called "TABLE with persons who work at the Metallurgical Factory in Cugir" with 122 names, followed by other tables with the names of commuters to Cugir from each of three villages; Vlaicu had the largest number of commuters. Each entry on each list gives the names of the person's parents, his/her date and place of birth, and in a few cases, the further mention "Possesses a file in the Informer Archive." A formidable amount of work went into constructing these lists—gathering dates and places of birth, parents' names, and specific occupations—all with the aim of contacting every one of them and warning them about me. Added to the episode with my motorbike, my proximity to this town remained a source of deep suspicion throughout my times in Vlaicu, as everyone but me seemed to have forgotten that I had not chosen to work in that part of the county but been assigned there.

It would turn out that my doppelganger followed me out to this village. Despite many years of living or visiting there, I never succeeded in putting to rest the persistent rumor among some in the village that I was a spy. A number of my respondents told me, both before and after the regime fell in 1989, that everyone knew I was a spy, though they didn't really know what for. They just knew that everyone said I was one. Occasionally someone would say it to my face, but mostly the rumor circulated behind my back. After 1989, one friend told me that earlier, when she invited me over for lunch, others reproached her: "Don't speak with her! She's a spy! Why aren't you afraid to invite her over?" Another, whose son I had hired to do some interviews for me, was admonished by her brother-in-law, a military man: "Don't let him work for her! She's a spy!"[7]

My local reputation as a spy was partly a consequence of the Communist Party's efforts to spread information and disinformation, including through films and literature that, as in Western countries, popularized the notion of the spy. Indeed, the idea that I was spying was probably planted by the Securitate's "rumor factory." They did it first through the informers they recruited, who were taught how to recognize a spy. And they also did it through the local police, as I realized one day in 1985 when a respondent told me that a policeman had been warning everyone to be careful what they said to me, since I was a spy and carried a concealed tape recorder.

I might have anticipated this had I been better informed about the Romanian educational system, which was preoccupied with spies and provided a significant socialization into spying as both adventure and source of worry.[8] For instance, a children's book called The White Spaceship, published in the 1970s, includes a scene in which a group of children manages to decode a message critical for national security. It revealed that foreign spies were conspiring to steal an ancient treasure crucial to Romanian identity—and they arrived at this truth after going through preliminary suspicions in which foreign spies were stealing other Romanian valuables. The book was later made into a popular TV series with comparable scenes. Similarly, an associate told me that the schools were a vital center for instilling a concern with foreign spies: "Kids in school and everyone else were socialized into the idea of infiltration by foreign bodies as the cause of our problems. Now, with you, the police could say, 'This is what a spy looks like. Here she is, in flesh and bone.' You were a godsend for them." With this start, it is little surprise that in the village where I settled, many people might think I was a spy.

Meri, Moaşa, and Moşu

Mrs. M., Professor Pop, and I drove into Vlaicu on the chilly wet afternoon of 21 November 1973. Unlike the more picturesque villages in the nearby hills with their view of the river Mureş and its floodplain, Vlaicu sits flat on that plain, bounded by the river on one side. Both the railroad and the highway connecting central Transylvania with Hungary to the west run right along the edge of the village, providing ready transportation out and accounting for all those commuters to Cugir and other towns. The main street into the village crosses the railway tracks, then runs past colorful houses—brown, gray, yellow, green, even orange, with contrasting trim—built on a variety of patterns. Winding past an old flourmill and then past the Lutheran church and the outbuildings of the collective farm, the road continues on toward aviator Aurel Vlaicu's natal house, the Romanian Orthodox church, and the elementary school.

Our van stopped just past the collective farm, and we piled out into the house of Mrs. M.'s relatives, whose meal we interrupted. The wife, Maria, was in her midforties, a warm and smiling presence with crisp curly gray hair (I was to learn that, unlike most village women, she almost never covered it with a headscarf except in the coldest weather). She had a way of slightly narrowing her eyes that somehow gave her an appealing saintly air, for which I baptized

Meri and Kathy, dressed
for Pentecost, 1974.
Author's photo.

her "Meri" (pronounced "Mary") to distinguish her from her sister-in-law,
also Maria. Her husband, Iosif ("Joseph," appropriately enough), also in his
midforties, was a robust fellow with thick glasses and a pleasant youthful face
capped by a startling shock of snow-white hair, a feature his son would inherit.
Iosif worked as a foreman at Cugir, and this would soon prove an impediment.

Professor Pop explained that I was from America on an exchange grant
to do my doctorate, I had all the necessary support from Bucharest and the
county authorities, and we hoped to find a good family to host me. Non-
plussed, the couple stalled while the professor skillfully wheeled the conversation around to their recently married daughter in Bucharest, their relatives
in Vlaicu, and so on, finally saying, "Well, what about it?" Meri looked at her
husband and asked, "What do we say?" to which he replied, "I say, let's take
her." Although I didn't know it yet, I had just won the lottery.

The next day, at Professor Pop's suggestion, Meri invited her aging parents and the village schoolteacher, whom the professor interviewed deftly and at length about marriage customs and kinship, village history, the local elite, and other topics, providing me with a wonderful model of how to connect with these people. I had had very little training in field techniques, so his example was particularly valuable. That he was willing to take this long train ride from Bucharest and spend two days getting me settled won him my lifelong gratitude. When he left the next morning—after advising me to stay away from Cugir and not to look into the collective farm—I felt quite bereft.

The feeling did not last, however, for my new landlady took me in hand and spent the day chatting with me. I took an immediate liking to her, which was reciprocal; we became fast friends and remained so for over forty years. I had reduced the village to a stack of 3 × 5 slips, and we would spend hours on end together going through the slips as she told me where the people in each house were from, their local nicknames, their godparents (an important aspect of Romanian kinship), their jobs, and so on. If there was any interesting gossip about them she would tell me that, too, with relish. She sent me to several families who became my best respondents for my work, and she introduced me to her group of five or six women friends who would come together during winter evenings for knitting or doing needlework, eating cakes, and telling bawdy stories. I soon proved I could hold my own with all but the needlework and became an honorary member. In addition, I became and remain close friends with her son Florin and his family, who still live in Vlaicu, and with her daughter Angela in Bucharest. Won the lottery, indeed!

Unfortunately my living arrangements (though not my association with Meri) soon came to an end. A couple of weeks after I had settled in, Meri told me that she was moving me to her close friend Veca, just down the road, who often hosted the social evenings I attended. The reason she gave was that with her daughter newly married in Bucharest, she planned to visit there often and would not be able to host me properly. When I told Mrs. M. of the change in plans, she ordered me to wait until she could clear Veca's family with the mayor, who, it turned out, was adamantly opposed: Veca's husband had been an active fascist in the war (a common allegation, I learned much later, often baseless) and could not be trusted. What that doubtless meant

Moasha looking out from her bedroom, 1974. Author's photo.

Moasha and Moshu, ca. 1970.
Family photo.

My bedroom in Vlaicu, traditional style. Photo by Nicolae Mărgineanu.

was that they couldn't be certain of getting information about me from him, and that was, of course, crucial to the Securitate.

After much backstage maneuvering to which I was not privy, I was turned over to Meri's sister-in-law, known as "Moaşa" (MWAH sha, midwife) for her role in numerous village births before hospitals took over that function; this gave her a special ritual status with the infants she midwifed. Although childless herself, she therefore had many "children" in Vlaicu of a ritual kind. Moaşa was sixty when I first met her at Meri's. With a youthful face, blue-green eyes, and always-rosy cheeks, she impressed me at first as rather cool and self-contained. She came from another village and, with her midwifery training and some years in a factory job, definitely thought herself a cut above members of the collective farm, where I never saw her work. Her husband, Lazar, known to all as "Moşu" (ancestor, grandfather) partly because of his wife's occupation, was recently retired from the same Cugir factory where Meri's Iosif worked. A portly, balding man also about sixty, Moşu was unfailingly good-humored and sociable (I had had a chance to observe this already) and loved to drink, which he did with anyone he could persuade to join him. This frequently included the vice president of the People's Council in Geoagiu and other local politicos. I was often to come home in the evening to find him conversing amiably if incoherently with the radio after an evening with his friends, of which he (in contrast to his less gregarious wife) had an extraordinary number.

Since there was nothing I could do, I accepted the new arrangement, but once I settled in, Moaşa and I gradually became very close. She was one of a handful of people I felt I could trust completely. Both she and Moşhu seemed glad to have a "daughter" in their house.

Only after I received my file did I come to understand what had precipitated the move: rules concerning surveillance. As a result of a power struggle in the 1950s between Communist Party leaders and the Securitate, a law prohibited the latter from having Party members like Iosif under surveillance without first securing permission from Party officials. The relevant document phrases it thus: "In order that he not be under surveillance by the state organs, since he is a Party member, he managed to move the American citizen to his brother Lazăr." In my case, because Iosif worked in the armaments factory, they doubtless preferred not to seek permission but to move me instead. Thus, his Party and work connections led to his being insulated from both me and Securitate oversight. I did not realize this at the time, of course, but learning it now makes clear that there were limits to Securitate surveillance: they could not do absolutely anything they wanted, and this had been evident right from the start of my life in Vlaicu. Nonetheless, for local police who came later and did not know that my housing was initially arranged by Mrs. M. through her kinship connections, the suspicion lingered that I had purposely selected Iosif and his brother's family because of their relations to Cugir. My earlier misadventure with the Mobra, then, would continue to influence perceptions.

Moaşa and Meri were both from respected families in Vlaicu, and their affectionate disposition toward me offered resistance to whatever rumors the Securitate was sowing to scare people away from me. So did the openly welcoming opinion of the much-loved village schoolteacher and his wife, Ştefan and Mărioara Popescu, whom I visited often, and of my venerable neighbor, Petru Bota, to whom Meri sent me right after I arrived and with whom I sat for hours every week. I made friends among women of various ages: Helga the seamstress, her neighbor Dorica (my special pal), Maria lu' Relu, Mărioara lu' Pompi[9]—these last two became crucial contributors to my research over subsequent decades—and, among the Germans, the Schmidt, Schön, and Hellerman families in particular. Gradually my network in the village expanded, countering the invisible network of informers who were being recruited or deployed to keep tabs on me. How much overlap there was between these networks—one cultivated from below, the other from the political center— would remain mostly a mystery, one I did little to unravel. I realize now, however, that my arrival in Vlaicu (and the arrival of other U.S. anthropologists later in the decade) was a great boon to the Securitate: villages were not easy for them to penetrate, and we helped them get in, like fleas on a stray dog.

If the Securitate would come to provide me with multiple identities as a spy, Meri and Moaşa offered me an alternative and much more appealing identity: that of kin. In an interview Meri did for a documentary film made about me in 2012, she explained something about our friendship that I had never realized: "From the moment I saw her I really liked her. My daughter had just gotten married and moved to Bucharest and in my heart I felt a sort of hole [lit., I was left with my heart fried] because she had gone. And so when [KV] came, I thought to myself that it was good to have someone here with me."[10] Translating our connection into the kinship idiom so common throughout the world, she has often said that she loves me as if I were her own daughter—and indeed, for a time I took on her daughter's role. Moaşa too would come to treat me like a daughter, and my friends Maria lu' Relu and Dorica, as well as Meri's daughter Angela, would say I was like a sister to them. This is one of the greatest pleasures of ethnography: to be adopted into the relations most meaningful to our hosts.

Kathy

Let us stop for a moment and ask about this person who has finally arrived at her field site in socialist Romania, in November 1973, to begin a year's research. What do we know about her? She is twenty-five and is called Kathy; "Katherine" would come with her first job, in 1977, when she decided it was time to grow up. Unlike many her age, she did not take time during or after her studies to travel or simply hang out but went straight on to graduate work after college; she took off only the intervening summer to travel in Scotland and Wales on a kind of kiddie fieldwork. It mainly taught her to drink hard liquor—scotch. She'd never been big on spirits before, and this new habit would stand her in very good stead in Romania, where her fieldwork demanded drinking as part of building trust. On that trip she also learned to expect fieldwork to include some lonely times, a lesson underscored by two months' research in Greece the following summer, in 1971.

Although she thinks of herself as a bit of a rebel, having participated in actions against the Vietnam War, Kathy was well socialized as a responsible older sister in an Episcopalian family. She carries many unexamined and typically American assumptions—in which her anthropological training has not made much of a dent—such as a mistrust of communism, even though she is curious about it and is open to changing her views. Like many Americans, she thinks of herself as a well-meaning person of unquestionable honesty and integrity, and she expects others to see her that way. This expectation will get her into real trouble in Romania. So will her thoroughgoing commitment to sincerity, openness, and transparency, which we have already seen.

Of the hidden forms of deceit in her character she is barely aware, and this tends to nourish some self-righteousness, which will occasionally get in her way during fieldwork.

Kathy is a child of the 1960s and tends to dress very informally, still in the mentality of a student. In Vlaicu she mainly wears jeans and a sweater, with her waist-long hair either loose or (when it gets greasy) covered by a bandanna like the Romanian women she spends time with (try washing long hair in a small enamel basin and you too will do it less often). Vlaiceni are somewhat baffled by this outfit, since in Romania a person getting a PhD, referred to as *doctorand*, has fairly high status and should dress better than that. Kathy doesn't care, and besides, she thinks villagers will be more responsive to her this way. Indeed, in 1979 she called a village meeting to tell people what she had found out about Vlaicu in the Transylvanian archives in Cluj, and she dressed up in her best suit and heels. People said afterward that it was a good thing she didn't look like that all the time or they would have been afraid to talk with her.

Kathy's family is solidly middle class, though not wealthy (that had ended with the stock market crash in 1929, which wiped out a considerable fortune). Her father had recently left his corporate job and become a real estate agent on Cape Cod; her mother stopped being an elementary school teacher then and kept the home; her younger brother, David, is a rock musician in Ithaca, New York, having opted out of college; and her much-younger sister, Margaret, is still in school (she will later become a horse trainer, and then a financial planner). Though the Securitate is eager to have these details, their informers—especially "Lazar" and "Silviu" (see below)—will repeatedly mess them up, perhaps indicating how far her family's choices were from what these men would recognize as career possibilities.

How, after all, did Kathy choose to become an anthropologist? It was her mother B.'s doing. Having dropped out of college in 1944 to get married, B. had worked at a number of secretarial and sales jobs until 1956, when she decided to finish her degree and become a teacher. To complete her distribution requirements in social science, she signed up for a summer-school course in anthropology. She loved it. All that summer Kathy's mother, generally a rather unpredictable and difficult person, was much more cheerful than usual because she was so enthusiastic about what she was learning, and she filled her children's heads with stories of Piltdown Man, *Australopithecus*, New Guinea, and Margaret Mead. This gave Kathy some pretty fancy stuff to talk about with her third- and fourth-grade classmates. She decided right there that when she got to college (which turned out to be Reed, a good place for anthropology), she would at least take a course in the subject that could render her mother so changed. She did—and another, and another. Although she'd thought of following a career in social work, her two most influential professors pooh-poohed that idea, pressing her instead to go to graduate school. Eventually she decided anthropology was the best discipline in the world, because you can study almost anything and still call yourself an anthropologist.

And how did she get to Romania, of all places? Although she had already shown an interest in the margins of Europe with her summer's fieldwork in the Celtic fringe, perhaps the beginning was the day in 1972 when a fellow graduate student, knowing her love of maps, came in with a large map of Eastern Europe. He put it on the floor and for hours they pored over what seemed crazy-looking place names in Hungarian, Serbo-Croatian, Czech and Slovak, Polish, and Romanian, many of them decidedly short on vowels and loaded with diacritics. (Remembering it brings to mind the joke circulating during the Yugoslav wars, "Clinton orders vowel drop for Bosnia.") The more they looked, and the closer they got to the Black Sea, the more excited Kathy grew: she was truly aroused by the prospect of working in a "communist" country having all those terrific names. Add to this the fact that she had long had a fearful-cum-fascinated relation to the idea of communism, having written two major papers about it in high school; clearly her relation to Eastern Europe was in some sense foreordained.

Since she had no specific research problem in mind yet—she was just curious about what life "behind the Iron Curtain" would be like—nothing dictated the choice of a specific country to work in. She picked Romania because in the early 1970s, it was the only Eastern European country where one could do field research with relative ease. The others, for a variety of reasons, had closed themselves off, whereas in those years the Romanian regime had chosen a path of greater openness. Not only was anthropological fieldwork permitted: according to the Fulbright handbooks, it was even welcomed. Since one of her professors had always insisted that picking a field site was basically ser-endipitous, this welcome seemed reason enough to choose Romania, so she set about beginning to learn the language, relieved to find it much easier than those other languages would have been. It was only in the 1980s that this welcome would wear thin. All along, though, the authorities apparently saw no contradiction between such openness and extensive surveillance.

Here are a few things that Kathy's friends from grad school and college recall about her. First, they say, she was smart. (Her relation to this talent was contradictory: not a little conceited, like so many academic women she

Kathy in 1973.
Author's photo.

nonetheless often felt stupid. Underlying this lack of confidence, she would learn decades later, was a reading disability that hindered recall and caused her distress throughout her academic career.) A lover of music, she enjoyed folk dancing and sang in community choruses. Friends remember her as warm and funny, with a hearty laugh and a proclivity for dirty puns, a habit inherited from her witty father. Brash and sometimes impatient, she tended to intellectualize things, making her more likely to explain them by theories or reasons rather than through social relationships or feelings. (I think this is partly because she is often at the mercy of strong feelings she doesn't understand or know how to deal with.) As a result, to some people she might seem cold or aloof. This quality will not help her in the field, but on the other hand those she meets will respond well to her vital intensity, her genuine interest in talking with them, and her exceedingly warm, open smile.

Kathy is an emotional person with occasional mood swings, but during these years she is generally cheerful and positive. She develops powerful attachments to people and can become distracted by them; on the whole, though, she maintains her forward drive and outward orientation well. All of this is, of course, my self-presentation and thus not fully trustworthy, but it will serve to anchor a view of her other than the cold-eyed view of the Securitate.

I sometimes write of Kathy as "naive," but perhaps "innocent" is the better word: the Securitate and their helpers are involved in actions all around her, and she is on another planet. Having led a fairly privileged existence that has exposed her to few hardships, she is an idealist and romantic who knows rather little about the world. Life has not yet knocked her about very much; she goes to Romania, meets her advisor, people in Vlaicu appear to like her, all seems great, she writes her thesis and gets a good job. She is used to things going her way and is not always gracious when they don't. Later on, though, as Katherine, she will find Romania a considerable challenge and will be forced to think more deeply about herself and her relation to her work.

A Novice Ethnographer

I am not a naturally born field-worker. I know this from having watched some who are, most especially Gloria Davis, my fellow Stanford student and dearest friend, who was a fieldwork genius. She visited me in Vlaicu and learned more in a few days than I had in weeks—and she didn't even speak the language. Gail Kligman is another one who, with her perpetual smile and engaged listening, can get information from a stone (she even impressed the Securitate, who noted her abilities). Although I have never seen my Hopkins colleague Gillian Feeley-Harnik in the field, it is evident from her writing and conversation that she is yet another. For me, though, doing research has always been something of a struggle, rewarding though it is. This was especially true during that first year, when I was exploring the identity of "ethnographer" and trying to grow into it. Not only am I a fundamentally shy person who doesn't easily approach others, but I was always getting tangled up in questions of theory that I couldn't figure out how to operationalize. How do I find out about this or that? What do I ask? When I began teaching at Johns Hopkins I found in my colleague Emily Martin another superb ethnographer who is masterly at operationalizing research questions. Then there were questions like, How do I make sense of what's happening in my data? My Hopkins colleague Ashraf Ghani, later president of Afghanistan, is brilliant at that kind of ethnographic interpretation. So I know from experience what these talents look like.

By now, I also know that they are rare, so my fumbling attempts to become an ethnographer may well resonate with others who have tried it. The main things I had going for me were the positive qualities I just described—vitality, a sense of humor, openness and receptivity, and a kind of intensity that many people I met seem to have found appealing. At least that was something. A few examples of how I tried to turn myself into an ethnographer show how I was creating that identity in ways that would eventually dovetail with some of the doppelgangers the Securitate was experimenting with across this decade and the next. My examples come from not only my Securitate file and my field notes but also some of my letters from the field to my partner, Wm.

The conditions under which I began my quest to become a field-worker posed a number of obstacles. First, a law passed in 1971 required any Romanians who had a conversation with a foreigner to report that conversation at their workplace. Although this law was rarely enforced during the 1970s and many Romanians were ignorant of it, the police could always pull it out as needed (especially as a means of recruiting informers). Another restrictive law was passed in 1974 that prohibited foreigners from staying in Romanian homes except by special permission. In 1985, the 1971 law was renewed with more stringent terms. Second, as I learned from my file, the Securitate regularly opened anything I mailed through the Romanian postal service (though I mainly used the embassy's diplomatic pouch) and intercepted incoming letters, some of which never reached me; periodically searched my room when I was away; and eavesdropped on any phone calls I made from Vlaicu, public phones, or my hotel room in town. Third, several of the people I had regular contact with were recruited as informers and gave more-or-less regular, more-or-less thorough reports. Finally, the Securitate primed people I encountered to influence how I thought about things, as well as trying to insinuate their people into my inner circle (e.g., "The penetration of informer 'Paul' into the intimacy of K.W.'s circle of relations will be attempted").

I did assume my mail was checked but was unaware of these other activities, which would become even more intensive during my next visit at the end of the 1970s. If some of the vignettes that follow seem to have little to do with surveillance, that reflects how I experienced them. These Secus were good at covering their tracks, and I wasn't really looking for them anyway. What was swirling around me wasn't visible—or I chose not to notice.

Although it may seem that only two forms of actual or potential spying were going on—mine concerning Romanian life, and the Securitate's concerning me—in fact there was also a third: villagers spied on me as well. Some of them did so as informers for the Securitate, others for the simple pleasure of knowing something neighbors might not yet know. Local social control was based on gossip, also known as "the village mouth" (*gura satului*). It might grow from the standard form of greeting on the street: "Where are you going?" (*Unde mergi?*) or "Where have you been?" (*De unde vii?*). Then, if people saw me heading out on my Mobra (and they couldn't miss it), word would travel, creating speculation as to where I was going and for what. If an unfamiliar automobile driven by a handsome man came into Vlaicu (in one instance, a Danish engineer I had met in Budapest), the village mouth would savor it. Rumor swirled around me much of the time, some of it planted by *securiști* and some of it simple gossip. In brief, everyone was collecting information, with various means and for various purposes. Anthropologists are often subjected to such scrutiny, though not usually by police informers. I was fairly oblivious to it.

> > >

Why, exactly, had I come to Romania? Near the front of my file for 1973 lies my first research proposal, in English with a Romanian translation made by the Securitate that replaced, with numerous errors, the translation I had submitted with my application. Their version was embellished with underlining from a Securitate reader, who found these parts especially significant. Here is some of their translation (retranslated by me), underlining intact:

[My] investigations are directed towards two problems: what is the basic unit of cultural homogeneity, and how are social or cultural boundaries connected with social solidarity? I believe that a settlement or group of settlements have maximum solidarity and a powerful sense of local identity when the borders around each cultural trait coincide, such that the boundaries delimiting a specific house style would coincide with the lines that mark costume, dialect, etc. When these lines do not coincide I would assume that the people in question do not have a stable direction of cultural identity. . . .

I underscore that my project entails establishing residence not in a large city but in a medium one or a village. In addition, I plan to travel frequently among settlements in my study region.

The bowdlerized translation makes my plans even murkier than they already were. It is unlikely that any officer reading this proposal would understand what I was planning to do and how. Certainly I myself, in my effort to come up with a politically unproblematic project (which, as it turned out, this one would not have been), had become tremendously confused by getting involved with folklore and traditional culture, about which I had never much cared. I wanted somehow to shoehorn all that into a kind of spatial analysis, which would have been more interesting but still required a breadth of knowledge of Romanian ethnography that I lacked.

In any event, my being excluded from the only area where this project made even remote sense nixed the whole thing, for the area around Geoagiu where I ended up was completely inappropriate for it. Although for a while I continued using these terms (culture, tradition, etc.), my field investigations fairly soon departed from that project. My case officers would learn of this primarily from informers' reports, for it seems they never succeeded in photocopying my field notes during that first year, only some letters and other papers. (Officers in the 1980s would have better luck opening the special lock on the suitcase where I kept my notes between trips to Bucharest.)

Encounters with "Communism"

To describe my becoming an ethnographer entails some stories that do not immediately involve the Securitate and thus seem off track, but they are important for giving a sense both of the kinds of things I was learning that officers might find of concern and of what life in Romania was like for me. A number of these episodes have to do with my encountering some aspect of that specter so frightening to Americans raised during the Cold War, "communism"—whether in Romanian daily life or in the ideology it professed or that we Americans associated with it. If there is no mention of these events in my file, this does not mean the Securitate was unaware of them: the relevant reports might have been purged as part of routine maintenance or lost during the 1989 "revolution."

One of my first efforts to "do some fieldwork" came on 23 August, a month after I had arrived in Bucharest, and involved not villagers but the urban working class. The Communist Party celebrated that day as a kind of independence day, marking Romania's shift of allegiance from the Nazis to the Allied forces in World War II. Here is how I described that day to my partner, Wm.

Letter to Wm, 22–23 Aug. 73
The city is being decorated more and more every day; banners and signs and portraits in every piazza, flags hanging on half the houses. . . . There was a terrific

vignette on the bus this morning. Passing a building on which were three enormous portraits of Marx, Engels, and Lenin, a little boy behind me on the bus asked his granny who the men were and was told their names. Then he asked what they had done and was told, "They wrote a lot, a lot."

I seem to be the only one interested in watching the festivities: everyone I asked what I should do on Aug. 23 said, "Go to the mountains" or "Stay home and read a good book." But on the 23rd I headed instead for the main boulevard at about 8:15 to watch people assembling for their obligatory demonstration; I then started for the area where the Dignitaries' reviewing stand is located—maybe 1½–2 mi. off. I was stopped half-way there by cops and order-keepers, told I couldn't walk on the sidewalk. . . . One of the Order guys responded to my saying I wanted to see the proceedings by whispering, "If you want to see, get in the parade—you'll see every-thing that way." So I piled in with some fellows who were standing on the fringe talking to me. They turned out to be workers from a food factory. Some men stood on the statue in Aviators' Square and harangued the parade endlessly with mega-phones, urging them to practice "agitație" (i.e., to chant goodies about the homeland and the president) and generally arousing biting sotto voce remarks from the fellows I was with. People managed to pull together a sort of feeble chorus of "Ceaușescu—PCR [Romanian Communist Party], Ceaușescu—PCR, hurrah!" I got a good look at Him—from a distance of about 150 yards—as well as the whole Central Committee, but I was too chicken to take a snapshot.

The most fun of all was when I got into the line, asked one of the fellows where he was from and was told "Sector 2" (one of Bucharest's 8 residential sectors), then he asked where I was from and I said "California," which came as a shock to the whole bunch. They had apparently not pegged me as a foreigner, largely because the idea of a non-Romanian marching in the parade was beyond the realm of the think-able. Most of them do their best to get out of having to march in the line. I'm told it's fun to watch the initial lining-up because half the people are trying to sneak out and go back home.

So here was an early lesson in "communist consciousness," which had shown me that the working class—or the segment of it I fell in with—was not very interested in cheering for the Party and its leaders. Had they found these notes, I imagine my Securitate officers would have been quite alarmed, as were the ones in Cluj when I joined a similar 23 August parade there a decade later.

I was far from immune to the feeling of danger associated with the idea of communism, and I was sometimes aware that my reactions smacked of clas-sic Cold War conditioning. Here's an example.

Letter to Wm, 8 Sept. 73

Had a somewhat mind-blowing talk with Bear, my first about politics here. I'd been reading a paper he wrote on transformation of peasant consciousness and went to talk with him about it; during the conversation I asked what he means concretely when he uses the term "socialist consciousness." In the course of this there came a moment when it was logical to ask if he's a member of the Communist Party, and he said yes. Somehow that moment was electric beyond words, though later he insisted that it's not a very important question—that everyone in a high position in academics here is a Party member, that it's fairly easy to be one. But for me—raised in part in the McCarthy and post-McCarthy commie-phobia of the US, and the author of high school English compositions on the menace of communism—there was something indescribably exciting about that instant, a rush of thrill and danger, feeling inside me for a split second the collision of earlier cognitive baggage about the Communist Party and my more recent intellectualizations about it.

I'd been hearing scary stories about communists all my life, and here I was suddenly surrounded by them. It took getting used to.

Among the most important skills I would have to learn for getting through daily life was to give one or another person "a little attention" (*o mică atenție*)—supposedly unnecessary in socialism, but essential for realizing one's goals. A little attention was particularly essential for those of us who had no local contacts to help us resolve problems like getting better service—obtaining a hotel room or train ticket (put money in your passport and hand it to the receptionist or sales clerk) or "finding" goods otherwise unavailable (put your hand on the counter with a bill barely visible under it), and so on. I generally found this hard to do; an entrenched capitalist reflex told me I shouldn't have to pay to be served, and it took me a long time to figure out what was wrong with this attitude. So I tried to manage by being very friendly or by revealing my U.S. identity, which often worked just as well for me.

Nonetheless, sometimes it was not enough. Barely a month into my life in Vlaicu, I was taught to bribe train conductors when I tried to buy a ticket from the far western to the far eastern end of Hunedoara County.

Field notes, 20 Dec. 73. Vlaicu. I learn to bribe.
I went to buy my train ticket back to Vlaicu, only to learn that you can't buy a ticket for the whole route. You have to get off at a switching point, Simeria, buy another

ticket, and then get back on. But the train would stand in the station for only two minutes. I asked the ticket seller what would happen if I got on and stayed beyond Simeria, not having time to get off: a 75-lei fine (significant, on my small grant). I asked her what to do: she said, "Talk with the conductor when you get on."

Fortunately a young woman waiting in line offered to help. She told me to get out 10 lei. We got onto the train and intercepted the conductor in between cars, where she explained the problem; he replied that he understood—no ticket to Vlaicu and no time to buy one at Simeria. He was grinning. What to do, sell me a ticket? I said, OK; he said, "75 lei. But if I close my eyes . . ." "Give him the money," whispered my new friend, and he received it with a polite bow and a smile, then went on into the next car. Thereafter, I understood that the expression "close my eyes" meant "Give me some money."

Although money was a frequent form of "attention," the most important means of it was a pack (or, for bigger favors, a carton or more) of Kent cigarettes. The first U.S. tobacco franchise to open in Romania after World War II, Kent fortuitously became the highest-status cigarette to smoke there throughout the communist era—in part because unlike Chesterfield, another early entrant, the name was easy to say. Kents, which were often not smoked but traded, could be purchased only at special shops with hard currency (illegal for Romanians to hold). In large cities one often saw Kents, but out in the village a sighting was rare. Even though my hard-currency budget was tight, I became the principal source of Kents for people in Vlaicu. My relationship to Kents would prove expensive but useful, for I regularly supplied myself with cartons of them for use in "special favors," for "small attentions," or to get out of tight spots. Sometimes they marked the thin line between suspicion and cordiality, the basis of forming trusting relations, in a society with a civic culture of mistrust. Not being a smoker, I had to develop a style that enabled me to open a pack, take one out for myself, and offer the rest to whomever I was trying to influence. I became expert at blowing smoke rings to keep from inhaling.

Socialist Inequality

I turn now to life in the village, to show something of the people who were my constant companions during the 1970s and the work I did with them. Through Professor Pop, county officials had counseled me to avoid the collective farm in Vlaicu, which was not a success. On the whole, I complied—of necessity, to some extent, for the farm president consistently put me off. But that didn't keep me from gleaning the occasional crumb in other ways. Many of them came from the feast of information provided by my first landlady, Meri. One concerned politics in the collective farm and how the president had consolidated his position, in part by excluding women from leadership roles. (So much for socialist democracy and gender parity.) Another concerned a topic lying deep in the underbelly of Romanian socialism: inequality. It was a theme I found endlessly interesting, having read a lot about social stratification in graduate courses. I would eventually do some exercises with Vlaiceni about the status rankings of their fellow villagers, which proved indisputably that twenty-five years of socialism had not created a "classless society" lacking invidious distinctions.

Letter to Wm, 24 Dec. 73
In talking with people about pre-war organization I have asked several times for the names of families that had a lot of land, that were respected, etc., and I find that people are very reluctant to answer questions about what families or people are currently respected. They respond with characteristics but not with names—the most concrete answer I've gotten is that the people respected today are the president of the collective farm, the technical personnel there, the teachers . . . Positions, not names—and in this village the incumbents of those positions are generally a pretty weak lot. Then I asked my principal German family about past and present statuses among Germans and got the same reluctance; but then they added gaily, "We're not like those Romanians, who are always saying, 'I wouldn't be caught dead at the same table with family so-and-so' or 'My daughter is engaged to someone from family so-and-so, an important family.'" They were initially hesitant but ultimately gave names of Romanian families who are very status-conscious. When I ask Romanians who are the most respected Germans, only a couple overlap with what Germans say. (The Romanians like the ones who intermarry, surprise surprise.) Later I asked Meri if it would be a nonsensical idea to give her a bunch of names and ask her to put them in hierarchical order, and she said it wouldn't be a nonsensical idea but she wouldn't especially want to do it.

I would continue to explore this topic for the next several months.

Letter to Wm, 20 Jan. 74
I've found a real gas of a task—writing down info from the tombstones in the cemetery. No need to interview anybody, no impression management, no problems of any kind except that some of them are illegible. The best tombstone so far has all the family members from the N. family and lists as well the occupations of the most recent generation even though they're still alive!

The lovely thing about the cemetery here is that there are two of them, one on a hill and one next to the church. When I asked someone what the difference was, he said, "Nothing in particular, the church got filled up so they put people on the hill." Which is untrue, since the church is not filled up yet. So I asked Meri, who said with her usual ingenuous smile, "The ones buried at the church are generally from the rich families, since it costs money to be buried there and it's free on the hill." So now I'm happily back to collecting tombstones.

With this as encouragement and using some of the information from the tombstones, I tried the ranking exercise again. Meri agreed to take a pile of index cards bearing the names of villagers and divide them into as many groups as she wanted according to their status in the village. She did it quickly and seemed to enjoy it, as she did the many similar ones I tried with her, but ended by saying, "For heaven's sake don't tell my husband! He'd be furious if he knew I was dividing the village up into social classes." This exercise followed by a scant six weeks some of my earlier unsuccessful attempts to get Vlaiceni to talk about social status. It seems that all I needed was to become more of a local presence, and I would be able to ask about taboo subjects like this; my network of relations was growing.

Since social inequality was a hot topic for a regime proclaiming to efface it, Secu officers eagerly followed my interest in the subject, though their notes show that they doubted its relevance to my research proposal. For example, in a note from October 1974, an informer describes in detail one of my ranking exercises: giving people index cards that divided the village into groups (widows, nuclear families with one salary, with two salaries, extended families, etc.) and asking them to sort each group into piles according to various criteria; at the end I would ask which families have Party members. I was doing the exercise mainly with women, because, as I apparently explained to this informer, "they go off the subject and begin to tell things that are very important. Sometimes without realizing it they begin to gossip, from which I get a better understanding of the exercise they did."

Four levels of Securitate officers became involved with this note, referring it to the first vice president of the county's Party administration.

Note of the Informer's Officer [N.O.]: The note presents interest for our organs, especially for its system of collecting and cataloguing the data. Source is instructed to continue his attentions to her . . . and if possible to enter into possession of her manuscript. Maj. Belgiu.

Note of the Superior Officer [N.S.]: Especially noteworthy is the selection of Party members from among the persons ranked by prestige, salary, character, etc. From what she learns, the target will be able to make tendentious speculations. Send the note to the Securitate leadership. Lt. Col. Petrescu.

Marginal note [M.N.] of county Securitate Head to Head of Service 3: The note presents operative interest. See if comrade Lazar has VK's work program and if this surpasses her mandate. Col. Golea.

In other words, I was not sticking to my project but straying into the domain of what they would later refer to as "socio-political information." I would have to be watched.

What Am I Doing Here?

By the beginning of the new year, I had settled in relatively well but was starting to realize that I still had no project nor any good idea of how to get one. I'd already gone through the two I had come with, both precluded by my assigned location—itself occasioned, of course, by my adventure with my Mobra. In February I wrote my friend Gloria, "You asked me to tell you what my project is. Damned if I know!" I also discussed it with Wm:

> Letter to Wm, 20 Jan. 74
> Am suffering at the moment from dreadful lethargy, can't seem to think of what to be doing with my people here, want to sit in my room and read books and not go talking. Keep feeling I must already have asked them everything and can't see the point in asking hundreds of people the same questions. Then after a day of inactivity I kick myself for the loss of time, panic at the thought of all I still have to do, and generally worsen my state.

The problem would be resolved in March, when Wm came to visit me in the field and we spent some time sussing out the situation. By the time he left, we had agreed on what I was going to do: scrap the whole spatial analysis thing (for which he had been the inspiration) and just do a social history of this village, with an emphasis on changes over time in ethnic relations, inequality, and social mobility. It was a tremendous relief to me that someone I loved could not only come and comfort me when I was feeling inept but also give shape and legitimacy to what I had been doing so far. Although I would continue to feel uncertain about my work, after he left I drew up a list of things I wanted to know about the past of every household, began visiting a broader range of people, and hired three students as research assistants. Having learned a few things by now, I got the mayor's permission before hiring my three employees and showed him the questionnaire they would be using (it appears in my file).

By April I was beginning to get a better sense of what I was up to, and a number of my respondents seemed to positively relish my visits, which gave them an opportunity to gossip about their fellow villagers, a favorite pastime. As part of my work, I began spending more and more time with several elderly villagers who remembered the earlier periods of village history going back to before World War I. My neighbor, "Uncle" Petru Bota, was eighty when I arrived and had an excellent memory for things like the interwar Romanian economy and political life. He was also a marvelous storyteller, giving me a superb life history interview (parts of which I published verbatim when he died in 1987) about his adventures as a soldier in the Hapsburg army and then as a prisoner of war in Russia.[11] At one point he had refused the scythe given him, loftily retorting, "We Austrians don't mow hay with a scythe but with machines!"—an idea he had invented on the spot, never having seen a mowing machine. For much of the year, I went to visit him and his wife, Ana, at least once a week, sometimes staying for several hours. His three children and their families also became valued interlocutors in my later research on property restitution, and I dedicated my first book to him.

Another superlative respondent for this oral history work was "Aunt" Lina Iancu, whose sharp memory of conflicts between Romanians and their Hungarian overlords prior to 1918 enlivened my understanding of that period. In future projects, conversations with her daughter Mărioara and her granddaughter Marilena would greatly enrich my work. Uncle Petru's age and Aunt Lina's infirmity afforded them plenty of time for lengthy conversations, which they seemed to enjoy as much as I did. And a third marvelous interlocutor was retired schoolteacher Ştefan Popescu, who knew a great deal about village history and was himself thinking of writing a monograph. As with my two landladies (Meri and Moaşa), my acceptance by these respected people facilitated my entry into other Vlaicu households throughout that year. I had finally settled into the identity of ethnographer.

This did not mean, however, that everything would now be easy. Fears related to my being a foreigner and likely spy could trip me up without warning and lead to some unnerving moments.

Field notes, 9 Oct. 74

Visiting with an elderly German man and wife. We've been talking about different groups in the village: the locally born, the in-migrants, and the Germans. He comments that Romanians are wrong to look down on the in-migrant hill people. "Romanians do that to everybody—toward Germans, toward each other. It's a kind

Aunt Lina Iancu, 1958. Courtesy of
Marilena Popescu.

Uncle Petru Bota, ca. 1980. Author's photo.

*of chauvinism." He goes on: the formerly rich form a clique, look down on others,
hold themselves high. He gives specific examples of poorer villagers who have gotten
ahead through hard work and deserve respect they don't get.*

*I ask who the formerly rich clique is, and he goes berserk. "Oh no! I won't go there!
I'm an old man, I don't have any children, I don't want trouble." He says someone
must have sent me, he's afraid. "I don't want to hear someone ringing the doorbell at
night." His wife is already saying he talks too much.*

I was quite shocked at this sudden change, which drew on images of the secret police (ringing the doorbell) in his refusal to discuss further what we
had been amicably discussing just a second before. Clearly, surveillance and
scrutiny were on people's minds.

Exploring Ethnic Differences

Yet another subject whose real-world manifestations often departed from
the socialist plan and which would become an increasingly larger part of my
research was ethnic identity. According to the Party, ethnicity was a form of
false consciousness that would drop away as socialism was built. Living in a
bi-ethnic village helped give the lie to this precept. For instance, one of the
principal markers of identity for Romanians was their view of themselves

as more hospitable than Germans. If I happened to tell a Romanian that I had been visiting a German household, the invariable reply was, "I bet they didn't give you anything to eat or drink!" followed by amazement when I described what I had been served. There was indeed a difference, though: unlike Romanians, Germans were less insistent that the guest eat or drink, inviting me to help myself to what they offered. A principal marker of identity for Germans, by contrast, involved punctuality. I heard several times (though never saw for myself) that when the collective farm leaders wanted to have a General Assembly meeting, they posted an announcement that said, "General Assembly meeting Saturday, 9:00 AM, 10:00 AM for Germans."

As time passed, I began learning more about patterned differences in behavior between Romanians and Germans. Here, I had just attended a pig-killing at one of the German families' homes, to complement my participation in a Romanian pig-killing the year before.

Field notes, 27 Nov. 74, Interethnic attitudes
When I tell Moaşa that German women don't wash the pig's intestines, as Romanian women do, she immediately says, "German women are less hard-working by a long shot, they don't do anything much [with the pig], unlike us." Same reaction from the woman next door: she says German women are nowhere near as hard-working as Romanian women. Ioan B. on the train back from Deva says, "German women don't clean the intestines and German men don't do a very good job of it. The gut [used for making sausage] remains with a shitty taste." He goes on, "German food is nowhere near as tasty as Romanian food, though Germans have now begun to learn something from Romanians, as we have from them."

[Two days later] Visit to Katharina, a German woman, whose explanation of why German men clean the guts and women do it among Romanians is this: Among Germans, the butcher is responsible for his work and if he lets the women do it and people later complain that the sausages tasted like shit, his reputation suffers. So he does the whole job himself. Moşu says later that Romanian women work harder, and they like to make sure that the guts are really clean. If the butcher has another pig-killing that day he may be in a hurry and not do a good job.

Thus, it looks as if the Germans professionalized the whole pig-killing task more than the Romanians, who used more relatives and neighbors rather than hiring butchers to do the entire job. Germans by contrast expected to make a business of it and to compete as well.

On a later occasion another Romanian with whom I was discussing the "backward" hill people said that the big difference here was the Germans. His example is that Germans taught Romanians to grind meat for sausages instead of just chopping it up and sticking it into the intestines in chunks. Germans had sausage grinders and machines for filling the intestines. "We learned these habits from them. Without Germans, we would be as backward as the hill people."

In short, having two ethnic groups in the village was among the most stimulating aspects of my first fieldwork. There was always something that would bring out people's perceptions of the differences, and talking with the other side would usually reverse the values (Germans, of course, saw themselves as much more hard-working than Romanians). The more time I spent there, the more I could see the points of articulation between two loosely connected but distinctive modes of rural livelihood, linked to the two nationalities' different histories and positions in Transylvanian society. Since Romania's ethnic Germans, unlike its Hungarians, were not a problem for the government, my interest in them seems not to have rung any alarm bells for the Securitate. The alarm bells would ring later, as I "became" Hungarian.

> > >

Ministry of the Interior   TOP SECRET
Hunedoara Country Inspectorate   30 August 1974, 10:00 A.M.
Source "Lazar"

Informer's note

. . . I have already informed you that the American took some German lessons from professor *Bierman of Deva. She told Source that she doesn't know how she managed to live without the professor up to now, so attached has she become to her. . . . She said that she's not crazy about the husband when he goes around in shorts.

Source believes the American stayed at the Biermans' house in Deva on August 21–22nd, since she didn't come home to Aurel Vlaicu.

N.O.: Measures: Effect a verification of the Biermans, to see if they submitted the required report from their discussions with her to the leadership of the units where they work. Contact the said Bierman to obtain data about her connection with the American citizen.

My interest in ethnic questions led me one day to an elderly couple who were to become stalwarts of my research: the parents of the Biermans in this note. The session began inauspiciously:

Field notes, 1 May 74
Asked for their kids' histories and why they decided to send their son to university, the first Vlaicu German to go (1961–66). The wife said "I'll tell you . . ." The husband, meanwhile, got up and went out; I realized later that he was bawling in the corridor, and she had trouble getting through the story herself, for weeping. They regrouped, though he kept having relapses. On why they decided to send their kids to school: she had been deported to Russia for five years [as were many Germans, in war reparations demanded by the Soviet Union] and their land was confiscated. She decided if she ever got home she would do everything possible to send her kids to school, "because no one can take away what's in their heads." So as she worked her fingers to the bone when she got back to send the kids to school, she destroyed her health but the kids are in good shape. They would never ever base their future on land again.

Even more impressive to me than the answer to my question was the raw emotion it generated from memories recalled decades after the fact.

This couple contributed far more to me than some good interviews about the Germans' local history, for their son *Ralf and his wife, *Ana, were to become my especially close friends, despite the entanglement this generated with the Securitate. In the summer of 1974, after my interview with Ralf's parents, Ana, who taught German in Deva, came to spend part of her summer vacation with them. At precisely this time, I had decided I really should learn some German if I were working in that village, and I had begun lessons with an elderly German villager; she soon handed me off to Ana. Though one might have assumed that Ana would not want to do that on her vacation, she agreed to meet regularly with me.

Ana and I formed a remarkable bond of sympathy in a very short time. A beautiful young woman in her late twenties, with curly dark brown hair and mesmerizingly blue eyes, she appealed to me partly for the feeling of warmth and inner calm she projected (always attractive to people whose inner life feels chaotic). Ralf once perfectly described her for me as having "a soul of extraordinary goodness." In addition, she offered me a living example of the complexities of Transylvanian ethnic history. In her parents' and grandparents' families there were people identifying as Croats, Hungarians, Germans (of two kinds), Romanians, and Czechs. Until Ana married a German and changed her surname, she had identified more as a Hungarian—or as a "mongrel," she would sometimes say—but now considered herself mainly German. Their two adorable small children grew up speaking German, Hungarian, and Romanian with equal facility.

Ralf would appear on weekends during the summer, and I came to love him as well, despite his shorts. He too is a "mongrel," though not as richly assorted as Ana. His mother's family intermarried with Romanians, as did his sister, niece, and several cousins. For this reason if not more generally for his outgoing manner toward all, Romanians in Vlaicu always spoke well of him. With this couple, then, I had captured the essence of Transylvania's once-celebrated multiculturalism. Perhaps their family's broad embrace of ethnic difference helped to consolidate our friendship.

Ana would win my undying loyalty when, one day in 1987, she took the train from Deva to Vlaicu solely to tell me that she and Ralf were trying to escape to Germany and would have to ask me not to phone or see them anymore. They had told only one other person, their daughter, but not their parents, siblings, or son. After several attempts, Ana succeeded in 1988, with Ralf following in 1990. I have visited them in Germany numerous times since, and they me in New York.

The Securitate picked up on our friendship fairly quickly, from the informer's note by my landlord, Moşu, reproduced above. The officers' notes on that report show clearly that any important friendship I tried to develop risked bringing the Securitate down upon the friend in question. A scant two days after Moşu's report there appears a note from his case officer with extensive details about the couple. Among other things, it shows that Ana, who, as the best teacher of German in Deva, had been giving lessons to the police department, lost that job on account of her friendship with me.

This would not be the Securitate's last pursuit of the Biermans.[12]

The Securitate Launches My Surveillance File

Ministry of the Interior	TOP SECRET
Hunedoara County Inspectorate, service III	19 Mar 74

REPORT concerning VERDERY KATHERINE MAUREEN

At the end of the month of July 1973 there came into the Socialist Republic of Romania the American citizen VERDERY KATHERINE MAUREEN. In the context of cultural exchange with the U.S.A. she was assigned to Hunedoara

Title page of newly opened dossier of informative pursual for "THE FOLKLORIST." Courtesy of the Archive of the Consiliul Național pentru Studierea Arhivelor Securității, Fond Informativ (ACNSAS-FI).

county for documentation about problems of anthropology, ethnography and folklore. . . .

From communication of Directorate III in Bucharest,[13] which has been watching her, it results that VERDERY KATHERINE MAUREEN is also occupied with collecting military information.

In view of this situation, I consider that active informative pursual of this person is necessary, in the form of organized evidence.

Maj. Iosif Pall

A person can be under surveillance for quite some time without becoming the subject of an organized "action plan." Only once officers ascertain that there is sufficient evidence to begin this more organized form of following with a "dossier of informative pursual" (DUI) will the most formal kind of tracking begin. In my case, it has been six months since I entered the county appearing to be a spy, and only now is counterespionage officer Pall opening a DUI. This is four months after the Bucharest Directorate for counterespionage had "ordered measures of intense following as long as she is in range of our activity because she is occupied with collecting information from the military domain." A few days after his opening proposal, Major Pall presented his requested "action plan," referring to the trip I had made in his county in September. I quote him at length to show the language he uses and the measures employed.

Ministry of the Interior   TOP SECRET
Hunedoara County Inspectorate, Service III   1 Apr 74

ACTION PLAN
concerning the informative-operative measures that will be
undertaken in the DUI "FOLCLORISTA" ["the Folklorist"]

On 20 March 1974 DUI no. 1723 was opened concerning VERDERY KATHER-INE MAUREEN, born 9 July 1948 in Bangor, Maine, U.S.A. . . . [details of my arrival in Romania and in Hunedoara]

VERDERY KATHERINE MAUREEN, through her travels in the communes of Hunedoara county came into contact with numerous persons, the majority being intellectuals and teaching personnel.

On 25–26 September 1973, although in her program she was to travel to the communes of Demsuş and Rachitova, this person was in Lunca Cernii, near which is also found military unit 01736, with special profile. . . .

From the data our organs hold two hypotheses can be raised:

I. VERDERY KATHERINE MAUREEN is occupied with collecting military information for which she travels in zones with special military units, discusses with the residents of these zones specific problems as well as with employees of the Mechanical Factory [UM] in Cugir.

II. VERDERY KATHERINE MAUREEN collects information limited to the problems that are the object of her dissertation, in which sense she contacts citizens among the intellectuals who can furnish conclusive data about customs, local folklore and problems of anthropology.

He lists a few items in support of the first hypothesis and then proposes concrete steps to clarify the situation. They include:

---

1. Use of the existing informers' network, thus:
   a. "ŞTEFAN MIRCEA" . . . He will be oriented to discuss with the target about the data obtained so far, the way in which she has succeeded in synthesizing them, whether she has found competent sources from which to obtain conclusive data for her topic and what her future intentions are along these lines.
   b. "SURTEA AUREL" and "BADEA VASILE," . . . who will have the task, within the limits of possibility, to observe the target's preoccupations and especially the trips she makes, where and with whom she makes contact . . .
   c. Sources "MULER MARTIN," of German nationality, collective farm worker, "MOLDOVAN IOSIF," ████, and "AUREL," pensioner . . . will be used to signal her travels and the connections she makes, especially the identification of those among them who are employees at UM Cugir. . . .
2. The creation of new sources of information, such as ████ and ████, who was observed having intimate relations with the target.
3. Use of some occasional sources, thus:
   a. B.—Lazăr, her host. He will be contacted and will discuss problems tied with possible interests manifested by VERDERY KATHERINE MAUREEN toward production at Cugir, the employees of this firm or other problems of a military order.
4. . . . A trip to Cugir will be organized in which . . . employees of this firm will be verified who are residents of the communes visited by VERDERY KATHERINE MAUREEN and even contacting them to establish:
   —if they work in sectors with special production . . . ,
   —whether among them are already informers who can be used with the target,

—recruitment as informers of those at the workplace who have come
into contact with the American citizen,

—study of the possibilities of interposing an informer who is unmarried.

Those measures would supplement the usual (intercepting my correspondence, shadowing me if I went somewhere, assigning me to hotel rooms with listening devices, etc.).

These documents, with their arrestingly cool, almost scientific tone, were the very first things I encountered when I opened my Securitate file in 2008: they had initiated my first round of surveillance. They spoke of a silent presence that had accompanied me, through the informers listed, from early in my research. If you had told me then that some forty years later I would be shaking the hand of one of those officers in Deva, offering him a bouquet of chrysanthemums, and engaging in friendly conversation for nearly two hours, I would have thought you insane.

Over the next nine months, officer Pall would pursue me methodically, without some of the exaggerations of his fellow officers but nonetheless thoroughly. His preparations included one that stunned me when I read it. In an undated document written sometime between 23 August and my departure on 16 December 1974 are the details of how to arrest me, if that proved necessary.

Ministry of the Interior   TOP SECRET
Hunedoara County Inspectorate
[Form filled out with personal information concerning Katherine Verdery. Under the rubric "present position" it says:] In the context of the research she is doing in our country she is also occupied with collecting military information.

Under which organ or service is she being followed: Service III
[counterespionage]

Urgency of arrest: Top

Team that will participate in her arrest [and other details]: ____

Annexes to this document: 1. her close connections. 2. the manner of action for retaining her. 3. sketch of the building. 4. photo of the element

ANNEX 1. Close contacts of the said VERDERY KATHERINE MAUREEN where she could hide.

1. The American Embassy in Bucharest, Tudor Arghezi St no. 9.

ANNEX 2. the manner of action for retaining
VERDERY KATHERINE MAUREEN
Variant I—from her domicile:

The retaining team will travel to Aurel Vlaicu village no. 73 where it will penetrate the residence through the front (and only) entrance blocking the window of the respective bedroom, which has possibilities of evacuation.

Variant II—when she leaves the locality:

When the target is away from the locality of her domicile the place where she is to be found will be established, an officer being sent who knows the respective locality, to make contact with the respective organ [of the Securitate] requesting their support with an eye to action toward retaining the target.

Variant III

The person in question being a foreign citizen, she can be invited to the passport office of the police, or to the commune People's Council, which supports her research activity, where it will be possible to retain her if needed.

Perhaps this document shows merely a bureaucrat executing normal job requirements, but I assume it indicates that the Securitate was deadly serious about my potential espionage, "proofs" of which were my motorbike trip into a military zone, my question about other such zones, and my suspicious "interest" in living near the weapons factory in Cugir. Although I realized the first two mistakes had created a problem, I somehow believed that my having been allowed to work in the county in a place selected by its officials meant that these mistakes were being overlooked. Moreover, it never occurred to me that a village located precisely in the area the officials had selected would be seen as evidence of my spying intent. I was blinded by two things. The first was my inability to imagine myself as a spy, which was connected with both my lack of political savvy and a too culture-bound sense of what "spying" could mean in this context—in short, I didn't realize then that *spying must be understood in culturally specific terms*, involving particular kinds of social relationships. Nor did I understand "identity" in a sufficiently flexible way, as a series of precarious minglings of various possible dimensions (philosophical, political, gendered, social, etc.) that changed situationally. My self-concept was way too rigid for the context I was in.

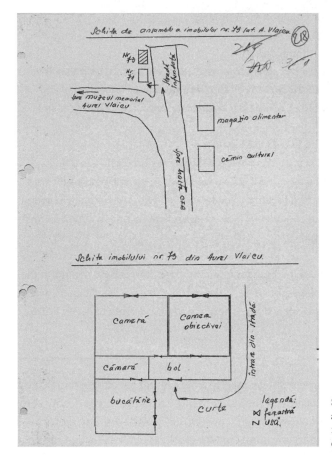

Sketch of my residence and nearby buildings, 1974. Courtesy of ACNSAS-FI.

The second "blinder" was my understanding of how politics worked. I saw the socialist system as more or less seamless from top to bottom, assuming that officials at any one level knew what officials at other levels were doing. In fact, the political hierarchy was fissured at every junction, authorities at the commune level being potentially uninformed about significant aspects of my introduction into the county. This sort of disjuncture created a great deal of room for local officials to follow their own path, not necessarily dictated from above. In subsequent research in the 1980s, I would begin to realize this insight more fully, but it was a hard-won realization.

Sex in the Field, Part I

So far we have seen Kathy struggling to become an ethnographer while the Securitate busy themselves with creating her spy doppelganger, "THE FOLK-LORIST." A decade later those two identities would become superimposed, in the person of "VERA": a spy with multiple identities whose ethnographic practices seemed to prove her spying. But during the 1970s things were already complicated enough: she was creating other personae for herself. Being in Romania made her feel different from the person she was accustomed to being at home. In the Romanian environment she found herself becoming less shy, more adventurous. In fact, these very changes would enable her to *be* the ethnographer she was striving to become. These new experiences of self were not simply a matter of situational self-fashioning in the field; they resulted from the effects of immersion in Romanian society in the Cold War context.

> Field notes, 28 Sept. 74. What I've learned about getting around.
> Wm visiting, we want to go to the East German Opera's performance of Mozart this evening. There are no tickets to be found anywhere, and my friendship networks didn't solve it, so taking a cue from the lady at the ticket agency, we went to the opera at 7:00 dressed to the teeth, found no tickets had been turned in, so I asked to speak to the director. I gave him a big story about how I was from the Folklore Institute and this US university professor of music had come upon us and I was to take care of him. He wanted to see the opera, etc. Within a couple of minutes we found ourselves with box seats, an extra chair was brought for the lady who really belonged there, and all was fine.

When I read things like this in my notes I am simply amazed. "VERA" is certainly not the person I am used to being at home; she is much more resourceful and willing to play-act and lie through her teeth to reach a goal. As I will find on numerous occasions throughout my work in Romania, being there has some liberating effects on me. It seems to create a detour around my superego (generally much less developed among Romanians than Americans), enabling me to be more quick-witted and imaginative than I usually am. One effect of this transformation is, as I have said, that I became more childlike. This quality, I'm convinced, contributed to my ability to create good relations with people rapidly, which is normally hard for me. Of course, a great deal of social science literature talks about the liberating effects of uprooting oneself from one's normal routines and social entanglements—after all, migrants the world over do kinds of work they would never do back at home. For me, the "kind of work" this enabled was fieldwork.

Part of my new persona was an expanded sexuality—expanded in the sense of both kinds of partners and frequency of sexual activity. This is not a topic that often appears in anthropology books. I put it in this one, despite some hesitation, because it is directly related to the themes of secrecy and identity in my life as a spy. A product of the 1960s, I was fairly active sexually at home, but here I was more so. Indeed, fieldwork offered me a chance to explore my sexuality: largely because the idea of "having a sexual identity" was not well developed there, Romanians could have an erotic encounter with someone of the same sex without thinking that it made them "homosexual." Although I now think that my sexual activity was mostly not a good idea and I would not recommend it for field-workers, it represents yet another way in which my self-identification responded to the social relations of the field.

It started, in fact, with the women's group into which Meri had introduced me, at which several of us would gather on winter evenings to drink wine, eat cakes, and make lewd commentary, talking about sex in both the abstract and the particular. These evenings established among the women my aptitude for vulgarity, and perhaps the word spread from there to other villagers through the "village mouth." In any event, I received multiple propositions from men in Vlaicu, Geoagiu, and Deva, my glistening wedding band notwithstanding.

Naturally, the people most interested in my sex life, of which they got a glimpse fairly early on, were the Securitate. When I first read this report, I cringed, deeply upset at having exposed an attractive new friend to the gaze of *securiști*.

Ministry of the Interior   Service "T" [eavesdropping]
Sarmis Hotel room 213
On 19.12.73 at 8:40 in room 213 are heard discussions between a man and a woman. At the beginning they discuss pornographically and sentimentally, then the woman explains to the man about some contraceptive pills. . . .

The man tells a pornographic joke, at which the woman is very amused and laughs heartily.

[Miscellaneous conversation]. . . . No more discussions are heard except imperceptible words, very slow, and then noise after which both leave. For the rest of the day in the listening post there was no activity.

N.O.: From the first verifications it appears that she was with [full details correctly identifying the person with me].

Whenever I stayed at the Sarmis hotel in Deva, I was given one of a limited number of rooms. The officer who was eavesdropping might have been doing it through the telephone, but more likely these special rooms were endowed with microphones, which were listened to all day long. Noteworthy is the speed with which my friend was identified. We had not left his identity card at the desk, as we were supposed to do, but had climbed up the back stairs from the restaurant, where the receptionist could not see us. Gleefully thinking we had outwitted any possible surveillance, we had a number of other trysts at this hotel during my year's research, though these do not appear in my file. Nonetheless, officers easily linked him to me.

Ministry of the Interior   TOP SECRET
Hunedoara County Inspectorate, Service III

INFORMATION SHEET
Concerning VERDERY KATHERINE MAUREEN from U.S.A.

... Our sources characterize her as a voluble person, intelligent, predisposed toward amorous adventures. She doesn't dislike drink, sometimes being observed a bit tipsy. From unverified information, it is presumed that she has relations of an amorous nature with ...

Advice to students: no, *really*, in this kind of setting it is *not* a good idea to get involved with people in your field site even if you travel to the city for it. If it doesn't get you yourself into trouble, it can cause a lot of trouble for the person you're with. For instance: in an action plan drawn up for me in April 1974, one point concerns the fellow I had been with, who

---

has been identified having intimate relations with [KV]. To use this person with an eye to clarifying the activity of VERDERY KATHERINE MAUREEN, the study and verification of him will be completed, moving on to recruiting him as an informer.

Being recruited as an informer could be a frightening experience, especially for a young person who couldn't have known what his fling with me might bring down upon his head. For the field-worker—especially the field-worker under surveillance—"responsible sex" requires a great deal of forethought and is best managed by abstinence. With sex, one potentially enters the most intimate areas of social life, where both the researcher and local people find multiple areas of identity and self-fashioning complexly interwoven. Managing that with tact was certainly beyond me at the time.

So, how to think about all this?

First, we should remember that Kathy had come of age as a sexual person in the 1960s, surrounded by a climate of sexual self-indulgence. She went to Reed, a college renowned for its permissive atmosphere. Although she was not overly promiscuous compared with her fellow students there and in graduate school, she had had sexual experience and was in a sexual partnership when she left for her fieldwork. Her partner had wisely proposed that for the period of her absence they have an "open relationship," and he would occasionally encourage her not to hold herself back and to explore all sides of her sexuality. Thus, whatever urges she might have toward sexual self-expression in the field were empowered.

In addition to all this was the allure the exotic American woman held for Romanian men, for whom America as an object of desire would come to roost in sex with me.[14] Aggravated by government pro-natalist policies that, by prohibiting abortion and all forms of contraception, made conjugal relations a torment (or so my women friends told me), men were pushed to look for other sources of release. I was sexy, with a lot of vitality, and many Romanian men found me attractive; if the attraction was mutual I was probably willing. I could be presumed to "take care" of myself and not produce an unwanted pregnancy. And with numerous Romanians trying to figure out how to get out of Romania, marrying a foreigner was at the top of the list. (This was why I wore that too-big wedding ring and presented my partner as my husband: to avoid complications.)

Finally, as officer Pall's "action plan" from April 1974 makes plain, with its proposal to study the possibilities of "interposing an informer who is unmarried," the Securitate actively tried to recruit men to become intimate with me as a way of finding out what I was really up to. This tactic will appear even more often in the 1980s. Male receptionists at hotels where I stayed, among others, were often urged to "get close" to me, and several tried. At the time, I was not asking myself how many of those who approached me sexually were put up to it, but I should have been: there were a lot of them. In this way the Securitate could colonize my sexuality to gain new traction among populations where I lived. According to my informer "Beniamin," his officer repeatedly asked if he knew whom I was sleeping with, and when he said he didn't know, the officer would tell him those whom they knew of, so as to impress him with their omniscience. "You see, we know everything about her, so you can't try to hide anything you know." My sexual habits were a way of giving them power over *their own informer network*, not to mention over the people I slept with, who could, like that first one in December, be targeted for recruitment. For this reason, the subject of sex leads us directly to the subject of informers.

Portraits of Informers, Part I

Anyone who comes into contact with the "target," more or less by chance, is at once brought under surveillance, written up, shadowed. [Thus] any person on the territory of Romania who, through the play of chance or fate, becomes a "target" also becomes radioactive: he irradiates all those with whom he connects.

—Gabriel Liiceanu, *My Dear Snitch*

The murky world of Securitate informers was an integral part of doing fieldwork in the context of secrecy. From 1973 to 1988, at least seventy people in Deva, Vlaicu, Cluj, Iaşi, and Bucharest (only twelve of them women) gave information on me to the Securitate. Many were casual acquaintances who wrote a small number of notes, some were people I met only in passing (such as hotel receptionists), and some were colleagues and friends, even intimates. The CNSAS staff decoded a few of their pseudonyms for me; I identified most of the others from internal evidence in the file. Some remain unknown. Of all these people, only two told me before 1989 that they had been asked to file reports on me.

I've said that I found myself becoming emotionally attached to a much larger number of people than was true of me in my normal life at home. Although I have always had a proclivity for developing strong attachments, during my fieldwork and especially in the mid-1980s I noticed in myself an unprecedented emotional promiscuity, only some of it sexual. This habit left me wide open to being colonized by the Securitate through their use of informers. When they find I am growing close to someone, they are likely to try to recruit that person to inform, if he or she is not already in their network. Here are two of them; we will meet more later on.

Ministry of the Interior   TOP SECRET

County Hunedoara Inspectorate, Serv. III.   19 Apr 1974

Source "Lazăr"

NOTE

On 19 April 1974, at noon, contact with "Lazăr" was initiated [he had been recruited on 9 April, soon after my official file, the DUI, was set up], on which occasion he related the following:

Since the last meeting he was attentive to Verdery Katherine Maurer, so as to see what she does, where she goes and with whom she makes contact. From what Source has seen, she goes from house to house and makes contact with everyone.

She types her material in three copies. She sends one copy through the mail, takes one copy personally, and keeps one for herself.[15] She said she does this because from discussions with other colleagues it resulted that they had had situations when the material sent was lost.

From the discussions carried on by Source with those who are contacted by Verdery Katherine Maurer, it results that she is not interested in other problems besides establishing genealogies. Up to now no one has found her to be interested in military problems, the Cugir factory, military units, etc. . . .

Source in this period discussed with Verdery Katherine Maurer about her family as well as her interests, establishing the fact that before university she worked as a waitress, since she needed money. [details—many incorrect— about the lives and work of my relatives]

When my file was opened in late March 1974, it meant recruiting informers to report on my daily activities. Although I had been unaware of it at the time, the discovery that my landlord, Moşu ("Lazăr," to his officer), had been filing regular reports on me during 1974 was not a surprise. He could scarcely have avoided being asked, given his friendships with the commune authorities who often came to drink with him—not to mention the fact that I lived in his house. (He had also, his niece reminded me, long been at risk of surveillance himself because of his expertise with guns, of which he had once illegally owned several, at the cost of quite a few beatings.) What surprised me, rather, was the striking *extent* of his reporting. For example:

Ministry of the Interior   TOP SECRET

Hunedoara County Inspectorate   10 May 1974, 12:00 noon

Source "Lazăr," Discussion taped

NOTE

Since our last meeting (30 April 1974) the American citizen Verdery Katherine Maureen carried on her activity as follows:

On 1 May 1974 she was at P—S— and M—L—. Source spoke with both of them. She asked P—S— only about his kin. He works as an electrician at I.G.O. Cugir, is about 37–38 years old. She asked him if he's from Vlaicu, to which he replied that he inherited his house from his father-in-law, being himself from Bacainti. He has two sisters, one an engineer and the other at university.

M—L— is from Moldova, is elderly, deaf, and myopic. He has a daughter by marriage. The American said she couldn't get anywhere with him.

On 2 May 1974 she went to V—T—, who cleans up the stables. He is 74. The American said that he is mentally weak and she couldn't find anything to discuss with him. . . .

On 3 May 1974 she went to V—A—, brother of V—T—. He used to be a big nationalist. He's about 80, and walks with difficulty. Source spoke with him. He said the American asked him about his kin and whether he is from Vlaicu.

In the rest of his informer note—rather damning of my interviewing style, unless I was being purposely vague (as often happened)—Moşu went on to report on my activities and his follow-up discussions with my respondents for the remaining six days until his next meeting with the case officer who handled him, officer "Grigorescu," whom we will meet later. Moşu had come with notes; their conversation was taped and then typed up later in the office. Such meetings were repeated about every ten days. The previous week, the officer's instructions had been that when the American left home he should go into her room, see who had written letters to her, and read the ones in Romanian, retaining their content, and he should also observe where she went and whom she saw. When she came home in the evening, he should discuss with her what she had talked about with them. Thus, he is to know what the American does every single day.

It is true that I often talked about my day with my hosts in the evening, but I never imagined that he was retaining what I said, noting it down, and perhaps checking it out with whomever I had visited. Once I saw these entries in my file, I began to think that few ethnographers have been so minutely recorded in their work. Starting with the next meeting with his officer on 28 May, "Lazăr's" reports are made day by day ("12 May 1974, she was at the German church at a baptism as well as at the feast after it. After this she went to L—M— and B—V—. 13 May 1974 she went to . . .").

In April, Moşu was new to this game (it seems he had not been used as an informer until now) and was still being broken in. The fact that officer "Grigorescu" used Moşu's real name (in quotation marks) rather than giving him a pseudonym indicates that he was what they called an occasional source, one with a single use: me. After a couple of months, the officer would ask him to come with his notes already written but then complain that they were superficial and incomplete. By September he had gotten the hang of it. On 20 September 1974, I threw a party for Wm, who had come to visit me again in the field. In Moşu's report of it, he listed every single person of the forty I had invited to the party and described what we had eaten.

They served a kind of biscuits with cheese from Holland and nuts, sandwiches with liver paté from Romania, store-bought ţuica (6 kg) and 2 kg liqueur. The wine was from California—12 bottles, with mineral water, and she thanked everyone for the hospitality with which she had been received in their homes.

Being mentioned on such a list could have repercussions, as we saw with his report of 30 August 1974, in which he told of my attachment to Ana Bierman. It had resulted in "Grigorescu" requesting verification of the Biermans and of her connection with me.

Moşu's reports made it clear that I could not have uttered a single throw-away line over breakfast or mentioned anyone in passing without my words potentially traveling on to the officer—generally in garbled form. In this way Moşu helped make me "radioactive," spreading my contaminating effects more widely. As I read his reports, however, I began to think that after the first month or so, he was not actually talking with everyone as he told the officer he was; maybe he got the gist in the first couple of weeks, then gradually narrowed the topics discussed to "She asked them about kinship." And though I winced at reading the notes, their cumulative effect was rather to exculpate me, for he repeatedly stated that I had not asked anyone about the armaments factory at Cugir or the work of people employed there. Because the Deva senior officer, Pall, was primarily concerned with my spying on military installations such as Cugir (which had gotten me into this pickle in the first place) and did not expand his inquiry into other areas when that seemed not to pan out, Moşu contributed a lot to the concluding report that absolved me of spying.

Following one report, the officer observes that this is "Lazăr's" first written note and is therefore pretty rough. He reminds "Lazăr" to write down *everything* he learns about VK's day. He has also checked out whether some of the people VK saw submitted the required statement about their conversation with her. He ends his report with the following:

It was arranged with the informer that when he finds that the American will leave the village, he is to telephone me so as to organize a search of her things. Noteworthy is that at present all her notes and other papers are locked in a suitcase whose lock is difficult to open. When she goes away for a short time her things are spread around her room, thus it is possible to proceed.

N.S.: Arrange with the informer to enable you to see the foreigner's documents.

An item following this says that on 5 June the attached material was photocopied and placed in "Folclorista's" file. The material consisted almost entirely of long and hilarious letters between me and Gloria, which I am delighted to reread now. The Securitate did not copy even one page of my field notes, for I had carried all three copies of this set with me to Bucharest while they were penetrating my room.

On 14 June, "Lazăr" produced another informative note, running day by day from 30 May to 13 June. This time, his officer admonished him for the poor quality of his notes:

The problems referring to Verdery Katherine Mauren are represented very superficially, for which reason it is not possible to draw a firm conclusion with respect to the activity of the American citizen. He was instructed once again about the manner of drawing up these notes.

A couple of months later he was admonished again and called to give a "completion" to his earlier notes, which he did, in great detail. The relation of an informer to his officer was understood as "pedagogical." We see from the progression of "Lazăr's" notes how "Grigorescu" is trying to train him to be a better observer and reporter on the officer's subjects of interest.

Moşu died before I saw my file. I would have liked to talk with him about it. Instead, in 2008 I asked Meri and Moaşa (his sister-in-law and his wife) whether they knew he was informing and how he had felt about it. Both said yes, though neither had ever breathed a word of it to me despite our supposedly close relations, perhaps suggesting the pervasiveness of suspicion and secrecy among Romanians as well as with me. Meri observed, "He knew which way the wind blew. But he liked you, so he wouldn't have said anything harmful. It didn't bother him much [nu l-a supărat], he liked going to the restaurant on the highway, getting something to eat, having a chance to ogle the waitresses—the reason he'd give for going there was 'I'm giving my eyes a treat.'" Moaşa's answer was similar: "You know how he was! He was always looking for company and a drink, and he enjoyed going out for a beer or a meal. The officer always met him at restaurants, and he had a good time." Neither woman believed that it had been a terrible burden for him or a source of anxiety. I'll never know.

"Iacob"

Field notes, 24 Nov. 74 [a year after I arrived and shortly before I left]. Friendships in the field.

Went to 258 for some photos; nothing new, except when I left he ["Iacob"] conducted me to the gate. I got partway home and then his wife caught up with me, going to her parents. When I asked why she hadn't left with me, she replied, "I wouldn't have deprived my husband of the pleasure of seeing you to the gate, since he seems to enjoy it so much." But she still wanted to leave right after in hopes of catching up with me so we could keep on chatting. This led to our wandering up and down the street several times, gabbing for an additional 20 min., during which she tried to say that she really digs me, that she has feelings but can never "exteriorize" them, is crazy about her son but has never been able to cuddle him or express her feelings. She says this while hanging onto my arm and having spent our past three visits holding hands.

This family was one of my very favorites, and when I lived in Vlaicu I visited them often—both at their express invitation and on my own initiative—as well as several times after they moved to town to live with their son. The husband was an exceptionally bright man, who always caught the drift of any question I posed him and gave me lengthy, informative answers. His lovely wife, while less verbal, was equally engaging. I looked forward to every evening spent with them. In truth, I had something of a crush on them both and must somehow have communicated as much, given her approach to me that evening.

Ministry of the Interior, D.S.S.   TOP SECRET

Hunedoara County Inspectorate, Service III   22.11.1979

To Directorate 3, Bucharest

On 17.11.1979 there arrived in Hunedoara County the American citizen VERDERY KATHERINE MAUREEN, assistant at the University of "JOHN HOPKINS" in Baltimore. . . . On the evening of her arrival, she was well received by the locals, who know her since 1974, manifesting their happiness to see her again.

On this occasion, informer "Iacob," according to the instruction given him, invited her the following day to visit his family at home. Among discussions of a general sort . . . the foreigner asked if Source knew the date of the first documentary evidence of this locality, to which he replied no. VERDERY KATHERINE specified that she had read a book called "SIEBENBURGER URKUNDE," in which it says that the first documentary mention of the village dates from 1290. She also stated that in the Ottoman period these territories were depopulated, to which the informer presented counterarguments based on historical reality. . . . The informer related to her that in the locality of Aurel Vlaicu there was no Hungarian population in past or present.[16]

This report is based on the informer's note of two days earlier, to which the officer had appended the comment:

The informer furnished this material at our request on the occasion of a meeting effected to instruct him concerning the American citizen Verdery

Katherina. . . . The informer was instructed to maintain connection with the foreigner and to observe her preoccupations, what problems interest her, with whom she has frequent contacts.

Maj. Crăciun Viorel

The officer's note from a later report by "Iacob" states: "The source has the task of cultivating further his relations with the respective citizen."

When I read these notes, I was devastated. Although "Iacob's" six or seven reports in my file were on the whole inoffensive, including positive comment about me along with mentioning my "historical errors," the thought that some of those happy evenings with them had been an assignment from the Securitate disturbed me deeply. Only in 2013 (five years after I first saw the reports) did it occur to me that maybe it was precisely his informer status that enabled him to invite me so often, because it gave him cover. Surveillance, after all, is often just a form of socializing. Until that point, I had felt wounded. And it took me even longer to realize that his reporting appeared to be confined to my second field trip, not the first (when our friendship was formed). With these thoughts, I could try to return to the belief that our friendship might have been real, not opportunistic.

It can take time to develop perspective on a friend's informing—in this case, five years. Gradually I remembered that after all, I had cared for these people and wanted to keep doing so. Such perspective is easier to achieve if the informer is still alive and willing to talk. By the time I read his notes, however, both "Iacob" and his wife were dead—the case with a number of the people who had informed on me. One of "Iacob's" kinsmen is my friend *Nico, with whom I had been discussing my file for some time. Asking him first if he would want to see reports written by his kin, I took him one of "Iacob's" notes. Nico was, like me, very distressed to see the note, and for that day and the next he, his wife *Sofi, and I talked at length about how we might explain "Iacob's" informing. Given his job (related, inevitably, to UM Cugir), it was possible that "Iacob" had come up short on classified inventory at some point—that often happened—and been given a choice between jail and informing. Maybe he was caught coming home with "too much" corn from the collective farm and given the same choice. Maybe his influence in the village made him especially desirable for recruitment, so they would have put a lot of pressure on him. Then Sofi says, "and he was a fearful person. For this reason it's possible that . . . But I'm convinced that doing it, he suffered." Later she uses the same word to describe another person everyone suspected of being an informer: he was very fearful, cowardly.

The next day I ask them if there was any fallout from that discussion: Nico has had a few thoughts but pushed them away, and both had dreams about it. In his, he was being followed by the KGB, who lost track of him and then found him again. Nico and Sofi emphasize their certainty that "Iacob" must have had some sort of vulnerability enabling his recruitment. Then he notes how much time we're spending trying to exculpate "Iacob," to uncover the excuses that will help us understand his behavior—which we all find troubling. They feel a desperate need to explain their loved and respected kinsman to themselves, a man who had been a moral exemplar for them. And so begins the nuancing of the informer: we can make excuses for some; some are not as bad as others because they didn't write ugly things about their target; even though he did it he probably suffered for his informing; and so on.

Later, from "Iacob's" informer file, I learned that he had been recruited in 1964 when he was on the church council, which the Securitate needed to penetrate. His reports then largely concerned church business. But information concerning him goes back to 1943—that is, to the pre-communist secret police, the Siguranța, whose reports the Securitate had preserved in their pursuit of active supporters of fascism, of which it seems "Iacob" was one. (In the 1940s there were plenty of people in Romania—both Romanians and Germans—who were interested in one or another indigenous fascist organization.) Indeed, the instructions for a number of these intelligence services after World War II, such as the East German Stasi and the Securitate, urged recruitment of members of the Gestapo, SS, and Wehrmacht, as well as indigenous fascist groups such as the Iron Guard, from whom it was feared the Western intelligence services would try to recruit; better to get them first.[17] Moreover, "Iacob's" real name closely resembled that of another Vlaicean who had also been an active fascist, and some of the information on "Iacob" from the 1940s is wrong: it actually concerns this other person. It seems likely, then, that he had been vulnerable to recruitment by the communist secret police for his wartime activities (partly confused with those of his co-villager) and had remained in the informer "reserves" for later use, concerning special cases like me. But this is just a guess.

> > >

Discovering people who had informed on me was the most painful aspect of reading my file—I will give further signs of that later—and trying to come to terms with it the most difficult. My reactions varied wildly from case to case, moving from rage to despair to bewilderment, always underpinned by wondering what made them do it. Fascinating to watch in myself and others I have discussed this with is our intense effort to explain the informing, to exculpate them somehow, as Nico, Sofi, and I did with "Iacob." It is easier when the reports are largely neutral, as "Iacob's" were, offering little that incriminates. But when they provide information that is damaging—information that is precisely what the Securitate is looking for to classify someone as an "enemy"—then the work of exculpation becomes more demanding. The matter of informers will become even more intense during the 1980s.

Aside from my personal feelings about them, in a broader sense informers' reports raise the important and sobering possibility that I, along with the several other anthropologists who came to Romania during the 1970s,[18] served as new points of entry for the Securitate into rural areas, where it had been sorely underrepresented. In those years, approximately 15 percent of informers were to be found in villages, where 50–60 percent of the population lived.[19] Any change in the village's social configuration—and the arrival of an anthropologist was certainly that—could serve as an opportunity for drawing more people into the informer network. At least two of those regularly used to report on me were recruited precisely for that task, as was another friend who was often questioned about me but did not write reports. Moreover, keeping track of me brought the local police force into closer relations with villagers, whom they would ask about my doings without formally recruiting them as informers.

Thus, the Securitate used us foreign anthropologists to further subject the rural population, enabling them to penetrate spaces and groups they might otherwise have had difficulty entering into. This suggests that although we might assume that the ethnographer would be largely a nuisance to the socialist state, as its secret police dithered at first over what to do with her, over time the Securitate became practiced at leveraging her presence. In a word, anthropologists brought some benefits to the police.[20] "Radioactive," indeed.

Betrayals

Did I feel betrayed by those who informed on me? That is certainly how many Romanians and others in the former Soviet bloc feel about their friends who provided reports on them, rousing some to a fierce quest for retribution—if only by revealing their informers' names. The stance to take toward informers is a complicated question, perhaps best left until I have introduced more of them in chapter 3. But some idea of the complexities transpires from my own behavior in the field.

Given how little I understood about Romania throughout much of my first stay, the irrepressible and highly responsive person I became made me a danger, a source of betrayals of my own. Consider the following report from a man I had met while copying documents at the notary's office in 1974. After we worked together for several weeks, during which we had begun to flirt a bit, we went out for a beer and flirted some more. Then I offered to drop him at his house en route to my next appointment, asking him if he knew the location of the building where I was going next. In my superficial way, I felt that he and I were becoming good friends, so I told him whom I was going to visit, thereby breaking the cardinal rule for foreigners in Cold War Romania: *never* mention one friend to another unless you are certain they know each other and you have their permission. His report concerning me covers two closely typed pages, among which is this paragraph:

Mrs. Verdery has a "Mobra" motorbike with a red license plate on which I went to the Gojd quarter of town to [address], where I left her since not knowing the city, she asked me to show her where it was. She told me that in that building live her friends, the Schilling family (I don't recall the name exactly).

The case officer's subsequent report corrects the final sentence: "She went to the Bierman family, with whom action will be taken in the manner ordered by the leadership of the Counterespionage Service."

What on earth possessed me to give their name to someone I hardly knew? I was a loose cannon! With this kind of carelessness, the closer I grew to the Biermans (and others like them), the more dangerous I became to them. It's true that the Securitate held Romanian scholars under surveillance too, but since they were less likely to be considered spies than foreigners were, the consequences of contact with them were likely to be less severe for their friends and associates.

My "radioactive" quality grew more malignant in 1984–85, when contrary to my previous practice of not keeping a personal diary, lest it be found, I began writing personal observations on the facing pages of my field index (where I kept each day's discussion topics and the corresponding pages in my field notes). At first the notations were fairly innocuous, indicating changes in my moods. But then, as my emotional promiscuity began to flourish, the notes became a telegraphic record of moments of intense connection with the various people I had fastened onto, as well as of the occasional dreams through which I was processing all this. It seems that I needed to preserve my memories of the rich emotional life I was having, in the hope that they might later help me resolve some perennial difficulties in my psyche. Imagining that I might not be the only person interested in the notebook, I carried it with me at all times. Nonetheless, the Securitate obtained it and translated the first few months (happily for me, before things had fully heated up). With that, my potential for betraying my friends increased even further. The changed circumstances of Romania in the 1980s would bring it fully to fruition.

In summer 2012 I launched a conversation about informers with my friend Silvia. What position should I take toward them? I'm hoping I can get some informers to talk with me, I said—that is, I will take an ethnographic approach to them, not an ethical one. She replied, "They're ashamed," implying that my sample might not be large. I said that I don't feel I have the right to judge, because I wasn't put in the situation my informers were in; I'm not from here, and I didn't have officers compelling me to inform. Silvia objected: "I find this a stupid opinion. Of course you have the right to judge. You spent a lot of time here, you've had a significant engagement with this country, and people did this to you, some of it quite harmful." In twenty-first-century Romania, informing remains an urgent moral question, pressing one to take a position that I at this point find elusive.

Identities in Flux

In the fall of 1974, when I had been in the field for almost a year, I climbed onto the train in Deva and headed for Vlaicu. A man behind me in the ticket line had overheard me stating my destination, and once we embarked he approached me to talk. He said he worked for the railway and had been stationed for some time at the Vlaicu train stop right after the war, and he was wondering if I could tell him anything about some of the people he had come to know in the village. We talked for almost the entire forty-five-minute ride, as I answered his questions about one or another person, what had happened with this or that one's children, who had moved away to town, what their kin were doing. There was nothing he asked that I couldn't answer. As the train approached Vlaicu, he suddenly stopped and asked, "But . . . who are *you*?" I decided not to get into the whole America thing that I often found tedious and said simply that I was a teacher at the school—a job that could easily bring me a lot of information without my being from the village. When I reported this episode to Meri, she laughed heartily and said, "There's *no one* in Vlaicu right now who would have done better than you!" From her point of view, I had fully consolidated my identity as an ethnographer.

A few months after this, I would lose my identity as a spy. Officer Pall—the one with the two hypotheses—gathered and synthesized the evidence he and his subordinate officers had collected. I quote at length to show his reasoning.

Ministry of the Interior   TOP SECRET
Hunedoara County Inspectorate, Service III   8 March 1975

REPORT with proposals to close the DUI concerning
American citizen VERDERY KATHERINE MAUREEN

On 20 March 1974, a dossier of informative pursual was opened concerning American citizen VERDERY KATHERINE MAUREEN [who came to Romania] to draw up her doctoral thesis having as its theme problems of Transylvanian anthropology, ethnography, and folklore.

To obtain the necessary data, the American citizen participated in cultural-artistic manifestations in the environs of Aurel Vlaicu, but her principal preoccupation consisted of contacting all residents of the village and asking them about their family origin and family composition, ages, occupations, character, etc. Likewise, another chapter consisted of establishing the origins of their property, the manner of gaining and transmitting it.

To gain the best possible documentation, she maintained connections with the village intellectuals as well as the elderly people, whom she consulted not only concerning their situation but also in connection with the other families. She also appealed to some secure sources such as the civil registers of the People's Council, evidence from the Orthodox and Lutheran churches, as well as various published annual statistics. [further detailed description of my sources and actions]

As a result of the informative-operative measures we took for this DUI there resulted a number of aspects, namely:

—Verdery Katherine Maureen contacted a large number of persons.

—She documented herself thoroughly from the social-economic and political point of view in Aurel Vlaicu, becoming familiar from all points of view with the life, preoccupations, manifestations, and so forth of the residents of this village.

—Although in her zone of residence many persons live who work at the factory in Cugir, and others who have relatives holding various state functions or in the military, from the material obtained it results that she was not interested in their activity in the workplace even though she came into direct contact with some of them.

—American students, doctoral candidates, and professors who come to Romania with the cultural exchange are in permanent connection with their embassy in Bucharest, which keeps constant track of their activities. . . .

From the materials administered . . . , it does not result that she carried on infractional activity against [Romania]. The relations created during her stay do not have a suspect character along the lines of counterespionage. . . .

Given the things reported, we propose with your approval to close the DUI concerning Verdery Katherine Maureen and to file the material in the archive. Her close relations will be held in attention for a period by our organs, being incorporated into the informer network.

The material will be preserved in the archive for 10 years.

Lt. Col. Iosif Pall

My surveillance had continued right up to and even after my departure. Two informers were primed to hang out around me in those last days, to report on whom I was contacting then and to get a copy of my writings, if possible. Officer Pall formed his conclusions from meticulous analysis of the data gathered on me, keeping his eye strictly on the task assigned him from Bucharest: to ascertain whether or not I was spying on military installations. From the evidence, he had decided I was not, and nothing else about me had made him uneasy. In his personnel file for 1973, officer Pall is described as "an intelligent officer with great powers of analysis and synthesis"—a judgment supported, in my view, by this final report, which is thorough and largely accurate. His colleagues during my next few trips would not be so goal-oriented but would keep looking until they found something bad—lots of things, actually, both invented and real.

> > >

One day in 1974 I was hanging out with Meri and her friend Veca. Talk turned to the subject of țigani, or Gypsies (as we called them then). Though they often came as seasonal labor in the collective farm, Vlaicu did not have a large population of them—but that did not keep Meri and Veca from extended negative commentary. Gypsies are lazy, they have a funny smell, you can't trust them, they steal all the time. . . . Instead of trying to explore more deeply these women's feelings about and images of Gypsies, as a good ethnographer should, I got a bit testy and began to explain why this group's position in the social structure contributed to their behavior—in short, I gave them a lecture on the "culture of poverty." They listened; then one of them turned to the other and said, "She's more of a socialist than we are!"

One of the great ironies of my first field trip was that, having departed from home in 1973 with no particular interest in the Left, either politically or intellectually, I came home in 1974 primed to receive the Marxist influence that was then expanding within anthropology. When I got back to Stanford at the end of my research, everyone around me was reading Immanuel Wallerstein's The Modern World-System, along with various debates concerning it in Marxist historiography. Within weeks, along with a number of others in the Stanford anthropology department where I was studying, I had joined the swelling current of those aligned with neo-Marxism. When I finished my thesis, I was hired at Johns Hopkins, whose anthropology department was at the forefront of that tendency, under the inspiration of Sidney Mintz. I would eventually retire from another such department, at the Graduate Center of the City University of New York. Although my Marxist credentials were never very stringent, throughout my career I have considered my intellectual home to be a form of the political economy orientation that neo-Marxist anthropology provided. Here is yet another modification of my identity, another aspect of the multiple "selves" precipitated at least in part by my experience of living for seventeen months "behind the Iron Curtain."

How did it happen that spending time in Romania had this effect? It was certainly not from the example of ideological commitment that I found there: to the contrary. There were precious few dedicated communists in my environment in Vlaicu (certainly none who talked about it with me), just a motley collection of petty socialist bureaucrats. Nor, in 1974, did the results of a quarter-century of Communist Party rule offer a particularly inspiring example. If anything, what impressed me most was that trying to create a communist social order without having first raised people's political consciousness to desire it was doomed to failure. That is, communism by Soviet conquest was not the way to go. The message, to me, was that the "revolution" would have to come from what Mao Zedong called "walking on two legs": working diligently to change consciousness while also changing the relations of production.

Then again, perhaps my new intellectual orientation had nothing to do with Romania at all: back home in my department, I might have been equally influenced by the enthusiasm of my colleagues. In that case, I might say that the time I had spent in Romania had loosened me up, enabling me to adopt a new intellectual profile. The political education I received there had broadened both my intellectual and my political horizons, convincing me that there had to be something better than the civic culture based on mistrust that I saw in Romania; perhaps neo-Marxist anthropology would help me think about it.

The Late 1970s
Am I Also a Hungarian?
Officer Pall's cheering verdict in 1975 absolving me of espionage was not to stand for long. I returned to Vlaicu in November 1979, five years after I had left, staying through February 1980. I had now finished my PhD and begun teaching. To publish my dissertation I needed to fill in some gaps, but I also wanted to see how things were going in Vlaicu. Before I even set foot in the country, however, two documents were created that did not bode well.

Military unit 0625   TOP SECRET
Source "Silviu"   19 June 1979

NOTE
concerning former IREX grantee VERDERY Katherine

In the whole period of her [previous] stay and at the institutions with which she worked, in particular the State Notary's office in Deva, reservations existed concerning the American scholar VERDERY K. especially for the fact that by origin she is Hungarian and her research refers to the period that concerns the Austro-Hungarian empire.

Ministry of the Interior   TOP SECRET

Hunedoara County Inspectorate, compartment 0544   8 October 1979

To the Counterespionage Service

In the context of the relations of cooperation and cultural exchange between Romania and the U.S.A., a number of researchers are about to arrive in the country for documentation, of which four are of Hungarian origin, namely: VERDERY KATHERINE MAUREEN, IANKY LAJOS, IANKY SUSSANE and SZEKELY ZOLTAN. . . .

In conformity with the order approved by comrade minister secretary of state of the Department of State Security, you will arrange for undertaking measures to establish:

—The professional probity of the elements in question;

—the mode of collecting, interpreting, and utilizing the data obtained and of the sources of documentation used;

—possible indications received and actions to influence those from the U.S.A. by circles hostile to R.S. Romania. . . .

—Their intentions and preoccupations for entering into possession of other data and material than those to which their access will be authorized.

A superior's marginal note has several additional measures, including that Verdery must be housed with someone "acceptable from our point of view" and preparations must be made for "the intrusion of two well-trained informers of the counterespionage service (teachers of history, Romanian, German or Hungarian) through whom we can influence her."

My transformation into a Hungarian had begun.

Why was this a problem? For several centuries, Hungarian and Romanian politicians have disputed sovereignty over the territory of Transylvania (now part of Romania) lying between those two states, and Romanians often express resentment at their centuries of being serfs of Hungarian nobles. Throughout my fieldwork in Vlaicu, people would interject into conversation, "But we were serfs, you know! Serfs of the Hungarians!" as if it had just ended last week. Decades of political action by the National Peasant Party between the nineteenth century and World War II had had long-term effects on Romanian peasant consciousness.

Although this is not the place for a history of Transylvanian ethnic relations (my book *Transylvanian Villagers* provides that), I note that there is no agreement on population figures for the ethnic composition of the region. But even if we use Hungarian censuses like that of 1910, at which time Transylvania was part of the kingdom of Hungary, the proportions are 55 percent Romanians, 34 percent Hungarians, and 9 percent Germans. Romanian claims are based on asserting prior settlement and superior numbers, Hungarian claims on right of conquest and rejecting Romanians' prior settlement.

While relations between the two groups have historically involved considerable friction, there was less conflict during the early 1970s than at other times. As Romania's economy began to deteriorate during the late 1970s, however, Transylvania's Hungarians began to protest one or another policy as ethnically discriminatory. They were supported in this by a strong Hungarian diaspora in Western countries, especially the United States, which among other actions opposed renewing Romania's special trade arrangement (Most Favored Nation status, or MFN) in the 1980s, arguing ethnic discrimination. A particularly stinging protest by Károly Király, a Party official of Hungarian ethnicity from Transylvania, appeared in 1977 (not long before I returned); other forms of unrest were rumored for that year as well and would continue into the next decade. From the point of view of the authorities, and particularly of the Securitate in Transylvania, it was not good for me to be thought a Hungarian.

Whether because of these protests or for other reasons, my return to Hunedoara and Vlaicu was met with exceedingly rigorous preparations. In late November 1979, the Orăştie Securitate filed a report concerning instructions to four informers "used in the case of 'the Folklorist,'" with twenty points on which these informers should follow up. They included any visits I make outside the village (their duration, aim, and persons I planned to meet); whom I contact among intellectuals and what I discuss with them; who visits me from elsewhere; my trips to the U.S. Embassy; what things I photograph; the contents of my suitcases, whether they contain religious material, and how I distribute it; the contents of my field notebook; whether I am interested in "nationalist-irredentist problems" (the Securitate code for Hungarians); whether I make contact with workers at Cugir; information about my family and any relatives abroad; my political party affiliation; and whether my published works represent the situation in Romania realistically or distort it.

There was also mention of my previously being suspected of collecting military information—without mentioning that I had been cleared of it.

These concerns suggest that I had now come under much more rigorous surveillance than before. One possible reason might be that officer Pall of Deva counterespionage was himself an ethnic Hungarian who would not have suspected me of being one, but after 1974 he had been replaced by Romanians. They might well have suspected me because of my name, which looks (to someone who is not a Hungarian) as if it might be; Hungarian surnames often end in y and are accented on the first syllable, like mine. Another possibility is that the number of the unit filing the report that labeled me one of four Hungarians, unit 0544, indicates the *foreign* intelligence service, centrally concerned with the Hungarian question—and it had just been completely reorganized the previous year after the defection of its deputy head, Gen. Ion Mihai Pacepa. With its best officers withdrawn, perhaps their replacements who had written the report were ill qualified and made elementary mistakes. Their errors would affect my life for years thereafter.

To the possibility of my new Hungarian identity I offered a ludicrous response, in a letter to the IREX grants administrator in Bucharest, Mr. Beiu, on 9 October 1979. In it I said, inter alia, that several people had commented on the seemingly Hungarian form of my name, that "from the Romanian point of view, it wouldn't be so great to have a researcher with a Hungarian name working with historical data from Transylvania," and that I wished to affirm very seriously that my name is French, not Hungarian.

Yet another paroxysm of "transparency," which was doubtless seen as an attempt at disinformation on my part. The very fact that I would even mention the problem of doing historical research in Transylvania with a "Hungarian" name revealed, once again, my remarkable naiveté.

Romanian sensitivities concerning Hungarians inform their definition of spying. As I deepen my culturally specific understanding of it, I realize that my hosts did not care about only one kind of spying—the kind involving military or political intelligence, which is the kind at the center of most U.S. spy culture (such as the TV serial *The Americans* or the novels of John le Carré). For Romania's Securitate that was important, but being cleared of it in 1975 was not enough. This flows from a fundamental difference between working among people in the Soviet Union, an unquestionably great power, and among Romanians, who are a fairly small nation perpetually consumed with their image in the world (as I learned to my cost).

One of the Securitate's most persistent concerns in my file is that I will contribute to denigrating Romania, and when I unwittingly did so, I was not forgiven. They are patriots and see themselves as defending a positive image for their country. Conversely, they worry that I will strengthen the voice of Hungarians against Romania and fuel the Hungarian cause—which they always see as inimical to their own. They are also concerned that I am creating bad press not against Romania but against the socialist system. This was, after all, the Cold War. Information about socialism was highly politicized on both sides and often considered secret. A person collecting "socio-political information," as I seemed to be, might find out inconvenient truths. These may not seem like forms of spying, but in the context of the Cold War, with its hostile blocs of "capitalism" and "communism" and the absorption of small countries into larger power blocs, they became so.

> > >

I began my four-month trip in mid-November in Vlaicu and then spent January in Cluj, returning to Vlaicu for a final month after that. Although the effects of the recession that had begun in Europe in 1973 had spread into Romania and it seemed my urban friends were grumbling more than they had previously, there appeared little significant change in Vlaicu. In my first conversation with Moaşa, I asked her what people were saying about things these days, which she took to mean life in general. She replied, "You know, life was never as good as it is now," adding that many people held this opinion—one I consider genuine, in her case. Meri, however, was more circumspect. She mentioned the disaster resulting from General Pacepa's defection and was fairly reserved in her talk, alluding to the straitened circumstances "since the nation was betrayed by Someone this summer." In addition, she said there were still those who doubted my mission from before. She expected I would have more trouble this time than last, and was surprised that I had even been allowed to return: a *securist* of her acquaintance had thought it unlikely.

I spent my three months in Vlaicu intensively following up questions about village history, especially with my elderly informants. When I headed for Cluj, it was to dig in the archives of Hungarian nobles from earlier centuries who had held estates in Vlaicu. This possibility, which I had not initially envisioned, had arisen from a wholly chance meeting that would have a powerful effect on my subsequent relation to Romania. The meeting was with eminent Cluj historian David Prodan.

Academician David Prodan

On my way into Romania, I had stopped for a few days in Budapest to try to obtain some statistics held in the Transylvanian section of the Hungarian State Archives. In contrast to how things worked in Bucharest, it was possible for me to request documents in Budapest even though I had no status as a grantee, for the archive there was under the Ministry of Education rather than the Ministry of the Interior, as it was in Romania. I obtained a lot of useful data and, foolishly, did not hesitate to say so when I got to Cluj, thereby setting myself up as "philo-Hungarian." Several informers' reports insinuate my pro-Hungarian leanings on the basis of my visit to Budapest.

By far my most important accomplishment in Budapest, however, was completely fortuitous. When I went to the archive one morning, the director told me that Professor David Prodan[21] from Cluj was working there just now and asked if I would like to meet him. I had been reading enough history to know that Professor Prodan was Romania's preeminent historian of the Transylvanian peasantry, so I accepted eagerly. Sometime later I was escorted into a hallway, where I saw a diminutive elderly man (he was then seventy-eight; I was thirty-one) with luxuriant gray hair, barely contained by the beret he wore, and eyes that sparkled with a fierce intelligence through his heavy glasses. He smiled and offered his hand. When I took it, I experienced something like a powerful electric current flowing from him, and I was a goner from that moment on. Of all the emotional connections I made in Romania during those years, my connection with him was particularly intense—and, unfortunately, the most fraught.

Since Professor Prodan had cordially offered to help me enter the archives in Cluj, I contacted him upon my arrival. During my few weeks there, he got me in with minimal delay and even managed to persuade a recalcitrant archive director to provide me with a translator for Hungarian, which I cannot read. I was thus able to discover some fascinating things about Transylvania's feudal economy prior to the abolition of serfdom in 1848. Far more meaningful to me, though, was my attachment to Professor Prodan himself. It is perhaps presumptuous of me to say that this attachment was reciprocal, but I believe that to a considerable extent it was; otherwise it would be hard to understand the disaster that ensued a few years later. Indeed, I was gratified to see that the Securitate officer who transcribed the telephone intercepts placed at the Prodans' in the 1980s characterized it in just this way, following the transcript of a long conversation between us (the transcriber has dubbed him "PAN"). I had been teasing him about when he'll let me marry him:

They joke, but the affection—notwithstanding their ages—is reciprocal. The two of them are very open, with a frankness that denotes a deep preoccupation with the subjects they approach. The friendship of these two is foundational [*de structură*].

And following another transcript from the birthday dinner they gave me:

Everyone is completely relaxed; K evidently feels good, she likes the flattery, she's attentive, polite and deferential, dominated by PAN—and it's clear that she likes his company. They complete one another reciprocally, with humor and good taste.

During the month I spent in Cluj in the winter of 1979 (unrepresented in telephone intercepts), Professor and Mrs. Prodan integrated me into their social life, baptizing me "Katiusha" and inviting me to gatherings at their house with his colleagues from the Academy Library, where he worked every day. A few years later, in 1984–5, when I would spend eight months in Cluj, some of those colleagues would become my special friends. The Prodans would often include me in their regular Sunday excursions out to the countryside, his witty colleague Liviu serving as our chauffeur. The professor had a rare capacity for deep communion with nature—and also with music, including me in frequent concerts at the Cluj Philharmonic. I recall his chastising me for saying I wasn't crazy about Chopin: "But Chopin is the poet of the piano!" (I've loved Chopin ever since.) When I read in Sheila Fitzpatrick's wonderful memoir of her research in Russia about her close connection with her mentor, Igor Alexandrovich Sats,[22] it felt a lot like mine with David Prodan—except he never got tipsy and professed his love. I don't know what I would have done if he had.

Aside from the powerful electric current that initiated my attachment to him in 1979, our connection as it deepened in the 1980s may have come in part from my professional development. I finished my dissertation and published a book from it, for which I had learned considerable Transylvanian history;

Professor David Prodan with "Katiusha" in 1985. Prodan family photo.

I got a good job at Johns Hopkins University and was well past my confused state as a graduate student trying to figure out how to do fieldwork. That these accomplishments were bringing me some validation from Romanian experts of the quality of Professor Prodan was very gratifying for me, and I reveled in his patronage. Moreover, and more personally, I was deeply fascinated by his favorite subject—the Transylvanian peasantry, from which he himself was immediately descended. I had fair hair and blue eyes (not common among Romanians), a combination to which he was generally partial and which I shared with his mother, who had died when he was a child. Finally, because he had resigned his professorship in 1962 rather than promote the dim-witted sons of Party hacks, he had sacrificed the fulfillment of having good students, a position I readily slipped into. All these things tightened the bond between us.

To me, Professor Prodan's most appealing quality, aside from his extraordinary intelligence, was the remarkable intensity of his engagements, both positive and negative. When he was enjoying a piece of music or a spectacular view of the mountains, his face took on a blissful expression as he participated wholly in the moment. When he was angry about something, he was frightening to behold. He reminded me of no one so much as Leonard Bernstein, under whose baton I once had the privilege of singing Mahler's

"Resurrection Symphony" in a benefit concert in Washington. Bernstein used his remarkably mobile face to tell the chorus what he wanted—a moment of uplift, for instance, signaled by a beatific expression. If we failed him, his face showed his intense displeasure, and without giving us further verbal instruction, he would simply tell us to do it again, repeating the procedure until we finally supported the emotion he was showing us so vividly. Professor Prodan was my Bernstein, and I adored him.

> > >

When I received my file, I was also given a dossier containing many pages of telephone wiretap transcriptions from the Prodans' house. I was thankful to find that they seemed not to be occasioned by me, given their location in the archive (that is, he was under surveillance not on my account but on his own), and they provided me with some comic relief. To begin with, the Securitate officer who made the transcriptions, Captain FI, complained that whoever placed the bugs in the Prodans' phone had done so in the kitchen, where few interesting conversations ever took place, and the professor's study (where they did) was too far away for the microphone to catch them. In addition, the officer liked to editorialize in a manner I have not seen in other wiretap transcriptions. She[23] is well disposed to Professor Prodan:

He has a distinctive personality and remarkable moral probity. . . . He also has a great sense of humor. He's a warm person, agreeable and very likable.

By contrast, she was not crazy about Mrs. Prodan and seemed to have taken a strong dislike to Mrs. Prodan's niece, who often came to cook for them. A wonderful example of her editorializing came in mid-November 1987, when the officer had finally had it with listening to the two Prodan women "chirping like birds" on this hidden microphone:

The man is 86 years old! Even if he's still active at this age, there are no grounds for maintaining this listening post. Basically, his scientific work [does not dispose him] to carry on any activity concerning state security, which he is not doing. I PROPOSE CLOSING THIS DOWN.

The recommendation was accepted.

Although I was relieved to learn that the wiretaps had stopped, it meant that I have no other lengthy, often verbatim, transcripts of my conversations with Prodan—of which there were a few despite the ill-placed microphones—in which we talked intimately about Transylvanian history, music, and other things we cared about. For me, these were moments of singular connection, among the most memorable of my life for their mix of intensity, passion, intellect, and emotional force. A devoted collector of Romanian art, the professor gave me a number of beautiful paintings that adorn my walls even now, keeping him vividly alive for me.

By the end of my second trip, I had made many friends in Aurel Vlaicu and a few in Cluj. I had learned a tremendous amount about rural social organization during the nineteenth and twentieth centuries, mostly avoiding the socialist era. Even if I occasionally found Romania exasperating, something in my temperament, some emotional affinity with their own emotionality, had opened doors for me. I had become quite attached to a number of people as well as to Romania itself, where I enjoyed working. I was less aware of the hand of surveillance than I should have been—not because it wasn't there (it was indeed quite present) but because its secret was well hidden. Moreover, I think I preferred to be fairly oblivious of it, in the interests of keeping my equilibrium. When I returned in 1984 for another year with a new project, however, that would no longer be possible. Both my situation and circumstances in Romania overall had changed dramatically.

The 1980s

The Enemy's Many Masks

In matters of ethos, the surest and most perfect
instrument of understanding is our own emotional response,
provided that we can make a disciplined use of it.
—Margaret Mead

In August 1984 I returned to Romania for another year's research, this time
on the historical formation of national ideology. The Securitate, however,
soon began developing other plans for me. Here they are, in some detail, to
show the climate that would now surround my work.

Ministry of the Interior   TOP SECRET
Cluj County Inspectorate, Securitate   24.10.1984

To the Ministry of the Interior
Department of State Security, Third Directorate
Confidential for comrade Lt. Col. DIACONESCU GHEORGHE

Our organs opened a DUI concerning American citizen VERDERY KATH-
ERINE, 36 years old, professor in the Department of Anthropology of "JOHN
HOPKINS" University in Balttimore, U.S.A., who . . . came to the Romanian S.R.
in August 1984 for a period of ten months to carry out a sociological study
referring to the manner in which national history is reflected in the consciousness of the Romanian people. . . .

Following her arrival in Cluj-Napoca for her present research stay, she was contacted by the American diplomat ███, political counselor at the U.S.A. embassy in Bucharest, a C.I.A cadre, with whom she had discussions partly verified by us. It resulted that the diplomat is preoccupied with obtaining information about the present situation of the population of Hungarian nationality in our country, drawing KATHERINE VERDERY into this action. . . .

From surveillance of the named KATHERINE VERDERY and from her notes obtained in photocopy on the occasion of secret searches, it results indubitably that she is collecting information of a social-political character, which she interprets in a falsified and hostile manner and although it is not secret, can be used against the interests of our country. . . .

With the aim of obtaining information she has contacted elements with a nationalist attitude from among Hungarian intellectuals, such as ███ . . . whom she stimulates in maintaining a resistant attitude toward state authorities. . . .

Given this operative situation, we consider it necessary to act urgently toward achieving the following objectives:

1) Impeding the actions she undertakes to form "trustworthy persons" among Romanian citizens . . . [which] might lead to her recruiting some of these persons into organized plots against our country.

2) Preventing the publication of the work she intends to write [which would] disinform public opinion concerning the Romanian people and realities in Romania.

To realize these goals we propose the following variants:

1) Informing the American embassy in Bucharest . . . about her preoccupations, with the proposal of interrupting her stay in our country.

2) If this measure is not opportune owing to some special situations in our relations with the U.S.A., we propose . . . that she be warned not to go beyond the framework of investigation of the theme approved for her study, lest we be forced to interrupt her stay.

In this variant, through a plausible scheme we will make her notes "disappear" so she cannot use them in writing the work she is preparing. . . .

For the Head of the Securitate   Head of Service 3
Col. OPREA IOAN   Lt. Col. VULCAN FILITAŞ

This document is one of several from October 1984 to January 1985 in which the top Cluj Securitate officers are planning my expulsion. Some of the documents appear to be drafts, often using identical language. All of them contain observations supporting the conclusion that I am a CIA agent and elaborating on what this might mean. Moreover, they propose further measures, such as placing well-prepared informants around U.S. citizens in Cluj to make sure they know that the Securitate is in possession of my notes; destroying the entourage of contacts that I have cultivated; and using this case with the university leadership to insist on the need for heightened vigilance against the actions of foreign espionage services.

How had it come to this? In March 1975, in my identity as "FOLCLORISTA," I had been cleared of the suspicion of spying on military objectives in Hunedoara County. Now, a decade later, I am living primarily in the city of Cluj, where I have become "VERA," a very powerful spy suspected of something altogether different: stirring up Transylvania's Hungarian minority against the regime, and propagating tendentious views of Romanian socialism through the information I am collecting—suspicions completely lacking in my file from the 1970s. "Spying" appears to be a capacious label—indeed, before the decade was out, I would be suspected of yet another form of it. What had happened?

First, the international context had changed. During the 1970s, there was less concern about spying than there would be after the election of Ronald Reagan, with his Star Wars initiative, his Cold War rhetoric, and his explicitly anticommunist agenda. Fears of conflict between East and West increased, just as they had decreased during the political relaxation that enabled my earlier dissertation research. Alongside this were growing reform movements in the Soviet bloc, which culminated in Mikhail Gorbachev's election as general secretary of the Soviet Communist Party in 1985—a tremendous threat to those communist parties like Romania's that were opposing systemic reform. The 1970s, by contrast, had been fairly calm.

Second, I had moved from the countryside to a city, Cluj, where I was easier to follow. My project for 1984–85 had me living in a hotel for a total of eight months, and back in Hunedoara—this time in the commune center, Geoagiu, rather than in Vlaicu—for four months. Beyond this, Romanian-Hungarian relations have often been problematic in Cluj, and the Hungarian minority there is sizable. And according to a CNSAS colleague who has read my file, the Deva officers who worked on me in 1974 seem less well trained and of lower quality than those in Cluj in 1984, who spent much more effort and were more thoroughly prepared: they would make a more convincing case.

Third, I had shifted my earlier research from folklore and village life onto the terrain of history—an exceedingly important and politicized field, for which my qualifications were more than a little dubious. Although I had read some history, I was now trying to approach historiography as an object of study, to understand its place in the formation of Romanian national ideology. Trying to wrestle this ambitious project into some kind of manageable shape involved almost as many tribulations as my first fieldwork in the 1970s, but of a different kind. They were compounded by the fact that when I arrived in 1984 bringing my first book, *Transylvanian Villagers*, I soon discovered that I had made a terrible mistake with it that led many people, Romanian intellectuals and Secus alike, to feel I had betrayed them. So even though I was now supposedly a grown-up scholar, I was once again reduced to being a "child," both by the difficulty of my project and by Romanian scholars' opinion that the book was, basically, a failure. All these and other reasons we will soon encounter justify treating my work in Romania in the 1980s differently from that of a decade before.

"Vera" Settles In

My home in Cluj—from my arrival in August 1984 through mid-December and again from mid-April to my departure in late July 1985—would be the Continental Hotel. Although it took them a while to get organized for my first period of residence (August through December), for the second (April through July) they were ready to welcome me at once with pre-installed recording equipment, or *Tehnica Operativa*, known as TO [pronounced teh oh]. From the initials TO, officers had formed the pseudonym "Teofil" or, affectionately, "Teo," by which they referred to this technology. "Teo" took several forms, including video cameras and various means of interception (telephone, microphone, battery-operated equipment [IDEB], etc.). The following note marks his arrival:

Ministry of the Interior   TOP SECRET
Cluj County Inspectorate, Service "T"

PLAN OF ACTION
with respect to the measures necessary
for executing installation of T.O.

By agreement with comrade Lt. Col. Ținca O. from Service III we have established the following: Type of installation <u>Video SO</u>, room no. *1*. The doors will be opened by Lt. Col. Ținca. The work will be done on 19.xi.84.

1980s postcard of the Continental Hotel, Cluj. My room is on the front left, second floor.

Measures required for penetrating, conspiring, and executing the action: The element being followed left today for Sibiu, where she will stay for two days. Assistance will be requested from the Sibiu County Inspectorate which will inform us in case she leaves early. The room next door to hers is empty.

Officers had already secured permission for a listening device during my short stay of March 11–14. Right through 1988, the documents reveal, "Teo" would be my constant companion at the Continental whenever I stayed there, and he would move with me to my other places of residence as well. Friends I visited in cities also acknowledged "Teo's" presence, by putting pillows or blankets over their telephones at home whenever they wanted to talk seriously.

> > >

While the Securitate settled in to watching me, a couple of months after my arrival in Cluj I wrote a letter to friends at home that indicates how I myself was settling in and what I was noticing about Romania. It's clear I didn't yet realize what was secretly going on around me and was expecting to enjoy my research as I had before.

General letter to friends, 7 Nov. 84

I continue to be struck by how this environment diminishes my capacity for discipline and increases my interest in having a good time. Add to that the insidious effects of Romania's non-capitalist attitude toward time, and we have a recipe for academic disaster at home. It is impossible to get much done in a day when no one else is in any hurry and when everyone's readiness to quit working so as to gossip and drink coffee impedes my usual manic stance toward work. Entire days disappear that have been filled with what turns out to be, in retrospect, utterly pointless activity. . . .

I am now heading off for a slug of absolutely wonderful plum brandy—have really been getting into the swing of nonmonetary exchanges, giving cartons of cigarettes for unbelievably good booze (home brew), chocolate bars for home-made eggplant salad, coffee in exchange for books I can't find to buy, etc. So I'm working on the human alternative to the market here, and it's been phenomenally successful so far. A bit more time-consuming than money-mediated exchanges, but also more interesting. And besides: time is not scarce. Except for those of us who straddle two temporal economies.

Although I would continue to struggle with Romanian attitudes toward time, throughout my research that year I would eagerly embrace some of the behaviors of my friends, such as ways of not working hard (the brandy would help with that) along with engaging in nonmonetary exchanges and "gray" markets, that revealed once again both features of Romanian life and the new self I assumed there.

"Foster the Target's Self-Doubt"

Thus established in Cluj, I begin to read for my project, which is much more heavily based on library research than my previous one. But I am not reading alone: Secus are present as well, already hard at work with their informers. Some of them are based in the library and look at my reading notes whenever I leave the room, noting down what they find there and passing it along. Another informer, a researcher at the Folklore Institute, tries to cut me off at the pass, unhappy with what he understands of my project's theoretical orientation.

---

5 Sept. 1984, Informer's Note. On 4 September, Source had a conversation with KATHRINE VERDERY, at her request. To Source's question what her research theme is, she responded that she would like to see to what extent ordinary people identify with national history, what they know about it and where

their knowledge comes from. In other words, a kind of folklore inquiry. To puncture her enthusiasm for her field research, Source told her that there has been a good deal of research on such a theme and more is in process.

And a second researcher/informer is being employed to exercise "positive influence":

---

18 October 1984, Source "Păun." Officer's note: Source was given the task of occupying himself closely with guiding and orienting her work, so she will conceive it in the spirit of historical truth and present it objectively, without tendencies and mystifications. The process of positive influence is to be continuous.

Positive influence, I was to learn from my research at CNSAS, could mean not just pushing me in particular directions. Here is an officer's note from Iaşi concerning a U.S. sociologist working there:

By interposing [informant] "ŞTEFAN" we achieved permanent control over the activity of researcher ■■■ in Iaşi. Through special measures success was achieved in having her enter into possession of information that does not disadvantage us, in the communities she studied. In this sense, "ŞTEFAN" had a decisive role, as she appealed to him to help her correctly interpret her research results. ■■■ manifested trust in Source.

This was "positive influence" close up, and I experienced it too, all in the name of generating research results to the Securitate's liking instead of the distortions they feared.

> > >

If I had sailed through my 1970s fieldwork relatively unmarked by the experience except for my leftist intellectual turn, the 1980s were a time of more intense dialogic self-fashioning, in which the Securitate defined me as not simply a spy on military matters but a friend of internal enemies and a danger to Romania's national image abroad. The former could involve me in attempts to overthrow the Ceauşescu government, the latter could affect renewal of "Most favored Nation" status for Romania, which was absolutely crucial to the country's economic prospects. In consequence, the Securitate interfered more directly with my friends and my research in an effort to contain me, to make me reliably pro-Romanian, and to push me out of conversations with people and into the library, where I would read what trustworthy colleagues would recommend. As one of my *securişti* for that year told me in 2014, "We wanted to make you love Romania." Toward this end, I was to stop being an ethnographer and become a historian—preferably one without distasteful theoretical predispositions, such as my view that national identity is a conditioned historical effect rather than the foundation of human existence, as most Romanians (including many of its historians) believe.

Realizing this gives new meaning to a note in my field index for that year, in the back of which I sometimes jotted notes about how I was feeling. I wonder if they gloated when they found this. Reading it reminds me of what Robert Gellately says was the main goal of East Germany's secret police, the Stasi: to foster the target's self-doubt.[1]

22 Nov. 1984
Energy for work zero. Sit and look at pages of school manuals and absorb nothing, can no longer recall why I'm supposed to read them. Looking at [Henri] Stahl's memoirs this evening; he talks about the psychological crisis of realizing all your theories bear zero relation to the confusion of facts. Started to bawl. Came to study a problem in the formation of a particular piece of ideology, no longer have any idea how to handle it. How simple my last project was! All the interesting things worth saying about this place can't be proved, what can be proved is either uninteresting or unpublishable or can be better done by locals. Why am I doing this? Why don't I go home?—better to enjoy the year and then go home, results will be the same: caput "career." How to "build a career" on a bunch of theories that are probably just as culture-bound as the history written here? For example I continue to be troubled by the subject of "popor" [people, in an ethnic sense]. My vision on this says that it's all contingent, there is no "blood," different societies have different materializations/culturalizations of this phenomenon. Their vision has "people" from way back—from the very beginning—and maybe they're right. Maybe the American "melting pot" experience is all that lies behind the relativity of the notion of "peoples," for us.

So early in the year, and already I'm being unhinged by the reading assignments provided me through the process of "positive influence."

The Biggest Betrayal

General letter to friends
Against the many congenial aspects of the socialist system must be weighed the tremendous load of uncertainty with which everything, especially—for me—human relationships, is invested. Any explanation for this that I can muster is small comfort when I find out that yet another person I have positive feelings about might be reporting on me to the secret police. Romanians I know seem to be able to separate trust from intimacy in a way that I can't: they package and distribute these things differently, anyway. Living in a hotel aggravates my feeling of surveillance from all quarters and contributes to a terrible inner restlessness and unease despite my wonderfully warm and receptive set of friends. I go to dinner, eat and drink and laugh far too much, have a fantastic time, discover interesting things, and then go home to brood about which of those people will report some innocent remark of mine into some portentous file. (And my friends for their part doubtless wonder what notes I took on the conversation, and how they will feel the effects.)

In 1983, following two visits to Romania of varying length (1973–4, 1979–80) and a lot of reading in libraries at home, I published my first book, dedicated to Petru Bota, the marvelous old peasant who had provided so much of the data for it. It was a social history of Vlaicu within Transylvania from the eighteenth to the twentieth century, emphasizing ethnic relations, migration, social mobility, and the development of the Transylvanian economy from feudalism to socialism. Not a modest goal, and it gives a sense of the intellectual ambition that got me through graduate school and into my first job, as well as into a lot of trouble. The book manuscript was quite different from my dissertation (which a few Romanian scholars, including Professor Pop, had read), with a much broader conception and much more history. I took a draft of the book to Professor Prodan when I went to Romania briefly in 1982, and he gave it to his colleague who knew English. It passed this reading as "favorable to us [note this criterion for scholarly work] and to the Transylvanian peasant" and a reasonably accurate history.

In an excess of enthusiasm for what I had accomplished, however, I decided to "advertise" its theme by means of two jokes, which I placed in the front of the book. They showed identical ethnic stereotypes of Transylvania's Hungarians, Germans, and Romanians in 1880 and 1980, separated by a century. In all the Romanian jokes of this type, of which there are many, the Hungarians always come off as hotheaded and violent, the Germans as stingy and scheming, and the Romanians as clever thieves. I thought the two jokes would be a concise way of stating the problem of the book: How could ethnic ideas have remained so much the same even as their environment evolved from feudalism to capitalism to socialism? That I was pleased with my solution shows just how little I had learned in the field about ethnic sensibilities—or even about the basic truth that an outsider can never tell an ethnic joke without deeply offending the people in question, even if it is a joke they themselves often tell.

Although it embarrasses me now to tell these jokes, here is one of them, reported by Emily Gerard in the 1880s:

> A deputation consisting of a Magyar, a Saxon [German], and a Romanian was sent from Transylvania to Palestine to retrieve the body of the Savior. Upon reaching Jerusalem, they were dismayed to find the Sepulcher heavily guarded by numerous Roman soldiers, and they stopped to discuss what to do. The Magyar urged the others to let him cut into the soldiers at once with his sword, but the Saxon restrained him, observing that they were outnumbered and might be harmed; it would be wiser to try bartering for the body. The Romanian had still another solution: "Let's wait until nightfall and then just steal it."[2]

I can try to excuse myself. Most of my fieldwork had occurred in a village rather than a city like Cluj, home to intellectuals with long pedigrees in the national ideology and a deep yearning for recognition from abroad. Vlaiceni hadn't gotten all that exercised by the question of ethnic antagonism, telling me repeatedly that their relations with village Germans had become much better under socialism, which had eliminated the two groups' differential wealth. Few of them remembered any Hungarians, and my friend Meri hadn't much reacted when I told her the jokes. They were more concerned with local kinship relations than with that kinship-writ-large that is "the nation." In my three weeks in Cluj in 1980, I had not seen enough to understand the national sensibilities of intellectuals, of which I would soon become all too aware. It was also true that my style of anthropology up to then had attended more to political and economic behavior than to how people felt about their nationality (that would now change, as the opprobrium cast on me greatly enhanced my understanding of Romanian national feeling). And finally, I acknowledge that as a person of privileged Franglo-Saxon Protestant ancestry, I didn't really know what it was like to be the object of unflattering ethnic jokes. I didn't understand that Romanians reading them would feel differently from the way they felt when they told the jokes themselves; I got the punchline but missed the painful sensibilities that accompanied it.

The bottom line, then, was that my sense of intellectual authority and desire to give the reader a quick précis of the book's theme had led me to put two jokes in the front that every last Romanian saw as my view of their character and at which they took violent offense. If riding my motorbike into a restricted zone had cast a huge shadow over my first fieldwork, this mistake cast an even bigger one over my work after 1983. It revealed great insensitivity and a terrible lack of judgment, and it ruined my relations with many Romanian intellectuals. Our divergent understandings were evident in the terms we used: I called them "jokes," Romanians called them "mottoes." The reaction began soon after my arrival in August, when a colleague in Bucharest went to the editor of Romania's *Historical Review* and told him, "We have to review this book." The editor opened it, saw the jokes, and replied, "How can this be!? I can't permit a review unless it's critical."

As is clear from numerous officers' reports, the jokes also damaged my relations with the Securitate in Cluj, where I would carry out much of my research in the 1980s, causing them to open a new surveillance file on me. For instance:

Ministry of the Interior   TOP SECRET

Cluj County Inspectorate, service 3   —.12.1984

REPORT with proposals to finalize the case of "VERA"

VERDERY KATHERINE, 36 years of age, professor in the Anthropology Department of "JOHN HOPKINS" University . . . came to Romania in August 1984 to effect a sociological study. . . . The above-named also effected research in our country in 1974 and 1979–80, publishing in the U.S.A. in 1983 a book about Transylvanian villages from the 18th–20th centuries, in general positive, but in which certain mottoes make insulting judgments against the Romanian people. . . .

We propose to interrupt her stay in this country.

In addition, the Securitate moved to influence me further—successfully, they thought—by asking their informer "ŞTEFANESCU" to write a negative review of the book and its tendentious mottoes. The result: "This article caused 'VERA' to apologize . . . and to treat objectively and correctly the themes with which she will occupy herself subsequently." Nevertheless, "Ştefanescu" later informed his officer that a very laudatory counter-review had been broadcast by Radio Free Europe (RFE), the regime's nemesis and the last place from which I would have wanted praise. Indeed, a superior officer's marginal note says, "RFE wants to popularize KV so as to strengthen her position among her connections in the country." These views fed the swelling current of negative opinion about me among some of my colleagues in Cluj and among its Securitate.

The highest price I paid for those jokes, however, was the devastation they wrought upon my special relationship with Professor David Prodan. He was absolutely livid—at the inevitable repercussions I had brought upon myself, at the embarrassment to him since others knew he had been supporting my work, at the injury to his own deep national pride. He had found out about the jokes before I arrived, and his reception when I showed up on a hot August day was, to understate the case, frosty. Explaining why putting them in was a bad idea, he said, "Romanians joke about themselves all the time, but in their heart of hearts they have a profound self-dislike, and they take very seriously what others say about them." To my comment that they nonetheless had let me back in, he replied, "Yes, but they'll be coming around asking us questions more often than otherwise about you. Why give them something to look at when they can't read the rest?" Things went downhill from there. A series of notes in my field journal reports my frequent arguments with him and a lot of weeping. For instance,

Oct. 25, 1984
DP tells me he's not very impressed with this American sociology that gets all the facts but misses the essence, that ignores the sensibilities of a people, their literature, philosophy, etc. Nothing I say about how U.S. anthropology grew up with "primitives" who had no literature, so we aren't used to having our research population read our work; about how one doesn't necessarily expect a 20-year-old student to get all this right the first time; etc.—none of this matters. He interrupts and returns to the theme of "greşeală," a mistake. Mrs. P says that he took too strongly to me and reposed great hopes that have been disappointed. He feels generally angry at his fate, deprived of doctoral students, disciples, all lean too far toward his chief rival [Ştefan Pascu]. The passion in his work comes from an absolute overidentification with the powerless situation of Romanian serfs.

Following many more such episodes, on 31 October I took him to the Russian ballet; he was absolutely enthralled and was warm to me afterward. The next day he observed, "It's nice that Americans come here to know us, they have only to recall that they find us in a period of dissolution. If people live by theft, it's conjunctural." It seems he had reprocessed our fight and was ready to make peace.

The rapprochement had taken four months, and even longer for some in the professor's entourage of colleagues and friends. Defending both him and their own sense of insult, they chided me over and over. I had countless discussions on this theme. My research collaborator, Liviu Maior, moved by my distress, offered the following observation: "National consciousness is so unconscious with us, so deeply formed, that we don't even know when it's influencing our reactions." Less helpfully, at the professor's eighty-fifth birthday party, one of his editors took me aside to tell me, "as a friendly gesture," that because of the jokes, no one loves me; he himself sometimes hates me and can't understand why Prodan is so attached. What everyone wants is for me to tell the world that Romanians are a great people stuck in a horrible system. Why won't I do that?

My reaction to all this is best seen in an informer's report:

---

21 October 1984, Source "Marcu." Note. In a recent conversation with Catherine Verdery, she complained of having a serious nervous collapse: she has powerful insomnia and she cannot work. <u>She contacted a doctor who is doing a relaxation treatment with her</u>.

Beginning in September, with all this quarreling and chastisement along with my feelings of guilt and remorse, I suffered insomnia so bad that I would lie awake all night and then doze off constantly while trying to read in the library. Eventually I sought the help of a psychologist, Dorina, who had a good reputation for treating insomnia. After getting permission from her department head to treat me, not only did she enable me to get back to my work, but we became very good friends afterward. When I was feeling upset, it was a godsend to have at hand someone whose way of thinking about personal issues resembled those of a U.S. psychotherapist, an idiom with which I was at home. Moreover, she was a talented portraitist and painted the portrait of me that still hangs in my living room.

The question of the mottoes could resurface even years later. In 2011, I reencountered for the first time after twenty-six years a well-known Bucharest historian who had been asked in 1984 to recommend my book for translation. He had refused to do so because of those jokes. Now, his second sentence after "Nice to see you again" was, "I was offering my mea culpa the other day about those mottoes in your book, because given the colossal scale of theft in our country these days, it's clear you were right." I was astounded: after nearly thirty years, a regime change, and five more books I'd written about Romania, what stood out in his memory of me was those jokes. And despite the many apologies I had made, he was still seeing them as my statement about Romanian character, rather than about the book's argument.

In 2012, a friend from the Academy Library where I had worked, Mişu, described for a documentary film the effect of my jokes on his own hitherto-close relations with Professor Prodan. He had been the one assigned to read the manuscript and clear it for the professor. Although the version he saw did not have the jokes, an ill-wisher convinced the professor that it was all Mişu's fault for not telling him about the mottoes. "He didn't speak to me for six months, in reproach. My decades-long relation with Professor Prodan had collapsed. For six months I suffered like a dog."

With all this upheaval in people's relationships on my account, it seems absurd to insist that those who informed on me betrayed me, as many of my friends expect me to do. Rather, as our relations deepened, my associates and I betrayed one another, sometimes knowingly and sometimes not, sometimes shaped by ignorance or circumstance—or sheer thoughtlessness. A note in my journal poses the question,

> Why does this stuff about whom I can trust cut so deep? Because I'm not entirely certain of myself within, so I have to know whom to rely on without? Because I don't trust myself?

These thoughts neatly turn inside out a basic problem I'm dealing with: many people had liked me and thought I could be trusted, but I had betrayed them with my jokes. Although my notes periodically wonder about other people's trustworthiness, is it not my own that is really at issue? And if my trustworthiness is in question, doesn't that make it more likely that I am spying? Isn't that partly what a spy is—someone who can't be counted on to take one's side? In making "VERA" out to be a spy, the Securitate were fabricating a person one couldn't trust. It seemed they had good grounds for doing so. Paradoxically, however, the jokes enhanced "VERA's" evil reputation.

Less self-critically, my insensitivity rested on ignorance that came partly from the Cold War system of international relations, which had cramped my knowledge of what went on "behind the Iron Curtain" and required that I learn everything from scratch, and partly because the Cold War had made leaders of Soviet bloc countries anxious about the negative image of socialism that people like me could propagate in the West. Moreover, it had politicized the question of the "satellite" countries' national images, sharpening their sensitivity to possible slights to the national character. In a bipolar world with superpowers and client states, both the image of socialism and the question of one's national image became matters of national security.

You may be thinking, all this stuff about jokes isn't really about her Securitate file. On the contrary: the supervisor's note on the first report of the jokes on 15 August 1984 reads, "We will send up a report to Directorate III in which we will propose that she be removed from our country." The jokes "proved" to the Securitate that I was an enemy of Romania—precisely their bailiwick—and therefore just the kind of person they should be following closely, maybe even expelling. Because of those jokes, they would not let me out of their sights for the rest of the decade.

My chastisement over the jokes made me very unhappy and remorseful at the time, for my attachment to Professor Prodan caused me to accept his definition of the situation, which made a huge error out of what might have been seen simply as an innocent gaffe. As I gain greater distance from the young Katherine of that period, I realize that because of my remorse, I initially failed to see that I was taking a crash course in Romanian national ideology. The episode revealed among my intellectual associates—and I see now from my file, among Securitate officers even more so—a thoroughgoing preoccupation with Romanian identity, one that assumed such an identity naturally deserves the central position they accorded it. I discerned little sign that they recognized the relativity of Romanian values and culture in the U.S. context, or the possibility that an American public might react differently. This—let me call it—ethnocentrism in people, some of whom were widely traveled and well-read, suggests to me that I had run up against not simply a sense of personal affront but a deeply ingrained aspect of Romanian national ideas. That gave me the theme of my next book project. Moreover, the episode of the jokes was part of a much bigger story, with multiple agendas in play. Romania needed foreigners—even if they were "spies"—to promote a positive image so the country could look better than other Eastern European countries, gaining it favor with "the West," including such plums as Most Favored Nation status. In this environment, I was caught in a sticky web. It's no wonder I messed up.

A related insight came more recently, from reading in my file the following telephone wiretap of a 1987 conversation between two of my friends in Cluj, transcribed by Captain FI with occasional comments ("t.n.," transcriber's note). M. and G. are discussing how to make me agree to translate G.'s latest book into English. I've already refused once—the book is two fat volumes, totaling 893 pages—but they're plotting a new strategy. Then they turn to talking about me and my work.

M: "I have the impression that the ethnography she does (she hesitates, looking for a word that will not be too unfavorable—t.n.) <u>picks and chooses</u> (our emphasis—t.n.) from a number of domains, without going into depth in the European style. I don't know if this is good or bad, but I've seen . . . like, with [her discussion of] philosophy: three words from here, four from there. . . ."

G: "Pretty much. Probably it's an excellent instrument for informing the public over there, because she synthesizes things admirably, you know. . . . It's just that it's as if taken <u>from an airplane</u> (his emphasis—t.n.). I won't tell her that, of course, though she's asked me to give her my opinion. . . . I'll tell her . . . that there's a lot more one could say. I don't know what her intentions are. I have the impression all this is just preliminaries. So then I shouldn't bother to. . . ."

M: Before, she focused on older stuff. Probably she's continuing up to the present. Who knows, but in any case, she's very intelligent (Yes—t.n.) and it would be great if . . . (M. breathes deeply—t.n.) <u>if she loved us</u> (her emphasis—t.n.)."

"If she loved us." Here, in a nutshell, was my dilemma among both Romanian intellectuals and *securiști*, who felt I had betrayed them with my jokes. Despite Ceaușescu's efforts to isolate the country from Western currents, Romania had first-class thinkers like Professor Prodan, M., and G., knowledgeable about their own intellectual traditions and far better read than I in European literature, history, and philosophy. Plagued, however, by the stigma of belonging to a small country surrounded by bigger, more aggressive and important ones, they hungered for recognition by outsiders. For all that distinguished the Securitate from my intellectual friends, both groups wanted to contain and channel me: to make me take their side and give them or their country international respectability. While Secus wanted to influence me "in a positive direction," scholars such as M. and G. wanted me to become their partisans in the larger world: to love them, to bring their work to an English-speaking public, to help them make the leap from their own small stage to a larger one.

Instead, I was a disappointment both great and small: small, because I did this superficial kind of ethnography from an airplane and declined to translate their work (which would do me no good in my quest for tenure in a competitive U.S. academic market); great, because I put those offensive jokes in the front of my book. The jokes branded me with a permanent stigma. The sad irony is that not only did Romanian colleagues want me to love them: I wanted them to love me too. There was plenty of disappointment to go around.

Under the Magnifying Glass

During this year, in contrast to my prior visits, I was increasingly aware of the surveillance exercised upon me, in both Geoagiu and Cluj. Because my home in Cluj was a hotel, *securişti* could maintain near-total surveillance of my activities, since I could not go in or out unobserved. This was less true in Geoagiu, but even there I was much more visible than I had been in Vlaicu, for Geoagiu, as the commune's administrative center, had a police post with several officers, at least one of whom was a Secu. In rural areas the Securitate customarily used local police to do its work, which included managing informers, spreading rumors and disinformation, and intimidating people with questions—and some of those questioned told me about it.

I complained about surveillance regularly to the IREX grant supervisor in Bucharest, Dan Ghibernea. According to one of his informative notes to my case officer there, I alleged that following every discussion I had with someone in Geoagiu, the person would receive a visit, after which I would no longer find them at home in a welcoming mood. In my field notes I mention going to see the local priest, who asked if I had permission to go wherever I wanted. When I expressed surprise, he continued that a Secu officer, having heard I'd been to church and to see him, had come and asked him what we'd discussed. He was warned not to tell me about the visit but thought it a good idea I should know. Meanwhile, the Cluj Secu were following my situation through my informer "Marcu," who kept his officer there apprised of what was happening:

She felt permanently under surveillance; she said that a friend from Geoagiu had told her that she saw the car of the police in the village every day, which is not normal. On the other hand, she acknowledges that she is tired and it might be a matter of nervous irritation (she has insomnia and her nerves are at the limit), so she says she is disposed to interpret things darkly.

What I would learn only after 1989 was that in Geoagiu, the house across the street from the room I lived in became the headquarters for a round-the-clock Securitate stakeout, from which they watched everyone who came or went and listened through the walls (using fancy technology) to what was happening in my room. The old fellow (the mayor's widowed father) who lived alone in that house probably liked all the attention; now he had people around.

Back in Cluj in April 1985, I tell my sociologist colleague Ion Aluaş about the Secu activity in Geoagiu, and he says, "Here too." Shortly after I'd left Cluj for Geoagiu in December, they had come to talk with him, saying they'd been in my room and his blood would curdle to see what nasty things I say about people in my notes. It was true that they'd been in my room. The telephone operator at the hotel (who had ensnared me in a relationship early in my stay and would periodically hit me up for Kents, for which she sometimes volunteered information in exchange) had let me know that the minute I had left for Bucharest the previous week, my room was searched top to bottom. She was not wrong: the seal on my locked suitcase was broken and the suitcase now had a slight buckle to it. She reported that they kept calling headquarters to say they weren't finding anything, something about envelopes (my field notes?); they were very upset because they were finding nothing. She had overheard it all.

Another hotel receptionist, Dumi, who often proclaimed himself my only trustworthy friend there and to whom I told this episode, insisted that no one had been in my room and I should trust him: the Secu had no interest in my doings. He denied that we grantees were seriously followed and volunteered that if anyone came from the Secu to ask him about me, he would tell me at once. But others insisted that Dumi was up to his neck with the Securitate, always hanging out in the back room with one or another of them, talking and joking. An informer's disturbing note that could only have come from him confirms it now. And finally, another Cluj friend, when asked whether she had been approached, said that her daughter had been—but then they found out that the fellow was an impostor, pretending to be a *securist* in order to get information he could use for his own ends! So (my field note concludes)

> there are three categories: people who are clean, securişti, and people passing as securişti. This really blows the mind.

As a result, trying to maintain psychological equilibrium during that year was a challenge. Research in Geoagiu involved constantly hearing from people that they thought I was a spy. A woman I visited often once asked me outright what I'm interested in; I explained it's about people's ways of viewing the past. Then she told me that someone at work had said to her, "Be careful what you discuss with the American! You can't be sure she's not doing espionage." She was at a meeting at which the county Party secretary had delivered some unpleasant news, at which point her neighbor whispered to her, "The American should be here now, she'd have something to tape record."

One day in early March I got several distressing reports of Securitate interference. They began in Vlaicu. My friend Veca told me that her niece had been questioned by a Secu about my research and was frightened; he told her he'd go to her workplace the next day for an official declaration. Veca had passed this on to Meri, who had not brought it up with me, and Veca also thought that the same guy had gone to the seamstress Helga, where I often hung out.

Field notes, 9 March 85
All this so depressed me that I could hardly function all day, bawling, long tense conversation with landlady. Wiped out. Hate this country, especially Geoagiu; want to write a nasty article. [!] Am convinced that cop Belu is using me so as to cover for bad things he's done (like, colluding with forestry thieves). When I talk with Mr. M., he says "Tell me your friends and I'll tell you who's ratting on you"—which of course makes me suspect him too. Back to the old problem of trust again.

I still remember one particular day on which I was utterly paralyzed by these tales of surveillance. I lay on my bed for a very long time, immobilized; I simply could not get up, feeling pinned to the spot by all the gazes concentrated in my direction and by the talk of who was my true friend and who merely pretending to be. I remembered something anthropologist Renato

Rosaldo had told me from his fieldwork among the Ilongot, a group of head-hunters in the Philippines about whom he knew that they would sometimes lavishly entertain guests from other groups and then, in the middle of the night, cut their heads off. He and his wife, Shelly, would have wonderful evenings with these people, eating and talking together. Then they would go to bed, and Renato would lie awake for hours wondering if they planned to cut off his head. Eventually his nerves broke. No one was cutting off my head, of course, but they were certainly creating a frightening environment, one in which I felt great sympathy for Renato.

After I returned to Cluj from Geoagiu in April 1985, receptionist Dumi took me aside and said that *securişti* from Deva had come all the way to Cluj to ask the head of the hotel about me—did I engage in commerce, who am I having sex with, what do I think about the problems with car traffic this year, etc. So having left Geoagiu to escape surveillance, now I learn that my surveillance has slipped out of Hunedoara and into Cluj, where it had at first seemed less glaring. Oh, naive K! Little did she know.

"Vera" as a Spy

There was nothing we weren't interested in.
—Stasi officer interviewed by Gary Bruce, in *The Firm: The Inside Story of the Stasi*

Evidence

Throughout the documents in my file we find the Securitate creating the spy identity of KATHERINE VERDERY's double, "VERA." How are they going about it? To begin with, officers provide their evidence that I have intelligence experience, confirming their suspicion that I am a CIA agent.

From analysis of photocopies made of nearly all her reports it results that the element being followed has experience in informative work. Thus, she has created her own code for writing out her material, and she has given pseudonyms to the persons contacted. They are called "informers" [and have] conspiratorial names. . . . Alongside the information collected, she mentions the place and context of the discussion, the informer's "attitude," the direct and subsidiary questions she asks in directing the conversation toward the subject of interest. [Some examples] She is constantly preoccupied with learning which of the people around her work for the Securitate. All of this denotes experience in informative work.

[Her reports are] typed in three copies and sent to the U.S.A. Embassy in Bucharest by special courier. . . . We note that "VERA" does not keep a single copy, as would be normal if she were using them to write a scientific work.

As a CNSAS colleague observed, "The Securitate didn't believe that someone could come to Romania only for scholarly purposes—just as they themselves instructed Romanians going abroad to get information!" In another document they praise my talents in espionage and even criticize the procedures of other officers. The superior's marginal note on an August 1988 report from the Iaşi Securitate to Bucharest reads in part, "**We must pay close attention because she covers her espionage activity very well. . . . She must be handled in a professional way with a great deal of care.**"

In fact, my identity as a spy is inscribed from the moment I am assigned to the Third Directorate, the Securitate's branch for counterespionage, whose goal is to discover and liquidate citizens of espionage services acting against Romania. In 2014 I ask a colleague at the CNSAS, "Did they really think we were spies?" "Yes and no," he responds. "The evolution of the system complicates it—the opening up of the mid-1960s, allowing more foreigners in. 'Spy' was a very good 'work hat' for them: it covered their activity. Lots of officers worked eagerly on foreigners, consumed lots of energy, and then had to justify why they were spending so much energy on these people. The officers had to demonstrate that the targets were worth it." "Discovering" they were spies would do that.

A secret police file is the traces of a state creating a person; the "organ" (as they called themselves) for doing so in communist Romania was the Securitate. When I gained access to my file, I was able to see that process, to discover a reciprocal self-fashioning in which the Securitate made me a spy as I made myself an ethnographer, each act of creation influencing the other. Each of us sought anchors enabling us to define and classify our research object—for me, the peasantry of a Romanian village, and for them, "VERA." Our practices differed, of course, in many respects. For one thing, anthropological knowledge ends up in publications available to anyone, whereas the Securitate's reports remained secret; for another, anthropologists do not coerce those from whom they gather information in the way *securişti* did. Moreover, whereas I conducted most of my activities in plain sight (shrouded, perhaps, by a professional jargon that somewhat obscured my research aims), they made theirs invisible to all but themselves and their collaborators. It occurs to me that instead of being unnerved by the picture they paint of me, I should be flattered: "VERA" is becoming ever more fearsome. But I, KV, take no pleasure in this.

What, after all, do *securişti* think a spy is? How can we develop a cultural understanding of it for this case? Some of my officers will address this question later, but for now I would say it is an enemy, whether the class alien, the foreigner, the anticommunist, anyone whose purposes are different from theirs. It reflects an incapacity to deal with difference, a fundamental premise that "different" equals "opposed to our interests." A spy does not have Romania's interests at heart. Virgiliu tells me about a conversation with a *securist* in which he asked what the officer thought U.S. citizens and other foreigners could have been spying on, given that satellites can take photographs with such astounding resolution. "They could be gathering data and presenting it in a tendentious manner!" How? "One of them was writing about there being no food in stores, about the ban on driving so as to save gasoline for sale abroad, etc." Virgiliu asked, "How was this tendentious? It was the truth!" "It was denigrating us, making us look bad!" Virgiliu sums this up: "That comes from a specific mind-set that equates foreigners with danger." This xenophobia has a venerable history not only in Romania but also in the attitudes of the KGB that trained the Securitate.

Indeed, in his reactions to reading his file, French anthropologist Claude Karnoouh stressed that what made the Securitate consider him a spy was his *foreignness*. But I think there's something else, something that does not appear in so many words, namely that a spy is someone who has no one to defend her—no relatives, at best an "entourage" into which *securişti* can make inroads. She has no network other than one she has fashioned on the fly, not through Romanians' lengthy mechanisms of trust-building. Her social support lies elsewhere, in another country. To be seen as a spy is to be seen as a social isolate whose connections can be manipulated. For this reason, I am doubly grateful to those who "incorporated" me as if I were kin: Meri, Moaşa, my Geoagiu family Mărioara and Ioan, and many others. They were my best defense against the identity being so diligently fashioned for "VERA."

But what if there is in fact *no* specific content to their notion of spy? What if "spy" is a role we are assigned that has a particular function in the apparatus of rule? *Securişti* create a number of formulae to give form to that function and then attribute them to a person's behavior, to make her a target in a system of repression. They have a standard language, such as "her view of our history is deformed, contrary to historical reality," "she makes denigratory interpretations of our realities," "she is a CIA agent," "she is collecting sociopolitical information that will create a negative image of Romania." Do all these descriptions—and they are standard in the files I consulted—simply signal the moment when Securitate officers initiate, concerning some person, a certain set of practices for which "evidence" is beside the point? This question will come up again.

> > >

During my research stay, I found all the talk of my identity as a spy rather wearing but was unable simply to throw it off. My field notes for 17 April 1985 observe,

> *Conversation with Dorina suggests that what is so unsettling in all this talk of spying etc. is that my own fragile sense of identity is threatened; I get no confirmation from without of my sense of who I am, what my values are: others say and think otherwise.*

This, of course, makes me resemble the Romanians who so hoped for external validation of their worth from my book and instead got those jokes. I remember a conversation with my beloved friend and mentor Ernestine Friedl, who while overseeing my summer fieldwork in Greece in 1971 told me why she found fieldwork so difficult. She had always thought of herself as a decent person, principled and honest, and here she was among people who didn't necessarily feel that way about her at all, and in any case didn't value those qualities as she did. Hearing all these rumors of my spying made me now understand her perfectly: I had always thought of myself as a good, straightforward person, and now I am thrown off balance when I find this is not the working assumption of many around me, nor do they value it.

But then again, didn't I justify their doubts? A spy is someone who acts suspiciously, and I was certainly capable of that. In the spring of 1985, my friends Ralf and Ana and I decided it would be fun to go someplace together and get out from under the likely surveillance in Deva and Vlaicu. We decided to have a weekend in Cluj and made a plan for me to go and visit an acquaintance who lived in a town en route from Vlaicu to Cluj; then, at a specific hour, I would leave, saying I had to catch the train to Cluj. Instead, however, I would go to the highway and hitchhike at precisely the moment when Ralf and Ana would be driving by. Here is part of two related reports about the incident, both from the Securitate of the county in which I was hitchhiking:

On 4 June 1985, the foreigner visited ▮▮▮ at her domicile, but at her departure she had a suspect comportment, seeking to mask as much as possible her presence in this locality and then her meeting with the BIERMAN family from Deva who picked her up with their car a Lada 1500, license ▮▮▮▮, at the periphery of the town and headed for Cluj-Napoca leaving the impression that they do not know one another, though a prior understanding existed among them. We specify that the meeting between the foreigner and the Bierman family was established a day ahead.

(The Hunedoara Securitate had known about it, of course, because the Biermans' phone was bugged.) Greater detail can be found in the shadowing report from the day of our meeting. It begins at 6:30 A.M. with Ralf's discovery that his car battery is dead, so he runs off to get a new one. Then he and Ana depart for our rendezvous, accompanied by a Securitate car bearing the shadowing team. It notes every stop they make, their shopping, the coffee they drank, his telephone calls, and so on. I will let the officers tell the denouement of the incident, which almost gets lost in their contorted "conclusions":

"MANU" [Ralf's pseudonym] and his wife left the coffee-shop at 13:05 . . . and took off in their car through 1 May Square, 23 August St., Razboieni St., and at about 50 meters after they passed the bus station they stopped in front of the said VERDERY KATHERINE (target "KATY") who signaled her presence by making a sign with her hand for them to stop.

"MANU" got out of the car, helped her to put her baggage on the back seat, then got behind the wheel and together they continued to drive in the direction of Turda.

CONCLUSIONS

From the shadowing carried out on the target it was determined that the meeting with the said VARDERY KATHERINE was in fact an organized meeting, perfected by telephone along the way, so as to leave the impression of a casual encounter. Given that the respective moment occurred in a very short time, almost while traveling, it could not be documented by photo, because the conditions of our cover did not permit us to follow them at a short distance, for the route was completely uncrowded, thus the operative did not have the necessary time to get close to the meeting place with the camera, the moment being consummated before he could achieve a distance consonant with the limits of the technical parameters of the photo apparatus, and part of the team was concentrated at the address where the informative organs had indicated that the meeting would probably take place.

In short, they were in the wrong location, too far away to get a good picture.

Oblivious of all their exertions, the three of us enjoyed a lovely weekend in Cluj, taking a picnic to the park on a beautiful sunny day, walking in the botanical garden (where Ana thought she spotted someone hiding in a bush near where we were talking), and taking pleasure in one another's company, even if on the last day Ralf hadn't been feeling well. Although there is no report of the weekend in either Ralf's file or mine, we should not be complacent: the bug in their telephone captured our next conversation.

K: Alo, "MANU"? I wanted to know if you got home safely.

M: Great. The drive was excellent and we got home well, everything is fine. . . .

K: And you're feeling OK?

M: Yes, today was good. I went to work and I felt fine.

K: And what did you tell people, that you went to get a medical check-up?

Our suspicious outing would put the Biermans firmly on the Securitate's map—where they already figured marginally, hence the wiretap that had earlier caught the conversations in which we had planned the whole adventure. Nine days later the Secus would begin "informative surveillance" on Ralf, justifying it by our trip to Cluj, which "proved" that I was spying and he was my accomplice. Then—having first requested the Party's permission, since he was a Party member—they would open a DUI on him in autumn

1986, prior to my return the following year. An undated telex from 1987 summarizes their view of him:

In 1979 he met the American researcher Verdery Katherine, suspected of being a C.I.A. agent. . . . He met with the foreign citizen in suspect conditions in Cluj-Napoca.

It was thus extraordinarily fortunate that when Ana told me that same year of their plan to flee and asked me not to call them anymore, she did so in person, not by telephone.

Characterizations

These documents that confirm "VERA's" spying reveal a process of sculpting an image of her and some of her sidekicks ("VERONA," "VANESSA," "KITTY," etc.). How does she emerge from this process? A common practice for the Securitate was to provide "characterizations," a genre they taught to their informers as well. As Cristina Vatulescu tells us, the aim of keeping files was not just to find evidence of a particular crime but to examine a person's complete biography in order to look for suspect tendencies.[3] Characterizations might help to establish them. The following examples are in chronological order; most come from 1987 and 1988, and most are from my academic colleagues. The positive tone of some may reflect the Securitate's success in recruiting informers from among my friends.

[From an officer's summary of a conversation with a historian, Cluj]: Source considers that she is an interesting character, complex, unusually intelligent with whom you have to be very well trained to be able to answer the questions she puts. Source remarked on the diversity of this woman's relations in Romanian society, her dynamic mobility, and considers that she could be channeled onto a well-established route. . . .

[Case officer's summary, Cluj]: She knows the Romanian language very well and is up to date with the realities in our country. She is characterized as having aplomb, she likes to be considered important.

[Shadowing officer's report, Cluj]: Target "KORA" is a lively individual, she always seems to be in a crisis for time and therefore she leaves the impression that she does not verify herself [i.e., look over her shoulder to check for the presence of shadowing] and is not attentive to who is around her.

[Note from ethnographer, Iași]: Voluble, expansive, intelligent, and diplomatic, she talked about everything and nothing. I listened, I "got enthusiastic," . . . we "became friends." . . . Personally, I believe that this K.V. is a person who must be seriously taken into consideration for everything she studies in our country and I also think we could have unpleasant surprises. She is exceedingly intelligent, experienced, skillful. She knows how to make herself likable when she wants to. . . . She isn't wasting her time here for nothing. Not at all to be underestimated as an adversary!! She will gather her material and after she "quits" us the attack from abroad will begin. That's what I presuppose and I hope I'm not right!

[Note from unknown informer, Iași]: What does Source think of her: She is cold as ice, calculating in every word and gesture, everything is intended to incite a reply. She is unusually curious about everything around her and aggressive when responding to something that interests her.

[Note from historian, Iași]: She speaks exceptionally good Romanian; a very intelligent person, cultured, well informed in many domains, with a "sparkling" conversation, amiable and friendly.

[Note from the officer shadowing "VERA" on 27.10.88]: She has a simple bearing, therefore she can be confused with the natives.

In short, if she is indeed working as a spy, "VERA" emerges as a very dangerous adversary, an intelligent, well-trained, and formidable opponent, able to attract Romanians into her confidence and to conceal her true purposes. Although I didn't much like her at first, I see her becoming a powerful force the Securitate must respect and reckon with—as I must too.

The Adventures of "Teo"

In order to gather ever-better data on "VERA's" presumed spying, securiști make liberal use of their friend and my constant companion, "Teo"—the recording equipment that will reveal what I am really up to. "Teo" in his various manifestations is their number one source toward this end. How reliable an ally is he? To ask about this is to consider the Securitate's technical endowment for creating doppelgangers. On the evidence in my file, "Teo" did yeoman work for them much of the time, but he was not beyond reproach. He has particular trouble competing with a television (a lesson my friends

Marina and Silvia had taught me back in 1973), and often his equipment doesn't function too well, or he has been improperly installed. (Anyone who has ever worked with a tape recorder can sympathize with these problems.)

[Report on "VERA," conversation in hotel room with a man.] Date of recording: 13.08.84. They turn on the television, the discussion can no longer be understood.

[From a conversation in a restaurant, being overheard by mobile "Teo."] The frequency keeps slipping, it's inaudible [mentioned five times during the conversation].

[Conversation with Steven Burg, an acquaintance from the U.S. State Department; overheard using mobile "Teo."] Superior officer's note: Because of lousy T.O. equipment the recording was of bad quality, for which reason a lot of data were lost that could have brought us clarity concerning the preoccupations of these two people.

[Meeting of an officer with one of my informers.] On 21 iii 89 I met with Source "Banu," a meeting for which the discussion took place in the presence of Source "Teofil" but, since the battery ran out, it could be played back only in part.

Finally, writer George Ardeleanu, in his biography of priest Nicolae Steinhardt based on the priest's Securitate file, reports on my visit there in October 1988 and provides the following piquant summary:

> In the end, observing this episode in retrospect, we find a comic note as well. We have the image of a tremendous machinery being unleashed (the First and Third Directorates, the Bucharest Headquarters Inspectorate and the Cluj County Inspectorate, Military Unit 0800, the Special Unit "T" for intercepting conversations, the special services for following ("F"), correspondence ("S"), and "111," the heavies [generals] Giani Bucurescu, Aurelian Mortoiu, col. Gheorghe Ardeleanu [no relation] the commandant of the Special Unit for Antiterrorist Warfare, etc. etc. for what? To record a simple meeting between two people in which the essential element—the conversation in Steinhardt's house—slipped through their fingers.[4]

Why? In all their mobilization of forces, they had forgotten to ask for "Teo"! He generally works well, but not if people fail to invite him.

It's important to note that except for video cameras, "Teo" never works alone but always with a transcriber. This is partly so officers can have readier access to the material but also because they need to reuse the tapes. In the above cases, his transcriber is conscientious and capable but that is not always the case. Here is an example concerning a colleague of mine working in another county, Salaj:

We forward to you seven tapes recorded in English . . . made of the doctoral student ▮▮▮▮, who is in our attention. We report that at our inspectorate it was attempted to transcribe the respective tapes, but owing to the fluency of the conversation and lack of expertise of the officers who know English the transcription was not successful. We ask that after exploiting the tapes they be sent back to us, communicating any interesting operative aspects that might result.

When Securitate documents refer to informers as the number one weapon in their arsenal, then, part of the reason may be that their technological endowment and even their own capacities are not fully up to the task. These were not, in any case, adequate to the organization's needs. Before a recording device could be used, the case officer had to request permission to install it—not just because installation could be tricky, but also because there were not enough machines for everyone who needed them. "Teo" always had to be approved—and if he was not, then his work might be delayed.

Austerity: "VERA" as Socio-Political Spy

I spent the winter of 1984–85 in the commune center of Geoagiu, where I lived with a marvelous couple from the collective farm, Ioan and Mărioara—he a first-rate raconteur, she a superb cook with a warm and mischievous spirit. My reason for going to Geoagiu was to talk to people about the national history that was being presented so broadly to the public in frequent news stories, television shows and movies about historical figures, references in political speeches, and so on. In Geoagiu—which I picked because it had wider educational and occupational diversity than Vlaicu—I would see if I could discern any effects of all this publicity. Discerning them might not be easy, I knew, but that was my aim.

Ioan and Mărioara,
my Geoagiu hosts,
1984–85. Author's
photo.

The Hunedoara Securitate recorded my arrival, noted my topic, asked (through the county Party secretary) for my research plan and a copy of my questionnaire, and at length approved my request to do ethnography in Geoagiu. In my file, they added the extensive measures they would be taking:

Ministry of the Interior   TOP SECRET
Hunedoara County Inspectorate, Service III   16-1-85

To Ministry of the Interior, Third Directorate,
Bucharest, Serv. I

To observe and to know the activities and contacts she establishes, the entire network of informers of the commune was given instruction. With a similar preventive aim, counterintelligence preparation was given to the secretary of the county People's Council, the president, vice-president, and secretary of the Geoagiu commune People's Council, the director of the post office, and the orthodox priest. Continued action is being taken for counterintelligence preparation of personnel in education, the community center, cinema, post office, etc., with whom she intends to have discussions.

In order to forestall unfavorable conclusions the American researcher might reach, comrade First Secretary of the county Party Committee was informed, so that the relevant employees could analyze the possibility of intensifying and diversifying cultural-artistic manifestations in the commune concerning historical themes. [!]

On 12.01.1985 a secret search was conducted at her domicile, on which occasion some material was photocopied. Similarly, it was established that she possesses a SANYO minicassette recording device identical to those used by our units. . . . While she is in Bucharest we will continue to photocopy the materials and to introduce special listening devices. . . . In addition, through the informer network and other means of Securitate work, we will proceed toward preventing her collection of data and information of a secret character, as well as seeking to influence her positively.

The instructions were familiar from my previous surveillance but less specifically focused on my interests in the military.

But the conditions of my work were quite different from before. With Poland's Solidarity movement had come a change in Ceaușescu's policies concerning foreign borrowing, in which Romania had engaged during the 1970s—and which the fate of Poland in 1980–81 had shown could be very risky. Polish Party leader Edward Gierek had lost his job in the wake of the Solidarity strikes, and the consequent renegotiation of the Polish debt showed just how much leverage "foreign interests" could have over debtor nations. Already by 1982, during a brief visit to Romania, my field notes show signs of the new austerity measures.

Field notes, 27 Jul. 1982
Romania has gotten a World Bank loan, whose condition is that there be no imports. This means that 60% of coffee sold consists of oats, so coffee is called by a name that means "neigh." No stockings, no sprays, because something in their manufacture has to be imported. No soap. As long as no imports, whole sections of factories are at a standstill, so the budget has to be wrung from the villages. The problem with wringing from the villages is that international treaty says no exporting of food if the local population is going hungry. Therefore rationing, which is supposed to be secret. General expenses keep rising.

The austerity worsened throughout the 1980s, such that people began to refer to the country as "Ceauschwitz" [CHOW shwits]. The worst time of all, however, was the year I was there. The foulest winter in decades had disastrous consequences for the Romanian economy; as a result, the government took austerity measures that squeezed the population even further. Writer Stelian Tănase describes it in his journal:

> Winter 1984–85, terrible and grotesque winter. Who can forget people's amazement that something like this could happen to them, that they should suffer so much? Lack of heat, no water in apartments, no heating gas. Driving prohibited for all vehicles but public transport. Food inexistent in the stores. Long lines, which last whole days and nights. So many dramatic situations. Old people and children, dead. Ambulances not circulating. The dispatcher asks you if the person is pregnant and about to give birth, otherwise they refuse your call. They ask how old the person is, then refuse the call. What a time! What a nightmare! It's dreadfully cold in the house. The electricity is constantly interrupted, and electric heaters have been taken off the market. Someone is punishing us, is seeing to it that we die.[5]

Novelist Herta Müller, writing of her relation to the Securitate in her book The Appointment, also captured brilliantly the insanity of the times.[6] The book's last line: "The trick is not to go mad."

While neighboring Hungary experimented rather successfully with economic reforms, the Romanian economy was in increasingly desperate shape. Because the winter was also among the coldest on record throughout Europe, Ceauşescu and his advisors took advantage of the situation to reduce the country's foreign debt: now, with Italy, Germany, and other Western European countries freezing, Romania would secure extra foreign currency to pay off its debt by exporting natural gas and oil products. As a result, train and bus service was cut back, new regulations curtailed driving by private citizens so as to save on gasoline now destined for export, and temperatures in all office and apartment buildings were dropped in order to export natural gas. Moreover, the government could profit even more by increasing the export of foodstuffs, particularly meat products; this led to severe shortages of food. Finally, salaries and pensions were reduced, and schools and factories were often closed, cutting employees' pay. Many spoke of Romania as a giant prison. Unlike normal prisons, this one had no actual incarceration, but it had forms of managed mobility, and its prisoners were tethered with listening devices.

My field notes show diverse responses to the crisis, most of them based on that stalwart of information broadcast under communism: rumors. Rumors spread about what had happened when a Secu, hiding in a long queue for food so as to overhear people's complaints, tried to pull a complainer out of the line for questioning: the crowd turned on the Secu and nearly tore him to bits. The unavailability of gasoline caused all manner of problems that aggravated the strict limits placed on the days when one could drive. One acquaintance of mine took eleven hours one day to fill up his tank: five hours waiting for the gas station to open, then another six hours slowly pushing his car forward in the enormous queue that had formed. On one such occasion, a riot reportedly broke out when the station manager tried to tell people there was no more gas. The police were called, but when the crowd saw them arrive everyone took off after them, overturning the police car. After the beginning of the new year, private citizens were not allowed to drive at all, ostensibly to keep them safe. Everyone speculated constantly as to when the ban would be lifted, but it continued. Then suddenly, on 26 March 1985, it was announced that cars could now circulate. Rumor had it that people had begun driving without carrying their license, papers, or license plates, so that when they were stopped they could not be identified and fined. They had gotten sick of sitting around, and their action had finally forced the hand of those in charge. Or so people said.

Alongside combustibles and food, electricity too was rationed for export. One never knew when the lights would go out, though in the villages, at least, a pattern gradually emerged in which there would be two hours of television in the early evening (most of it featuring Ceauşescu) and after it the lights would go off. People joked about plans to increase the birth rate as a consequence of forced time in bed. But there were rumors of factories closing from lack of electricity, and for schoolchildren who needed to study at night or others who worked late, the electricity cuts were very inconvenient. Among their multiple consequences, they also affected people's back-up plan for keeping warm: turning on heating coils (which many people had at hand for making coffee) or electric heaters. The cold was much worse in cities, where central control over combustibles could be strictly maintained.

Field notes, 8-5-85
Marina says winter in Bucharest was terrible; for three weeks running, there was no gas in her building at all, so residents drained the water to keep the radiators from freezing. The official reason for the cuts was to save industry, but coincidentally lots of old people died in the cold—she wonders whether that was part of the plan. Also

lots of infants—in three hospitals, all the incubators cut out. Marina's pregnant friend told her of a new law: it used to be that the father of the child would go to declare it at the civil registry on the day after its birth, but now he will go on the twentieth day, so statistics will not show all the infant deaths. Radiators in a number of schools burst during winter break and were not repaired by the beginning of school in February. Marina went to classes in a hat, fur coat, and gloves. She says there has never been anything like this in her lifetime. Diplomats from the French and Italian embassies were evacuated to Bulgaria and Serbia; before going, they protested officially to the Romanian government about their work conditions.

And then there was Romanians' characteristic reaction to everything: an entirely new genre of jokes on the theme of austerity, such as these from my field notes, which help to show why I had so much fun in my fieldwork despite the surveillance. They were always told with caution, for fear that securişti might hear them and arrest the teller.

A guy goes into a food store and asks for chicken. The butcher replies: "We have nothing but backs, necks, and feet." "How can this be!? Don't you have any breasts?" "No, no breasts." "Don't you have any thighs?" "Mister, this is a grocery store, not a whore house!" (Alternate punchline: "What a memory you have!")

Have you heard that refrigerators have gotten more expensive this winter? They're now up to 200,000 lei for the ones with four rooms.

Q: How did people light their homes before gas lanterns? A: With electricity.

As obtaining food becomes a serious problem, a young couple is discussing what to do. Because both are too busy at work to struggle with cooking, obtaining the ever-less-available food, and so on, the husband suggests, "Let's just have tea for breakfast, something cold for lunch, and in the evening we'll nourish ourselves with love." They agree. The next day, tea for breakfast; for lunch some cheese, bread, and salami. In the evening when he gets home, he sees his wife in the nude going upstairs, sliding down the banister; upstairs, down the banister, up, down, up down. . . . "What on earth are you doing?!" he asks. "I'm warming up your dinner."

Romanians had many complex forms of resistance, but their jokes were the most delightful—full of kookiness, self-ridicule, and sarcasm. To me, their capacity to suffer adversity while finding ways to laugh at it is among their most engaging and admirable traits, and it helped me to weather that terrible year.

> > >

In general, austerity was less pronounced in the villages, where people had food from their personal plots and the animals they kept, heated with wood or (where that was lacking) with big canisters of sawdust obtained on the sly from furniture factories, and so on. Therefore, the implications of austerity for me personally were minimal. For the worst of the winter I was living in a household where there was plenty to eat and a nice wood-burning stove, for which I had procured wood on the black market. I had no car so I was not affected by the gasoline crisis, nor did the shortage of buses and trains much affect me because I rarely needed to travel. Although I had to write my research notes by a propane lantern, plenty of anthropologists before me had done that. I would return home from this field trip fatter than when I left, austerity notwithstanding, for I always had to eat and drink when I visited people, and in the village, that could be four or five households in a day. Back in Cluj, I had access to food from the hotel restaurant, and I took to buying delicacies for the intrepid souls who invited me over; I had made firm friends, of course, with the head waiter, who helped me procure the treats.

If my personal experience of austerity was fairly unproblematic, it nonetheless had implications for my surveillance, for the climate of increasing discontent among Romanians made securiști worry that I could more easily recruit disaffected persons to plot against the regime. In consequence, they would have to monitor my conversations even more closely than before. Here was yet another explanation for why my experience of surveillance in the 1980s was so much greater than it had been in the 1970s: a set of policies specific to the economic crisis of the 1980s that had not existed in the previous decade.

In my field notes, some of which they had photocopied and translated, they underline things like this:

28 xii 84. Twice in the past 3 days someone has come bringing milk, hidden in a plastic sack, and the person then hangs around for a while, to hide the purpose of the visit. Both times P. commented that this is how you have to handle under-the-counter milk sales these days: as if carrying contraband. . . . [This paragraph is marked "Yes" by its Secu reader.]

6 iii 85. More hassling about bus service. Allotments of fuel must go to Hunedoara's extensive industry and transport of export products, public transport last. But the result of this is increased clashes between local officials and IRTA [the bus service]. D. said some time ago that no one was going to work because there were no buses. . . . Someone said IRTA had been warned that bus drivers would be dying at the hands of people from Geoagiu if there's not more reliable service for factory workers; second

shift has had no bus all week, had to walk home from the highway (1½ hours) at midnight.

Austerity afforded me even more examples, then, of a kind of field note that proved to them my fundamental lack of goodwill toward their country: I was collecting "socio-political information" that could be used to tarnish the image of Romanian socialism abroad. Of all the suspicions harbored against me, this is the one I most readily own: it is the *job* of anthropologists to collect "socio-political information," and I did so unremittingly, no matter where I was or what specific research project I was conducting. No detail, I felt, could be too small for helping me understand the society I was living in, even if those details did not fit my research "properly speaking," as officers put it. For anthropologists, the goal of understanding is always larger than a particular project. We vacuum up everything we can.

Indeed, here was my biggest problem with the Securitate, who expected a specific research agenda with circumscribed boundaries, into which they were always trying to shoehorn my sprawling inquiries. I wrote down my conversations with my landlord's son, who would take over an hour to commute to his factory where he would be told to work a half day or go back home with a pay cut, because there wasn't enough work for everyone (this note was underlined by the Secu reader). I wrote about an argument of two friends who held low-level political positions, one of whom said that to solve problems you have to curry favor with the people above you, the other that you have to get your subordinates on your side (guess which one was the Party secretary). I wrote down innumerable details of the black market, which was in full flower all around me, about how people in Geoagiu were disconnecting their electricity meters to reduce their bill, about how they (and I as well) procured stolen wood from the forestry service to heat their homes. I wrote down the discussion between two collective farm members about why the crop yields of farm land had dropped by two-thirds (improper application of fertilizer, they thought—the Secu reader gave this one a "yes"). I wrote down jokes, even though people asked me not to: the jokes were too funny to lose.

I wrote down a friend's story about a local mayor and his cronies wanting to go trout fishing but not having any equipment. Actually, they wanted to *eat* the fish more than to *catch* it. So the mayor said, "You guys come with me." They went down to the river, where he knew a bunch of locals were poaching trout without permits. The mayor said to them, "The comrade inspectors are here from Bucharest! Hand over your permits! . . . Don't have them? OK, confiscate the trout!" Their meal was delicious. I wrote down the way my "driver" in Geoagiu managed to get us Pepsi one evening in the local restaurant, which supposedly didn't have any: the waitress brought it to us in a teapot with cups, something one never saw in a restaurant except at breakfast. He said, "There's no other way. There isn't any Pepsi, and if others see we have it, they'll cause a riot."

And back in Cluj, I would write about how the clever director of the library where I worked, Liviu Ursuțiu, sought to convince the authorities that his unit was indeed cutting its use of electricity, a reduction of 50 percent having been ordered for all institutions. When his friend in the electrical plant called him one day to warn him that an inspector was on the way, Liviu ordered that all the lights in the entire building be turned off at once. The porter directed the inspector to Liviu's office, from which Liviu could hear the fellow thrashing and banging his way down a long, absolutely pitch-black corridor. Finally a knock at the door: "I'm here to check on the 50% reduction in use of lights, but please turn a light on." Liviu replied, "No, I give the orders around here. You've come to check the reduction, so what are you going to write? *100% reduction!* That's right, 100%!" As soon as the inspector left, he turned all the lights back on.

It was stories like these that made me love being in Romania, surveillance notwithstanding. As with their jokes, their endless capacity for humor and irony enlivened and made bearable the dismal situation of the 1980s. The stories also show that despite people's victimization by the regime's austerity policies, Romanians had many ways of making do—of exercising some agency in these unpropitious circumstances. What I learned from such moments, however, made me perilous for Romania's image in the world, just as the Securitate said. No wonder they were always trying to copy my field notes. Along with the several other U.S. anthropologists there in those years, I gave them priceless information about their countrymen, which (according to Gen. Iulian Vlad in an interview) was very useful to them—another reason why they might not want to throw me out.

Village Research Comes to an End

From the very outset, the ethnographic component to my project on national history ran into snags. My first interviewee was a retired local schoolteacher, Mr. *Bogdan, and although he seemed upset by our encounter (with good reason, it turned out), he knew how to talk about history. But he wasn't eager to have our dialogue recorded, which I thought was necessary for this particular task, and neither was anyone else. Most people would balk at the exercise itself, saying history was not their business: I should be asking schoolteachers about this. In other words, what university professor asks peasants for the national history? I could not slough off my professional status, and this revealed a flaw in my research design. Aside from a few illuminating conversations—such as one in which a peasant woman insisted to me that the rebel movement of Pintea the Brave (1703) had taken place *after* the peasant uprising led by the peasant Horea (1784) because the TV program about Horea had come before the one about Pintea—my project was not going well. In late January I went to Bucharest to mail field notes and consult with some Romanian colleagues, including Professor Pop, about my difficulties. All of them said I should tape-record without telling people—interesting advice from scholars working in a surveillance state. I tried it a couple of times but felt so awful I had to stop. A field entry shows how my research was now providing the idioms for such personal decisions:

> Field notes, Geoagiu, 4 February 1985
> Attempt at meditation. Fauré Requiem comes to mind, "Luceat eis." Give them light; gives way to the line [from a Gerard Manley Hopkins sonnet], Send my roots rain. Roots, tree, Oak tree of Horea [leader of 1784 peasant revolt; betrayed and executed]. Betrayal—of Horea, of trust. Trust being betrayed all around, here. Sudden feeling of claustrophobia, I jump up and take the bus to Orăştie to call Ana and Dorina. Just the idea of getting out of there was liberating.

Clearly, I could not continue to betray respondents with my tape recorder, which was making the atmosphere for work even more suffocating than it already was from austerity. I still regret having tried.

My conversations weren't going all that well, and despite repeated visits to various families I could not seem to get past the cushion of reserve into greater ease with them, as I had in Vlaicu. Mrs. M., whom I had first met in 1973 and whom I now saw often, said she thought the mayor was spreading nasty rumors about me; someone else said it was the policeman named Belu. Finally I resorted to an expedient she suggested: asking the People's Council's Vice President for Culture to accompany me on a few visits, so people could see that I had the support of the local authorities, after which I could go on my own. This seemed to help, but I noted to myself that "I am reluctant to project my authority adequately to work well: I could get away with much more than I do by simply *proceeding*." In any case, trying to build trusting relations by mobilizing local officialdom hardly seemed the right path.

3 Feb 85: *For several days have been feeling ill at ease about interviews, feel dread-fully manipulative, homing in on some poor unassuming family, hitting them up for friendly conversation when I know the whole point is to see if they can be of use to me. Feel parasitic. Ill at ease too about abusing norms of good social conduct—pushing ▮ past the point where manners would have stopped, because I feared he wouldn't be willing to do this again. And ill at ease at possibility of people's being questioned, about my being a resource for petty politics here, etc. I can hardly wait to get out of here. Atmosphere of suspicion becoming really oppressive. Went to see 279, they say how much they like me, others say I'm here to do some kind of espionage.*

22 Mar 85: *Frustrating day again. A.M. appointment not at home. Others I sought weren't in—hard to tell if avoiding me or not. Easy to be paranoid. Went to Mrs. M., who told me to beware of drivers: they can be directed to keep track of me, to boast about sex [even if there is none, I guess]. Went to 279, who fed me more: says 42 is spreading rumors about me. So much of this that I am now becoming amused. Nice evening with R. Don't care if he's a plant. He showed up with a candle for when the electricity goes off!*
  Next day: once more, appointments fall through. Getting more paranoid.

8 Apr 85. *Horrible day. Went to work at ▮▮▮, who at the end of a perfectly nice chat asked if I tape record all these talks. I denied it but he looked like a thundercloud, clearly unconvinced. Then told me old Mr. Bogdan had been very frightened, because he was questioned by the Securitate right after his talk with me. If he spread the word so early in my stay, no wonder there's such successful gossip about my spying. I decided to go home; the atmosphere was too heavy. They tried to hold me back but I left, almost barfing with anxiety.*

The next day I went to Deva to register a complaint with the county Party secretary. I told a friend there, Iulia, what had happened, and she replied, "They'd kill me if they knew I said this to you, but the Secu car from Deva was at the Geoagiu cops every week, and the commune vice president was questioned left and right by them once—said he'd never experienced anything like it." A string of people whom I asked later that same day all admitted to having been approached by the policeman Belu, who would tell them, "Be careful what you discuss with her," or "She carries a hidden tape recorder wherever she goes."

The pig-eyed Party secretary in Deva to whom I complained about the surveillance the next day replied, smirking, "Let's overlook this, you still managed to do a lot of work." I decided that my fieldwork in Geoagiu was over—and indeed, I never made use of the data I collected in those four months. The couple who stood me up for my next (and last) appointment presented their excuses while offering me a jug filled with two liters of excellent plum brandy. I went home and—to Mărioara's consternation ("People don't drink alone!" she admonished me, refusing to take a glass)—got drunk. It was my last attempt at village fieldwork until after the communist regime fell.

"VERA" Spies for Hungarians

I returned to Cluj in April, not knowing that their top *securişti* had already sent up the hierarchy a recommendation to expel me. They immediately picked up where they had left off, anxious about my socio-political spying but also about something else troubling them before I had left for Geoagiu: my emerging identity as a "Hungarian." An informer in Geoagiu had reported on it in an informative note of 27 February 1985:

For all the harmony of opinions that devolved from her correct interpretation of historical facts, facts that showed the terribly difficult situation of Romanians in the Habsburg empire, I acknowledge that I always had a certain suspicion, though without proofs: was she possibly—whether formally, or from courtesy, friendship towards me, or politeness—hiding from me a sympathy for our Hungarian adversaries?

Suspicions to this effect had appeared as early as 1979 (and in some quarters, endure to this day). For one thing, there was my "anti-Romanian" book, and for another, there was my Hungarian-looking name. No matter how much I insisted that my name is French, the suspicion lingered that in saying so I was sowing disinformation, to mislead people as to my "true" identity.

Then there is my budding relationship with Hungarian academics in Cluj, to whom I was recommended by a colleague at home. Two of them are very enlightening companions and I visit them several times. There I am caught in the recording devices already installed in their apartments to keep tabs on the Hungarian minority—always a source of worry for *securişti*. My colleague's recommendation makes me careless, and what I intend as a "transparent" prelude to friendship in one case enters their documents as a particularly worrisome indication that I am on the wrong side of the Romanian-Hungarian conflict. They are particularly concerned about my relations with the colleague they call "Csaba." Here is a précis of how "Teo" saw my first visit at "Csaba's" home on 5 October 1984. "Teo's" transcriber used a combination of summaries and direct quotes, and the case officer underlined the most interesting parts. My excerpt is approximate; the underlining is theirs.

[After extended discussion of a variety of topics], KATHERINE VERDERY says, "I have great confidence in you and I'll tell you openly the problems I'm interested in. For you it's unpleasant not to trust people, but for us it's even more difficult because we don't know whom we can talk with. And it's very important that with those 1–2 people we talk with, we can tell them what's on our minds without problems arising from that." Further conversation touches on a number of other problematic issues. For instance, they talk about the relation of the Orthodox Church to national identity, to the state, and to people's daily problems; whether church attendance is rising or falling (she asks, "Do you think that in a way going to church is a sign of disdain for the government?," and Csaba replies, "Absolutely. And it means a certain decrease in governmental authority."). She tells him about entering the August 23rd "parade" incognito and talking with people around her, telling them she is from the library; he replied that he used to go to all these obligatory events until about three years ago, when he decided to oppose it as a waste of people's time. Then "Csaba" and his wife tell her some political jokes about the 13th Party Congress. They give her advice (not to call them from the hotel, not to leave certain things in her room, how to find the person who can sell her books that are unavailable otherwise).

At several points it does indeed seem that KATHERINE VERDERY is looking for forms of resistance against the regime, or for sources of popular discontent. As I look back on this conversation now, I sense the underlying Cold War reflex, though I was agnostic about the virtues of communism at the time. My *securiști* don't know that, however. They also don't know that it is a standard practice in fieldwork to agree with your respondents no matter what they are saying, so as to probe deeper for their views. The agreement doesn't mean you *share* the views. When I explore "Csaba's" Hungarian nationalist sentiments, I have no thought of inciting him to any further action, I just want to see what he thinks. *Securişti*, however, are very literal-minded. They "know" that "Csaba" is an "irredentist element," and I am spending time with him. This so alarms them that in two subsequent visits that "Teo" picks up in his house, the transcriber even states that the conversation is being transcribed "from the Hungarian language," which I don't speak. She also mistakenly attributes to *me* (by using feminine pronouns) the negative views of "Csaba."

In one of those later visits, I describe for "Csaba" and his wife the surveillance I was under in Geoagiu and say how disgusted I am by all the gossip and rumors circulating about me, but especially by the fact that no one tells me what they think to my face, which would be the honest thing to do. (Another setback for transparency.) "Csaba" then makes a comment whose importance I appreciate only later: he hopes that my friendship with him isn't going to prove damaging to my situation in Romania. To this I reply (as captured crystal clear by "Teo," in their living room), "We've succeeded in hiding our connection pretty well." It would of course turn out that all my efforts to keep from contaminating "Csaba" with my foreign presence were completely beside the point: it was indeed he who was contaminating me. The rumor of my Hungarian connections spread: a source in Iaşi expressed her opinion that she could hear a Hungarian accent in my Romanian. The same conjecture underlay the reaction of a top Cluj Securitate colonel, who made a marginal note on the following statement, part of a report sent by Cluj to Bucharest counterintelligence in 1988:

On the occasion of effecting a secret search two papers were found, one written by VERDERY KATHERINE, referring to "The Phenomenon of Romanian Regional Stereotypes," with a content that is objective and favorable to Romania. . . .

Marginal note of superior officer: "Have you considered that she left it there for us <u>on purpose</u>?"

In the fall of 1985, after I had left, my friend Gail Kligman went to Romania, returning to tell me that she was harangued about my book the whole time: no one was talking about the jokes, they were simply complaining that it was pro-Hungarian, though they couldn't "prove" that with arguments (they hadn't read it). One person Gail spoke with was mad because I didn't come out and say that Romanians are right and Hungarians wrong about Transylvania's history, which means I must be pro-Hungarian. This report made me furious. Here were all these Romanian scholars expecting foreigners to get them out of the bind they'd created for themselves by toadying to the Communist Party, as a result of which they had no credibility abroad. They want Americans to give the Hungarians a bashing so they can stand back and cheer, but when I ask why they don't speak up themselves, they say their hands are tied. The question of people's attitudes toward my book, which began by making me feel terribly guilty for my insensitivity, eventually turned into a source of persistent irritation. They probably thought my touchiness on the subject confirmed my Hungarian sympathies.

"VERA's" Fame in the Securitate Spreads

The fact that I had left Cluj for Geoagiu in December did not mean that the Cluj Securitate could now relax. To the contrary: they were working on their drafts for a recommendation to the higher levels in Bucharest that I be expelled. The idea was already being discussed as early as August—that is, shortly after my arrival, and in direct response to those jokes, which one of my Cluj informers had written about to his officer as soon as I gave the book to him. On his informative note of 15 August appears a marginal notation by officer Filitaş Vulcan, head of the counterespionage service of Cluj: "We will forward a report to the Third Directorate proposing that she be removed from the country." The same officer wrote the next day, "The book she published in 1983 slanders us, insults us, and falsifies our country's realities."

From October to December they perfect the documents recommending my expulsion. They detail the themes I have followed, starting with Romanian-Hungarian relations, and they use the headings of 165 pages of my field notes (about half of my total by that date) as further evidence. Having translated these notes, they find that the information I obtain has "a character hostile to our country." The correspondence involves all the top brass of the Cluj Securitate and several of the highest generals in Bucharest. Their report, entitled "Proposals for Finalizing the Case of 'V E R A,'" bears the marginal note "Agreed," with the signature of Maj. Gen. Ştefan Alexie, then Romania's chief of counterespionage. It would appear to have moved from him to his immediate superior in the Bucharest Securitate, Col.-Gen. Iulian Vlad, then adjunct minister of the Interior, who two years later would become head of the entire Securitate for Romania. In my Cluj dossier is a brief message from him a month later, responding to the report.

Ministry of the Interior   12.01.85

Cabinet of the Adjunct Minister

Comrade General Alexie,

Comrade Lieutenant Colonel Diaconescu,

   1. The case is very important and any negative evolution, any proliferation must be stopped immediately.

   2. Respond urgently with concrete proposals for finalization.

Colonel-General

[signature]

Iulian Vlad

5.01.1985

Two years later, a similar set of recommendations would go up to him, to which he replied with a handwritten marginal note.

Go, "VERA"! It's as if I'd gotten access to my FBI file and found the signature of J. Edgar Hoover on two of the documents. Here is concrete evidence that the Securitate have made "VERA" not only a spy but a very important one.

My first reaction to seeing these notes was total disbelief. What could possibly have made "VERA" so important that she ended up at the top of the Securitate's food chain? And if she was this dangerous, why was she allowed to remain and even to return in 1987 and again in 1988, whereas other anthropologists (with much smaller files) were prevented from returning? Concerning this second question, a CNSAS researcher suggested, "It wouldn't look good internationally. That would be just what we needed! As it was, the image of Romania was deteriorating, though relations with the U.S. were still OK; Romania would have to keep on its good side." At lower levels, however, she said, local case officers continued to do their duty, ferreting out spies and recommending them for expulsion. The top brass were the ones with connections to the embassy; it was they who would have to use their judgment about whether to cause an incident by expelling a U.S. citizen. This meant that officers lower down could be radical in defense of their positions, as mine were being, while superior officers put on the brakes. Two of my Securitate case officers, as we will see later, had other explanations for why I was not thrown out.

Why had I become so important? The Securitate had considered many U.S. researchers to be spies, CIA personnel, or otherwise *personae non grata*, but it

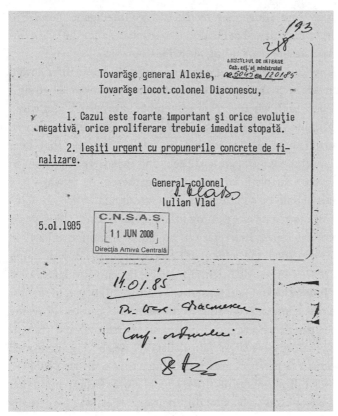

1985 document concerning "VERA" signed by Col.-Gen. Iulian Vlad.
Courtesy of the Archive of the Consiliul Naţional pentru Studierea
Arhivelor Securităţii, Fond Informativ (ACNSAS-FI).

was rare for them to get as far up as General Vlad. Two colleagues offered possible answers as to why I had. First, a CNSAS researcher suggested that whenever renewal of Romania's Most Favored Nation (MFN) status with the United States was coming up, "spirits became agitated" and surveillance of foreigners who might influence this was tightened. The Hungarian émigré community had been giving a lot of publicity to Ceauşescu's plan to move or destroy hill villages all across the country, including areas inhabited by Hungarians, who were protesting it as an anti-Hungarian measure. In consequence, my apparent interest in restive Hungarian colleagues like "Csaba" made me a potential threat. Since hearings and a decision on renewing Romania's MFN status would be occurring in 1986 and 1987, the timing would have been right for this explanation. That the Securitate cared about my views on the MFN question is apparent from a document by the Foreign Intelligence Service in 1987, in which they summarize what I had said to someone after the U.S. Congress had passed a measure suspending MFN for Romania.

Second, a U.S. colleague with good connections in Romania interviewed General Vlad himself in 2014, having inquired first if there was anything I wanted him to ask (I said, whether Vlad remembered my name and why I would have been so interesting to them). The reply he reported to me was that General Vlad did not recall me by name, but he did remember that there were a lot of U.S. anthropologists around then, and they were important to the Securitate for the valuable information they gathered. As to why I and other U.S. scholars should be so interesting, he said it had to do with Gorbachev, whose reformist ideas were gaining influence in the early 1980s, peaking with his election as general secretary of the Soviet Communist Party in March 1985. As he ascended, the leaders of Eastern Europe's non-reforming "Gang of Four" (East Germany's Erich Honecker, Czechoslovakia's Miloš Jakeš, Bulgaria's Todor Zhivkov, and Romania's Ceaușescu) began to fear for their thrones. In this context, according to the general, Ceaușescu became convinced that the people who would instigate his overthrow were Transylvania's Hungarian minority, his latest nationalist excesses having aggravated already bad relations. His paranoia greatly expanded the Securitate's room to work, and they took full advantage of it. We should always bear in mind that the Securitate as a whole, as well as its different branches, was perpetually jockeying for position with other segments of the ruling bureaucracy. Opportunities to expand their mandate were always a boon—as were people like me, rich with "enemy" possibilities that could augment their domain.

During the year of my research, they were busy ferreting out terrorist activity. For example, someone planted a bomb next to an important Romanian statue in Transylvania, and for that whole year (1984–85) the Securitate was in a frenzy, trying to track down the perpetrators. They later "showed" that it was a network of Hungarian nationalists, who allegedly had plans for other such spectacular actions. The Securitate maintained particularly tight surveillance over Hungarians and over anyone thought to be in collusion with them. This part of General Vlad's answer, and the nationalist logic of it that is so characteristic of Securitate thinking, could easily help to explain the degree of scrutiny I got. And it was indeed considerable: the CNSAS colleague who went through parts of my file with me said I should be proud to have received so much more attention than most others! By the same token, we might say they should have been grateful for me, as I helped them further enlarge their bureaucratic territory.

General Vlad's order concerning me produced a flurry of activity to develop the measures he had asked for. Within two weeks, officer Ținca went from Cluj to Deva to see what they had on me (recall that during this time the Securitate car from Deva was in Geoagiu constantly). Copies of the resulting report were sent to various offices, with illustrative copies of some of my field notes, and identification sheets were compiled for my main contacts in Cluj. In May 1985, yet another report came from Cluj, with much the same content as the earlier ones and with proposals to finalize my case. They included some of the usual measures plus some new ones, such as having informers spread the word that the Securitate had copies of my notes, and "destroying my entourage" by using my field notes to warn my contacts against me. In the hierarchy of actions against a presumed enemy, there were only two left: launching a penal action and throwing me out.

When I returned to Romania in summer 1987 and again in 1988, the same measures as before were set in place and intensified, as indicated in a note to the head of the Cluj Securitate from the head of the Third Directorate, Maj. Gen. Aurelian Mortoiu, "in conformity with the order of comrade Colonel-General IULIAN VLAD." Cluj had previously sent confirmation of what they were doing concerning " 'VERA,' C.I.A. agent" since her arrival in mid-June. In April 1987 the Cluj office had drawn up an action plan to deal with my impending return. It named four informers, all good friends of mine, who would be tasked with specific responsibilities concerning me; specified the recording devices to be placed in the homes of people I visited frequently as well as in my room (a video-cassettophone with a TV camera to follow her activity continuously [for twenty-five days]); ordered frequent shadowing and the use of mobile eavesdropping for my meetings in public places, along with secret searches of my room every one to two days so as to photocopy my field notes; and so on. Their reports from shadowing covered entire fourteen-, sixteen-, and eighteen-hour days, in which they note every time I leave one building and enter another, often providing photographs. Some reports are sent directly to General Mortoiu personally. The motivation for these actions remained the same as before: in my earlier trips I had "conducted an intense activity of collecting information of a socio-political character" (in at least this one report, the Hungarian theme had dropped out), so I must be closely watched.

The report General Mortoiu sent up to General Vlad in July 1987 noted that in the six weeks since I had arrived, I had seen many fewer of the people I had contacted in the past, and in their secret search of my hotel room and their monitoring of "Teo," they had found that I was spending the majority of my time studying problems in my specialty in the library or my hotel. Since the secret searches had not turned up anything, they were now going to search my car. Informers had not noted an interest in topics other than my project, and their secret searches turned up reading notes that contained *only* (their emphasis) jottings concerning my topic. Instead of seeing this as my having finally figured out what I was doing, they drew a different conclusion, based on a complex double-reverse psychology (that they can understand what I'm really doing only if I am pretending):

VERDERY KATHARINE is acting on the basis of rigorous instruction that has as its goal . . . strengthening the convictions of the Romanian authorities that she is exclusively interested in scientific activity and in supporting Romania's interests in the U.S.A.

Damned if you do, damned if you don't. I'm behaving in un-spy-like fashion not because I'm not a spy but because I'm following orders not to look like one. The same wording appears in a document from the Cluj Securitate to Bucharest in early October 1988. Among their other plans was this, proposed by the Cluj Inspectorate to Directorate III in Bucharest:

We should consider the variant of simulating a theft, along with some objects of value we take her hostile informative materials, and when we catch the "thief" we will also find these. Likewise, we must document any activities that can compromise her as a person.

Informers were now providing their handlers with other information about me that perhaps made me seem more of a danger than before: I had been promoted to full professor, I was now department chair, and I was the American Anthropological Association's deputy liaison to the Moscow Ethnography Institute. In that last capacity I was co-organizing a panel on ethno-national identity with the eminent head of that institute for the International Congress of Anthropological and Ethnological Sciences, scheduled for Zagreb in 1988. Here is part of a travel report from Pompiliu Teodor, my academic collaborator for 1987:

KHATERIN VERDERY, anthropologist, now full professor at John Hopkins University, known and influential in the U.S.A. She has relations at the level of coordinating institutions, friends and colleagues at the great universities. JOHN HOPKINS is an institution of genuine prestige, with influence in American academic life.

In short, I had become important, and if I were not Romania's friend, that would be grave.

Along with this, of course, were the usual items, including an informative note from my colleague/informer "Păun," who wrote about me and several other U.S. scholars,

The data we hold attest to the fact that they have connections with the American espionage service and their research is used as a source of documentation for actions that concern Romania.

In preparation for the Zagreb Congress, my so-called friend "Anca" from Iaşi was being instructed in counterintelligence so that she could be "interposed near the American citizen for the entire time. . . ." (Indeed, "Anca" kept turning up wherever I was during the Congress.) She was also given the job of discrediting in my eyes the principal scholar whose work had become essential to my framing of my next book, Mihai Dinu Gheorghiu. We went to a restaurant where her handlers had instructed her to warn me that I should avoid him because he's a provocateur and Securitate operative. She wrote in her informer report,

VERDERY K. proved at first to be fairly cautious, but gradually, after she had consumed an appreciable quantity of red wine, she became voluble. . . . Talking about matters of love, VERDERY mentioned that [unnamed] had made a pass at her, at which moment Source told her, "Be careful with Mihai.

He's a *securist.*" Vera seemed surprised, underscoring the fact that she had "read some polemical essays by him that she thought were very smart. Now . . . she doesn't know what to think!"

This classic form of disinformation goes beyond merely reporting what I have said, deliberately deceiving me about someone whom Secus see as exercising influence, but not of the "positive" kind. I myself, however, had found his influence positive indeed and he himself among the most brilliant and help-ful of all my Romanian colleagues. I have no evidence of the effect of "Anca's" warning on me but can only imagine that I was distressed.

Sex in the Field, Part II

"Anca's" warning me to avoid amorous adventures with this sociologist leads back to the subject of sex—a classic means that the Securitate used to verify my identity as a spy. In requesting a video camera to be placed in my Cluj hotel in 1986, officer Ovidiu Ţinca argued that it would show "the activity she will carry out in her room." The request was approved. That the activity they were interested in might cover more than watching me make up my bed (though they got that too) is evident from a number of documents during the 1980s. And they were not above trying to influence what went on in that bed, either. On 30 August 1984, for example, an informer reported on my (non-erotic) collaboration with a historian, to which officer Filitaş Vulcan, the head of the Cluj counterespionage service, wrote the following marginal note for the case officer: "**Study the possibility of introducing an informer who will maintain intimate relations with her so we can control her more ef-ficiently.**" After I went to Geoagiu, Mr. M. told me one day to "avoid drivers," to which I replied that I have nothing but coffee and cigarettes with mine. He replied, "I don't know who is spreading the word in Geoagiu that you have sex with that person, but if you do, you should know he's probably been put up to it." (As any viewer of spy movies knows, this is standard secret police procedure.) His comment reminded me that I was subject to surveillance by more than just the Securitate: village gossips in Geoagiu had me under surveillance too, as had those in Vlaicu at an earlier time.

In May 1985, my diligent secret informer "Marcu" reported to his Cluj of-ficer on a conversation we had had in which I hinted at some events in my close friendship with a woman I knew. He concluded his report, "Although she has spoken on several occasions of various men in her life, I do not ex-

Surveillance photo of "VERA" in her hotel room, 1985. Courtesy of ACNSAS-FI.

clude, nonetheless, that she might be disposed sometimes to practice les-
bianism." His officer gave him the task of "continuing his relations with her
to become as intimate with her as possible, with the aim of deciphering her
present preoccupations, the contacts she has created, and their nature." This
report was sent up to the desk of Lieutenant Colonel Diaconescu himself,
deputy head of Directorate III for Romania.

An informer's report observes, "Verdery has a talkative nature." What an
understatement. It seems I could keep nothing to myself. And the note ended
up, I repeat, on the desk of the third most powerful man in Romania's Securitate. I wonder what he thought of it.

In a final example of the Securitate's use of sex, a document from the Bucharest Ministry of the Interior in 1987 identifies the residence of one G.A.,

code name "Alin," whom I knew in an official capacity. It describes his personal details and concludes: "The address was visited by the American doctoral student of Romanian origin and Hungarian nationality [sic], named VERDERY KATHERINE, target 'VERA.'" It accompanies a lengthy report by "Alin" concerning several conversations we had had as well as a visit I had made to his apartment once for a drink, when we had been unable to find a table at the restaurants we tried. At the end is the case officer's note:

The material was solicited from "Alin" concerning certain aspects connected to the presence in our country of K. Verdery [which] were presented in the previous notes to clarify the meeting he had with her at his domicile, on 26 June. . . . Alin was warned that another "mistake" of this kind will lead to the withdrawal of his approval for entering into contact with foreign citizens and of course, moving him to another work place.

The officer's superior disagreed with his punitive judgment, however, imaginatively suggesting in the margins: "Why not use this situation in the context of a long-term scheme, under our direction?" I imagine that "Teo" would be there to help.

> > >

Although my sexual activity during the 1980s was considerably more subdued than it had been during the previous decade, the same cannot be said of my affective engagements and fantasy life. I seemed once again to have crushes on a number of people. First, I found a few men attractive and engaged in a fair amount of flirting with them. Moreover, a polymorphous quality in my character seemed to evoke an erotic response from at least three of my women friends. A brief note in my field index for 11 November 1984 suggests it:

> Great time with F, who whether she knows it or not is flirting with me. She was nervous as a cat when I arrived, . . . is affectionate, hugs and cuddles. Next day she says to me that although common wisdom here is that one doesn't tell people of one's affection or it diminishes, she has the impulse to keep telling me. . . . She admits to being drawn to me in an unusual way.

A handsome, sensual woman, this "F" and I always held hands in a manner I found sexy, though she never pushed it further.

One who did was a friend I will refer to as Mariana, who taught sociology at the university. Immediately attracted by her warmth and her beauty when I met her (she was tall and statuesque, with thick dark hair and startling green eyes), I found myself seeking ways to run into her and to be interesting so she would want to develop some kind of friendship. She did. Her husband often worked late at night, so on occasional evenings I would take a taxi or bus to an address a couple of blocks away from her residence—as I learned from my file, the *securişti* were not fooled—and walk to her apartment. We talked for hours about everything, from my life at home and her childhood in Romania to our jobs and memorable affairs in our pasts. Unusually verbal, smart, funny, and self-aware, a wonderful cook and marvelous companion, she became my closest friend that year, as we mutually acknowledged a powerful connection with a hint of eroticism. It gave me a greater understanding of the *amitiés amoureuses* among women in eighteenth- and nineteenth-century fiction, which both were and were not about sex. I did not then ask myself—and certainly not her—whether she reported on me to the Securitate (that will come later). I was too busy trying to create a deep trusting relation with her.

It was a great surprise to me that my first erotic experiences with women occurred in Romania, with people who likewise had never had them before. I was astonished when I went one day to visit a friend, who said cheerily, "Come on, let's go to bed." "Why?" I asked. "It's perfectly warm in the house. Why should we go to bed?" (In that cold winter of 1984–85, people often got into bed to warm up.) "For *you!*" she replied. "Have you found someone to have sex with yet?" I declined but asked whether she was used to doing this sort of thing, and she said, "Not at all," leaving me mystified. Homosexual behavior was severely censured: harsh laws strictly prohibited homosexual acts, which if discovered could be a basis for recruiting the perpetrator into informing so as to avoid prison. Concerning foreigners, in the large Securitate file on U.S. researchers is a series of documents in which Secus had discovered that a Fulbright lecturer was having sex with a young man he had brought along as his "adopted son." They lost no time in setting him up with one of their captive homosexual informers to entrap him, "discover" him in flagrante, and throw him out. (I must remember this later when the Secus I talk with seem like such nice guys.)

It was evident that being in Romania empowered something that life at home kept in closer check. But more than this, one can say that precisely in oppressive regimes where people try to have secret lives hidden from the Securitate, we would *expect* erotic adventures of this kind. The "secret" police worked to ferret out secrets that the population strove to hide. In other words, something about life in regimes of secrecy encourages transgression, and that seemed to affect both me and some Romanians I met. Once again, the conditions of the Cold War created a certain kind of environment for anthropology that affected my personality, but they fed experimentation by curious Romanians like Mariana as well. She had not had an easy life. It included failed pregnancies and unhappy marriages, fragile health, exclusion from the career she wanted because of relatives who had displeased the regime, and problems at work from a difficult boss. But she found something novel in our friendship, something that stirred her in disquieting ways and made her wonder at the path she had taken in life.

These transgressive effects also fed my thinking about Romanian society. I would sometimes talk about it with Dorina, the psychologist who had helped with my insomnia.

Field notes, 1–2 Jan. 85
Talked to Dorina about the funny reorganization of parts of my personality in Romania. The undisciplined kid is in the ascendant and gets virtually no direction from the harsh parent. Reading and thinking about this, I see a huge gain to be had by giving subjectivity free rein here; it contributes to the insight—which I think is a true one—that Romanian society is fundamentally anarchic and not centralized.

I was able to deepen that insight later in the spring one day, when some Romanian friends and I enjoyed ourselves defeating some of the endless impediments the regime placed in everyone's way. Despite all the cold, the lack of food, and the constant surveillance, I found I was having fun, and it had to do with the satisfaction of defeating authority. I realized suddenly that thoroughgoing anarchy of the sort we were engaged in subverted the Party's claims to total power over Romanian society—that is, the Ceauşescu regime was not "totalitarian" but struggled to impose itself on the populace, with only partial success. Somehow I found such an atmosphere very invigorating. I would eventually build this insight into an academic paper arguing against a "totalitarian" understanding of Romanian communism.

Moreover, I realized that this special appeal was a basis for my feeling of deep affinity to that country—something that is key to an ethnographer's coping with life in another place. I see my affinity as having two main sources: the conflict between authority and rebellion, and the constant questioning of identity—Who am I, in relation to others? Both are deeply rooted in me, and in Romanian social life as well. But the affinity went beyond this. I loved people's zany sense of humor, their intensity, their capacity for enjoyment, and the different ways of being that they encouraged in me, including a greater willingness to misbehave and get a kick out of doing so (possibly provoked by that atmosphere of secrecy). Trying to live a life of honesty, transparency, integrity, and hard work could get pretty tiring; here I could have respite from it. This is not to say that these values were lacking in Romania, but rather that they were differently concatenated. Perhaps these realizations are what Margaret Mead had in mind when she said that our emotional response, if we can make disciplined use of it, is the surest and most perfect instrument of understanding another way of life.

> > >

Despite these various pleasures, after I left in 1985 I felt traumatized for months. My file records that on a later visit I told a friend, whose home enjoyed the presence of "Teo," how I had felt after leaving, that year: "The most interesting thing for me was how long it took to lose my instinct that I was under surveillance: it took me four months, after just one year of living here." At home in Baltimore I found myself constantly worrying about microphones in my apartment, and I panicked when a friend began telling me on the phone about another friend who was doing something with cocaine. I was convinced my phone was bugged and the police would overhear it.

My final field note from 1985 gives a sense of my frame of mind.

At home, on top of jet lag, serious resistance to all the advertising, which seems utterly nauseating. Have a constant sensation of wanting to cry but can't. But more than usual, I feel the effects of having been constrained and dependent for so long. People around me talk of grand plans that involve all sorts of ACTION and initiative; makes me feel desperately inadequate. Panicked as Ashraf tells me all sorts of plans for the future of the department, etc. Feel not in command, not grown up. In another vein, walking with Richard C., someone waves to him, and my automatic reflex is, "Will Richard be compromised by being seen with me?" Go to a restaurant; fast, courteous service. I'm blown away by the contrast.

In addition to all these, a sense that life here is plastic, the values shallow. Academics in Romania have something to fight for, to represent. What do we have? "Building the department" isn't enough.

If this was what happened after one year in Romania, I wondered, what would be the effects on those who lived there for a lifetime?

"VERA" and Dissident Opposition: The Securitate at Fever Pitch

---

312/NS   TOP SECRET

REPORT

On 21 October 1988 in accord with orders received, entry by the American citizen KATHERINE VERDERY to the domicile of the said PALEOLOGU ALEXANDRU of Bucharest, 34 Armenească St. was prevented.

From the discussions conducted with the above-named on this occasion the following resulted:

She was in the area to visit a friend who is expecting her. She communicated to me that she is an American citizen and with an IREX grant she is effecting a specialization in our country.

I asked her if the Education Ministry knows about this meeting and if she has approval of this body to actualize it.

She told me no.

I recommended that any interviews she wishes to conduct must have the approval of the competent organs that coordinate her research activity.

The entire discussion with the American citizen was recorded in secret.

Maj. "S. Dragomir"

I returned to Romania for two more research stays in summer 1987 and fall 1988, totaling five months. They were spent entirely in Cluj except for a few side trips to Vlaicu and two weeks in Bucharest at the end. The Cluj Securitate seems to have settled into a routine of checking my socio-political information and my visits to Hungarians, but nothing new emerged for them: in their view, those were my two spying identities. One more such identity awaited me, however, in my final days in Bucharest. I was still "VERA" (my pseudonym in Cluj, which carried over to the capital), but now I was seen as someone actively fomenting opposition to the regime by consorting with the few dissidents emerging in the country. I was housed at the Hotel Lido for those two weeks, where "Teo" awaited me as usual in both microphone and video forms, and in my visits to restaurants he would often be present as well ("mobile technical means will be used to verify 'VERA's' contacts in various restaurants of the Capital").

As context for what follows, I note that by 1980 there was increasing dissident activity against communist rule in neighboring countries, which the Securitate struggled to keep from spilling over the borders—Poland's Solidarity Movement, the Czech "Charter 77," and so on. A feeble opposition had already appeared in Romania also, first in a movement around soon-to-be-émigré writer Paul Goma in 1977, then in a 1979 attempt to form a free trade union, a year before Poland's Solidarity. Its leaders ended up in jail or dead in "accidents." A handful of dissidents gradually emerged nonetheless, and by the late 1980s intellectuals were beginning to unite against Ceauşescu's policies. In 1987, a strike at a major tractor factory showed that Romanian workers too were discontented.

It happens that my movements were indeed suspect, completely by chance, for friends in Cluj and Iaşi had recommended that I see several important Bucharest intellectuals, who were then becoming politically active. Although I did not know this at the time of my visits, I was to learn it after 1989. On 18 October 1988, at Professor Prodan's recommendation, I went to visit Orthodox priest Nicolae Steinhardt; on 21 October I had an appointment to see an important writer, Alexandru Paleologu, at the recommendation of his friend historian Alexandru Zub, with whom I had been consulting for my project; and on 23 October, I went with Professor Zub to meet philosopher Gabriel Liiceanu. With each one I planned to discuss what was happening in contemporary Romanian cultural life that seemed connected with my research. But I was unaware that the first two had signed a letter of protest to Ceauşescu that had been drawn up in early October and was being circulated by younger writers in the Writers' Union—all of whom were being watched day and night. The third was under close surveillance for being a disciple of Constantin Noica, a philosopher and former political prisoner (like both Paleologu and Steinhardt), whose views were not at all to the regime's liking.

Here is how the first of these meetings entered into their archive.

TELEX 0619/1068. Person being watched: Verdery Katherine Maureen
Information: From the data we have it results that the person in question is a
C.I.A. cadre come to R.S. Romania with the aim of contacting persons known
to have a hostile or dissident position. In this sense on 17.10.1988 she met

with the said Steinhardt Nicu-Aurel, former political prisoner, with the aim of collecting data. . . . [He] had been sentenced for plotting against the security of the state. In 1973 he published a work with content hostile to the social political system of our country. He maintains relations with reactionary emigres such as Eugen Ionescu, Emil Cioran.

The case officer's report based on my shadowing—they had intercepted my call to Father Steinhardt when I made the appointment—mentions that I came out of Steinhardt's building with something I did not take into it: a white envelope, which I dropped into a mailbox and the Securitate promptly took out. (Dismayingly for them, it proved to be a postcard I sent to a friend, not something I was mailing for Father Steinhardt.)

A conversation with a journalist in 2012 revealed to me why they were so anxious about my meeting with Steinhardt. He had written the manuscript of his memoir, *Happiness Journal* (*Jurnalul Fericirii*), in three copies, but when the Securitate had raided his apartment to get it they found only one. Expecting that he might be trying to publish it abroad, they were constantly on the lookout for the other two copies, and I might well have had it. (I didn't.) This could explain, however, why reports of shadowing me always mentioned what I was carrying (a purse, a bag, a plastic sack) and noted if it seemed bigger or smaller when I came out of someplace than when I had gone in.

> > >

On 21 October, my shadow followed me out of my hotel at 8:55 A.M., noting that I carried a purse and a plastic bag. The shadow noted every street I entered and then observed that I was turning onto Armenească Street:

And near the building with number 34 she was stopped by a worker from the informative organs. After discussing with him, "VERA" left, seeming troubled and went back to Post Office 13. There she had a telephone conversation with the individual from Armenească St. no. 34, from which was heard: "that she tried to visit him but was stopped by a balding individual who smokes a lot and did not wish to say who he was."

"VERA" meets a *securist*. Surveillance photo, 1988. Courtesy of ACNSAS-FI.

Here was my only known encounter with an officer of the Securitate during the communist years. As with Father Steinhardt, I had made my appointment with Alexandru Paleologu by phone, whence the Securitate had learned of it. With all the secret-but-known oppositional activity in the Writers' Union, my timing for a visit to him could scarcely have been worse. As I approached the building, there emerged from it a rather scruffy fellow of medium build in an overcoat, hair thinning in front, with a mustache and cigarette-stained teeth, one of which was chipped. In a rather belligerent tone, he asked what I was doing there and whether I had permission for the visit, then advised me to leave until I did. His version of the encounter heads this section, along with the information that he had recorded it secretly. Accompanying it were three photographs of me with him. When I met officer "Dragomir" again many years later, it would be under quite different circumstances, and the question of recording in secret would once again be on the table.

My phone call to Paleologu resulted in his coming out onto the street to meet with me and make a plan for lunch the following afternoon (we had a lengthy conversation, fully recorded and transcribed by the same officer). The shadow accompanied me for the rest of the day, noting the exact times of my movements, what I was carrying, when I mailed a letter and in which postbox; he also took photos of me and Paleologu. (When I first saw these at

"VERA" with Alexandru Zub and Alexandru Paleologu. Surveillance photo, 1988. Courtesy of
ACNSAS-FI.

CNSAS in 2008, the employee who was helping me said, "How nice! Now you
have pictures of yourself with this wonderful fellow!"—as indeed he was.) I
went on to see my grants handler, Dan Ghibernea, to complain about this
episode. As he reported in his informative note, he instructed me firmly that
what I was doing was against the law; I was supposed to get permission for
any such meeting, or ask him to arrange it. The officer's marginal comment
to this note was, "Verdery's position is evident, her interest in contacting certain people known for problems with the Securitate, hostile." He proposed that my contacts be investigated and warned about their violating the
laws concerning relations with foreigners.

It would seem that our "VERA" was now in deep trouble. Starting on 9 October 1988, she was subjected to the first of nine events of considerable grav-
ity. All nine appear as handwritten texts identified only with "Ministry of the
Interior" at the top left and sometimes with a numeral indicating one of the
Securitate's special units. All bear the heading "RECORD of findings from
effecting certain precursory acts," and all begin by writing out the date, the
locality, the officers' names, and their unit, followed by the phrase "in view
of gathering the data necessary to the beginning of penal pursuit."[7] Then fol-

low the instructions they had received ("being informed that X, of x address, will meet on y date at z hour, location, with the said KATHERINE VERDERY [her details]") and their resolution of it by waiting incognito at the assigned location and writing down what they saw. What they saw in each case conformed to what they had been told to expect. Person X did indeed show up at the appointed time, I did indeed go to the telephone booth at the expected hour, etc. In each case but the two in Cluj, they took photographs of me together with the people I was to meet. The first two episodes in Cluj (9 and 12 October) took them to the telephone booth near my hotel, where they noted the numbers I dialed. The seven in Bucharest took place on the 19th (twice), 20th, 21st, and 22nd (thrice) of October: immediately after my visit to Father Steinhardt and continuing until the day after my visit with Alexandru Paleologu. I remained in Bucharest for another week before leaving for home, but no more of these actions appear in my file.

A CNSAS colleague with whom I discussed those documents said she had never before seen such a thing in my type of file and had no idea what it meant. Another person saw them as a slight shift in the practice of shadowing me, according to which "normal" shadowing might be transformed into evidence for bringing a legal case against me (especially since Steinhardt and Paleologu both had penal antecedents and were potentially engaging in anti-state action now). The fact that this kind of document preceded my meetings with these people, however, starting shortly before them in Cluj, is puzzling. To me, it suggests that someone had decided "VERA" was a serious enough problem to warrant arrest, for such "precursory actions" were often a prelude to bringing penal charges.

Whatever the explanation, it would seem that I was beginning to crack from the strain, for my grants administrator wrote a lengthy informative note saying that my nerves seemed stretched to the limit, that I was protesting vehemently to him about things that seemed inconsequential, and that I had broken down in tears when a sociologist started criticizing my book. He ended his note thus: "In any case, at this moment I think that she finds herself in a state of collapse, is really panicked by the fact that we have picked up on some of her games, and she reacts violently." The note was heavily underlined by his handler, Major "Dragomir."

Because I left Romania soon thereafter and would not return until after Ceauşescu fell, I mercifully did not experience whatever the next steps would have been.

Securişti *Follow Me Home*

That I had left did not mean I was free of scrutiny. Overlapping with the measures being ordered up in Romania for my visits in 1987 and 1988 were other measures back in the United States. After gathering some information about me during my stay in 1987, the Foreign Intelligence Service of the Securitate had decided in April 1988 that I warranted formal surveillance. That is, after many years of being followed by their equivalent of the FBI, I was now being watched by their "CIA" as well, through messages sent back and forth between Bucharest and their group in Washington, D.C. My change in stature came with new pseudonyms, "VANESSA," "VERONA," and "VADU." Their characterization of me mentions my book (but nothing about the jokes in it) and my current project; notes that I'm a good specialist and have a favorable attitude toward Romania, having spoken up at a seminar in Washington in favor of extending Romania's MFN status; and affirms that I have publicly opposed the theses of Hungarian historians concerning historical rights over Transylvania.

Nonetheless, they also note that "suspicions exist that she is carrying out activities to collect information during her repeated visits to the country, for which aim she is used by espionage diplomats." A few of the messages they sent back and forth between Bucharest and Washington were in a rather ludicrous coded form, such as this (code equivalents in parentheses):

Telegram from 0544 to Group in Washington, concerning IREX grantees. Act to obtain stamps (information) at the level of how they are known by the local council (embassy) ... their attitude toward the evolved sectors (socialist countries) including *Ceahlău* (Romania), things they have published about Ceahlău and other data that would make their presence in the sector inopportune. The stamps obtained should be selected urgently at the work site (central office).

(The CNSAS researcher who helped me read this said, "Terrific! Superb! A coded message!" but couldn't figure it out at first.)

Their access to me was eased by a six-month fellowship I enjoyed at the Eastern European program of the Woodrow Wilson Center in Washington, D.C., from January through June 1988. There I met, among others, Romanian dissident Mihai Botez, then living in Washington and regularly attending Wilson Center seminars. While I was at the Wilson Center, an émigré Romanian historian sought me out for conversation; I suspect that he was one (perhaps the one code-named "Gorun"?) who wrote informative notes describing my views about Botez, about MFN, and so on. By the end of April they had developed an action plan, which included identifying my contacts in Romania and beginning surveillance on them; directing sources to influence me during my forthcoming trip to Romania in fall 1988, "so she adopts a realistic attitude and promotes the historical truth about Romania"; engaging me in "new actions of popularization and promotion of Romanian cultural values in the U.S."; and finally, using their personnel abroad "to continue contacts with her" toward various specified ends, including information about Botez. My case officer was, unusually, a woman, in a Securitate that was about 90 percent male.

Informer "Gorun" told them about my publications, which he judged as "favorable," and he expressed his view that I could be drawn into opposing the hostile actions of Hungarians in America. Either "Gorun" or another of their external agents attended a seminar I gave the following year in which I talked about emerging currents of disagreement within Marxist philosophy in Romania. The person reporting asserted that the Wilson Center, "known as an undercover institution of the C.I.A., is engaged in actions of disinformation and drawing Romania's émigré intellectuals into hostile attitudes, as well as propagating the idea of a latent intellectual opposition to the regime in Romania itself." In conclusion, the reporter noted, "We are continuing to act . . . to influence KATHERINE VERDERY positively not to let herself be drawn into manifestations with a hostile content toward Romania."

Two things disturbed me about these reports. First, it had never even remotely crossed my mind that I should be wary of Securitate action at home, and it made me think differently about the several Romanians who had sought me out in Baltimore and elsewhere, sometimes out of the blue, to propose friendly conversation. Second, and more important, during 1988–89 the Foreign Intelligence Service was largely seeing me as well disposed, taking Romania's side against Hungarians on international questions—and it was true. Had I arrived at these positions on my own, or had I been skillfully manipulated into them by Securitate actions both in Romania and at home? I suspect that some of my Hungarian colleagues who found me too pro-Romanian would agree with the latter possibility. What a distressing prospect.

> > >

I closed out the 1980s with a brief visit in May 1989. On my way to a conference in Yugoslavia, I slipped across the border to spend a weekend with Mariana, who traveled from Cluj to meet me in a city nearby. The weather was glorious and the flowers freshly scented. She stayed with friends and I at a hotel, and we wandered all over the city, spending time in the botanical garden and the zoo, where the animals enjoyed watching us eat and drink, talk unceasingly, and laugh with delight. Our friendship had never been richer than in that weekend. I particularly remember a fantastic peacock; I had never seen one that close. Naturally, the Securitate were hot on our heels, taking pictures and putting under surveillance the people we visited (another "radioactive" moment for "VERA"), one of whom they categorized as a "known irredentist," that is, Hungarian. Although they had no trouble identifying Mariana, they mistakenly noted that we went around town speaking Hungarian. Before I left, I put two packages in the mail, a book to friends in Cluj and a small gift for my landlady in Geoagiu. Neither package reached its recipient; the originals of the accompanying letters are in my file, indicating they were never delivered.

Also in my file is Mariana's informer note describing the weekend in detail.

Parting Thoughts

The Securitate created its knowledge about people like me by changing the sign of our social relationships. Relationships were its currency—as they were mine, and as is especially true for anyone living under a regime of secrecy. Propagating the idea of my being a spy was already aimed at isolating me, channeling me into the Securitate's paths. Then, using informers who were my contacts and supposed friends effectively divided those people's allegiance, drawing them into complicity with the organization and attenuating their relation to me. Nonetheless, a reciprocal impetus to connect with people and they with me outlasted the regime, endowing me with many valuable friendships that I still treasure.

By 1989 I had progressed through four different spying identities: conducting military espionage, gathering socio-political information, mediating Hungarian opposition, and conspiring with dissidents. Although the first of these was fairly self-contained, the others entailed extensive and deep involvement in Romanian questions, making the matter of my spying increasingly complex. With this progression, however, I became ever more powerful in the Securitate's eyes. "VERA" was a good partner to me: she showed them how important I was. At the same time, for other Romanians the possibility she represented was something they would have to overcome. It was remarkable that people still wanted to associate with me, given "VERA's" secret reputation. Does that desire show people's bravery, or curiosity, or perhaps that the Securitate had successfully calibrated the secrecy with which they surrounded her?

With all these identities was I "the same" person? I certainly felt that I was, but no. There were several of me, at any one time (the child, the surrogate daughter, the researcher, the department chair, "the Folklorist," etc.) and across time as well. Speaking personally, I was in some sense the product, at different moments, of the people I became tied to and of the person being in Romania had made of me—more labile, more sociable. Although those configurations changed, what united me in them was an emotional vulnerability and neediness that drove me to seek social connection. Professionally speaking, I went from groveling as a result of my mistakes with my book to feeling myself an increasingly important person, someone to be reckoned with, and although I let myself be influenced "positively" in my reading for my new project in the 1980s, I gradually pulled myself out of it onto my own turf. I think I became a better field-worker, more sensitive to the views and positions of those I spent time with. And I ceased to research the history of Romanian national ideas for which so much positive influence had been exerted, exploring instead exactly what the Securitate feared: the nature of Romanian socialism and the place of national ideology within it. What unified me across these different times and spaces was an intense professional ambition that would diminish only as the end of the regime deprived me of my object of study—socialism—and crushing personal losses sapped my resilience.

Thinking about the effects of Securitate practices on people's relations encourages further reflection on their methods. My Securitate file consists of the traces of the Romanian state fabricating a person—KATHERINE VERDERY, a.k.a. "VERA"—as a certain kind of threat. In their work during the 1980s, I can see this happening more clearly than in the previous decade, because the process has become more urgent and the traces more visible. My ethnographic eye picks out the "proofs" they muster for various constructions of the threat I present to them, different for each historical moment and spatial location in which the work is going on: Hungarians were a problem in the mid-1980s because of Ceaușescu's fearful reaction to Gorbachev's reformism, and they were situated in Cluj; dissidents were a problem later in the decade, and they were preponderantly in Bucharest. In Hunedoara County they had stopped thinking I was spying on military objectives but continued to assume I was spying on *something*—and spread this rumor in the villages I lived in. In each place and time, Securitate officers high and low sought various ways to anchor me, and they came up with different Katherine Verderys, nearly all of them perfidious.

Like Gabriel Liiceanu, astonished to discover from his file that they were actually right to see him as a threat because he insisted on thinking "differently,"[8] I cannot deny that at least half of the spying identities the Securitate crafted for me had some basis in reality. I was not spying for the military nor was I a partisan of Hungarian interests, but I did indeed collect socio-political information that would teach me about socialism, and I presented a picture of it that was not rosy. Furthermore, I had indeed begun to ally myself with opponents of the Ceaușescu regime, unwittingly at first. In my writing from 1975 to 1988, I had hesitated to criticize lest I be prevented from coming back, and I had in any case felt it was more important to give a view different from the usual Cold War censure of communism. But in my second book, *National Ideology under Socialism*—mailed to the press the day before the Berlin Wall came down—I finally took the position the Securitate had expected all along: as an enemy of that regime.[9] My exposure to the hardships it visited upon its citizens had brought me to champion those intellectuals I discussed in the book who were resisting more and more openly and with whom my association had provoked my first and only meeting with a Securitate officer, as my "entourage" came increasingly to coincide with their lists of enemies. I took that oppositional stance reluctantly, for I believed it would make me, finally, *persona non grata*.

On 22 December 1989, Nicolae Ceaușescu and his clique of supporters were overthrown. A new social order was to be launched, in which part of the Securitate would turn out to play a significant role in both political and economic transformation. What was their representation of me as they stood on that threshold? It depends whom you ask.

In October and November 1989, the routine of the Cluj branch continued with their usual tasks, soliciting informers' reports and writing yet another action plan in November. The usual summary preceded it, with the history of my visits to Romania, my relations with Hungarian scholars, my book with its mottoes, the conclusion that I was collecting socio-political information for the U.S. information services, and new contacts they were now following because of relations with me—specifically, my friends Andrei and Delia Marga, for whom a DUI was now opened on my account. *Plus ça change.*

The Foreign Intelligence Service (CIE), however, decided to close down my file. The final document is dated 24 May 1990, so it seems they were still tying up loose ends after the December revolution. For them, their "research" on me had shown beyond doubt that I was really a scholar working on historical problems and was thus of no further interest, even though the internal service might still see me as a spy. The CIE did not seem to care about that—or, at least, not any longer.

24.05.1990   TOP SECRET

INFORMATION SHEET CONCERNING
KATHERINE MAUREEN VERDERY

1. DATA CONCERNING IDENTITY AND KNOWLEDGE:
   Name, Forename:—KATHERINE MAUREEN VERDERY
   Place and date of birth: 09.07.1948—Bangor, Maine, USA
   Education: Stanford University—Social Anthropology section
   Profession: University Professor
   Place of work: John Hopkins University, Baltimore
2. She is recognized as the best American specialist on southeast
   European problems.
   She knows the Romanian language very well, oral and written, down
      to the details.
   She is extremely able and succeeded in creating relationships for
      herself in the most diverse social environments.
3. DATE OF BEGINNING TO STUDY HER: 28.04.1988
   DATE OF REMOVING HER FROM CONCERN: 24.05.1990
4. DATA OF OPERATIONAL INTEREST:
   Up to the present she has undertaken no actions that might harm Roma-
      nia's interests in the USA, nor are her writings hostile to our country.
   She situates herself on the position of Romanian historiography con-
      cerning Transylvania.

The counterespionage division holds data according to which she is
an agent of the American special services.
5. She is no longer of interest to our unit.

Cpt. Maria Petculescu

In the changed circumstances, *National Ideology under Socialism* did not make
me *persona non grata*: on the contrary. The book was translated in record time by
some of those it supported—former dissidents once harassed by the Securitate
who were now heading major public institutions and welcomed the positive
image I had given them. By focusing on intellectual debates taking place in
the 1980s, the book had managed to avoid some of the "positive influence"
aimed at me, as well as the problems I had encountered in trying to master
too much Romanian history writing. To analyze those debates, I developed a
theory of socialism that linked the complexities of my life in 1980s Romania
to the national ideology I had been both researching and experiencing on
my own skin, because of the jokes. The book contained—along with those
old ethnographic standbys, gossip and rumor—the results of long conversations with various oppositional figures, all bound together by the Securitate's
nightmare: "socio-political information."

Professor Prodan lived just long enough to see that it was dedicated to him.

I returned to Vlaicu briefly in the summers of 1991 and 1992, then for the
academic year 1993–94. My subject this time was the dismantling of the collective farm and the return of its lands to the villagers who had been forced
to "donate" them in the 1950s. Given Moaşa's advancing age, I had a new host
family, Ileana and Petru, who would provide wonderfully for me in that and
subsequent visits. In March 1994 I flew home for my father's funeral. When
I returned, my hosts informed me that during my absence, two *securişti*—
one a distant cousin of Ileana's, hoping that kinship would gain him her
compliance—had come and asked to be let into my room. My hosts refused,
lying that I had locked the door and taken the key with me. When I returned
again to Vlaicu two years later—that is, six full years after the "revolution"—
three different friends let me know that the same officer as before, Colonel
Belgiu, had come around asking them why I was there. The Securitate was
still alive, even if under another name, the Romanian Information Service.

For all the joy my Romanian friends and I felt at the change of regime, I myself would come to experience it as a radical deskilling, which contributed to a growing sense that I had lost my moxie. Until 1989, I was fairly self-confident about my intellectual capacities and the work I had done. I had found homes for myself in Vlaicu and Cluj and had made lifelong friendships. I had learned something about socialism and developed some theories about it. Moreover, I had both an intellectual and an emotional commitment to my research, hoping to contribute to the critique of capitalism by studying its chief alternative. Through my research in Romania, in short, I had found my feet.

After 1989, I began to feel more tentative. With the collapse of communist regimes throughout Eastern Europe, I no longer had either my object of study or a sense of political purpose in my work. I struggled for over a decade to write my next book, The Vanishing Hectare. Following that, I took refuge in the past, as I returned to the study of socialism through its Party and Securitate archives. With this, I assumed yet another identity: I "became" a historian. Immersion in these archives gave me a rather different picture of the social world of Romanian communism, a world in which serendipity, clientelism, incompetence, improvisation, and failures of communication play a much greater role than does the totalitarian autocracy I was raised to expect—and whose traces in my imagination I still occasionally discover, testimony to the defining power of Cold War ideology.

Reflections on Reading One's File

I don't advise anyone to confront their Securitate file.
It is an absolutely personal decision, difficult and not without
consequences. For me, at least, reading my file was traumatic.
—Radu Ioanid

What is it like to read a secret police file? I can do no better than to recommend the remarkable novel *Dossier 51*, by Gilles Perrault, pseudonym of a French writer of adventure and spy novels.[1] Composed in the form of an intelligence dossier without additional commentary, it shows us the kinds of codes these files employ, the infighting among parts of the secret service, the recruitment and deployment of collaborators close to the target, the wiretap transcripts and reports of shadowing, the administrative correspondence, and the attempted blackmail that ultimately destroys a French diplomat. Reading it after reading a number of files at the CNSAS, I felt right at home (though fortunately I escaped the diplomat's shocking fate). The main difference from an actual Securitate dossier is that the prose he adopts is somewhat less deadening to the senses than the prose of my file, which I have tried to render close to the originals, yet without putting the reader to sleep.

Dossier 51 is a better guide than we get from the much-admired 2006 film by Florian Henckel von Donnersmarck, *The Lives of Others*. An East German secret police (Stasi) officer, Gerd Wiesler, is assigned to monitor the activities of a famous East German writer and his wife. The officer is gradually drawn into their lives, seeing them in an increasingly sympathetic light, and ultimately tries to protect them from the activities of his Stasi comrades. It is a superb film, but many East Germans and other Eastern Europeans were not enthusiastic: as against the film's romantic reception in the West, they considered it ludicrous, something so far-fetched it could not possibly happen. For one thing, no Stasi officer would become sympathetic to his target. (Certainly none of the three Securitate officers with whom I eventually made contact had developed that kind of attitude toward me.) If we see the film as part of a process of "cleaning up" the Stasi so that Germans can live together in one state, then Weisler's attraction to his target is simply a plot device enabling that. It is a fantasy underpinning Germany's unification.

Perhaps, however, it is also a fantasy of those of us with files. Gabriel Liiceanu, in his meditation *My Dear Snitch*, invents a picture of the officer who transcribed text from all the microphones in his apartment: his officer says that he finds his target and the target's wife "very simpatico" and that the Liiceanus still inhabit him after he finishes his day's work. As for me, when I watch *The Lives of Others*, I am envious of that writer under surveillance. I too would like my officers to admire me.

I received my file in 2008 and went through it cursorily so as to decide what to copy for later reading. I had some powerful reactions to it then, to things like discovering informers among my friends and realizing the extraordinary degree of surveillance to which I had been subjected, far more than I had ever imagined. But only after two years, benefiting from a semester's leave, did I sit down to go through it in detail, page by page. Until then I had been finishing other work and postponing my discovery of what the file might contain.

That careful reading (the first of several), which occupied September and October, was the most difficult "research" I have ever done. My reactions were so varied and contradictory that after a while I began writing them down as I experienced them. They are all over the map, ricocheting wildly from one feeling to another, but over time they reveal my gradually "normalizing" what I read. Because they show the enormous challenge the file posed to ethnographic practice—to ethnographers' constant effort to feel and experience with their whole beings while seeking to stand back and analyze those feelings and experiences—I include here a few of my reactions.

18-9-10. Reading Dan Ghibernea's reports about how I react violently to conversations with him; descriptions of me as cold and calculating. I feel like shit. Mad at "Anca," who is really a cad. I look her up on the web and find this as her self-characterization (2014): "I don't like lies, hypocrisy, falsity, or ostentation."[2] Right! So should I read these people in terms of the personality characteristics I bring out in them (mîrşav [base], viclean [wily]), which they attribute instead to me?

19-9-10. Reading my Cluj file makes me want to cry, for the various friends brought in on my case as either informers or themselves under surveillance. I come upon photos of myself from the "Teo" in my room at the Continental Hotel in Cluj. I am in my underwear, making my bed and then using the mirror above it to fix my hair. The outlines of my body are quite clear, though the photos are lousy. Later I have a mental image of myself in my underwear, pinned like a butterfly on a collector's table with spotlights shining on me from several directions. Become embarrassed, then feel angry, then violated. Imagine if I had actually made love with someone in that bed . . . how appalling. These people are merciless.

20-9-10. Reading more bad reports on me: I should see this as how THEY imagine a person who is an "enemy of the people." Manipulative, calculating, etc.

22-9-10. Reading lots of informer's notes from "B.," feel very bad. He's so diligent, getting so much info. Makes me seethe, then be depressed. Have to remember: it was probably because of me that he got recruited in the first place. They have to colonize any relation close to me and turn it to their purposes.

Then lots of reports from Moşu, day by day, exactly whom I see, he goes and talks with them about what I asked, writes all this down. Is chastised if his report is not detailed enough. I feel claustrophobic, terrific sense of privacy being violated, appalled, angry, remorseful. Come home (no one there) and start shouting out loud. Drink some gin, put on Renee Fleming singing "Four Last Songs" and other Strauss; start to sing with it. I need a large choral piece or something so I can just do a controlled scream for a while [Fleming's description of singing]. I have to remember I got myself into this with the motorbike, but for god's sake!

23-9-10. Evening ended with a bunch of correspondence Moşu has gotten for them from my room. It's Gloria's, not mine, but includes a letter from me to her that is so hilarious it leaves me in stitches. That Kathy sure could write a great letter! This plus the catharsis of shouting and singing has definitely improved my mood.

Reading my file is a bit like spying on myself.

25-9-10. *Amazing* marathon of shadowing in Cluj, fall 1988; people are spending 10–17 hrs/day on me, day after day. Astounding level of activity. There seems a remarkable disproportion between the effort being mobilized and the magnitude of the threat—from my point of view, at least. Must understand why.

26-9-10. Reading all those shadowing reports yesterday, the effect is to cringe each time some friend shows up in these pages who will then enter their radar screen. I should have kept entirely to myself. But this is exactly their aim: to isolate people like me from Romanians. Reduce contamination. Friend and foe, inside/outside.

8-10-10. Having been invited to give a lecture in Leipzig, I contact Ralf and Ana [Bierman], hoping they might join me there for a couple of days so we can visit. In reading my file, I had found various things involving them, including the Securitate's extensive report of the trip we took to Cluj in April 1985, laughably imagining that we had outwitted my surveillance. When I asked whether they would be interested in seeing documents concerning them from my file, they said yes. After I arrived, we sat down one morning to take a look. To help us recall our reactions, we taped the conversation.

We begin with the report on our trip to Cluj and start to read it aloud. Ralf is reading the details of what he did the morning of the trip—going with some colleagues to pick up a new battery for his car, and so on. Suddenly he stops, puts his hand on his chest, and says, "I can't go on! My heart is beating too fast! I had *no idea* they followed people this closely." Realizing their phone was bugged is a big shock to them. He starts trembling and is almost crying; it takes him some time to compose himself. We continue later with an informer's note that he recognizes as written by a good friend of his; once again he becomes very agitated. As we talk about these notes, he says at one point, "I wonder who's listening to us now. . . . Oh, right: we're in Germany, not Romania!" I recognize in him some of my own reactions.

6-11-10. Movie "Fair Game," about Valerie Plame, CIA agent outed during the G.W. Bush administration. She's very tough, very humane, very pretty, very appealing, very dedicated. I think, That's what Secu thought I was, a CIA agent! For the first time, I find this an interesting possibility. Kind of cool to be someone like her. Here's a very different image to try on, not me as ambitious and aggressive academic but tough patriot. Hmmm.

16-11-10. Did a class at Princeton for Irina [Grudzinska-Gross]. Afterwards she responds to my saying I don't like myself in the file: "There is NO WAY you could like the person who emerges from it. This is how they work: they're looking for your bad side, feed on your weaknesses, so that's the picture that will come out." They take my liking people and turn it into something bad, pervert it. I shouldn't *expect* to like myself as I emerge from the file. She's upset about, yet interested by, my saying I actually was a spy, given their terms: "Look, this is how they achieve their effects! They get you to acknowledge something about yourself that was not true!"

23-11-10. Think about Secu ways of getting information compared to the data-mining of today, which one could see as equally violating/manipulative but just doesn't involve roping other people into it in the same way. Questions about trust.

26-11-10. I seem to be constantly irritated these days. Is it from this project, I wonder? Reading all this unpleasant stuff (Albu's book *The Informer*) about what people are doing to each other; find myself incapable of getting past fury with my informer "B.," wanting to unmask him.

Vatulescu book, talking about literary idea of estrangement in art: artist's job is to jolt readers out of routine by making familiar seem strange. This is what is happening to me as I read file: my familiar is made strange.

5-1-11. Conversations with two Princeton colleagues. I come away thinking more about Secu as fragmented, multi-voiced: "collective authorship." No narrator/narration. The miracle is that with all this segmentation, the Secu could convince people they were unified and omnipresent.

7-1-11. I recently found my field index for 1984–85. Today I read it through; surprised to discover it had a lot more personal stuff in it than I thought. Much more realization of surveillance in there than I had remembered, more warnings about how they're on me. But main impression is, huge amount of emotional stuff. Not a new realization, but very striking. Crazy about so many people, having such complex and intense relationships. Taken aback at how openly I write about all this stuff—anyone could have read it. I think I carried this field index with me all the time; only then can I understand how willing I am to implicate all kinds of people in the way this is written. Felt sad the whole day. Challenge: coming to terms with this person.

12-2-11. My website has been hacked by someone claiming to be an Iraqi. Asked Dick [my uncle, an Arabist] to take a look; he read me the comments on it—vituperative, incomprehensible. I can't imagine who representing "Rage for Iraq" would be hacking my site, then I think: it's Secu. This thought hasn't left me for several days. Now he calls and says he consulted with a colleague and they both agree that there are some grammatical oddities that make it seem it's not a native speaker. So my paranoia may be justified. Maybe they heard about my recent lecture in Leipzig and want to unnerve me. But why Iraq?! Am I being paranoid, or is this really possible?

THE FOLLOWING SUMMER

19-7-11. Doing documentary film for CNSAS with Cristina and Nicolae. We go to Vlaicu, have interviews with Meri, others; then to Cluj. . . . I find myself thinking at one point, I've spent more of my life here than anywhere else except U.S. , but with this file, I'm feeling some alienation from Romania. Feel very sad for much of this, as if something is closing. What interests me is the long-term effect this shadow operation had on people: I come in, introduce a perturbation. To what extent does that create ripple effects that last, interrupting people's relations?

I ask Cristina why I'm so sad: she goes back to documentary scene in the morning when I found photo of Moaşa and Moşu and me in Sibiu, was telling about their meeting Mum and Dad there, and started to choke up. What is clear now is that the ethnographer implicates herself completely. I threw myself into these relationships, went overboard, even. This is the brash young person that comes through but is also someone who didn't much defend herself. The ethnographer is her own work instrument; if you hold back, defend yourself, you won't succeed. But this means that in the shadow world of Secu informing, the possibility of betrayal takes on an even more immoral cast: it *profits from the work practices of the ethnographer to turn her against herself, in their service.* And against not only herself but also those others who then enter into the Secu's gaze.

The irony, however, is that for me, "communism" as an environment *enabled* that throwing of myself into things, that return to a more irrepressible self. Part of the sadness now is that this is gone, because without social-ism, the environment is irrevocably changed. Nostalgia for it?

14-10-11. Second time I'm reading this thing. The more of it I go through, the more stultifying it becomes: the extent of surveillance, the assumptions of bad faith. Thinking about the subterranean. Most of my professional life I've worked under the assumption that surface appearances are not where truth lies: that to understand something you have to get beneath the surface. Now, here are these guys doing it, and me *really* getting under the surface, finding things I had no idea were there—all these grantees being followed all the time, reports on them, correspondence going up and down the hierarchy, top people being involved in it. Overwhelming sense that it's too much—that seeing all this invisible stuff means having to acknowledge how much of it is actually going on all the time. Mafias hidden out of sight, secret services everywhere, all the spy activity that ac-tually happens. It calls into question what an anthropologist can possibly think she's learning about a place when she can't see any of that. What naivete is fieldwork built on, in a world of surveillance!

Dream 29-10-11. Return from a month in Romania on Oct. 28; next night the following dream. I convoke a gathering, which seems to be of research-ers who worked in Romania and of Secu officers. A preliminary meeting with a small number of each has made it seem that a larger gathering would be productive (though it's not clear toward what end). People arrive. Spa-tial arrangement is peculiar: chairs arranged in a meandering way, not a circle or tables. I worry suddenly that I forgot refreshments, am preoccu-pied with figuring out who's going to speak. People are milling around in mixed groups, several of the officers are animatedly talking with the re-searchers, seem very interested in being together; others sit off on the side, waiting to see what will happen. Too late, I think I should have brought my tape recorder, since it doesn't seem I have enough paper.

Someone begins talking before I have a chance to convene the gather-ing. I'd wanted everyone to go around doing introductions, but too late now. Inexplicably the room is getting fuller and fuller. Two people who've crashed the gathering are doing some kind of side show/advertisement; I try to get them out, apologizing to those who are watching: this is sup-posed to be a focused gathering, no place for that kind of thing. Noise level is growing, focus (whatever it was) is slipping away. I get up and start talk-ing. The idea behind my contribution is to take my Secu file and see what it tells us about the production of knowledge in the Cold War. How did they think of us, *really*? I was hoping, with this gathering, to talk about these kinds of things. And what we researchers thought of them, of socialism.

As I speak, more people are beginning to leave, talking among themselves. Almost no one is paying attention to me; my efforts to control this gathering are a complete failure. Suddenly a huge utilities truck pulls up right outside the window, making an enormous racket that drowns out any attempt at continuing the meeting in an organized way. The truck driver shrugs his shoulders in apology, says he's just checking things out, and drives slowly and noisily around the building. I wake up. Did the Secu send that truck to break up my meeting?

What exactly WILL I accomplish with this book? How can I create a focus when all these pieces are so disparate? What's the point of it anyway? Why should I think anyone will be interested in it? I can't even corral the attention of the group I've convened in the dream, whom I would expect to find it riveting—those who went to communist Romania and those who tried to contain the effects of their presence. Everybody is busy with other things now.

Spring 2012. Continued rereading, along with more stuff on intelligence services, memoirs of Romanian intelligence officers, stuff from *Securitate* magazine, etc. Trying to think about Secu as another tribe, I notice that what they do seems more and more normal to me: *of course* they want to prevent sabotage and spying, doesn't the U.S. too? Look at my actions, of course they got suspicious; etc. To recover my anger I will have to go back to reading something like Herta Müller's *Die Zeit* interview about how abysmally they treated her, or Belu Zilber's memoir,[3] his life completely ruined by false charges, to recall that these are *not* nice people. As I begin to get used to the bureaucratic routine, that realization can slip.

A YEAR LATER

9-9-13. Now I'm rereading the file chronologically instead of in the haphazard manner of its original form. I see the accumulation of evidence, relationships; understand why I looked like a spy. Feel increasingly claustrophobic—huge weight of shadowing. Plus discrepancy between my sense of self going to see friends and the reality of the surveillance on them, their being questioned, etc.

July 2014. As I read this file yet again and begin to write, I find I still don't much like this Kathy whom I encounter there. She is amazingly ignorant about how one should behave in a world of secrets and surveillance. I suppose that's unfair: she'd never been in a situation like this, full of secrets and surveillance, so how should she know what to do? But she seems to have little imagination for this kind of thing. Moreover, she has no conception that the "transparent" speech so valued by her 1960s generation has its own forms of politics and manipulation. Doggedly persisting in her good example of the open-and-honest American who will show those Romanians the virtue of such behavior, she's also determined to teach those Cold Warriors at home a lesson about what life in a communist country is really like. Clearly this is a person born into privilege who is used to seeing her vision of things prevail. In a word, she's not very grown up.

But then again, isn't that what Irina meant in saying this is exactly what Secus want? They want to generate a picture of an unlikable person who will merit their actions. Why be so hard on poor Kathy? She was doing the best she could. And it's not true that they don't love me: plenty of people do—and plenty loved her as well. She couldn't have done her research otherwise. Indeed, I find that working on this memoir has quickened my affections for people I'm writing about who were so ready with their own, and has brought back what I loved about being there.

> > >

What emerges for me from this series of meditations is a gradual transformation in my attitude toward the file, reflecting a development from my reacting quite personally, to my thinking about it as a researcher. First I'm appalled and depressed, then I feel violated and angry, and finally I find it interesting, see the Securitate in a more matter-of-fact way and agree that my behavior was suspicious. This is going to infuriate my Romanian readers. If I had problems there with my first book, this one could be a lot worse. Focusing as it does on an ugly aspect of Romania's history, the hated Securitate, this book too will be seen as creating a negative image of the country and the people (though I should note that the Securitate was no worse than those other KGB-cloned secret police in Eastern Europe). Romanian readers not concerned about that will find something else to dislike, most especially: Shouldn't I be condemning the informers, the officers, the institution? That's what many Romanians I know will want.

Here, in my view, we come face to face with some of the limitations of the anthropologist as compared with inhabitants of the places we study. They can be utterly indignant about aspects of their society in a way I feel I can't. It's not that I still believe anthropology is an "objective" science—clearly it isn't. But I am committed to resisting condemnation that would wall off possibilities for understanding. Maybe once I think I've gone as far as I can with understanding and explaining, I can pass judgment, as I did in *National Ideology*, but I'm not there yet with the Securitate. Until then, I feel I have to hold back.

Most Romanians, however, do not have the constraint of scholarly purpose. Instead, they have the constraint of living where they do. They can be horrified and indignant, because they have either to live with the situation or to emigrate, whereas I can simply go home. Although it's true that I too was vulnerable—to being arrested or thrown out—and therefore the stakes of my surveillance were not negligible, nonetheless these were *their lives* that were invaded, unlike my brief research trips. I can't know what this experience was really like for them. I can only glimpse it.

Not all anthropologists would emerge from fieldwork like mine with my circumspection. That is, doing anthropology does not require it—indeed, some "engaged anthropologists" find they work better in situations that make them angry. I do not like to be angry, however, and usually try to tame that with reason. Or perhaps my hesitation, the hesitation that will make this memoir unpopular with at least some in Romania, has something to do with my gender—a topic I have barely mentioned, because once I "got married" in August 1973 I didn't experience being female as much of a liability except for the sexual propositions (common enough at home, too). Perhaps, though, being female has meant a harder struggle to create scholarly authority, which I am then loath to compromise by making premature judgments. In chapter 4 I will wrestle again with this hesitation, as I move toward a more analytic view of the Securitate and of my relations with them and their informers.

Let me give the last word to two Romanians who have read their files and express reactions more extreme than mine. This is not to say their reactions are "true," just vividly expressed.

In 2010, exiled writer Dorin Tudoran began his book I, *Their Son*, about his Securitate file, thus:

> Here is the only book I should not have had to write. It was enough to have lived it. In fact, it wasn't I who wrote this book: it wrote me. Twice. The

first time was when I was its character. At that time I was called "objective," "element," "enemy of the people," etc. . . . The second time was when I plunged into the ocean of poison [his file] that I thought I could handle with humor. Now I know that no one can have sufficient humor to emerge unscathed from the impact of 10,000 waves of gall. You find yourself facing an immense monster that develops by fission—in place of the severed tentacle grow ten more. Until it dies from within, the beast cannot be defeated from without. And from within, it hasn't died. It has only changed the color of the paralyzing ink it throws on us.

. . . These documents say that, beginning in the mid-1970s, my private life disappeared. At the end of the operation, I became someone else. . . . I'm not sure if and when I'll escape from this strange being who has taken my place or sits with me on the same chair, drinks with me from the same glass and reads together with me the same book. . . . Isn't it true that I talk about myself too much, that there's too much about myself in what I write? That's what happens when someone has robbed you of yourself.[4]

Second, in 2013 Gabriel Liiceanu wrote that as he read his file,

I experienced growing amazement. I had never imagined that there could exist so compact a parcel of abjection, orchestrated, systematized, stapled, sewn up, institutionalized. From that instant, the relation I entered into with my own past was dreadful. . . . You lost faith in the autonomy of your own life, in everything you had lived while deluding yourself that somehow your being might possibly have a small space of intimacy. From that day of November 2006 when I opened my File, I began to feel chronically dispossessed. I discovered that in those almost two decades, my life had been stolen, that in fact I had lived for an unspeakably long time—with my secret discussions, my loves, my fears, my whispers, my thoughts shared only with writing paper—naked, in the bosom of the Securitate. From this, hatred toward those who stripped us down and subjected us to this exercise of humiliation. From this, repugnance toward those self-appointed representatives of a super-species who subjected us to their discretionary power.[5]

With this preparation, let us step more fully inside the mechanisms of surveillance, exploring the subterranean secret world of informers and that "super-species," the Securitate officers. To do so, I depart from my autoethnography and become once again a researcher doing fieldwork—for which the autoethnography will prove essential.

PART II

INSIDE THE MECHANISMS
OF SURVEILLANCE

Revelations

Truth is not a matter of exposure which destroys the secret,
but a revelation which does justice to it.
—Walter Benjamin

Ministry of the Interior   SECRET

Performance Review

Officer ▮▮▮ works very well with the informers in his personal network,
he prepares for each meeting, he directs it towards problems of counterespionage, he gives each informer concrete tasks and indicates the manner
of proceeding so as to realize them. In this way he succeeded in obtaining
information of operative value, especially concerning the foreign citizens
who come into the county.

I was not, of course, the only person with doubles in the Securitate's secret world. Another category of people had them too: informers, the officers' number one weapon in the search for enemies. These doubles were
marked, like mine, by new names, but unlike me they rarely had more than
one. Sometimes informers picked their own pseudonyms, sometimes the
names were assigned; some of them didn't even know they *had* a double with

a pseudonym, though it appears in my file. Up to now, I have been dealing with my own multiple identities. Now I turn to those of others.

The dyadic relationship between officer and informer plus the latter's relationship to a target was the "elementary structure" of Securitate work. Officers considered informers to be their most important weapon in the struggle against the enemies it was their job to contain. In some cases, their relations might develop into something like friendship; in others the informer might never get past the initial fear and anxiety of his (they were largely male) recruitment; either way, both parties maintained the relationship as secret. The informer had to sign an oath not to reveal it to anyone, not even family members, and an officer kept confidential the identity of his informers (except if he were moved to a new post and might transfer them to another officer). As the communist regimes crumbled, there were some reports, though hard to verify, of concern to protect informers' identities by destroying their files.[1]

Other Romanians, however, were less discreet. A major pastime after the files were opened in 2000 was outing informers. People would get their own files and identify the informers who had reported on them; some would then spill the person's real name in the press. This procedure assumed that there was a reality beneath the pseudonym and the task was to reveal it. The CNSAS operated on the same principle, offering to "deconspire" the pseudonyms in people's files. Usually the public deconspiring of an informer went along with accusations and censure, but I have chosen not to do this, as is apparent from my redactions in documents in this chapter (some redactions are by the CNSAS).

The decision to preserve my informers' anonymity was not made easily. As one of my CNSAS colleagues said when I told her of this decision, "Oh, great! So the Securitate protected their identities with pseudonyms beforehand, and now you're going to do the same?! These people did a lot of damage: they should not get away with it!" People like this colleague think informers should be outed, regardless of the situation that drove them to it. Although some informers may have signed on willingly with malicious intent, the ones I have been able to speak with were generally not willing informers (hence their agreeing to speak with me). They were subjected to pressure and coercion, perhaps related to something they had done that was illegal and that would incur prosecution if they said no. It is true that many people who served as informers are now claiming they were coerced when perhaps they were not, but I prefer the more conservative interpretation. Therefore, like Timothy Garton Ash in his book about his East German file[2] (but unlike a number of Romanian authors), I leave out their names.

Discovering who informed on me was, nonetheless, truly distressing. It produced a reorganization of my entire affective landscape, as far as Romania was concerned, and it required work to assimilate. As I present some of my informers, indicating what they told me informing had meant to them, I also indicate some of the emotional work their stories occasioned. The picture I present is biased by the fact that those who told me the most were also "good" informers: people who did not like the work, rather than those who relished denouncing their fellows. We must not lose sight of the fact that informers could do tremendous damage if they chose to, writing reports that could completely change someone's life chances. Most of mine, fortunately for me, did not.

Portraits of Informers, Part II

Terror is not, as Western intellectuals imagine, monumental; it is abject, it has a furtive glance, it destroys the fabric of human society and changes the relationships of millions of individuals into channels for blackmail.

—Czesław Miłosz, *Native Realm*

"Beniamin"

INFORMATIVE NOTE

Source informs you of the following: the American citizen was in Bucharest 15–25 July 19■ where she was to get some advice from ■. On 26 July 19■ she was sought by a car with number 7-B■ which from what Source knows belongs to ■. She spent the night of July 27 with the above-mentioned person at a hotel in Alba Iulia. Source knows that the American citizen also had intimate relations with ■. . . .

N.O.: The note results from tasks assigned. It brings new data concerning the relations and preoccupations of American citizen Verdery K. Source was instructed to have her under surveillance in the sense of knowing her movements, the ties she creates, her conceptions, and her daily activities.

It is difficult to write about my beloved friend "Beniamin," for not only was his informing on me a painful discovery but most of the facts that would clarify its emotional load will make him identifiable, and he does not want that. He is ashamed. To use our conversations here requires me to suppress details that would improve his and the other stories, but at least I can show something of how people motivate their informing and their reactions to doing so, as well as my own reactions to it.

It took me some time of reading my file before I figured out who "Beniamin" was. His parents were good friends of mine and I'd met him through them; he was a bit older than I. As an informer, he was diligent, contributing a sizable number of reports. His officer says he provided over thirty-five written notes on me, along with a large amount of verbal information. One can see that they were fairly detailed, though some of that might have come from the officer himself. In my file there are nineteen informative notes from him; others might have been purged in routine maintenance. But when I first read the notes in 2008, I was horrified to see the kinds of things he seemed to know, and I was furious at what I took to be his betrayal of me. He and "Silviu," below, were the two people whose informing distressed me the most. Though I would be unable to discuss it with "Silviu," who had died, I was determined to pursue "Beniamin" until he talked. In retrospect, the depth of my initial rage at him surprises me, given how much milder were my feelings about most of the other informers in my file.

In summer 2009, before I had identified him as "Beniamin," we got together and I told him about my file. A peculiar look that I didn't know how to read passed across his face, but he said nothing. Before I went to Romania the next summer, I figured out who he was, and as soon as I got there I tried to call him (as I always did) to set up a meeting. The following field notes from 2010–13 bear the heading "Fantasy and Fugue." They reveal both my frame of mind and some of the central practices of the Securitate with informers, their most valued weapon in the hunt for spies. To ease the telling, I have rearranged parts of two conversations (from notes taken during or after them); my own questions are usually in parentheses.

16 June 2010. From the time I arrived, trying to reach "B." for a visit. He never answers his two phones or returns my calls. Eventually around June 5 I get to him through a family member and he calls me back, says he was super-busy with reports at work and not answering any calls he doesn't know. He puts my new phone number in his mobile, so this excuse is now gone. He says he's truly eager to get together and proposes lunch at 1:00 on the 16th, place to be arranged. Around June 10 he calls me at a time when I can't talk, says he'll ring tomorrow morning between 8:00 and 9:00. No call, and no reply to my calls. For the next couple of days I try on and off, no answer. On Monday I call his daughter and ask her to have him call me; no call. Today at 12:30 I call her again and ask what's up, am expecting lunch in half an hour but don't know where. She says she'll call me when he returns her page. All day no call.

It now dawns on me that someone has told him he can't see me and he's told his family to put me off. Even though the Securitate no longer exists as such, he must still have a relationship with its successor and be taking orders from them. Maybe he learned that CNSAS had "deconspired" him and he's gone to ground. I check my suspicion with Silvia, who says once they get their claws into you, you never get away; she thinks I'm right that he's been warned off.

I go to bed with a stiff drink and a sleeping pill. Awaken 7:00 A.M. from a murky dream about "B." I have an image of Secus still working all over Romania, spreading their net across the country. But now they can work much more efficiently because Facebook and cell phones give them networks without having to go through actual informers. Image of millions of points of light, beeping in the dark, illuminating clusters of the surveilled. So is Secu alive and well but better camouflaged? In the era of cell phones and social media in the post 9–11 era, total surveillance is everywhere. Romania will be in the vanguard because Secu was so active before and so little destroyed. Is asking these questions and having these thoughts further evidence of my supposed metier as a "spy"?!

I go home without having seen "B." and brood about it on and off all year. In September 2011 I'm returning to Romania for a month, and on the plane I start imagining my approach to "B." I imagine setting this note on the table before him: "Dear 'B.,' We've known each other for many years. I've been good friends with many in your family. You and I enjoyed a special affection. But now at CNSAS I learn that you are 'Beniamin' and were an especially diligent informer reporting on me. Will you talk about this with me? It would help me greatly to understand the kinds of pressures people were under, etc., etc. Why am I putting this in front of you on paper instead of saying it? Because I think you might still be working for the Secu, and in case you're wearing a microphone, I want you to have the chance to turn it off so we can talk."

I start to ruminate: Should I tape him clandestinely? Isn't that forbidden by my professional ethics? Should I make veiled threats to reveal his informing on me to his family, to his boss? I obsess over the constant self-questioning, the ethics of trying to do this, the self-doubts. Why am I so much madder at him than at others who did the same thing? What am I missing here?

2-10-11. Lunch with Zoli, I tell him my problem. He thinks all methods are fair game, I should record "B." secretly, blackmail him—his behavior warrants this. Force him to meet with me as a condition for forgiving him. But later, dinner with Daniel is very different. He explains why "B." refused to see me after making the arrangement: because in the first flush of excitement he had to say, "Of course, get together, fantastic . . ." rather than saying "Can't," like an American, who is always thinking along several time horizons. And he has to maintain his face, which was that we were friends, as everyone knows. But once he's said yes to a plan, then he has a problem with how he can go through with it. He has no way of making an excuse, but he can't face me. To explain his disappearance, I don't even need to posit that Secu got in touch with him: he knew I had a file.

So should I try to see him? Should I tape him, blackmail him? Should I send word by a reliable third party that I want to see him regardless of what may have happened, tell him how to contact me, and wait? Should I not keep trying—it becomes embarrassing—but let him know ahead of time this won't be a blood bath? A better way to talk about all this, says Daniel, is not asking him how he felt but putting it in the abstract—how would a person feel when recruited?

But I am still mad.

5-10-11: conversation with CNSAS colleague who has deep experience with the Securitate. I explain about "B.'s" not keeping our date: she replies, "He feels guilty. He's embarrassed—not afraid, but embarrassed." "What should I do?" I ask. "It was very painful that he shut me out like that." "You should get a note to him saying not to be alarmed about stuff from the time when he had to make reports, let's get together." She thinks this would be meaningful to him. Earlier she has been talking about how hard it was for Secus after 1989, until things got settled. "What they did to us!" she says, revealingly, and comes back to that theme several more times. At this moment I feel a sudden closeness between her and me, as I share my sad feelings about "B." and she is identifying with his feeling embarrassed for what he did. But when I say it's my fault he was recruited, she is vehement: it's NOT your fault. They would have recruited him for something else if not for you.

The next day I email "B." as follows, and the message does not come back:

Dear B—,

I'm here and would like to see you. Never mind what happened in the past, we're old friends. Please call me. Katherine

No response.

14-10-11. Having gotten his phone number over a week ago but been unable to bring myself to call, I finally do. He answers. I give my name, want to see him; he doesn't hang up. We agree where and how to meet. There have been some pauses in here but he seems interested in working it out. Then I ask, "What happened to you last year?" A pause, then, "The worst thing of my entire life. I haven't told anybody, but it was simply terrible." He gave me the details later, and indeed he had suffered a devastating blow, which he continues to keep secret from everyone but his wife. And now me.

So the big message here is, what a paranoid and megalomaniacal state of mind this project I'm doing induces in me, *a state of mind that dictator Ceauşescu seems to have diffused outward from himself. I scarcely recognize "myself" in these reactions, now that "B." has told me what happened. Should I believe him?*—that his disappearance had nothing to do with his past Secu connections or anything to do with me: it was just an emergency involving his job? Though it had crossed my mind at the time that he might have something totally different going on, mainly I preferred to concentrate on this paranoid theory of his ongoing work for the Securitate, which sustained my anger. It seems, however, that it wasn't his past informing that led him to avoid me but his shame over what had happened to him. This being the case, how should I approach him?

So now it's the day when we're meeting for dinner. He shows up; I feel stilted; we walk arm in arm to the restaurant. We discuss what's happening now in Romanian politics, make small talk for a while. Then I look away. Putting a hand on his arm, I say, "I have to raise a painful subject. I know you wrote reports on me." "Yes, I wrote them," he replies evenly. "Are you willing to tell me about it, how they got you to do it, and so on?" "Yes, I am."

This was one of only two times that I directly put the question to an informer. Usually I did so in a more indirect way, leaving them plenty of room to deny it, but here my paranoid fantasies have made me more direct—more an aggrieved person and less a researcher. Parts of our first conversation went like this:

It was early in his last year at university; one of his professors told him someone wanted to talk with him, Major *Moldovan. "He flattered me, said I was a good student, wouldn't I like to tell them stuff about my fellow students and professors? 'There are lots of bad people around, and we want to find out about them, help our country . . .' and so on. I was terrified. What should I say? I had no idea what to say. He asked me about my physics professor, and I said, 'He's a very good professor, but he does like to drink.' He responded, 'This is what we want, stuff like that.'"

---

in resolving the tasks entrusted to me and to preserve in secret my relation with the organs of security. I am conscious of this fact and of the consequences that might arise in case I should violate this pledge.

"Beniamin"

(Tell me more about your recruitment. How did it go?) "At the beginning it was very 'soft,' friendly. He contacted me through my professor, who said 'No need to be afraid of Major Moldovan.' He told me to inform about what happened at university, with colleagues, but if I know something outside that. . . . Later he asked me what I wanted to do when I finished university and I told him some of my hopes, such as working in an engineering job close to my parents, to which he replied: 'We can't guarantee that.'" Gradually the officer drew him towards other occupations, maybe working as a securist—they could guarantee that. Moldovan kept insinuating that "Beniamin" was not good enough to get the work he wanted without their help and that his chances were reduced by the fact that his cousin had fled to the West. But what he recalls most is that he was terrified they would do something to keep him from getting good work near home if he didn't cooperate. He repeats the word, "panic-stricken." The whole thing created a state of terrible stress for him. Whenever he had to meet Moldovan the next day, he wouldn't sleep. His housemate would ask, "What's wrong with you?" He'd be too anxious, and his stomach would ache.

I note the skill with which Moldovan produced the very data that he needed B to regurgitate back: clearly they could not just write these files on their own but needed the informer to do it. Also note how they manipulate people's temporality: using his past against him (his cousin who fled), then trying to deny him his future unless it's on their terms. I'll see that again later, with Mariana.

(How did he argue for recruiting you?) "First of all, patriotism. He would give me lessons about how important that was. 'Not everyone has your moral qualities, that's why we want to work with you.' Second, he said he could help me in life." He continued, "A couple of months went by after that first conversation, I didn't do anything, then Moldovan called me in and said, 'You haven't been giving us any reports!' I think, 'Maybe he knows I know KV, I was very nervous, so I mentioned it a week or two later. Moldovan says, 'Very good! I knew you were the right person for us. We want to know about her. She's a spy, is going to do great damage to Romania.' I think they intended all along to use me for you but didn't tip their hand at first. He gave me a lot of complicated instructions and told me I had to be very careful with you, because you're very smart."

(How did you know who I slept with?) "They told me! They kept telling me they knew everything about you, all I was doing was verifying, they were testing me to see if I was truthful or not. This created tremendous pressure to say everything I knew. So they'd ask me if I knew who you were sleeping with, I'd say no, they'd tell me and ask if you had been seen talking with the person in question. When I said yes, they would say 'SEE?! We know!'" (Then what you wrote in the notes wasn't your idea?) "They would tell me what to write and ask for my additions." (So you didn't have to think about what to say and what to hide, like my friend M., who was always trying to figure out how to stay a step ahead of them?) "No, I was much too scared." (How did you feel when they talked about who I was sleeping with?) "Miserable. Miserable. Miserable!"

This revelation completely transforms my feelings about him. He claims he was not the person saying a lot of this nasty stuff: it was his handler! I found this plausible, for I'd wondered how he could possibly have known some of the things in his reports. The answer is, he didn't. Although one could be skeptical of all this after-the-fact remorse, somehow—knowing him for as long as I do—I want to believe him.

(What was the officer like? How did he talk with you? Was he aggressive? Tough?) "No, not like that, but his technique was to catch me off guard, like with the question about who you sleep with. He'd throw it at me, I'd be caught off guard, then he'd push his advantage."

After 1989 there was further stress for "B." from worrying who would find out. Did he ever talk about this with anyone? No. He was scared to, they told him not to. (If I hadn't brought it up now, would you have told me?) "Yes, I almost did when you first mentioned your file." (So this is our secret! Do your parents know?) He repeats emphatically he told no one, not his parents, not anyone. (Your best friend? He seemed to know.) Did not tell him. (Why didn't you tell anyone?) "Two reasons: 1) Fear. Moldovan was very insistent about this, 'Don't imagine you can tell . . .' He really scared me. 2) How could I tell anyone, when I was doing something horrible? It wasn't something I could be proud of, so why let anyone know?" (Did you know it was bad at the time?) "Yes, I knew it was bad even then, not just now. From my parents, from my grandparents' stories—my grandfather used to tell me, 'These guys will take you and send you to the gulag!' etc." His eyes grow moist. "And my father a few times said to me, 'Be careful what you do with the American.' As if he had smelled something."

(They were still following me in 1994, 1996. You?) "In 1992, I saw Moldovan on the street and headed right toward him. He turned and literally ran in the opposite direction!" (What did you want to say to him?) "I don't know. I just headed toward him."

We've been holding hands for the last part of this conversation. I feel genuine sympathy for him as he shows how frightened and confused he was. I say I'm really sorry about all this stress he had because of me; he replies that he brought it on himself by being so fearful. (But you were young and inexperienced, how could you know that people said no, and how to say it?) We walk back to my hotel arm in arm. "How do you feel now?" I ask. "Much better. I feel as if a great weight has been lifted from me." I do too, and I can once again feel my old affection for him.

Every informer has an informer file (*dosar de rețea*) in which his handler details his recruitment and his performance thereafter. The next time I see "B.," I have read his informer file closely, finding in it notes like this from the top two Secus of his county: "He revealed great passion for informative work, and all his materials were characterized by sincerity and objectivity." I make another lunch date with "B." Is he willing to continue the last conversation? He is.

I tell him I've seen his informer's file, and roughly what's in it: "It turns out that you were good! They liked your work." He replies, "That's what Moldovan used to say, 'An excellent collaborator!' He'd praise me. But I still hated it." Knowing how thorough and disciplined he was as a student, I found this credible, but someone else I discussed it with scoffed, "Everybody is now rewriting their histories! Stomach-aches now, but diligent work then. . . ."

(Tell me more about your work with him. You said your recruitment was 'soft.' Did he then get tougher?) Sometimes very tough, sometimes nicer. He was very insistent with his tasks, having no concern for what else "B." might have to do. Makes him feel he's responsible for everything. So insistent, asking what KV was doing, that "B." began to be very inhibited with me. I'd be wanting to talk, he'd be tongue-tied. He had to be with two faces: be natural with me and then turn around and squeal to Moldovan, which led to tremendous stress and tension.

(Was your relation with him a pedagogical one? Their instructions tell them to teach their collaborators.) "Yes. He would sit in his office, very relaxed, and he'd ask questions, then say, 'Let's write this out, summarize.' I would say something, he'd rephrase it, give me concise language for my various details. He would also tell me things like, 'Never use the names of Nicolae and Elena Ceaușescu: instead say 'the higher Party leadership.' But he also shaped my vision." (Did your powers of analysis grow?) "Yes, especially through his rephrasing. I was very admiring of how he could bring out the essence of my scattered thoughts. But he would also manipulate me in one or another direction, saying 'KV is an enemy, surely she has something hidden.'" (Did he plant doubts in your mind about me?) "Yes. He made it seem impossible you could just be coming to do what you said."

So in this case, the officer has not created a new identity but taken someone whose identity is not yet firmly established and molded it to his own
purposes. He's had considerable success, and that must have complicated
"B.'s" personality development, as his family was trying to warn him away
from the very sort of person who was shaping him.

*(You did this fairly often for over a year. Did you get close to him?) He hesitates, as
if he doesn't want to admit he did. "No, but I had the impression he knew everything
about me. He seemed smarter than average, especially in how he could synthesize
thoughts so well. He was not an idiot. He had authority with me, and others acted
that way too, when I would announce at the entrance that I'm here for Maj. Moldovan. It would make me feel important." (Did you?) "I never felt relaxed." (Did he
treat you with respect, aside from yelling at you sometimes?) "Yes. Aside from some
very subtle moments when he indicated that I had to do what he said, he acted as
if we were friends."*

*(How often did you meet?) "At least once a month, more like every two weeks or
ten days. It would last an hour or more." (Did you ever write your notes beforehand?)
"Sometimes he would say to do the notes at home, but usually it was in the office.
Especially at the beginning, 'while you're getting used to this,' and he would do this
rephrasing thing." (Where did you write the notes?) "At home." (Not worried someone would find them?) "Of course!"*

*"He would always ask, 'Did anyone see you coming in?'" (What were the effects
of having this secret?) "It created a knot in me, I was always worried someone would
find out." (So having a secret was not exciting.) "Not at all!"*

*(How did this experience affect you?) "I became more reserved. [He pauses.] I still
have a feeling of guilt—I believe I did you wrong [cred că ți-am făcut rău]. If I'd
known what would happen . . . but I wasn't sharp enough to avoid telling them everything, writing garbage. All of that 'We already know!'—so intimidating. Also, my
family had an acquaintance in the Securitate who would say things like, 'If there are
two cabins in the mountains, one is the Securitate's.' This would impress me. I would
never agree to do it now, but then I was frightened. I knew these guys killed people, sent
them to the gulag, to jail. I was really afraid, and I thought I had no option."*

Perhaps readers will experience the same confusion of values that I did from
these two lengthy conversations. "Beniamin" had illuminated for me a number of things about the officer-informer relationship and had given a very

believable account of himself, hinting at the complexities of a relationship that put a knot in his stomach yet made him feel important. I definitely felt much better about our relationship once I decided to see his informing not as a betrayal but as a cause of suffering for him (the same will be even truer of Mariana). He felt better too: an email sometime after I left for home read, "Thank you for all the warmth and tact with which you have overcome this dark moment in our friendship." For a bit I'd gotten snagged on that officer's mention of his "passion for informative work" and on the obvious truth that many Romanians, busily "rewriting their CVs" since 1989, don't exactly present a truthful view of their actions during those times. But then again, he'd taken a sociology course and seemed to have a vocation for it—in fact, he'd told me how much he had enjoyed it, wishing it weren't too late to change his major—which throws some light on his "passion for informative work." We should remember, too, that officers could write just about anything in those files: no one would correct them. By making "Beniamin" praiseworthy, maybe his officer wanted some reflected glory to substantiate his pedagogical skill with his informer. It's hard to know what to make of that praise.

Am I wrong not to condemn "Beniamin's" behavior? Many Romanians would say yes. In 2014, discussing with a Romanian writer the latest scandal in the newspapers in which an important politician is being attacked for having informed on me to the Securitate, I say I refused the newspaper's request to comment on the case because this person had given me a great deal of help and friendship in the past. My colleague replies, "Don't go too easy on him. It was precisely *because* you were friends that he would be asked to report." With "Beniamin," however, I am moved by his relative innocence and youth. He presents himself as fearful, and I believe it. I think back to Kathy when she was his age: would she have refused? Wouldn't she too have been frightened, even if she would also—characterologically, like him—want to "do a good job" of it? There's a scrap of evidence that she might have behaved similarly.

> > >

One day in 1987 as I was sitting in my office at Johns Hopkins University, the phone rang. The caller identified herself as someone working for the FBI and asked if she could speak with me. I invited her to continue, but she preferred to make an appointment to come and see me in person. Baffled by the call, I immediately began wondering about its cause. In 1986 I had taken my first trip to the Soviet Union, with another early in 1987; maybe that was the rea-

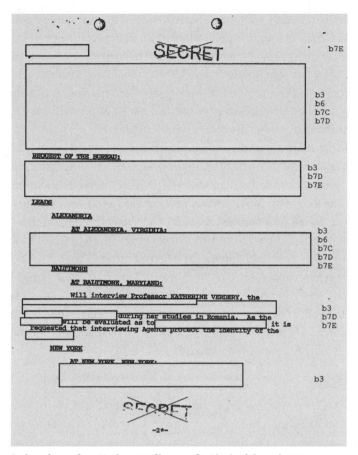

Redacted page from Verdery FBI file, ca. 1987. Obtained through FOIA request.

son for the visit. In addition, I was going out with a physicist who worked for the Hopkins Applied Physics Lab, which had contracts with the Department of Defense for the Trident missile program. Maybe they were doing a background check on his personal life.

With these thoughts in mind, I was thunderstruck by her first statement at our meeting: "It has recently come to our attention that you spend time in Romania." I replied that I had done so since 1973 and wondered why they were finding out about it only now. She was not at liberty to say. She proceeded to ask me a bunch of questions so naive, and revealing such profound ignorance of life in Romania, that given the Securitate pummeling I had experienced in my visits between 1984 and 1987, I feared the United States would lose the Cold War. These included her asking me whether Romanians had ever tried to get friendly with me or had ever asked me for things (both happened almost daily during my trips), whether I had ever met Romanians in the United States, and so on. After a while I asked her why she had come to see me; again, she was not at liberty to say. (When I would eventually obtain my very small FBI file through the FOIA—a total of sixteen pages, heavily redacted—I would learn that they were concerned not so much with me but rather with a Romanian I knew whom they were watching.)

What struck me most about my meeting with the FBI agent—the only meeting I ever knowingly had with a U.S. intelligence officer—was that even though I was sure I had done nothing wrong, I was very nervous and even fearful during the interview. My heart was beating fast, and I kept feeling I should ingratiate myself with her even though I had absolutely no reason to. I guess I hoped that in this way I would disarm whatever suspicions she had. This meeting was therefore quite important when, starting in 2008, I would read informers' reports about me, like those from "Beniamin," and thought I could imagine, even if in only a small way, the troubling effect that meeting with an intelligence officer could have on a person, especially one being recruited to inform. My reaction would also prove a foreshadowing of the meetings I would finally have with my securiști.

How Many Informers?

There is no agreement on how many informers Romania had. Estimates range from under half a million to three million, depending on whether we include those working with the regular police, in addition to those working with Securitate officers. I prefer the conservative figure of 486,000 (about one in thirty adults),[3] but it is not clear whether this refers to all informers for the entire communist period or only to those active in 1989. One datum is significant, however: a report from 1968 shows that the Securitate had determined that fully 50 percent of the adult population was suspicious and should be under surveillance![4] No wonder they needed so many informers—and no wonder Ceaușescu had decided it was time to rein the Securitate in.

As for full-time Securitate employees, the figure from CNSAS researchers is about 15,000 (some 10,000 of them officers), though that too is in doubt—and it leaves out the regular police, whom the Securitate often used as auxiliaries.[5] To compare, the equally uncertain figures for the Stasi in East Germany are 93,000 full-time employees and 178,000 informers and collaborators, for a population of 17 million (compared with Romania's 23 million): thus, East Germany with its smaller population had more officers and fewer informers than Romania did. Part of the difference may come from the tremendous expense of eavesdropping technology, which might force poorer Romania into greater reliance on informers. But all of these numbers are uncertain.

There is also no firm consensus on the categories of informers or who counted as one. I do not refer to the lists of kinds of informers as the Securitate saw them (agent of influence, "skilled" and "unskilled" informers, collaborators, residents, etc.) but to people engaged in various acts of reporting. I have already mentioned, for example, the law specifying that anyone who had a conversation with a foreigner had to report its contents to the Party organization in their workplace. So if there is a pro-forma report in my file about a dinner I had at someone's house, does that make my host an informer or simply a law-abiding citizen? Similarly, any Romanian who traveled abroad for any purpose—a piano competition, an international convention, a research trip, a visit to relatives, and so forth—also had to file a report upon return. Did this report make them informers? Several friends who mentioned it stated firmly that they did not think of it as an informer's report; it would have been one only if it included compromising information about someone else on the trip. These kinds of reports could form a slippery slope, though: a person writes a report on his trip; then one on his dinner with the American; and then it's easier to draw him into more serious informing on specific targets.

People in certain occupations were virtually required to give information when asked: postal and telephone employees, hotel receptionists, personnel officers in firms or offices, certain kinds of civil servants. Were they informers? How about someone who wrote an innocuous report with no damaging details: Was that person the same as one who wrote very damaging reports that implicated other Romanians (and thus made them vulnerable too)? Some informers reported under duress, others with enthusiasm; some wrote banalities, others were positively vicious. Should they all be tarred with the same brush? Sometimes a Party member could be brought in to give information on a case, but he would not have an informer file—and permission would have to be given by Party organs before he was approached. Was he an informer or a responsible Party member? Sometimes a person would refuse to be recruited as an informer but agree to show up from time to time and give verbal information, perhaps as the result of knowing the officer independently. Was she an informer? Was there a difference between informers who signed their own name as opposed to using the pseudonym they had been given? Questions like these show how difficult it is to know how many informers there were.

We should consider, too, the Securitate's different ways of siphoning information out of people, which might or might not qualify them for the label "informer." *Elena, a friend in Vlaicu who had an office job in town, told me that the *securist* for her institution would come into the office periodically and say, "So how's your friend, I see she's back. Have you seen her? What's she up to these days?" It was all very conversational. "I think I didn't actually realize some of the time that he was getting a report on you [i.e., that she was informing]. It seemed he was just chatting." I asked if she had signed an informer's pledge, but she hadn't (and indeed, at CNSAS I found no evidence of written reports or official informer status for her). We talked about whether people in Vlaicu knew who the informers were, and she said, "People in villages didn't really notice this kind of thing much back then." Because rural areas were under-endowed with informers, perhaps this kind of soft touch, through "just chatting," was more usual there.

Another of my acquaintances had rather the same experience. As he described it, because he knew some German he would occasionally be called to the Securitate office in town and asked to translate something. Then the officer would start chatting with him about me, asking what I was up to—easy to do with this friendly fellow. In his case, there were a number of written reports, but all were typed and his signature did not appear on any of them; the officer probably wrote them up as reports after the chat. Unlike my friend Elena, he had a pseudonym, "Valentin," but when I asked for his informer file there was nothing, which suggests that indeed he had never been formally recruited. I asked Meri whether she thought he had been informing, and she said no: "He was terrified of you! He did everything he could to avoid you, except for pleasant greetings on the street." Perhaps realizing how he was being used, he tried to have nothing to report.

This case, in particular, smells to me like the officer's attempt to build up his informer stable without doing all the necessary background work to recruit him properly. Everything about "Valentin's" reports looked as if he were being treated as an informer, except for the lack of a file indicating his recruitment and his actual signature on the notes. Although one of the *securişti* I spoke with denied that there was a "central plan" or other motivation for recruiting informers, I find that doubtful. At different times there were different orientative recruitment targets: each officer had to have twenty-five, or forty, later even fifty. Some Romanian researchers indicate on the basis of their work in the archive that, like everyone else in the Romanian economy, officers too were given a plan to recruit a certain number of informers. For instance, a performance review of one officer notes: "Quantitatively speaking, the number of his informers is insufficient." An officer might inherit some of them from other officers being moved on to a different job; some of them he might "invent," as is likely with "Valentin." Sociologist Maria Łoś says the same happened in Poland: officers raced to recruit informers, and superior officers encouraged them because having more informers would bring them more operational funding.[6]

The creation of informer doubles had certain general properties—that is, those recruited to inform on me were not a special case. There was a script, in a standard language used repetitively, intended to produce a specific reality: the patriot-informer trained to look for certain incriminating traits of his targets and willing to keep his informing secret ("I swear not to divulge . . ."). The informer was groomed to be complicit with his officer and duplicitous with his fellows, his self split between these personae. One means for accomplishing this is a peculiar aspect of informer reports, which officers insisted on in training them: the use of the third-person pronoun to refer to themselves. An informer was never to write "I saw Katherine Verdery with X on March 27," for instance, but rather, "Source informs you that Verdery Katherine was seen with X on March 27." The person who writes reports, then, is not "I" but someone else, someone called "Source." Because the word for "source" in Romanian is feminine (sursa), any self-referential pronouns the source used would also be feminine: "Source invited K. Verdery to [her] home for dinner." I wonder whether that practice might enable the pseudonymous informer to experience [her] identity as completely separate from [her] "real" self. Did it enable multiplying their subjectivities more readily, splitting off their reporting self from some other self? Since the majority of informers were male, I also wonder if this feminine pronoun helped to alienate them even further from themselves and the work they did.

Letter to Phyl, June 27, 2014
Today I spent the morning in the archive reading files of informers from Vlaicu in the late 1950s–60s. What's fascinating about them is the world they create: how the officers plan the recruitment, how they say they execute it, and how they then try to reform these people's habits—for example, the drunkard whose drinking they knew all about before recruiting him, then they try to reform him. It seems pretty clear that

often they purposely approach people with flaws and misdeeds so they can use those in recruitment, telling the candidate that they know all these things he's done and it would be a shame if he had to lose his job because of them.

Recruitment

Although one can't take anything in them at face value, the informer files in the CNSAS archive indeed open a fascinating window onto the phenomenon of informing as well as onto village life. Consider this paraphrase of the recruitment file of someone from Vlaicu who informed on me in the 1970s. His experience, which I present at some length, was typical.

Recruitment File for H.W. [a German], pseudonym "Muller Martin"

Report with proposal to recruit H.W., in the category of nationalist elements from Aurel Vlaicu.

AIM and NECESSITY of RECRUITING: In Vlaicu there are many nationalists from the GEG [German Ethnic Group, from which many men joined the Nazi army while Romania was Hitler's ally], such as ███. Individual informer actions have been opened in Vlaicu concerning ███, former GEG leader, but no informer has been found having possibilities to report on him. Among those in the entourage of elements of German nationality and in his circle of friends appears this H.W., former GEG member . . . who enjoys the sympathy of the above-mentioned people and is better trained than they from the professional and cultural points of view.

DATA about the CANDIDATE. Born in Vlaicu, has no property, etc. His activity: went to school, then hired on as an apprentice. Has worked in a variety of places. He is friends with the following GEG members [names].

UTILITY OF THE CANDIDATE. He lives there among those we want to follow and is a former GEG member. He is intelligent, has training suitable for an agent, and knows how to make friendly connections with people who interest the Securitate organs. He is an element without vices and is appreciated among the villagers as a steady person.

BASIS and METHOD of RECRUITMENT. Use compromising materials in our possession: he was in the GEG, then left as a volunteer with the German army to fight against the Soviet Union, where he was captured. He has hidden these facts of his biography from the places where he works. . . . Another informer tells us H.W. works clandestinely in his own workshop making repairs for villagers. This is against the law. He has two children 5 and 8 years, and if we brought him to justice it would destroy his children's future—we will use this in recruiting him. We think he will be amenable because he is a fearful person.

PLAN OF RECRUITMENT. We will ask him about the following three things: His role in the GEG, his volunteering for the German army, and his clandestine repair activities. The recruitment will take place in the office of the head of personnel at his factory. If he admits to the things we ask him about, we will move ahead with recruiting him. Otherwise, recruitment will be attempted with other GEG members.

He will be instructed about how to behave with his family and with elements located in the village, and about how to arrange meetings with his officer.

REPORT on the recruitment effort. He was picked up as he was walking from work and taken to headquarters. He admitted to everything we had uncovered and told us who is making hostile manifestations in Vlaicu; feeling he was appropriate, the recruitment proceeded, giving him the name "Muller Martin." He was provided extensive instruction.

The recruitment lasted from 11:30 to 17:45. [Long verbatim record of questions asked and answers given.] He said, "I admit that I have done wrong but ask the Securitate organs to give me a chance to rehabilitate myself, by reporting on anyone I hear making hostile manifestations." Then his pledge, which includes all his wrongdoings, and ends, "I will report on what I hear and will sign my information 'Muller Martin.' I pledge to preserve in secret my connection with the organs of the Securitate. If I break this pledge it will prove my insincerity. I ask to be punished in conformity with the laws in force." 24 iv 61. Signature.

[Reports, references and interrogations concerning him from various fellow villagers.]

From this report we learn a great deal about how Securitate officers drew someone into their informer network. They have studied him closely ahead of time, decided why to approach him rather than some other German, envisioned an exit strategy, and decided on a mixed recruitment plan, combining blackmail with an appeal to material interests. (The other typical route was a simple appeal to patriotism, as with "Beniamin.") Blackmail generally involved the officers' knowing of some illegal behavior the candidate had engaged in (performing/having an abortion, homosexuality, speculation, stealing from the collective, clandestine work for money as with "Muller") or some bureaucratic failure, such as not declaring previous fascist activity on an employment application. In exchange for his signing the pledge, the officers would not press charges. But key to any strategy was to convince the person that they already knew everything about him. Part of an officer's training in psychology was to identify a person's special weak spot—to be able to "read" people and profit from their weaknesses in seeking to recruit them. As we see, they took their time: "Muller" was in their hands for over seven hours, typical of other recruitment reports I have seen. There would be plenty of opportunity to ambush him with their knowledge of his weaknesses.

The informers I introduce here all passed through some such procedure. Now they have passed through another recruitment, this time by me. My approach to interviewing each one was different: in general, I did not "confront" them with the fact that I knew of their reports but said that I had my file, then gradually worked around to saying I was interested in talking with my informers to see how it was for them. Except for my conversations with "Beniamin" and Mariana, my notes were taken after the fact. Even if the people I discuss have denied it, there is no doubt in my mind that they were informing on me, given their handwriting, circumstantial evidence, or confirmation from the CNSAS. This does not mean, though, that everything about them in my or their own file is "true."

"Groza"

Source "Groza"   TOP SECRET
13.08.88

Informer's Note

On 12 August 1988, Source paid a visit to Academician David Prodan. After an hour he told me of KATHERINE VERDERY's visit to him. . . . He told me that she regrets hugely the foolishness with the mottoes in her book, which were absolutely stupid. In my view, DAVID PRODAN is [unrealistic] about KATHERINE VERDERY, convinced of her good faith. . . . In Source's opinion, what the old professor takes in is filtered through an honest man's trust, who can easily be deceived by KATHERINE VERDERY should she wish it. On one hand she gathers all sorts of historical and methodological information and on the other, her possible parallel activity has remained for D. PRODAN a figment of the imagination of suspicious people.

"Groza"

"Groza" was one of those informers whose information about me generally created trouble. It was he who had first informed the Securitate about the jokes in my book in August 1984, his report generating the recommendation to throw me out. Here, he is undercutting Professor Prodan's good opinion of me; he also badmouthed a report I wrote of a conference, informed about my relations with Hungarians, and passed along other tidbits to his officer. I had been friendly with him at first but got tired of his repeated passes at me, so I had pulled back, thereby hindering his informer activities. In 2012 I decided to talk with him about them, though I was promptly brought up short by the state of his health.

> Field notes, June 2012
> "Groza" and his wife greet me affectionately, though I haven't seen them in years. She puts three cups on the table, sits, asks him to get water, whispers that he has Alzheimer's and remembers very little. Then a bit later she goes out for something, I whisper to him, "Does your wife know you informed on me for the Secu?" He looks at me sharply and says, "Who told you that, her?" No, it's in my dossier. He denies it; she returns. The discussion was very fragmented, she keeps going off on tangents, monopolizing 85% of our conversation in her attempt to mask her husband's condition.
>   I don't recall how we got onto the subject of his father's having been a political prisoner. She interjects that Secus were living in their house, they had obligatory domicile because his father's sister was a Greek Catholic nun. His father was arrested in 1950, ostensibly for knowing about a subversive organization but not denouncing it; he did a year in prison. He appealed, and in 1962 was rehabilitated—they show me the paper—because he'd made three inventions at his prison job that improved productivity. "Because my father had been a prisoner, we were unable to do a whole lot of things," he volunteers. She adds, "The family never talked about this, and only very recently did we learn from his sister that her husband had been in the gulag!" Why didn't they talk about it? "You couldn't trust anybody."
>   The family fled to another city. After the communists banned the Greek Catholic Church, his grandmother kept a priest in the basement even though they had Secus in the house: she said she needed someone to confess to. Meanwhile, his father took

him around to different churches, so he could decide for himself where the truth lay. Both joined Protestant sects.

(Any consequences of your past?) "I lost many opportunities." She: "He applied to university twice, didn't get into medical school at all so did ██. He lucked out in getting a job: he was first assigned to a ██ museum as assistant to the director, a very powerful person who took a shine to him and recommended him to succeed her when she retired. He joined the Party to get the job."

His wife goes off on a tangent about some woman their family had helped in some way. "She worked as a waitress at the '██' restaurant, where he always went with foreign visitors. One day the woman said to his sister, 'After all your family has done for me, I have to tell you, warn your brother that they always put mikes under his plate." I tell him that when he and I went to restaurants, the conversations were often recorded; he wants to know what they were about but then loses interest.

(People were exposed to all sorts of pressures to become informers. Why did they succumb?) She: a work obligation; he: personal interests, probably. They leave the subject at once. He's been fairly restless throughout this visit and it's increasing; keeps getting up, going to the bookshelf, looking for things, sitting down. It could be the topic, or the Alzheimer's.

With the wife's constant interventions it has been difficult to do much with this conversation, but it does point to several things that could get a person into informing. In particular, having a political prisoner in the family was a major black mark, and to gain opportunities otherwise denied, one might try to expunge it by agreeing to inform. There was also the connection with the Greek Catholic (Uniate) Church, which the Romanian Communist Party had suppressed, since its ties to Roman Catholicism gave it too much international leverage. The same was true of the Protestant sects. As an intelligent and ambitious fellow, "Groza" must have felt overwhelming inner pressure to agree to inform, given his family's connections with undesirable religious groups. A note in his informer file states that he was recruited after being caught bringing religious literature into Romania.

As an informer, "Groza" has an informer file containing his reports and recruitment data, but as someone who has himself been under surveillance he also has a multivolume surveillance file (DUI) of his own, like mine, replete with officers' notes and informers' reports on him. This latter file is fascinating for what it reveals about someone who has done a lot of good informing but whom the Securitate does not trust and therefore continues to verify through intensive surveillance. In the 1980s he's suspected of being recruited by U.S. intelligence as a double agent—apparently I am one of the people working on him toward this end. He was probably a good informer: his reports on me are detailed and often lengthy, including a close translation of all the chapter headings and epigraphs of my book. But his imagination could also get the better of him, as in this conclusion to a long report of a lunch I had invited him to—a lunch with an agenda, I discover from reading his informer file, dictated by his Securitate officer, who had briefed him ahead of time and recorded our conversation. "Groza" ended his report of it thus:

From her entire comportment, with a provocation of the woman-man type at our parting—sometimes through gestured allusions—affirmations unexpressed with exactitude but communicated through silence and gaze, I think we are in a very advanced situation of possible collaboration. . . .

N.O.: Verified through special mobile eavesdropping devices. Source respected the briefing received.

N.S.: The meeting had taken place on the initiative of KATHERINE VERDERY who I think has the job of verifying "GROZA." From comparing his note with the recording we made, it results that Source related their discussion correctly to us with small differences of interpretation. Source is directed to let himself be recruited, since it seems this is the sense in which things are proceeding.

This remarkable report transmutes a casual question I asked "Groza," about his interest in traveling to the United States, into my having a mission to recruit him as a double agent, using sexual innuendo as part of the lure.

"Viorel"

[From a 1974 action plan to verify the purposes of "FOLCLORISTA"] Sources "MULER MARTIN," of German nationality, collective farm worker, "VIOREL," ▮, and "AUREL," pensioner . . . will be used to signal her travels and the connections she makes, especially the identification of those among them who are employees at UM Cugir.

Field notes, Summer 2012. He's sitting at a table in the pub drinking a beer and well into his cups. Volunteers something about listening to Radio Free Europe (I say, "Dangerous in those days!"). He says he wasn't a Party member. He invites me to sit down, tells me about the time I spoke on Voice of America [VOA]. No matter how many times I say I didn't, he won't budge: he knows I spoke on VOA. The conversation continues in this vein.

Then I say, "Because of your work, you had to give reports to the Securitate, right?" He looks uncomfortable. (You had no choice, you had to do it.) "Yes, but I managed with them. I'd get rid of them fast: lie to them, they'd go away." (Whom did you meet with—Secu or local police?) He demurs. (Where? Did they come to you or did you have to go somewhere?) "I went to them." (Where?) "That was a secret." (It was, but it isn't any longer.) He avoids answering, but at the end when I ask him again he says, "I didn't go to them, they came to me." He's still not saying who, but this seems more credible.

"But I had them in the palm of my hand!" he volunteers. (How?) "My boss gave me a camera, I could follow them, take pictures, they'd end up on the front page of that police broadsheet, The Reflector. You know what else I did? I had a connection with the drivers of the forestry trucks. They [the police] would say to me, 'Tomorrow we aren't coming.' I'd call the drivers and say, 'The coast is clear.' They'd come down and sell wood to people. If I knew the police were coming, I'd call the drivers and say, 'Don't come.' So I managed."

"You were very closely followed," he tells me. (Did you know? Did people in Vlaicu know?) "People said so. Remember Ioan D.? He followed you! His nephew—big cheese in the Securitate!" He then tells me a lot about my being followed: "how many copies of your notes did you make? Three: See? I knew!" Something about how they stole notes of mine in the train station: he knew that too. He knew about VOA. He maintains he once told me he'd heard me on the radio, and I'd asked, "Does anyone else know?" "No, only me." And I'd said, "Then don't tell anyone." So I too am paranoid, it seems, and keeping secrets, like him. He repeats again that he wasn't a Party member, made his wife one but not him. (How did you know all this stuff, about the three copies of my notes, and so on?) "They would tell me!"

(Tell me about them. Did you know one called Belgiu?) "That's who it was! Belgiu! A filthy fellow, a very bad man." He's not sure he remembers anyone else. Remembers the names of several policemen, but still didn't answer my question about whether he talked with police or directly with Secus.

Several times during this conversation he says not to tell anyone. I ask, "You had to swear an oath, right?" He nods. "Not to tell anything?" He nods. "But that's over now, you can talk about it." "Of course . . ." As we part he says again not to tell: "I don't want it to be known what I was."

"Viorel" was quite a character, with whom my relationship changed significantly after 1989. Before that, he played the blockhead and refused to speak to me except when absolutely necessary. Because of his work, he had to file regular reports on anything he saw in the village—that is, he would not likely have been recruited as an informer, since giving information was a requirement of his job. He appears periodically in action plans, but no notes from him appear in my file. I imagine he mostly spoke with the officers rather than writing anything down. I also suspect him of having purveyed rumors about me for his handlers to some of the many Vlaiceni he saw in the course of his work.

After 1989, when he retired, he would sometimes accost me on the street, more than a bit tipsy, and engage me in a conspiratorial way in conversation, usually about something "secret." He would say, for instance, how even under the communists he had always loved Americans, and how he was now getting very religious but I shouldn't tell anyone because it was a secret. These drunken confidences opened up to me an inner self that he was hiding (had long hidden?). His obsession with "the secret" when he was drunk seemed to me eloquent testimony to the role he had played for so many years. Particularly interesting in the conversation I report is his last sentence: "I don't want it to be known what I was." It suggests a sense of embarrassment about all the reporting he had done, which to some extent he owns. This is by no means the norm among informers.

"Alex"

Catherine Verdery maintains very close friendship relations with ███,
visiting her at home and considering her an intelligent woman. This person
feeds her with various gossip from town. . . . [KV] spoke very warmly to me
of one of the receptionists from the Continental, Maria Demeter, in whom
she has full confidence.

"Alex" was a longtime friend, with whom I had kept in touch first with the occasional letter, then via email. Having seen his handwriting from his letters, I was fairly sure I recognized it on some reports from the 1980s. (I later confirmed the handwriting with someone who knew it well.) His reports gave much more information than I would have wished about my activities, including the names of friends I visited—one in particular, whom he was jeopardizing with these repeated mentions.

Field notes, 6-13-08
Several of us sitting around, "Alex" brings up the book Historians and the Securitate; *how interesting to see all these people whose handwriting he recognizes. Talking about who was an informer; he's very sure ▮▮▮ was one—he had to be. When I mention having my file, he reminds me of the first time we met, when I invited him up to my hotel room to give him something, and he had to leave his ID at the desk. Soon thereafter, "Groza" appeared, he said; the message was obvious. He expected to be called in after that, but wasn't. Stories continue in which he is working hard to present himself as innocent.*

Two years later, I join "Alex" at lunch with friends one day. As I have done with several others, I talk about my file and say I'm going to write a memoir from it; I'm interested in talking with people who had to give reports. My goal, I explain, is not to have a showdown but just to see how it happened to them and how they felt about it. I've indicated this interest to a couple of people who've replied, "They came to me too." I say, "It must have been very difficult to be approached to become an informer; I can imagine I myself might have agreed to do it." I ask whether they think people will want to talk to me. All present reply that they think so: people will be glad to get it off their chests, maybe it will help them.

A couple of days later I go by "Alex's" house with some beer. After we chat for a while, I casually mention yet another friend who has said, "They came to me too."

Field notes, June 2010
He starts to speak: "I want to say something to you." I think, Here it comes, and I choke up, thinking he's about to admit it. Then he talks about a time when his mother needed medical help not available in Romania; he would do anything to get a visa. The securist told him he would get it if he agreed to collaborate with them. "I refused categorically," though he did promise to let the officer know if he encountered any "hostile manifestations" in his circle. When he was next asked, he hadn't. But they kept at him. They were especially interested in one of his colleagues, and he finally agreed: made one report, and felt absolutely terrible. "I was horrified at myself." He decided never to do it again and swears he never reported on me.
I say, "This is interesting, because I thought I saw your handwriting in my file—I thought maybe this was some fallout from the jokes in my book." He replies, "I swear

it wasn't me, and I'll give you a handwriting sample if you want." I decline, feeling the brinkmanship is too unpleasant. He goes on to say that one of my friends, *Felicia, was often saying I took the Hungarian position on things; he continues with other criticisms of her. This deflecting of blame onto others was something that had bothered me in his notes, too.

(Were people afraid of the Secu?) "TERRIBLY afraid. I would get a tight stomach, nausea, when they addressed me."

We then go to a restaurant for dinner, and among other things the subject of homosexuality comes up—Romania's candidacy for the EU had made this a burning issue and aroused tremendous opposition to decriminalizing it, as the EU required. I ask if Romanians have become more tolerant on this score. He says, "Let me tell you that I too have homosexual tendencies but didn't act on them, for the most part." I am so taken aback by this that I don't hear the last part well. He continues, "Even now, Romanians are not accepting of it; society rejects you. It's too complicated. Only a few people are more or less out, like [famous theatre director] Liviu Ciulei." I tell him it's too bad, since I myself have a happy household, and I ask why he's telling me this, after all this time, saying I feel honored. "I always planned to, in the spirit of honesty." Do his friends know? No.

Later, as we leave, he asks me, "Nonetheless, if I'd said to you that from time to time I have to give reports, what would you have thought?" I reply, "I always assumed people did. I would have appreciated the gesture, but at the time I knew people would get into trouble for telling me that." He agrees.

This startling conversation left me with even greater certainty that he had informed but couldn't bring himself to say so, and that his revelation was his way of telling me why he had to do it. He must have gotten caught in some compromising sexual situation and could not refuse the Secus' recruitment, lest he be prosecuted and outed to his family, colleagues, and friends—in a gay-bashing context even worse than the United States in the 1950s. Inconceivable: it would have destroyed him, as well as his family. It is easy to imagine that his horror of this would make him inform.

Later, I began to wonder whether even this story could be believed. He seemed determined to avoid responsibility for his actions, and given what he knew about me, he had the basis for a compelling story. In my field index I found something I had forgotten: an entry from a day in 1984 in which he had told me that he was very distressed because he had been called to the Securitate and asked to tell them whom I see and what I read. He said this had never happened before and he's so upset that he wants to leave Romania.

Up to then, no one else had told me of a Securitate approach, and this is a note in his favor, on which I had not followed up at the time. For now, I decide to accept his story, which enables me to understand something of the forces that might have propelled him into informing and thus to continue our friendship, even without his overt "confession." I only wished that his notes had been . . . nicer, not opening my sexual proclivities to the Securitate's gaze (he was the only one who did) and not constantly implicating my other friends, exposing them to surveillance and possible reprisals.

"Silviu"

Informer's note, 19.11.1979. When she was here the last time she went twice into areas prohibited to foreigners. Likewise, in this period she was interested in data from before World War I, in particular the Hungarian names of people.

From the account of Professor Pop from Bucharest it results that he saw her publications in the U.S. and they do not denature the realities of our country.

N.O: He was given the task of finding out . . . whether she has carried on nationalist irredentist activity [i.e., Hungarian agitation]; whether beneath the same mask of innocence she again penetrates into areas prohibited to foreigners; what is the aim of her creating so many contacts.

One of my very favorite people from my years in Romania was a middle-aged man whom I will call "Silviu"; he lived in Deva, and I had met him through my connections in Vlaicu. A warm, soft-spoken fellow, he became the person I went to first if I had any problems or needed advice. He appeared to have become very fond of me during my first research trip, and I had certainly grown very fond of him. I loved the feeling of calm centeredness that he projected. Sometimes he hinted that he felt a special kind of communion with me—telling me if I showed up unannounced that he had had a premonition I would come. True, he did intimate to me several times during those fifteen years that he was being harassed by the powers, but he implied that he was holding firm.

Therefore, I was quite unprepared for what I found in my file. For example, along with the previous note appeared the following informer reports, with Secus' underlining:

(22.11.1979). I saw her by chance in Deva in a car that she told me belongs to the Catholic or reformed bishopric of Arad. . . . It is interesting that speaking of the beauty of some European cities she observed that Budapest is a lovely city, which she saw in a visit before she came to Romania.

In the trips she took in the past, both inside and outside the county, she told me that she visited Cugir and Ilia even though there were signs indicating she should not enter. She said that she went to Cugir out of curiosity and to Ilia to a friend who is a teacher.

(18.12.1979) In the discussions I had with Werdery Katerine, I learned that she bought a car worth $4700 but had great luck with the owner of the firm, who is a Hungarian and gave it to her for $4000. . . . Another significant fact from her life is the meeting she had in New York with a history professor of Hungarian origin. She confessed that she liked him very much. . . .

N.O.: The present material is the result of tasks assigned and brings new elements of interest concerning the situation of WERDERY KATERINE especially along the lines of her relations with Hungarian emigrants. As follow-up the source was instructed to find possibilities to spend as much time as possible in her entourage.

Hunedoara County Inspectorate   TOP SECRET
15.07.1982

NOTE REPORT concerning the American citizen Werdery Katherine

On 24.07.82 I contacted the said "Silviu" in her entourage, who told me the following:
. . . She regrets that she does not know Hungarian because she had great difficulty reading some archival documents given her in Cluj-Napoca. Therefore she has decided to learn Hungarian. (Source has the impression that she knows Hungarian but pretends that she doesn't, so as to mislead.) Every time she comes here she travels through Hungary. . . .

                                                    Lt. Col. "Moldovan"

In these notes it is clear that "Silviu" has been given the job of cementing my newly emerging identity as a Hungarian, but he is also to confirm my CIA status.

(15.01.80) Having had the possibility of eating several meals with Verdery Katheryne . . . I have formed certain opinions about her activity. I remain of the view that her material situation is not especially good, but that she wishes to improve herself from both material and social points of view, being disposed to use any means to that end.

In this sense I have the opinion but not certainty that she has ties to the Pentagon or CIA. . . . Looking through a book of ours, she showed me a photo of a high functionary from the Pentagon whom she knows, the one who wrote about the horrors of the Vietnam war [I had met Daniel Ellsberg at a conference]. . . .

From the way she behaves, it appears she is only interested in data for her book, but from the information she receives, she can at any moment serve the U.S. authorities or other persons with data that are not favorable to us. . . .

It is quite possible that her first two trips to Romania might simply be preparation for the real work she plans to do.

"Silviu" cooperated with the Securitate in other respects as well, helping to remove me from Vlaicu so my field notes could be copied. With the assistance of my landlord, officers would enter my room, then locate and copy my notes while "Silviu" drove me around Orăştie and Deva under the Securitate's watchful eye.

Of all the informer's reports in my file, these enraged and distressed me the most—even more than "Beniamin's," which were largely accurate, whereas these incorporated bald-faced lies. The underlining indicates what the officers were excited to find, and it was coming from someone with impeccable credentials as a person of integrity and good judgment. He presents me as a liar and believes all the research I'm doing is simply a cover for something else. He repeats the falsehood that I had gone to Cugir and Ilia (where there were military installations) "out of curiosity," having confused those with my ill-fated trip through Topliţa in September 1974. He insinuates my Hungarian identity repeatedly, as well as noting my preoccupation with the Hungarian nobles in the area before World War I. Here is the Securitate nightmare come true: that I am an agent of the Hungarian diaspora who will denigrate Romania and tarnish its image in the world. Moreover, he states outright that he suspects me of being an intelligence agent and comes up with justifications for his view. His final report in 1980 (as I read it) sees me having prepared for the intelligence coup I am now ready to carry out. He then assists the officers in conducting a search of my room.

I first read these—hastily—in June 2008 and felt very hurt, but I did not have time to sit and read them closely; I simply came away with the sense that these were truly damning informer's reports from a man I had loved. I was on my way to Deva to see him with the thought of discussing these reports with him when I learned that he had suffered a heart attack (and indeed he died soon thereafter). A conversation with him about his reports would be difficult; I would have to make my peace with him in the absence of that.

Field notes, 7 June 08, ca. 4:30 P.M.
I phone his house, his wife is sobbing. He's doing much worse, mostly sleeps. She's upset that I didn't come sooner. When I hang up I start to cry; general feeling of desolation. Yesterday I lay down for a nap: huge buzz in my head. It had to be that loud to drown out my feelings of terrible loss. Image of a large howling mouth and an echo that I fear will never stop if I let it start. Then, "Silviu, how COULD you?!! How COULD you?" Crying, fighting against crying, against feeling of betrayal. "Can't say that; he must have had his reasons." But that's no reason for me not to feel betrayed.

He's in bed in another room. In the kitchen where his wife receives me she talks about all the accomplishments of her children and grandchildren, how bad she's feeling because she's so helpless. She takes me in to him, then returns to her cooking. I look down at his wasted shape. No reckoning possible here.

"We might not see one another again," I say. He puts his hands to his eyes, cries a little. He hasn't been able to speak for days.

"I won't forget you, and I loved you very much." He whispers, "Me too."

"I know you've had problems on my account. I'm very sorry for it." He makes a dismissive gesture, whispers, "That's over."

"Do you have anything to say to me?" He tries to say something but I can't catch it—too short, and inaudible. He looks away; has been holding my hand, brings his other hand up to touch my arm. I kiss him on the forehead, say something like, "May it go easily for you." He nods. I head for the door, turn, blow him a kiss, he does the same.

I sob on his wife's shoulder and then leave, crying.

I had asked her at an earlier time whether "Silviu" had ever been asked to inform on me. She had said no, but then remembered one time when an officer came to ask him to do just that. She paraphrased his angry response: "You pig! You ask me to do this kind of thing? You're paid for it, not I. Do I look like that kind of person?!" The officer went away and didn't come back, she said, continuing with how much she disliked him. But she added that "Silviu" was always convinced he was being followed, and I know he was also giving reports, despite her denial.

Not long after "Silviu's" death I talk with his son *Mihai, not letting on that I'd read my file—I say I'm about to, and I expect some surprises. He replies evenly, "I wouldn't be surprised if my dad is in there. He was a very fearful man. He'd give in if he thought it necessary. His past was full of reasons to be afraid. He had many qualities, but courage was not one of them." In another conversation three years later, Mihai repeated this thought, adding, "He presented himself as a very garrulous, hail-fellow-well-met type of guy, but he was very vulnerable. Psychologically speaking he was not a strong man." He then went on about the aspects of "Silviu's" family history that had put him at risk politically: interrogations concerning relatives; "unhealthy social origins"; treachery by his friends; and so on. We also talked about the perils of his love of drink, which opened him to the approach of a certain heavy-drinking securist who would liquor him up. Drink would encourage him to seek attention, tell stories and jokes, exaggerate things, embroider beyond them. Because he tended to fear people in authority, maybe to ingratiate himself with the officer he would then say things that he wouldn't have said otherwise. Mihai concluded, "He did it from weakness, not from malice."

I would add that the officer quite possibly provided or even dictated some or all of "Silviu's" reports for him to sign, rather than the other way around. This was common enough, and I know from another informer used by this same officer that he had proceeded in a similar way in that informer's case. Among those who knew this officer from their work in the county, he had the reputation of being nasty and a bully. (He was certainly insistent: as much as six years after the change of regime, he was still coming to Vlaicu and asking people what I was up to—only this time, they told me about it.)

With these thoughts I struggle to bring "Silviu" back, by divesting him of the ugly and damaging things he wrote and attributing them instead to his officer. But this resolution is precarious: I am subject to revisiting it for years thereafter. How could he have presented himself to me so affectionately and then written these calumnious smears? How should I understand my relations with him? Was he entirely put up to it, or was this the price he had to pay in order to express his affection? How had I so misjudged him, not recognizing his psychological frailty, which might have put me on the alert? So many unanswered questions.

On Friendship and Betrayal

This and my earlier examples would seem to constitute betrayals of my relationships with various friends, who either were already working for the Securitate when they met me or agreed to do so thereafter. Certainly upon reading their reports I felt betrayed, as is evident from my image of the howling mouth and my asking "How COULD you?" Reading my file had many such moments, though most of them were not as extreme as with "Silviu," because my feelings of trust in him were especially great, and I thought they were reciprocal. Because other people saw him as a person of unusual uprightness, I had convinced myself he was, and that would mean he wouldn't make outrageous claims to the Securitate about me—the most damaging claims of anyone who informed.

But were my expectations appropriate? Was our affectionate relationship sufficient for me to think of this as a betrayal? In her book *Betrayals*, Italian sociologist Gabriella Turnaturi writes that one can speak of betrayal only in relationships marked by prior expectations of loyalty, based on previously established trust; otherwise there is no betrayal.[7] Her emphasis on relationships, rather than specific individuals, helps me to place the relation between me and an informer in the context of all that person's other relationships, rather than focusing on the informer and me as two individuals, one betraying the other.

Although it is possible to have betrayal in the abstract, I think it requires that one or both parts perceive it as such. Therefore, if I discern from my friend's behavior—his reports in my file—that he has abandoned our relationship, I can define it either as a betrayal or as his having been overwhelmed by a greater exigency to which I was insignificant. In other words, the trick for me is to refuse to define the apparent abandonment as a betrayal. For that to happen, I must drop my very American tendency to think largely in terms of autonomous individuals—a cultural reflex so deep that even anthropologists, supposedly trained to question their premises, often exhibit it. My relations with various Romanians who arguably "broke my trust" have to be placed in the context of the larger set of relationships in which they are embedded, which these people may be trying to shelter when they agree to inform on me. For me to see their abandonment as betrayal would be to insist that I be more important to them than those others. To put the problem in this way is to diminish the force of "betrayal," for clearly it is absurd for me to imagine that I will be more important to my friends than their own families, friends, and ongoing lives—relations having much greater longevity for them than does ours, and which their reports on me protect.

Here, the difference in the circumstances—not to mention the cultural under-standings—of anthropologists and their local friends is crucial to thinking about whether our informers betrayed us. I developed a number of close friendships in the field, investing perhaps an inordinate number of them with strong feeling. In response, many people I met seemed positively drawn to me, in part because I represented "America" and freedom, and surely because I was a rarity. In addition, I worked hard to be appealing company. (Even the Secus noted this, observing that I was dangerous because I was good at form-ing connections.) I could be amusing and interesting, could offer people an impartial ear for things they might not have wanted to discuss with their kin or other villagers; I could tell them fascinating tidbits about "America" and answer their questions about drug use, crime, or kinky sex, thus enlivening their days. Sometimes I could even be a conduit to scarce goods. But their definitions of friendship and trust differed from mine—and this even before "friend" in the United States became completely debased by social media. Romanians often commented to me that Americans have too shallow an un-derstanding of friendship: a couple of conversations, a sense of interpersonal charisma, and—hey presto!—a new friend. Not so in Romania or other East-ern European countries of those times.

There are several reasons for these discrepancies in thinking about friend-ship. First, among Romanians, much more of the work of organizing inti-macy comes from kinship relations that begin at birth, and after that from native place, school, occupational, or workplace ties likely to be of long duration. Second, friendship as an alternative basis for social connection develops over a lengthy period, often within the framework of these other ties. Loyalties build up gradually and often lag behind the initial feeling of positive attraction between two people. It takes years—especially in the con-ditions of surveillance under socialism—of testing another's trustworthi-ness in tiny increments before that person can truly be called a "friend." My stays in Romania were too brief for that testing, but my actions nonetheless placed me on the terrain of genuine trust and possible betrayal. And once tested, a person might as easily be assimilated into the category of kin, rather than friend. For me, Meri became a beloved friend, but her way of expressing it after a number of years was to say that I'm like a daughter to her.

Third, friendships between Romanians and outsiders like me contained both obstacles and opportunities different from people's other relations. Al-though I could have a sense of them in the context of their lives, they could not possibly have that with me; hence, our understandings of one another, based on interpersonal meanings in context, could not be reciprocal. But precisely because I as an outsider was not bound by their contexts, people often told me things they would not have told another Romanian, enhancing our sense of a strong connection, though not necessarily resting it on trust. For Americans who take warm and hospitable behavior as evidence of friendship, it is easy to feel rather quickly that one "has a lot of friends" there, because so many Romanians have a wonderful capacity for making an intense connection that feels to us like friendship—a connection that Americans would expect to support relations of trust. But to expect trust from these relations too fast is to risk disappointment, not because the people are untrustworthy but because the relationship may be still too young and the social world around it too perilous. Their history as Romanians has ravaged the sense of predictability that underlies trust, a precious and fragile relationship. The Securitate aimed at precisely that, assaulting trust in the most deliberate manner (for instance, in a document from 1985 they write, "Our organs must take special measures to interrupt her trust relations").

In fact, the possibilities for trust kept shifting throughout my work, affecting the prospects for betrayal. In the 1970s repression was less manifest than in the 1980s, when the pressures on people to inform became much greater and the likelihood of trustworthiness diminished. At that point, submerged betrayals may have subtly affected relations among friends and kin, as changing political circumstances threw people back into a narrower circle of those who had passed the test of loyalty. Like all ethnographers, I sought to create trust and predictability for my associates, to learn roles intelligible to them that enabled me to be assimilated into their system of relationships. But during the 1980s, the growing hysteria of the Ceaușescu regime changed the terrain of relating for all of us, subjecting earlier-settled trust to new trials.

My friendship with the Biermans, for instance, which had deepened from 1974 into the next decade, was profoundly tested when, in 1986, two Securitate officers came to their weekend house in the country, put Ralf in their car, and drove off, leaving Ana to wait in rising panic for several hours. They took him to a field away from other houses—the sort of place, he said when telling me about it, where you could imagine they would shoot you—and told him that I was about to be arrested for extreme treachery (înalta trădare), and if he refused to inform on me, then he would be arrested as an accomplice. (He refused, and they took him home.) I doubt that these friends' trust in me would have been subjected to such an ordeal a few years before.

Where do these ruminations leave me concerning the betrayals with which I began? My reaction to learning, in 2008, that someone had reported on me depended to some degree on how close I felt to them, how hurtful I felt the reports to be, and whether I could imagine why they did it. The reports of "Silviu" were exceedingly hurtful: they took precisely the information that would be most damning to me in the eyes of the Securitate and wove it into an indictment. Those of "Groza" and "Marcu" played up the negative aspects of my activities and implicated my friends, while other reports such as those of "Iacob" were fairly benign, giving away little while appearing to be cooperative. I strive to remember that I could not be the most important relationship in their lives during those often-terrible years and to accept that something significant must have made them abandon our relationship, if only in secret.

This means that I do not share the vituperation that many in Romania's public space have heaped on "informers," demanding that they be unmasked and seeking revenge. I can afford this position, of course, but for Romanians who were betrayed, these often *were* their most important relations. Because the stakes are completely different for them and for me, I fully understand people's condemnation of those who reported on them. But my goals are different. Even though I am stuck, like others, with the work of having to reconsider past relationships that my file reveals in a changed light, I hope instead to comprehend—with those who will speak to me—the forces that led them into reporting. That is, I place my anthropologist self above my more personal self, whereas most Romanians do not have that choice.

Although it can be important from an ethical point of view to determine guilt and responsibility, I would rather ask what these cases teach us about surveillance and about why people informed—even though my sample is small and very biased. Given the unreliability of the files, we can't really know what informers did. I prefer to follow the lead of Romanian poetess Ana Blandiana, who writes,

> I am convinced that more powerful than the horror [of discovering one's informers] would be sympathy for those who were obligated, blackmailed, humiliated, spiritually deformed, pushed in one way or another to do all this: I would recall . . . that they had children, that they needed an apartment, that one had a sick wife and another had been excluded from doctoral studies—so very many excuses and explanations that together formed the poisonous and slippery slime in which they lived, and that said less about their souls than about the mechanism to which they had fallen prey.[8]

Refusing to Inform

In 1998 Romanian writer Nicolae Corbeanu, who had fled Romania for Germany in 1973, published his memoir *Recollections of a Coward*, in which he wrote of the time he had spent as a Securitate informer and its ongoing reverberations decades later. For years after he left, he asked himself why he did not refuse when the officer approached him, and one of his answers was, "If anyone had told me of even a single case of someone who refused to become a snitch without ending up in jail or worse, I think my attitude would have been different."[9] Today this is a very common response to questions about why people did not refuse to inform. Indeed, it has become a justification for informers to refuse responsibility for their past actions.

From 2008 to 2016, I found it easy enough to learn, even without asking directly, ways in which people could refuse to sign an informer's agreement; finding people who would talk about why they *did* sign one was far more difficult. My interlocutors would readily volunteer their stories of how they had avoided becoming informers. Here are some examples; the first is from a peasant woman, the second and third from academic colleagues, and the last from writer Herta Müller. I offer them to show some of the tactics officers reportedly used and the readiness with which such stories are volunteered. Although it is not possible to assess their truth value, I have found all of these people credible on other matters.

Field notes, June 2013

My Geoagiu landlady tells me again about when she was called to the People's Council by the Securitate after the authorities had placed me in her house in 1984. The officer began by chastising her for taking me in and threatened to throw her son out of his factory job, unless she agreed to inform. She responded in her forceful way: "I never asked for her, I didn't want her in the first place, and I don't want her now! I was forced to take her! She's the last thing I need, with my sick husband. The vice-mayor said they wanted a family that got along together so she would feel at home. Take her somewhere else! If you throw my son out of his job, next thing I'll throw all her clothes out in the street and that will be the end of it!" The officer admonished her, "DON'T do that!" She tells me the vice-mayor had to get her out of this pickle, because the securişti were pretty upset with her. But they left her alone after that.

I ask how she felt when this happened. "At first I was afraid, but when he started bullying me, I found my courage and wasn't afraid anymore."

In the following story, the importance of having a parent who successfully refused is crucial. I heard similar stories from a couple of others.

Field notes, October 2010

I ask Koni if he'd ever been asked to inform. He was, but had told them no, using the formula his father had suggested to him. His father had spent time in prison, and after he got out they'd asked him to collaborate. But he'd told them, "I spent two years in jail because someone reported on me, and I'm not doing that to anyone else." Later, he told this to his children: "Here's what I said to them when they tried to recruit me, and nothing bad happened to me because I refused. So if they ask you to inform, say the same." Koni followed his father's advice, and nothing happened to him, either.

The next respondent refuses to be afraid.

Oct. 2011

Zoli begins reminiscing about the 1960s. He was afraid of the Secu then; kids in his classes were being hauled off for telling jokes. But by the 1980s, he was doing everything openly. They asked him to collaborate, and he replied: "You guys know I did my degree in philosophy, I know my Marxism-Leninism, I know my rights and obligations as a citizen of Romania, and I know I'm supposed to report any problems I see to the Party, not to you." They offered to get a job for his wife, who needed one: he said, Not interested. They didn't come back.

Finally, here is Herta Müller's brief account from her Nobel Prize acceptance speech, of how she refused to become an informer, thereby losing her job. The officer had been browbeating her into writing her agreement to inform.

Without sitting down, I wrote what he dictated—my name, date of birth and address. Next, that I would tell no one, no matter how close a friend or relative, that I . . . and then came the terrible word: *colaborez*—I am collaborating. At that point I stopped writing. . . . I said: *N-am caracterul*—I don't *have the character for this.* I said it to the street outside. The word CHARACTER made the Securitate man hysterical. He tore up the sheet of paper and threw the pieces onto the floor. Then he probably realized he would have to show his boss that he had tried to recruit me, because he bent over, picked up the scraps and tossed them into his briefcase. The next day the tug of war began. They wanted me out of the factory.[10]

> > >

"If anyone had told me of even a single case . . . my attitude would have been different." It seems it was indeed possible to refuse—and some people *did* know of a single case. Forthrightness, lack of fear, craftiness: these are among the ways people could stay out of the Securitate's informer network and avoid the creation of a doppelganger, even though (as with Herta Müller) it might indeed cost them their job or bring other difficulties down on them. Other examples of refusals appear in Mihai Albu's book *The Informer*,[11] which also tells us that in every recruitment plan drawn up by Secu officers, there was an escape hatch in case the recruitment was not going well. Thus, although the people approached might not know they could refuse, the officers certainly did. But it seems that on the whole, they managed to convince most people that refusing was not possible. People could not always find escape routes; they assessed their options and the costs of refusing, and they imagined that they could comply in a way that would not be too harmful.

With their intensive psychological training, officers also had a flair for detecting people who were fearful and were thus especially vulnerable to recruitment. One such person was my dear friend Mariana, introduced in chapter 2.

Mariana

> He had given up [reported on] neighbors who had wished him a happy birthday every year of his life. And still he believed himself the victim as much as the perpetrator of his crimes.
>
> —Informer in Anthony Marra's *A Constellation of Vital Phenomena*

The informer was used in the informative pursual of the American researcher "VERA" about whom she furnished informative material of operative interest. She manifested conscientiousness in fulfilling her tasks, punctuality at meetings, and care in preserving confidentiality. In the future she will be used again for informative pursual of the American researcher "VERA." Given that her meetings with "VERA" take place at the informer's home, by the time of "VERA's" arrival in the country measures will be taken to introduce T.O. means at the informer's residence.

Like "Beniamin," Mariana agreed to discuss her informing with me on the condition that she not be identifiable; I have left out important details of her life and invented a few others. Our developing closeness during 1984–85 had not escaped the Securitate's notice. As I learned from her informer file, they baptized her "Elisabeta," following careful study and a grueling six- to seven-hour recruitment that spring.

When I returned to Romania in 1987 for a month, I went to see her and, to my dismay, found her strangely distant. We managed a visit or two but she was very stiff and wouldn't say why. Though I felt baffled and hurt, this was not sufficient to drive me away for good as she seemed to want. Then, when I went to Romania again the following year for three months, I got a message from her asking me to visit. She'd changed her mind and now wanted to spend time together. Eventually, after two months of frequent visits, she told me what had happened the previous year. From shortly after our friendship began, she had been asked to file informer's reports on me and had done so. She told me how terrible it made her feel, describing it as "devastating"; how after every visit of mine she would wait in dread for her officer's call to set up a meeting; how she would lie awake all night with stomach pains when she had an appointment with him the next day. She hated it so much that she concluded not even the pleasure of our friendship was worth this anxiety. Therefore, she had decided to cut me off the next time I came, and she did.

This confession overwhelmed me and cemented our relationship. We did not go into detail then about how she had been recruited or what she had said; that would come only later, after I read my file. It contained a number of reports from her, some lengthy. I was also able to read her informer file, including the report of the officer who recruited and then managed her, officer Ţinca. According to him, she had submitted over twenty informer's notes; five of them are preserved there, and in mine are another seven, all of them fairly innocuous. Of the seventy or so people who informed on me, only she and "Alex" told me *before* the communist regime fell that they had been asked to report, and only she confirmed that she had actually done so. In consequence, I have chosen to remove the stigmatizing quotation marks from the name I have given her.

Once I had read through my file, we got together with the understanding that her experience with the Securitate would be our main subject. She told me a lot about how she was recruited, her state of mind, and her feelings after the fact. For me these conversations were riveting. They showed at close range the effects on self-concept and identity of being drawn into the Securitate's orbit and of feeling compelled to keep that relationship secret.

Field notes, 9 June 2010

After lengthy small talk and catching up, I finally ask if we can talk about "the event." Can I take notes, or tape record; which would she prefer? She says taping makes her freeze; better take notes, adding that she's giving me a great gift with these confessions.

Her recruitment had happened soon after I began spending time with her. She was going home one day around 3 P.M. when a rather distinguished man addressed her: "We must have a discussion." He'd already been in her apartment and found her aunt there, so he'd waited outside. Now he says, "Let's go up, leave your bags, and tell your aunt you're coming with me." Her aunt asked when she's coming back, but she didn't know. Getting into his waiting car, they drove to the Securitate building near the train station, and then she knew what this was about; until then she hadn't been sure. People were always trying to avoid this building, and now she's going in!

They were joined by another man—she can still see them both in her mind (I can tell her now who they were: officers Vulcan and Ţinca). They were very ceremonious, polite. "We have to establish some coordinates. You have traumatic events in your past, your grandfather.[12] . . . Our Securitate now is different, but we still have to guard our country. You have a connection with a person from the U.S. We're not asking for much, just a few notes. We'll have to see each other from time to time." They asked her about my research, which strikes them as justifying their suspicions that I have "other tasks." So just in case, it's best that they know what I'm up to, and she'll help them.

Their discussion lasted seven hours, until 10:00 P.M. Before leaving, they ordered her not to tell anyone anything that had happened. I ask how they had done that: "through tone, context, firmness, atmosphere," suggesting that if she revealed it, something very grave would happen to her. "It was less what they said than the context: extraverbal communication, and my own nature, which they knew: fearful. They had said it right at the start: 'Let's be clear from the outset that this system of Securitate has nothing in common with the 1950's [when her beloved grandfather had been arrested and shot]; you don't have to be afraid. Fear is pointless, the relations are completely different. This new Securitate has a different style, different consequences. You would be doing something important for your country.'" But of course she continued to be terrified, and they knew it. Their talking about it had made it worse.

She has no idea what took them seven hours—some of the conversation was quite ordinary, things about her work. She was very stressed, kept drinking water; they kept telling her to relax. No, they weren't aggressive; made small talk, little politesses—"and this disturbed me most of all! I felt they were enveloping me in a method I couldn't see. I kept thinking, 'I have to manage, to outsmart them.'" They made no threats, though she began to worry about keeping her job because they kept asking about specific ideas she had promoted in her sociological research, saying they'd heard those were passé—"so they called my practice of my profession into question, very subtly. But I couldn't refuse them! Things were going on in my job right then, and if I refused, I might lose it. I had already lost one career to this system for being the grandchild of a political prisoner; I couldn't lose another. So I decided I would do it and I would simply have to be smarter than they. They're smart, but I'd have to outsmart them somehow." After the recruitment meeting, she was distraught for several days, insomniac, depressed. "I couldn't talk to anyone. Whenever I would think about it, I would freeze, then start to shake. I had awful nightmares."

Even when I wasn't in Romania they would be calling her at home, setting up meetings, at which the officer would tell her to talk to him about me. They kept after her about my name—is it Hungarian?—were always trying to get her to say I'm doing things I'm not supposed to, and continually asked her whom I meet with and why I always stop the taxi elsewhere, rather than at her building. "I tried like hell to avoid saying anything important," she assures me. They didn't take notes—she thinks they tape recorded it all—but would bring her water, listen, then ask her to write it down. "The worst part was when they would leave me a few minutes to write things down and then make me sign my name. That was the most difficult of all: signing my name." She recalls this as very important, remembering it clearly. "I felt that that moment was the most embarrassing and worrisome seal on the event. I wondered what psychological value there is to whether or not you sign your [actual] name."

Her notes were signed with her name, not her pseudonym.

Interesting in this recital is that in describing her meetings with her officer she consistently uses the pronoun "they," even though when asked, she confirms that except for the recruitment there was always only one. The plural may reflect her feeling overwhelmed by the situation, her conflating all meetings with the first terrible one, or perhaps her thinking in terms of "us" versus "them," as she said later. On another occasion she recalled how she would feel at her meetings with officer Ţinca:

"Every time I left that café I felt dizzy and disgusted. I'd try to repeat to myself how it had gone. I felt nauseous at that glass of juice or whatever it was he gave me. As I would go down the hill I was panicked at the thought that I might be followed. Everything culminated in an episode near my building where I had the feeling that two guys were posted there who didn't leave all evening. The next day I complained to a friend that I was afraid I was developing a persecution complex" (delir de urmărire).

She recalls telling them two things. The first was an incident I had reported to her about my room at the hotel being searched, and I filed a complaint, told people about it. Since they were always asking her for information, she told them about this, think-ing there was nothing new in it. Second, I left my field index at her house once, and she told them about that. "I wanted to give them something to chew on. 'Did you find anything interesting in it?' the officer asked, and I was thrilled to tell him I didn't find anything." She was very excited because she was saying nothing and thought she was protecting me by not telling them! "I thought I was as clean as a tear." But what she had done was to tell them it existed, making it a target of their searches.

"By 1987 I had already decided not to see you any more—I wanted to, but I just couldn't take it. Worst of all was that I couldn't talk to anyone, my friends Adri-ana and Ionel, my brother especially. I couldn't explain it to them, though I think they guessed. Two or three days after the revolution, my first subject of conversation with them was what had happened to me the night I was recruited. I had never told anyone, and it was deeply liberating to tell them now. We had always talked about 'us' and 'them,' and once I had made this confession I thought we could all re-main 'us'—I kept insisting that I was never involved in the reporting, I hadn't become 'them.' I had to make my confession or I couldn't remain friends with them. I was afraid of their disapproval, needed their understanding so there would be nothing separating us; needed their absolution. Like with a priest. I told another friend later, who replied, 'Don't worry, all intellectuals did that!' I had wondered if I was the only one! It's very important to know there were lots of others."

She had earlier refused their request that she report on people besides me, and after the revolution she refused even that. "After December another person appeared—I was at work at the end of the day—and it really shook me up. That time I was very brave and sent him away at once: I told him very firmly never to appear at my office again. Apologizing, he left immediately, and I've never seen him since, even on the street. Even now, though, I feel a shiver down my spine remembering it. The revolution notwithstanding, they still had their program!"

"After the revolution, I thought to myself, 'I was an informer!' It's horrible to me, but this is what people would say. I regret that I've been 'outed' by the CNSAS. Except for the stress of it, I never had the sense that I did something important or interest-ing. I never felt I was an informer, and I have trouble using the word concerning myself. It's very upsetting to know that this word is attached to me now in an official way. The word 'informer' is repugnant to me! Hearing it about myself . . . I refuse it! I don't identify with this label. Maybe this is why I can talk about it so easily."

She had been afraid to discuss this with me—a question of self-image—but she thinks I can understand, maybe even empathize with her situation. The most painful thing was telling me not to seek her out, but she couldn't stand the idea that they would keep calling her. The emotional momentum of this conversation now drives me to remark, "It's pointless to say this, but I'm unspeakably sorry that these things happened to you on my account." I choke up, look away.

After this long day, we have dinner and I eat ravenously, drink too much, go home and eat even more. I'm both exhausted and energized, feel very bad about her suffering but fascinated by these two ideas (on her acquiescing to the rule of silence and on not thinking of herself as an informer).

11 June 2010. We continue where we left off, filling in further details of the recruitment and its effects on our relations: "It complicated my friendship with you terribly, by founding it on a deception. You have no idea how awful it was to have this duplicitous relation with you—wanting to get closer to you and create trust, while constantly knowing that I was duplicitous. It set up a dreadful conflict in me—it changed my relation to myself. That was partly why I decided in 1987 I would give you up. Better that than to have this constant terror about the phone calls from the Securitate. Then I would have to try to outsmart them, my whole day would be destroyed, my nerves. . . . Any phone call made me nervous. If he called in the morning for an afternoon meeting, my day would be ruined; if he called in the evening for the next day, I wouldn't sleep a wink. But at the same time I had a powerful desire to see you, to develop our connection."

At the end of this conversation she has withdrawn and is defensive. She leaves the room, and when she comes back she asks me, "Did you turn off the tape recorder?" Then she adds, "Imagine if after all this time I ask you this question even in jest, what that means!" After a while, she says, "What a lot of harm you caused me!" Then, "I know you didn't do it, but Adriana, discussing all this with me, said, 'How could Katherine not know how much harm she could cause you?' "

After this I had a terrible night's sleep; wide awake, obsessing about it, feeling bad. Who betrayed whom? Whose responsibility was it to prevent this trauma? Such a ridiculous question. It was the Securitate's responsibility, or the Party's, or Churchill's and Roosevelt's at Yalta when they let Stalin keep Romania, but surely not any one individual's, certainly not just mine. Nonetheless, I feel guilty for having brought such a dreadful experience upon someone I cared for.

How's that again? She had informed on me, but I had harmed her? It reminds me of the film *The Autobiography of Nicolae Ceaușescu*, in which perpetrators keep being confused with victims, keep *becoming* victims—a widespread tendency in the way many informers have struggled to account for their actions: by presenting themselves as victims of the system. In fact, I am sympathetic to this position, especially for those whom officers blackmailed, but I would like it to accompany some acknowledgment of remorse. Here she is, rejecting the identity of informer and embracing that of victim, sought by so many in today's Romania. *Everyone* wants to be a victim, so as not to be accused of collaboration; it helps them preserve their relationships. Does this resistance to acknowledging one's actions come partly from writing of oneself in the third person, as "Source"? Maybe in a situation of extreme anxiety, that holding of the self at a remove diminishes the anxiety by splitting it off, helped by that use of the third person. "Source" is not me, it's someone else.

I could answer Mariana's question of why I didn't know how much harm I could cause her by saying I *didn't* know. I was in the first generation of U.S. ethnographers in Romania: we were ignorant. I always assumed people might be asked to report on me, but I had no conception at all of what that would be like. Although I knew I might be followed and my phone conversations overheard, I somehow thought I'd taken care of that by phoning from the street instead of my room and taking taxis to addresses a few blocks from my destination. Besides, so much in Romania was inefficient; I could tell myself that surveillance would be, too. It is comforting to learn from Romanian writers such as Stelian Tănase and Gabriel Liiceanu that reading their files had made them, too, realize how naive they had been in underestimating Securitate surveillance.[13]

Indeed, I could add that not even Mariana herself knew what harm I could do her. An entry in my field notes for 20 October 1984, before her recruitment, reports a comment that she made to me on the subject of surveillance: "The best thing is to carry out your affairs in such a way that there's nothing to hide." When I tell about my friends' wanting me not to phone and so forth, she continues: "You should tell them not to worry. Nothing will happen; you make an affective matter of these things, when at most they should only be a question of strategy. Part of your personality is to take excessive responsibility for things, for other people's decisions, but it's not necessary: you go through all these contortions because you want people to like you." My concluding note: "Either this woman is really naive, or this is a nifty example of how people fail to look out for one another." She would realize soon enough how wrong she had been.

But the most important conclusion from my conversation with Mariana is, as she so perceptively revealed, that the Securitate's methods changed how people related to themselves and altered their relationships with others. Like viruses corrupting a healthy organism, Securitate practices subverted positive sentiment and turned it into guilt, rejection, and avoidance, making me feel *guilty* for having loved my friends and for not protecting them enough. Mariana came close to saying I had harmed her by wanting to spend time with her, that *my affection* had turned her into something she did not want to be—an informer. In my view, we are mistaken to see this merely as her refusing responsibility for her actions (though it is also that): it is the effect of how the Securitate's power worked.

13 June 2010. *Two days later we continue this exhausting exchange. Before we begin, I ask her if our conversations so far have made things worse, better, or neutral. "Neither one nor other," she replies, "but in no case 'better.'" It has created unpleasant inner states, more insomnia—for both of us.*

We enter into the thorny question of who initiated our friendship and continue with how I could not have known what harm I was doing her. Her line is that I came to Romania with a disposition to connect with people, she was one of them, then I left. She was a casualty. I remind her that from the first time she invited me to her house, which she did voluntarily, she had already implicated herself and brought on that harm. She could have avoided it by not inviting me. She accepts this but returns to the various things that made her feel she couldn't refuse to inform, and to the ways she had been brave in her relations with her officer. Although she does not now repeat the most important justification for her informing, I see it as key in my desire to excuse her: that when the two officers escorted her to headquarters and held her for seven hours, it reactivated all the terror and shock she had experienced as a little girl when the securişti had broken into their home and hauled away her grandfather forever. After her recruitment she'd had nightmares about that for weeks, recalling those events, and echoes of the nightmares after meetings with her officer.

At 6 P.M. I phone her from the airport as I leave, say we should have had some sort of absolution for all the confession we had performed, to use her own words. For my part, I offer mine. I couldn't quite hear her response.

Absolution? What possible sense does that make? Who am I to absolve a person trapped in a global conflict not of her making—whose chief "sin" was to reciprocate my affection—of doing what she felt she had to do to survive, even if it meant keeping from me the secret of her double identity? I know she suffered for it. Of course, from the Securitate's point of view, her "sin" was different: she befriended a suspicious foreigner, a spy. But I am not the one to absolve her of that.

In June 2015 I decided on a whim to look up Mariana's Securitate officer, Ovidiu Ţinca, on the Internet. Up came a huge photo of him, wearing academic garb in his role as eminent dean of the Law School of Oradea University. There was also a YouTube video of him giving a lecture on labor contracts. After some deliberation, I wrote Mariana an email asking if she had any interest in seeing these reminders of her past. When she said yes, I sent her the URLs. Confirming that he was indeed the person who had recruited her and to whom she had to report (though he had used a different name), she wrote,

> In the first seconds, opening your email and seeing his face, I had a sensation of disgust so intense that it racked my whole body. So I closed it rapidly. I don't know what I was expecting. Maybe something better, so I could go on reading. I recognized his face at once, like a predatory fish covered with ice. He hasn't changed much in these decades. Seeing him caused me the same shudder of repugnance that I had each time. . . .
>
> You asked if he had behaved in an uncivilized manner, had tried to take advantage of me: no, which in no way diminishes my disgust because I always felt violated anyhow. As you know, the worst thing about it was that afterwards I couldn't talk with anyone about it.
>
> I would recognize his voice whenever he called for a meeting. It was as if a SECRET were happening, which once I agreed to it, no matter how ugly, could not be contested or opposed. As if this fact "was accepted"—what kind of ACCEPTANCE is that!? In any case, I carried the stigma of what I had consented to and had no escape.

She ended with the following sentence: "I think I now see even more clearly the nature of the evil I lived and how much these individuals (in fact, the *system*) contributed to strangling some of my potential . . . a life not fully lived, unfulfilled, anguished, oppressed by fear and by half measures beginning when I was a child." I wonder if she was rendered a victim at so young an age that she was permanently imprisoned in the role.

Victims and Blame

In Eastern Europe, the language of punishment and forgiveness in relations between targets and their informers occupies much space in public discourse. Similar discussions have taken place in Poland, Hungary, Germany, Romania, Slovakia—wherever informer files have been made available. In Hungary, for instance, Hungarian scholar Anikó Szűcs has written about the conversation around Sándor Tar, a writer who, knowing he was about to be outed, sent a letter denouncing himself to the person he had reported on, historian and philosopher Janos Kenedi.[14] Kenedi, in turn, immediately wrote him back and expressed his forgiveness. But this, Szűcs proposes, publicly advanced the position that, like the people they had reported on, informers were victims of the regime; therefore, they cannot and should not be held responsible for their betrayals in the past. Kenedi states outright that the perpetrator was the communist regime itself, not those who tried to make their way through it. Nevertheless, Kenedi later comes to think that he acted too hastily: because his gesture of forgiveness absolves the informer of guilt, the informer no longer need take any responsibility for what he did. The informer, in turn, can object that if responsibility is being sought, secret police officers too should be made to acknowledge theirs.

There is more than enough blame to go around. Part of it involves claims of victimhood: Who were the victims—the people targeted by the Securitate? The informers who reported on them but who can claim also to be victims of the repressive apparatus? Officers themselves, "victimized" by the system they upheld? With everyone a victim, no one is responsible. In the canonical Romanian folk ballad of the ewe-lamb, "Miorița," two shepherds plan to kill a third, jealous at his many sheep and fine dogs. A ewe warns the third of this plan, but instead of fleeing he accepts his fate, asking the ewe to tell his mother that he hasn't died but gotten married to an empress. In her commentary on this, poetess Ana Blandiana observes that Romanians identify with the murdered shepherd, ignoring the fact that his two fellows had killed him. Identifying with the dead shepherd makes the ballad a story about the beautiful death-wedding given to him, whereas perhaps it should instead be seen, she proposes bravely, as "an analysis of our traditional incapacity for solidarity . . . and a recognition of the evil that has inhabited us for millennia."[15] But hers is not a popular view.

One kind of language that appears all over these ruminations concerns, as with Mariana, the question of harm. Informers are apt to say—as are Securitate officers like the ones I spoke with later—"What harm did I do you, after all?" or "My guiding intention was to do no harm." This is a complex question to which I will return. In June 2014, I discuss it over dinner with my friend Andrei. I am telling him about someone's reports that seem to me very mild; I find nothing to object to in them. He disagrees. "Say we meet for coffee and then you're called to report on me," he proposes. "In your report you say, thinking you're just giving unimportant details, that we discussed irrelevant issues, then ordered coffee and put vodka in it. That detail may seem nothing, but then when the Securitate decides to recruit or investigate me, they start by saying, 'Would you like some coffee? We have a little vodka for it, because we know that's how you like it.' This tiny detail is very destabilizing, because immediately I would say to myself, 'If they know this about me, surely they know everything else.' So the minor fact becomes the basis for destabilizing me for investigation or recruitment." Among people who describe being recruited, the pivotal moment is precisely when they feel "everything is known" and are pushed toward capitulating. This is the harm an informer can do, making those they report on vulnerable.

In our conversation, Mariana turned the question on its head, claiming (to my surprise) that I had harmed her rather than the other way around. But an even more astounding refusal of responsibility came from officer Pătrulescu, the *securist* of Gabriel Liiceanu, whom Liiceanu sued for gross breach of privacy and violation of the Romanian constitution, as well as of the international accords Romania had signed. Pătrulescu's lawyer answered that Liiceanu should be ashamed of himself for complaining: he had been allowed to breathe the cool mountain air in the company of famous philosophers, had received a grant to study in Germany (albeit after two years of petitions), had not suffered anything special, and didn't even know he had been under surveillance. The officer had only done his duty.[16]

Romanian ethnographer Smaranda Vultur further explores the subject of informers and their victims:

I have met people followed in the 1970s and '80s who, after seeing their files, did not wish to reveal the names of those who had supplied even numerous reports on them, because they had written nothing bad. When the surveillance did not have grave consequences, in retrospect, the former victims may even have a feeling of gratitude for the person who reported . . . because the informer had tried to protect them. Others feel embarrassed to divulge the informer's name so as not to make their own form of denunciation, in turn. And sometimes people feel guilty for not being vigilant enough, talking too freely, or being insufficiently selective in their friends.[17]

What is striking here, as I have observed earlier, is the lengths to which people who were reported on will go to excuse their informers. It's as if retaining their social connections is more important to them than being self-righteous. This alerts us once more to the truth that, contrary to what most Westerners would think, informing in Romania was *social*. Becoming an informer was not a strictly individual decision dependent on a person's courage or cowardice, though these qualities could affect it. Rather, as I observed in thinking about betrayal, people might feel compelled to inform so as to protect their families and social networks. To accuse someone of cowardice for agreeing to inform presupposes an isolated individual making decisions from conscience who must now take individual responsibility for those decisions. That view makes less sense when not individuals but social connections are the basic unit of society. Perhaps the Securitate's fierce insistence on the oath of silence, even for those who refused to be recruited, was a response to Romanians' strong sociability. Otherwise, they would too readily break open the seal around the Securitate's secret world.

> > >

It is impossible to describe retrospectively the effects of trying to do ethnography in this context. At the time of my research, although I periodically worried that one or another friend might not be reliable, I tried not to think about it (being something of a whiz at suppressing bad feelings). This may in fact have kept me relatively sane. Given what I know now, however, it seems almost unbearable—like a form of torture—never to be sure whom you can trust. Perhaps better said, I would make good connections with people, and then they would be recruited, thereby *becoming* a trust concern that they may not have been at first. A note in my field index for spring 1985 says that Mariana had become irate when I asked her about trust and that I was finding her to be more hostile to me than she had been earlier in the year. Her file shows that her recruitment had occurred not long before. This compromising of trust relations has sobering consequences for ethnography as a method.

The Securitate hoped to discover what was in the soul of their target, but in contrast to confessional practices of earlier times, they did not seek it by interrogating the target to make her confess. Instead, they sought out people to whom the target would open her soul, and then strove to get *those* people to confess. For officers, the most valued kind of recruit was the "depth informer" (*informator de profunzime*), who was carefully placed in the immediate proximity of the target; they had been "recruited from among the target's intimates, having the full possibility of knowing everything they do, as well as their intentions."[18] In my case, Mariana was one such person. On the evidence of her reports in my file, though, their strategy did not pay off. She knew a lot about my actions and intentions, but she did not "confess" them, and in this respect my trust in her was vindicated. Nonetheless, the cost to her was great, justifying her sense of having been harmed. I would insist that it was not I who harmed her but the apparatus of surveillance in which we were both caught up, but who's to say for sure?

Portraits of Officers: Pygmalion Moments

> Whores in their old age join a convent; aging *securişti* begin to repent.
>
> —Romanian maxim

And what about Securitate officers, those forgers of identity and makers of people? If talking with informers has revealed something of the mechanisms of surveillance, what if anything can we learn from Secus themselves? First, we will have to find them.

Searching for Secus

16-5-1989

Pledge

I swear that I will not divulge anything of the secrets of my professional work during my employment with the Ministry of the Interior. If I should break this pledge, may I be subjected to the rigor of the laws of the Socialist Republic of Romania.

"I. Grigorescu"

One day in 2011, while sitting in my office in New York, I find that I urgently need the phone number of someone in Romania. On a whim, I do a computer search for "Romania, telephone numbers." To my surprise, a page called "whitepages. ro" comes up, and I find the number readily. With this unexpected resource in hand, I ask myself what other phone numbers I might want, and I type in the names of some of the *securişti* who appear as case officers in my file. Nothing comes up for many of them, but two of them are there—the one above, whom I will call officer "Grigorescu," from Deva, and officer "Dragomir," from Bucharest: the former with a phone number and a street address but no building or apartment number, the other with no phone but a full address.[19] I file these away with no specific plan but with a feeling of excitement: I have unexpectedly glimpsed something of the secret world that had been created around me.

A year later, in July 2012, I am in Deva and decide to phone officer "Grigorescu." I write down what I plan to say, and with my pulse racing and hands trembling with apprehension, I manage to form the number. A woman answers.

KV: Please excuse me for disturbing you. I'm looking for officer "Grigorescu," or perhaps his son [who bears the same name].

MRS. "GRIGORESCU": Yes, he's here. [He answers.]

KV: Officer "Grigorescu"?

IG: No, I'm retired.

KV [using the most respectful form of address]: My name is Katherine Verdery and I'm an American citizen. You and I are implicated together in my Securitate file, about which I'm writing a book. Since you'll be in it, I'd like very much to speak with you, so the book can present as objective a picture as possible.

IG: I haven't had any . . . I'm not involved with . . . Who did you say you are again?

KV: Katherine Verdery, an American citizen. I did research here in this county in the 1970s.

IG: No, since 1990, since 1989, I've had nothing to do with . . .

KV: I know, you retired in 1989. Please, sir . . .

IG: No. [He hangs up.]

I wipe the sweat off my face, wait for my pulse to subside and the shaking to stop, and look around, suddenly realizing any passerby or anyone in the building I'm standing next to could have overheard me. It takes hours before my nerves calm down.

> > >

This is not the first time I have thought about contacting my Secus. My earliest attempt was sometime around 2005, even before I received my file. Some Romanian friends with experience in low-level administration had been telling me about their good relations with the many senior Securitate officers they had known. When they spoke warmly of two of them from several decades earlier, both now retired in the county capital, I asked if they thought the first one would meet with me. They gave me his phone number and said I should use their name. Although I had not yet seen files from the Securitate archives and had no idea what kinds of things this officer might have signed off on, my friends liked him so I was cool as I rang the number. I gave my name and those of my friends and said I would like to meet him. A very sharp voice replied that he did not wish to meet me or hear from me again. He hung up abruptly.

A couple of years later I asked these same friends if they would mediate my attempt to meet with the second officer they had mentioned, whom they had presented as a longtime close friend. Eventually they told me they had spoken with him and his reply was this: "I worked in an institution for my whole life, and I don't think it's appropriate to talk about it now with an American," adding that he would be very upset if his colleagues found out that he had done so. (A few years later I arrived in town by chance on the day of his funeral, *after* which I learned that his widow had invited me to come! "I've heard so much about her and would love to meet her," she told our common friend.)

Once I received my file, and especially after my first thorough perusal of it in 2010, I became much more interested in finding out what these officers were like, but how? In 2011 a friend in Deva told me of a conversation she had about me with the man who headed the county Securitate in 1989. He said he would like to meet me, but when she tried to set something up, he got cold feet and backed out. The following year she tells me she tried again without success, adding that we'll try yet again the next time I come. As I leave her office, she says, "He lives right near me, by the park," and gives me the building number, F4.

I decide to try by myself. I go to F4 and walk around it, find the entrance in the back, and go up the stairs to the list of apartments, on which his name is barely visible: apartment 5. I stand there for a good while, maybe five minutes, feeling too anxious to proceed. Then I take out a business card and write on it, under my name, "I will leave at once if you prefer." I raise my hand to the buzzer but don't push it, standing there with my finger hovering over it for several more minutes. What will I say to him? "Grigorescu" is one thing; I have a history with him, but this guy? Why do I want to meet him? To ask if he really thought I was a spy? This is pretty silly; I take my hand away from the buzzer. Better to see if my friend can set up a meeting. As I leave, I ask myself, What is it I want from these men? With their special training in disinformation, I can't have any confidence in the answers they would give to my questions; at most, maybe their idioms will be revealing. Basically, I want to *see* them, after all these years of their being invisible as they watch me from the shadows. Just to see what they look like, sound like. If I get to talk with them too, so much the better. I have an image of locking gazes with this man, then handing him my business card.

Why such timid objectives? For one thing, there is my own fear of this organization, whose terrifying reputation I have absorbed not only from hearing about the KGB during my Cold War upbringing and from conversations over the years with Romanian acquaintances, but also from my harrowing read through the documents I consulted for my book on how the Communist Party created collective farms. And then there are all these negative images of me that they have devised in creating my file. They do not think well of me: *of course* I should be frightened! For another, there is the oath taken at the retirement of the officer, shown above, swearing never to divulge the secrets of his work. Because of this, an acquaintance familiar with the organization had doubted that I would find anyone to talk to me: "People swore to keep things secret, they'd be *cursed* for revealing the secrets of the trade!" I will have to tread very lightly.

As I ponder this thought of finding my Secus, I cannot foresee where it will lead: that my seeking them out will rebound into their "recruiting" me; that my quest for revelation will open onto different vistas from the one I imagine; and that I will uncover *securişti* not isolated from the populace by fear but integrated into it by favors.

> > >

In October 2011, I make a brief visit to Cluj. Looking for a phone number in the desk of my friend Felicia, I find the business card of retired officer "V. Blidaru," one of my case officers from 1984–85; the card has his home address and phones. A few days later, I think up a few questions for him, then get into a taxi and give the address. On the way there, I ask myself, How will I begin? "I wonder if you'd speak with me for a few minutes . . ." "The Romanian Securitate has been much maligned, and I'm writing a book about it. I'd like to get a better, more accurate picture; perhaps you can help . . ." "I just wanted to see what you look like, sound like . . ." He'll ask if I have a tape recorder; I do, and it's on.

His building is one of those anonymous gray Stalin-era apartment blocks, quite unprepossessing. Finding his name on the list, I ring the buzzer— several times—but no one answers. I imagine there's a video camera and he's looking out; maybe they never answer the door if they're not expecting anyone. What was I thinking in coming here? Of course he wouldn't just answer a ring! I bet he would be too suspicious (images from Cold War–era spy movies). I think I hoped to get into the building and knock directly on his door, but that's not possible. My taxi is waiting for me, so I get back in and go away. My mouth is dry, my pulse hammering. The next step would be to phone him and see what he says. But I don't.

Two days later I go to visit my colleague "Groza," whom I introduced earlier as one of those who informed on me. I plan to ask him about that, but the conversation takes an unexpected turn.

K: Every important institution had a *securist*, and yours was officer "Blidaru." Do you remember him?

G: Yes! In my first few days as director, guys kept coming into my office saying "I'm in charge for France," "I'm in charge for the U.S.," "I'm in charge for England . . ." So I went to the head of the county Securitate and said to him, "Who *are* all these guys? I've seen them around, but I don't want to have to deal with so many." A couple of days later officer "Blidaru" presented himself and said, "From now on, I cover your entire institution" [not just its relations with one or another country]. He showed me where the microphones were hidden in my office, which was very helpful.

K: What kind of a guy was he?

G: For me, he was an extraordinarily good fellow. He specialized in ▮▮▮ at university, and he has a really nice collection of folk paintings. We knew these people weren't allowed to appear in public, but I exhibited his collection for him.

K: You must have had to report to him about various people.

G: Yes, I talked with him often. [His wife adds, "They're all doing very well now, they all have firms, and they look down on you if you don't have money."]

K: I'd like to talk with him. Do you think he'd agree?

"Groza" picks up the phone; I give him the number. Getting no answer on the cell phone, he calls "Blidaru's" daughter, whose number is in the phone book. He identifies himself, greets her affectionately, and after a few minutes of friendly conversation, asks, "Where's V▮▮?" [So they're on a first-name basis!] "He's at a party watching some football game; he'll be home after 8:00." "Groza" promises to follow up and let me know the result.

I phone the next day. "Groza's" wife tells me, "We called him, and here's exactly what he said: 'Let me think about it.' " (I assume this means, "I have to ask my superiors.") They gave him my phone number, and he'll call if he decides to meet me. He doesn't call. But I think, now he has my phone number. Will they be tracing me, listening to my phone conversations? (Of course they will, and doubtless were, even before I gave him my number.)

One of these nights I have a dream, half-waking. I'm talking with officer "Blidaru," asking him what his life was like as an officer, what was a typical day. Did he have an office he went to, or was he always going around to other people's offices? What about work compartmentalization? How could they all be in one office and still maintain the secrecy of their work? Did they have a "plan" for recruitment, for the frequency and length of reports? As I become conscious of the dream, I realize it's a very interesting conversation and I'm enthusiastic about it. But it's not going to happen.

The next year, in summer 2012, I call my friend Felicia (who knows officer "Blidaru") to ask if she would invite him over for a drink. She agrees. When I get to Cluj, she reports on the conversation she'd had with him, as follows:

F: "Hello, V██, how are you? Do you know who this is?"
V: "Yes, I do. Who is it?"
F: "It's Felicia."
V: "I thought so. How are you?" [They exchange pleasantries.]
F: "V██, I have an invitation for you."
V: "That sounds exciting, but there might be a problem; I'm really busy right now. What is it?"
F: "It's for a coffee or a drink, but it's with a very special person, who's coming to visit. She misses you and wants to see you."
V: "Katherine?"
F: "Yes. We were hoping you could do it sometime this weekend."
V: "I'm really sorry, but I can't. I've got to go to a wedding, and I won't be back until Monday morning."
F: "What a shame. She'll be very disappointed."

Felicia believes he was being sincere—launched into his excuses with no hesitation. So now I don't know whether to keep trying or give up. But I'm taken aback by his having guessed (or actually known?) I'm here; it makes me wonder about Felicia's relation to him concerning me, though she has insisted that she never gave reports. After all, he recognized her by her voice. Yet again those old doubts about whom I can trust. I ask her to tell me about him and learn that he's an outgoing fellow who plays the clarinet; she would occasionally run into him at performances. She talks about him in a light and friendly way and seems to like him.

I discuss officer "Blidaru" with another friend, *Radu, whose wife turns out to know him quite well. Radu proposes I try another officer, who lives in his building and is very affable; he'll ask him.[20] I note that both Radu and Felicia seem to know *securiști* beyond those directly attached to their institutions. So where, I wonder, is secrecy, if regular citizens know these *securiști*?

Ministry of the Interior   WORK SECRET

29-11-1978

REPORT [concerning the proposed promotion of

Maj. "I. Grigorescu"]

The officer has the presence and authority necessary for a leader of a collective, he is critical and exigent with his subordinates when circumstances
require it but knows how to be modest and sociable with those who fulfill their
professional tasks honorably. . . . He is one of the best heads of department,
standing out for his discipline, skill, correctness and understanding. He always
judges things with patience and calm, and this is the quality of a leader for
he will always draw objective conclusions and will find the best operative
solutions. . . . He is a good organizer, with a talent for analysis and synthesis.

The following October I go briefly to Romania and decide to be more aggressive with officer "Grigorescu," who had hung up on me the year before. I
know the man's street address, and it's not a very long street, so I start at one
end and go from one stairwell to another, looking at the list of residents on
each. One stairwell has no names; some don't have them outside, so I have
to wait for someone to emerge from the building and let me in. Except for a
general unease, I do all this in a fairly mechanical way, unaware of particular
feelings, since the task seems so quixotic. After completing the first set of
buildings on the northern side, I cross the street and do the first half of the
southern side of the first block; nothing. On to the second half, and after
about twenty minutes, there he is. Building D, apartment 14. I'm both elated
and suddenly panic-stricken. What do I do now?

A colleague at home had suggested that if I were trying to meet these men,
it might be good to take some flowers or a box of chocolates, as any polite
Romanian visitor might do. That will indicate that I don't intend to make an
ugly scene. So I go to the nearest flower shop and buy a bouquet—not too
fancy, not too common. The selection isn't great, mainly huge bouquets or
single roses, not exactly the best flower for this occasion. I end up with some
golden-beige chrysanthemums, which, when I get them outside, look a bit
wilted. Too late now.

I return to building D, another of those nondescript Stalin-era blocks. I stand looking at the buzzer for a couple of minutes, trying to remember the approach I had imagined during the train ride to Deva. I push the buzzer, pulse racing. It rings several times; just as I'm beginning to feel relieved, a man's voice answers. "I have some flowers for you," I say. He buzzes me in. I walk up one flight, two flights, three flights, at the top of which an apartment door is open, the light behind it silhouetting a tall, powerfully built man with a fringe of hair on a balding head. He has stepped outside the apartment into the hall. His features gradually emerge from the shadow as I approach; his expression strikes me as both suspicious and quizzical. I'm amazed and exhilarated, thinking, "OH MY GOD, *this is actually working!*" I can't believe it. I give him the flowers, my heart pounding, and extend my hand: "Katherine Verdery." He shakes it, continuing with that look. "Didn't you come here before . . . ?" "I telephoned you last summer but you hung up on me. I thought I'd try again."

He's dressed very informally, wearing a mustard-colored jersey and tan trousers; he has a very close-trimmed white mustache that shows his upper lip well and seems not to have much by way of eyebrows. His teeth are in bad shape: he definitely needs dental work. I observe that he's been retired for a while and ask what he does with his time: he grows vegetables for the household. "Well, come in and sit down," he says, not exactly welcoming. I do. He seats me in the entryway by the door and remains standing in the entrance to the kitchen, a rather inhospitable arrangement, and it feeds my anxiety. "So, what is it?" he asks.

Before I went to his apartment, I had dithered about whether I should take a tape recorder or not. I have a very small one that can lie unobserved in my purse or pocket, which I would have to use surreptitiously, since he would surely not give me permission. After all, I tell myself, *they* recorded *my* conversations clandestinely, so why shouldn't I do the same? Then I remind myself that I am not in the same line of work, and in mine, recording without permission is unethical. It's true that in my first attempt with officer "Blidaru" I had taken it, but I had immediately regretted that. So now I left my tape recorder at home. As a result, and because I didn't think it appropriate to take notes as we spoke, I lost a great deal of the conversation and cannot reproduce its order or its exact content. Nor can I use this exchange to trace the evolution of my questions or the sequence of subject positions I took on. I had gone into this adventure somewhat half-cocked; I had a few things I wanted to find out, but I didn't have a precise interview plan, and I didn't much probe his responses. I was more interested in the experience of meeting these men than in the informational content of our talk, which for my purposes was somewhat irrelevant.

I begin by telling him that the law obliges me to say I've read his personnel file at the CNSAS, and I repeat that I'm writing a book about my file. He makes it clear that he doesn't want any publicity from this encounter. I'm very tense and am talking a mile a minute, smiling too much, being as garrulous and animated as possible. Soon he remembers what I did—"Geoagiu, Aurel Vlaicu, some project with ethnography . . ." He's warming up, remembers me well, says I haven't changed much. "So you knew what I looked like?" "Yes, of course. You roomed at Lazăr B.'s. You were a very interesting case." Note that this was forty years ago! After a few minutes, he says, "I don't think I did you any harm. My motto was, Do no harm." I reply, "I don't think so. In fact, reading your file I found you simpatico, which is why I wanted to meet you." He brings a stool out of the kitchen now and sits down on it. As the conversation unfolds, it's clear he's an intelligent man with a superb memory.

I continue with nervous chatter, giving a long account of what I had come to Romania to do back then, how two things prevented me from doing it: I didn't know enough about Romanian ethnography, and I rode my motorbike right into a military base. No wonder they thought I was up to no good. He smiles—in fact, he's smiling frequently and seems to have relaxed. "So my supervisor came and asked in Deva where I should go, and the authorities said 'Geoagiu commune.' But it had none of the characteristics required by my project. As a result, you were perfectly right to report that I wasn't keeping to my research proposal, because I couldn't. [He smiles *very* broadly now.] I noted down everything I learned, and you commented on that too."

I ask what he thought of me. He replies, "Whenever anyone came into the county, we had to try to figure out what they were really here for." Later I ask what "spy" meant to them: "It can mean a number of things: political, economic, social. . . . To decide if someone is a spy, you have to determine if they're collecting information. So you said you were here collecting ethnographic information, but what if that's just a cover for something else? So many of the embassy personnel were agents; we had to find out who else was." "What might I have been collecting?" He says, "Information about people's state of mind" (*starea de spirit*)—a matter of deep concern to the Securitate from its inception, and exactly the sort of thing I often learned from villagers. But eventually he determined that the information I was collecting was not problematic. I observe to him that in many respects we were doing the same thing: I got interested in socialism, would write down whatever I found out and then take all these bits of information home to try to make sense of them; he was doing the same with me and others, trying to put together bits of information to make sense of them. He grins very broadly at this idea. I ask if he liked the work: yes, he did.

"Tell me about my landlord, Moşu: Was he frightened at the meetings at which he had to report on what I was doing?" "Not at all: I'd known him from very early on, at the factory where we both worked before I joined the organization. We were friends." (This puts Moşu's detailed informer notes in a completely new light. I had imagined him quaking with fear when he had to meet the officer, as "Beniamin" and Mariana had, but that's clearly wrong.)

"What made you decide to join?" He grins sheepishly: "I wasn't very serious. I thought, let me join up and get good pay for a few years—I had a friend who did that, was a bit of a rascal, spent three years in the Securitate and got good pay, then they threw him out. I thought, I can do the same. I wasn't very interested in the job itself. But after a bit I got used to it."

For the first half hour or so we are alone, but then the door to the living room opens and his wife comes out in her bathrobe, surprised to see a stranger rather than her daughter-in-law, whose voice apparently resembles mine. She sits with us in the entryway for the remainder of the visit. By this time the tone of our exchanges is very warm; he continues to smile a lot, and I'm killing myself to be likable. At one point he says to his wife, "This lady was very courageous to come here!"

He asks me to bring him up to date on my research after he was moved to a different job and no longer handled my case. I describe all my projects and books, demonstrating my scholarly authority to him. When I talk about my book on land restitution, he asks if I think returning land to the former owners was a good idea; I say no, and he remarks, "Well, then, we seem to be of one mind." I say my politics were always leftist, and breaking up those collectives didn't seem like the way to go. They think the changes haven't been good. His wife adds, "You said you're of leftist sentiments: me too. I think people were doing pretty well, the workers had money and good jobs, their standard of living was going up. Now look what's happening." He agrees. "Did you have leftist sentiments when you signed on to the Secu?" I ask. "Yes. I was a worker, and even though I wasn't a raving communist, I agreed with the basic ideas and joined the Party for that reason. After 1989, many people took their Party cards out into the street and tore them up or burned them, but I didn't: I still have it."

At one point I ask him a question I no longer recall; he hesitates. "Please don't feel you have to answer if you're uncomfortable," I say, thinking of that oath he signed. He replies, slowly, "No, it's just that I haven't talked about my work with anyone since I retired twenty-five years ago. I said to myself, 'OK, that's that,' and put it aside." But he hasn't been reticent about answering the questions I ask, though admittedly I didn't push very far. We return to his hanging up on me last year: he says he didn't remember me then, and if he had he would have treated me less rudely. "I apologize for that, but now we've made up [ne-am împăcat]." I repeat this.

The visit has lasted well over an hour. I have tried a couple of times to go but he's continued talking. Now I say I fear I've overstayed my welcome. He stands up, offers his hand, smiling, and says, "Come back again! Maybe we'll go out somewhere in town." The next day I rang; his wife answered. "Your guest of yesterday. I want to thank you for the visit; it did me good." "I feel bad that I wasn't dressed properly," she responded, "but you'll come again and it will be different." So the invitation has been repeated twice, and I'll follow up next year.

> > >

This meeting casts my soul into chaos for days. I feel terribly confused—how can this be the hated Securitate? What should I think of them now? Are they just a bunch of regular people doing their job, as Hannah Arendt said of Eichmann? Or has he simply pulled the wool over my eyes very craftily by being super-friendly? Is he atypical? Is he a good actor who has convinced me that he's just a decent fellow? I somehow feel I have a special new friend. But this is insane! What can I be thinking?! These people were trained to be good psychologists and to be manipulative and duplicitous in their relations with others. How can I possibly imagine that this was a "genuine" encounter, that he was being forthright with me? Clearly, I want to. This is baffling. I am reminded of Slavenka Drakulić's book *They Would Never Hurt a Fly*, about the men prosecuted in the International Tribunal at The Hague for war crimes in the wars of Yugoslav succession. "The more I have occupied myself with the individual cases of war criminals," she writes, "the less I believe them to be monsters. . . . As the days pass you find the criminals become increasingly human, [and] you wonder how they could have committed such crimes, these waiters and taxi drivers, teachers and peasants. . . . And the more you realize that war criminals might be ordinary people, the more afraid you become."[21] It is more reassuring, she concludes, to think that they are monsters than to imagine them as regular folks.

On my way home I stop at the house of my friend Elena, who was often approached by officers on my account; I tell her about meeting "Grigorescu" and express my confusion. She says, "Officer Homorodean [with whom she had dealt] was like that too, nice, friendly. I never felt fearful when he came around, unlike Colonel Belgiu, who awakened dread in you when you met him. There was something about him that made you afraid." For several nights my sleep is broken, with quasi-dreams full of tension, in which officer "Grigorescu" appears. I'm preoccupied with the meeting for days, but at the same time I'm both sad and relieved. Why sad? Because I've been deprived of an image I've harbored for four decades? Because it calls into serious question my understanding of Romania? I'm not sure. The relief could have several sources: that I managed to meet one of these men and wasn't eaten alive, that I was able to create a positive relationship with him to counteract the sometimes-ugly things in my file, that it led to some sort of peacemaking. . . . But was that genuine? Not likely. Questions and doubts ricochet ceaselessly through my thoughts, with no resolution. The whole encounter has unhinged me.

> > >

In June 2014, I am once again going to Romania and plan to see "Grigorescu," as he had suggested. I send him a note ahead of time, saying when I'll be coming to his town; once there, I ring him up. His wife answers and calls him: "It's that lady from America." His voice on the phone is hesitant, withholding, even suspicious. I think I failed to make enough small talk, going straight to the question: Can we get together, or would he rather leave things as they were last year? He would prefer to leave things as they were. His daughter has been visiting for three days, he says, and he's going off with her tomorrow to the countryside. He ends by saying with a hint of exasperation, "Mrs. Katy, I can't schedule anything." I hang up, feeling upset—I had so many interesting things I'd thought of to discuss with him.

To make this call to him I had left a conversation with my friend *Solana, whose brother-in-law *Pavel was an auxiliary Securitate employee and aware of my efforts to meet them. I now return to the conversation, saying I won't be going to the city after all because the person I hoped to see there can't do it. She replies, "Was this one of your *securiști*? You can't trust anything they say. They lie. They lie and make things up all the time. You can support your-self on their word as on a rotting fence."

For the rest of the day I feel distracted by this failure: I had somehow not thought it would happen, thought we had a connection. What a fool! Am I just as naive now as when I first set foot in Romania? Perhaps our one meet-ing gave him whatever catharsis he may have found useful, perhaps his family was uneasy about further exposure, perhaps indeed his daughter is there and he doesn't want to interrupt his visit with her, perhaps he was reprimanded by the present-day intelligence service. Dreams and wakefulness that night feature him—we're having nice conversations—or else a feeling of distress. The weather the next morning is cold and rainy.

A year later I call to offer him a copy of my book, recently translated into Romanian.

KV: Mr. I.?
IG: Yes.
KV: This is "Folclorista," from America. [He chuckles.] How are you?
IG: [Voice suddenly cool] All right.
KV: I would like to bring you my book about collectivization. It just came out in Romanian. I'm coming to town tomorrow or the day after. . . .
IG: No. I don't want us to have any more contact.

Rotting fence, indeed.

"S. Dragomir"

Case Officer's note on informer's report from
"Alin," 1 September 1988

K. Verdery, agent of [U.S.] information services, is in the attention of Service 3, Cluj-Napoca, the case being processed under the control of our unit.

Measures will be taken for identification and complex verification of "Alin" [my grants contact].

The next discussion between "Alin" and K. Verdery will be verified through special means [that is, he will eavesdrop on his own informer].

S. "Dragomir"

Back to the previous October: following my initial triumph with officer "Grigorescu," I return to Bucharest to work in the archives and to approach another *securist*, officer "Dragomir." Since I have his complete address, I prepare for this meeting differently. I write him a letter in Romanian, which I email to a friend in Bucharest before my arrival there, and ask him to put it in the local mail:

Esteemed Mr. Dragomir,

I don't know if you're the person I'm looking for: the Mr. Dragomir who was a Securitate officer in the 1980s and who appears as a case officer in my CNSAS file (I even have a picture with him, when he met me on the sidewalk once). If this person does not live at this address, please excuse me for disturbing you.

If you are the person I'm looking for, I offer my greetings and an invitation. I will be in Bucharest between October 16–19, and I would like very much to meet with you. The reason is that I'm writing a book based on my file; I would like to present the viewpoint of some of my case officers, so the book can be as close as possible to the truth. You will appear in it in any case, with the photo; it would be great to be able to present your "human face," and not only the propaganda of dissidents from those times.

I realize that you have sworn an oath not to divulge information about your work, and I will respect your scruples if you do not wish to respond to one or another of the points I would like to discuss. They include your general situation (family, education, whether you have relatives who work for the organization); whether you remember me and what opinion you had then about my presence and that of other Americans in Romania; whether you can help me understand some things that appear in my file (e.g., "precursory acts to the beginning of a penal action"); and so on. I do not intend to create a scene; I am simply curious to meet you.

[Instructions for how I will get his answer.]

I very much hope that you will accept my invitation. It would be terrific.

On 17 October 2013, a friend left the letter in his mailbox. I plan to visit his address the next Wednesday, and I don't sleep very well the night before: too apprehensive. On Wednesday afternoon, I buy some flowers and, as if to postpone the meeting as long as possible, I walk the considerable distance to his apartment building; there's no answer, so outside his door I leave the flowers with my business card and phone number. The doorman says he's gone to the countryside.

The next day I'm working in the archive and turn on my phone at lunchtime; shortly thereafter, it rings. A man's voice: "S. Dragomir." "Unbelievable!" I exclaim, without thinking. He thanks me for the flowers, which are very nice. He's not in Bucharest now but will be back the day after tomorrow—his son had come home, found the flowers and my card, and called him up to give him my number. When he gets back, he'll call again to set up a time. "I can't thank you enough for calling me," I say. He responds, "I hope the pleasure will be mutual."

Excited by this phone encounter, I want to tell people about it as if it were a new crush. I'm having conversations in my head about what I'll say with him. Will he be mad that he's already in my book *Secrets and Truths*? What did he mean by the pleasure being "mutual"? Is he afraid I won't be nice? Two days later, he calls, as he'd promised he would. We settle on a meeting place. As I move to end the call, he adds in a somewhat harder tone, "Don't expect too much from this meeting. I don't know if the pleasure will be mutual."

At 3:00 P.M. I arrive at the appointed place and am about to open the taxi door when I feel it open at my elbow. Startled, I look up. There stands a fairly tall, well-built, completely bald man with a full white mustache, holding a bouquet of white chrysanthemums and smiling a lovely smile. I would guess he's about sixty-five to seventy years old, but vigorous. His dark-hazel eyes are warm and intelligent, and he is definitely better-looking than the last time I saw him, when he stepped out of a building and barred my entry into it in 1988. Like officer "Grigorescu," he seems to have bad teeth, a fact well camouflaged by his mustache. We enter the restaurant and order drinks, I don't remember what; maybe a Coke for him, tea for me. As with "Grigorescu," I elected not to turn on the tape recorder in my purse, and he gave no sign of wondering if I had one. (Who knows if *he* did . . .) My notes, excerpted here, are disordered and incomplete.

Did he remember me? No, but *any* foreigner coming here in those days had to be checked to be sure we weren't doing something against Romania's interests. They had to know what we were up to. I ask if he remembers the pseudonym "VERA," but he doesn't. He then observes that clearly I've had a long relation with Romania; moreover, they obviously hadn't put obstacles in my way, since I've done a lot: he'd looked me up on the web. I explain that I'd gotten his address the same way, and then I tell him how I'd gotten my file. As with "Grigorescu," there is an excess of smiling on both sides and (at least on my part) tremendous energy expended, again, in an effort to create an attractive impression. I'm as nervous as a cat.

He is retired, but I did not ask him as of when: although he would probably have been too young for retirement in 1989, I hesitate to probe for what
he had done after that. When I inquire where he was in the countryside this
week, he demurs—just in the provinces. Then I ask where he's from, and
he pauses. "This should be a secret: I'm a Transylvanian." (Why is this a secret? I wonder, startled.) His father was a miner, his younger brother—now
dead—as well. So: good working-class origins, like "Grigorescu." No one
else in his family has worked for the Securitate: "I'm the first and last."

"Why did you join the organization?" He smiles mischievously: "I always
liked the . . . invisible side of it!" "Did you like detective novels as a child?"
The only thing you could get then, he says, were Russian novels about World
War II, with spies and their pursuit. He loved those novels. (Maybe this fascination resembles mine with going "behind the Iron Curtain.") He went to
university to study law and was then recruited, with counterespionage as his
specialty.

I describe the series of suspicions for which I was under surveillance:
first for military spying—I explain how, and he smiles. Then for collecting
"socio-political information," but he doesn't find this compelling. Then
for suspicions about my being Hungarian, because of the y in my name. He
scoffs: he would certainly not have thought that! I don't mention the fourth
form of spying they suspected—consorting with dissidents—for which he
was the case officer. He says again, "We had to be sure you weren't a spy."
"What does that mean?" "Not something about socio-political information:
a spy in the sense of working for the CIA or FBI." So already he departs from
the opinions of the Cluj officers, who saw my gathering socio-political information as a prime spying offense. It seems there are at least two different
culturally appropriate definitions of spying.

I ask him about the informer "Alin" who was responsible for the bulk of
his work with me. He says, " 'Alin' was very refractory and wouldn't always
give me the information I needed." "You worked with informers: Did you
have to recruit them also?" "Of course—that came with the job. Informers
are very important. The CIA relies too much on technology and doesn't get
good intelligence because it doesn't use informers enough. But I never coerced people during recruitment or threatened them. I might spend a long
time with someone and part the best of friends even though they refused to
inform—and many people did." "But," I object, "the image one gets is that
people were terrified of the Securitate." He explains that up until 1964, things
were very different: they used lots of force. But when he started, he was in

the first generation of the new order, which recruited officers with university degrees. "Older guys would boast to us about how they used to do it, by intimidating people. But not our group." Is this plausible? It fits the timing of policy changes.

We discuss several other things having to do with normal practice for handling files, then I ask his help concerning those nine documents in my file: "record of a finding to effect certain precursory documents, with an eye to gathering data necessary for beginning a penal action." I show him my notes and read aloud the first one, which describes with exactitude a series of phone calls I made from a phone booth, though "it was not possible to establish the content of the conversations held," and refers to me as a doctoral candidate in history (by then I had had my PhD in anthropology for ten years: so much for competent information gathering). Officer "Dragomir" looks at the notes with interest, then says, "There were only certain officers empowered to initiate this kind of work; I was one. I would give the order, they would follow it up and write the report"—he says the words as if describing something utterly commonplace. "But presumably you didn't ask for that unless you thought there was something serious going on, right?" He shrugs it off.

Describing his work procedure, he says, "We'd get some information about someone that would make us decide to get more specific. We gathered a lot of information, put it through a sieve, trying to figure out something about the person." "So you were like ethnographers: we too get lots of information and put it through a sieve." "Then we have something in common," he replies. Once they figured out that the person was up to no good, they would declare him or her undesirable. "So why wasn't I thrown out in 1985 when the Cluj division sent that recommendation to Bucharest?" He smiles, seems a bit contemptuous of the officers in Cluj: they could sometimes get a bit hysterical. "An office would write up a report with a recommendation, send it up to Bucharest, and if we decided here that it wasn't warranted we'd send it back, saying no. But you have to remember that the 1980s were a very difficult time." I agree, then ask, "Did you know the end was coming in the late 1980s?" "Yes—in fact, I'll tell you a secret: I learned it from someone in the diplomatic corps, who told me he was always posted in places where there was a change of regime." Though he is telling me secrets, I do not reciprocate. He asks who my other officers were and have I met them; I tell him I've met just one, but I don't wish to say who it was.

By 4:30 the conversation is beginning to flag a bit; time to end it. I ask why he agreed to meet with me, to which he replies with a grin, "Why not?" Then I observe, "I don't understand why you said on the phone not to expect too much from this meeting. It was very important for me." "Who could say how it would go?" he replies. "It was a pleasure for me too." I take my flowers and leave.

Just as with officer "Grigorescu," I realize I have been going overboard to be engaging, leaning forward in my seat in a supplicant posture and smiling so continually that my face is sore, and I now feel—crazily, again—as if I've made a special new friend. I'm assailed by remorse concerning the photo of him in my book *Secrets and Truths*: when I mentioned it, he had expressed strong doubts that it could be he, yet the book identifies him by name. I wish I could take it out. I call my CNSAS colleague Cristina and say I'm feeling sorry about that photo, want to cut it. She laughs; I say, "Stockholm syndrome"? She agrees, adding that after December 1989, officer "Dragomir" actually managed to get himself a certificate as a revolutionary, despite all those surveillance reports he'd signed! If he is "outed" as a *securist*, though, that will be taken away—and she thinks several people have already formally requested that he be "outed." She is charmed by the idea of my going with flowers. I say it was to get me in the door, but she thinks it shows *smerenie*, humility—that I've achieved a certain distance from all this and am not going to make a scene. This will impress them.

What impresses *me*, however, is my excessive emotional reaction. Just as during my earlier fieldwork, I seem to have gotten crushes on these men. Preposterous! For the rest of the evening I keep seeing the warmth of his eyes and smile. So you can say one thing for the Securitate: it definitely knew how to select people who could make a good human connection. Silvia picks me up and I say this, expressing my confusion about how to think about these two interviews. She responds, "You've taken on part of what *we* experienced with them, learning to fear them. But they were trained to think of us all as enemies: this is what a *securist* I met some time ago told me." Then she goes on, with passion: "Fear of them was laid down in the population in strata: one era of terror, then another kind, and another . . . first through the people they killed, jailed, threw under cars or buses, or beat almost to death. . . . They ruined my life and the life of my family. I didn't start having a life until after 1989." The message is clear: don't you *dare* make their apology! I feel chastened.

Among other things, this conversation shows clearly the ambivalent position of the anthropologist: although not outsiders, we are not insiders either. Our work occurs in the space of difference that defines us as both part of and not part of the places we study. This is evident in Silvia's two reactions to my musings about officer "Dragomir": she sees me as perceiving the world like a Romanian—fearing yet identifying with my "captors"—and at the same time as completely un-Romanian, in my ridiculous feelings of remorse about the photograph with "Dragomir" and my desire to protect him.

Still, I keep thinking about his photo in my book and feeling compunction about it. Finally I take my copy of the photo and write on it something like this: "Esteemed Mr. Dragomir, Here is the photo. If you are convinced it is definitely not you, please let me know immediately." I give several ways for him to do this. I put it in the mail, then have a terrible night's sleep, once again overcome with the discrepancy between my image of evil *securiști* and the two nice fellows I have now met, all the while telling myself this is an asinine reaction. My feelings and thoughts about this meeting are so contradictory that I have trouble getting a fix on them.

I hear nothing from officer "Dragomir," but I write to my editor at the press where *Secrets and Truths* is in final page proofs and ask her, if it is not too late, to take his name out of the text.

> > >

Sunday, 15 June 2014. I am visiting the family of my friend Solana (of the "rotting fence" metaphor), and I bring them a copy of *Secrets and Truths*. Her brother-in-law, Pavel, who was connected to the organization in an auxiliary role, takes it and disappears. After an hour he comes back and says, "I want to give you a preliminary reaction: it's very balanced." He seems impressed. A couple of hours later he returns having finished it, and he uses the same word, adding, "You didn't come with accusations but try to say things in an even-handed way. That's very good. Even though you were a victim . . . you didn't come to point the finger." (I later think that I should have commented on how much less I have at stake than most of those who *have* pointed the finger.) On our way out I comment to Solana that Pavel's seeing it as "balanced" is an interesting reaction, to which she responds, "You have to remember, these people were taken into school and trained from the outset that the world is divided into 'us' and 'enemies.' Whoever is not us is the enemy. So when they see that you don't have this reflex, they're amazed."

Pavel's reaction initially buoys my spirits: at least *one* person in my most critical "target" audience isn't furious. But then I think, Is that a good thing? Just how much of a compliment is it to have them approve of what I've written?

Officer's Note on informer's report, 27.02.1988

The report was furnished according to tasks assigned, the person indicated is known under the "American Problem" and is worked up through a DUI. Source received the task of informing us concerning the extra-professional activities and preoccupations of the American doctoral candidate. Source will direct her toward historical sources that will help her make an objective documentation on her research theme.

"V. Blidaru"

With the October success under my belt, I have decided to use the same technique to try once more with officer "Blidaru" in Cluj, where the bulk of my file is from. Though other Cluj officers were more active in my case, he is the only one I've been able to track down. As before, I enlist a friend to mail the same letter for me, and she tells me later that he had called her to say I should ring him when I arrive. I get to Cluj on 16 June and telephone him that same morning. A woman answers the phone: he's not there. "When can I call and find him?" "You've looked for him at home, but he's at work." I ask for his work number, she asks for my name. I give it. She gives me the number.

A somewhat reedy voice of medium timbre answers the phone. I say who I am and he is very responsive: "I kiss your hand!" (a respectful old-school greeting). I say how glad I am to hear his voice and am hoping to see him. Tomorrow might be a good day, he suggests; I should call him tomorrow around the same time. All the way through he sounds exceedingly cordial. I hang up in a state of elation, then remember he can just as easily disappear tomorrow or change his mind, like officer "Grigorescu."

He doesn't. The next day we set a meeting at noon in Liberty Square. At noon on the dot he's there, a nice-looking white-haired man with glasses, about medium build, maybe five foot nine, wearing a dark leather jacket. He comes toward me with a positively joyful smile and firmly takes my arm to walk to a café, the embodiment of that classic Eastern European type, the charming older man. Since flowers are my signature in this operation, I bring him a bouquet. This confuses him—"I should be the one bringing *you* flowers!" Our conversation lasts over two hours and I don't take notes, so much is lost.[22] Once we sit down, he speaks uninterruptedly for quite a while, with only a few prompts from me. At first he talks very rapidly, I can't get a word in, and his right shoulder is twitching noticeably, but that subsides after a while. He volunteers the Securitate's mission: to gather information that was verified and to process it into knowledge, hoping it would be used wisely by the Party. He emphasizes the reliability of their information several times during the conversation (though I note that in his 1988 report, above, he still didn't know I got my PhD in 1977).

Surveillance here was stepped up considerably, he notes, when Jimmy Carter was succeeded by Reagan, who had made it clear he would bring down the Soviet system. "The Cold War was on then, creating a very tricky environment. Our job was to find spies—who aren't just covert intelligence officers. A spy gets information that is then employed to propagate a negative image of Romania abroad, using it against us." Note the discrepancy between his view of spying and those of the other two officers, the difference helping to explain the many kinds of spy I was found to be: they couldn't agree on a definition. I say that the Securitate was right to see me as "collecting socio-political information," to which he responds, "We don't mind if people come to learn about Romania and see it as it is, but they shouldn't denigrate it with tendentious interpretations. We knew there were at least some people who came here to do just that."

Like my other two officers, he smiles almost continually throughout the conversation, especially its first hour—except when he gets exercised over something, which happens a couple of times. He tells me where he was born, what he studied in university: "I wasn't an officer from the beginning. I did my degree and was then assigned to a teaching post in the countryside. I'd gotten married, my wife is from the city, and I had a choice: take her out to the village, which she wouldn't like, or get myself here. The latter seemed the better option, so I let myself be persuaded to join the Securitate." I had elsewhere heard of this as a rationale for joining, so I found the story plausible. Job assignments in rural areas were unappealing to most who received them, and joining the Securitate (or serving as an informer) was preferable. Later he indicates another motive for his choice. As did "Dragomir," he too liked working with "the invisible"; it was very interesting.

We talk about what a workday was like: "Twenty-four hours in twenty-four. We were never really off duty." Of course he knew officers in other divisions—shadowing, telephone wiretaps, censoring correspondence, etc.—because they all had to collaborate (so much for compartmentalization). His own specialty was analysis and synthesis. On a daily basis he sat in his office looking over the information collected and writing reports from it, or going around to institutions assigned to him (museums, libraries, university departments) to gather more. "Were relations with your neighbors affected by your job?" I ask. "No, and actually, the Securitate did *a lot* for people—solving problems of all kinds for them—and not just for those in our network." How about his social life? A fellow who really likes people, he is always ready to party, the one to organize festivities for New Year's or other holidays, and he has lots of friends not connected with the Securitate.

I bring up the thorny question of the jokes in my first book. "This was one of the few things we had to reproach you with," he says. "Those mottoes created real problems, because people were offended. They were the reason for our recommending that you be thrown out of the country, in 1984–5. They weren't a question of national security but of national sensibilities—a *moral* question, concerning the image of a people. At the time, the propaganda about Romania was very negative." "So why wasn't I thrown out?" "Because cooler heads prevailed. It was very important for us to have relations with Americans, and stupid to jeopardize that for something minor like a few jokes." "Did you think I was Hungarian?" He looks puzzled—it had never crossed his mind that my name might indicate that. This surprises me, for I had thought that was what caused such anger over the mottoes: they meant I was taking the "Hungarian side" against Romania.

I ask how he got his informers—"I had fifty or more of them!"—did he inherit them or create them himself? "When I first started, I inherited some, then built up my network myself." He describes how one might recruit someone who was a Party member to serve as an informer, for whom he would have to seek permission: " 'K.V. is coming, Mihu is a good informer for her, we request permission to use him for the period of her stay to be certain of her loyalties and make sure she becomes Romania's friend rather than enemy.' The goal was to use informers in order to draw you into loving Romania, having the right views. So informer 'ŞTEFANESCU' has a name but not an informer's file, like 'TRAIAN' and others." This means that plenty of people could have been reporting on me but not appear in the documents with informer files. The goal of making me love Romania gives me pause. I had often felt that Romanian friends were awfully pro-Romanian, far more so than I am pro-American. Was this put on for my benefit, yet another form of "positive influence"? Probably not. Another moment of paranoia. Perhaps it is a further manifestation of "small-country" patriotism, which affords citizens fewer choices than does patriotism in larger countries.[23]

He comments without prompting that after the revolution, all Securitate officers were sent into the reserves. Then in December 1990 or January 1991, they brought many back into the newly constituted Romanian Information Services (SRI)—he thinks about 40 percent of the previous officers.[24] Most of them were older, because the problem was the need for expertise in the new SRI, just as had happened when the communists took over and the Securitate was formed; the younger ones had to find other work. He himself was pensioned at age fifty, did manual labor in agriculture for much of that first year, then was brought back in and retired again in 1997. When he finally retired, he didn't turn over any of his informers to his successor.

He's very opposed to all the anti-Securitate propaganda, saying that CNSAS, the repository of the archive, "bewitches the Romanian people!" and will give me misinformation. Then he tells me about someone else besides me who found him in their file and denounced him as a member of the Securitate. He was called to trial in Bucharest but refused to go, instead writing them a letter with three points, two of them being: "1) Which law did I break? What we did was legal then. 2) My accuser can see what I wrote in his file, but I can't see what he wrote when he got home. It might have been something denigratory." As a result of all this, he says, his name was published in the official state publication, the *Monitor Oficial*, confirming publicly that he had been a Securitate employee. "They could have saved themselves a lot of trouble by going to the organizational chart of the Securitate!" He is growing increasingly upset while talking about the climate in which the CNSAS can destroy officers publicly, and he starts to weep as he says, "It irritates me *so much sometimes* . . . !"

Now he talks about the organizations of former *securişti*, asking if I know their magazine, *Vitralii* (meaning "stained-glass window," a nice religious image). He recommends a book by Gen. Filip Teodorescu, *A Risk Assumed*, which he will get for me and give me tomorrow. It argues that 1989 was not a revolution but a coup d'état organized by foreign intelligence services. Clearly he's trying to convert me to a positive view of the organization, and I must say he's rather persuasive. He often tells me they were "nice guys just trying to keep Romania safe." I ask him why the Securitate had such bad press and awakened so much fear. He responds that in the 1950s it was warranted, but after that, no. "We kept the situation under control without that."[25]

At several points he comes back to this: "We were just doing our job, making sure there were no spies. We weren't the horrible monsters we were made out to be. That idea was propagated about the Securitate of the 1950s, but in 1964 General Pleşiţa came to power and began removing all the Hungarians from the organization. Then things began getting better." He doesn't actually say that the presence of Hungarians was why things were so bad, but the implication is clear. As in this comment, he several times reacts to something in a way that suggests strong patriotic and pro-Romanian, anti-Hungarian sentiments. Another is in discussing the cession of Transylvania to Hungary during World War II, which led to his father's being thrown out of work; he appealed to a Hungarian for a job, but the fellow dismissed him rudely. While telling this story, "Blidaru" begins to weep again.

Was he glad to have been in the Securitate? "I'm very proud to have been an officer and am upset about all this denigration of the Securitate. If I had a choice, I'd go right back to being an officer." He is distressed that the Securitate is taking the fall for the bad policies of the Party leadership. They were the ones who set policy; all the Securitate did was to send up information for the Party to act on. In his talk he tends to vilify the Party and CNSAS, raising up the Securitate as a good organization.

At the end I say, "My goal is to balance things a bit, try to show something of the people behind the files. Can I use some of this conversation, presumably with a pseudonym?" He agrees, laughing out loud at the idea that I am giving him a pseudonym; we decide what it will be. How did he get mine, "VERA"? "It was easy, 'VER' from your surname and then add an 'a.' It's a nice Russian name." He takes my arm firmly again and escorts me to my next destination.

I find I'm completely exhausted afterward from the effort to retain what we discussed and to be an engaging companion for a person of extremely high energy. From our conversation it's obvious that he is an intelligent and thoughtful man, his loyalties and prejudices notwithstanding. I believe him when he says he has a lot of friends, and he would certainly have been very successful at recruiting and nurturing his informers. Compared with officers "Grigorescu" and "Dragomir," "Blidaru" volunteers more information and is more determined to create a good image of the Securitate. He seems very jovial at the end of our meeting, as if confident that he's succeeded in doing so. Although I've gained much more from this conversation than the others and liked him a lot, I don't have the feeling of special attachment I had with them. Perhaps the nature of our exchange helped to disperse that, as he became more real through it, or perhaps I'm gradually domesticating "my" *securişti*, getting used to them, somewhat as I did in reading my file. Nonetheless, "Blidaru" is yet another personnel triumph of the Securitate, selecting people who can make a good connection. He was great.

The next day we have a briefer visit, for him to give me two books he'd promised. We talk about "Groza," who was in "Blidaru's" informer network and who recently died. "Blidaru" was one of only three people outside the family who showed up for the funeral: "He was a close friend!" I'm startled by this violation of my stereotype of officer-informer relations, just as I was when "Groza" had asked for "Blidaru" on the phone by his first name. Then he goes on to describe how informers were recruited. "It was done in two ways: using patriotism and compromising material. We could appeal to your desire to serve your country, or if you'd gotten caught doing something against the law, we'd say 'Come work for us; if not, you'll be prosecuted and go to jail for it.' " With this choice, is it a wonder that many chose to inform?

At one point he observes that Cluj had a total of about 150 *securişti*, including both officers and auxiliaries (but not informers), adding, "So it's wrong that we were everywhere!" I reply that they obviously had a very successful disinformation machine, then, since the populace thought they *were* everywhere. He likes this but says he's upset that the word *securist* has become a term of opprobrium, used as an insult.

I ask about gender: Did they suspect women and men of the same or different things? The same things, he replies, but the procedures for dealing with the sexes were different. Although they might use men to seduce women targets, they also used other women for this purpose, trying to collect the gossip women are famous for. With men, however, they largely used romantic entrapments. Men and women have different habits: men drink more, want sex, whereas women are more careful, more tenacious, can put their charm into play. As to why there were so few female *securişti*, he said the work is very difficult and involves long hours, sometimes several days' absence from home; how can a mother do that? Their inclusion on a team also caused logistic problems. He stops to count: in over thirty years as an officer, he could remember only four female operatives. Most women worked instead in office jobs with an eight-hour day, not as operatives.

He has some questions for me too, though now I prove secretive. Who was the friend who sent him my letter? (I don't say.) Does our friend Felicia know we've met, and should he let on to her that we did? (Yes.) What about the other two guys you met: Where were they from, how did you get to them? (I am circumspect.) And he goes back to what he said yesterday concerning the goal of my surveillance: wanting me to like Romania. I ask why he agreed to meet with me: "From professional curiosity." To verify what he thought he knew about me.

As we leave he summarizes things: "There were some bad people in the Securitate, but after 1964 they were mostly good, correct, serious in their work." I respond that meeting with these three officers has affected my vision of the Securitate, and now I'm sorry that in the documentary film the CNSAS made with me, I gave *securişti* a blanket reproof for abusing the population. "We can't expect everyone to have the same vision," he replies. "The point is to try to be balanced, to hear all sides." He kisses me goodbye. I will have two more meetings with officer "Blidaru," in 2015 and 2016. Again he is charming and warm, and he answers a number of questions. I feel that we could almost be friends.

> > >

When I return from Cluj, Cristina asks if "Blidaru" told me anything new, adding, "They're still trying to complicate everything, give disinformation, create spider webs that catch people unaware, fragment identities through their schizophrenogenic methods." I realize that although "identity" is a good tool for this story, I have been thinking about it too simplistically. She reminds me that a prime effect of Securitate tactics is not just to multiply identities but to fragment them as well.

Nonetheless, these three officers and I have formed—howsoever briefly—a different kind of relation from the one we had before, now based not on invisibility and shadows but on a physical encounter. What did those meetings mean *for them*, I wonder? Did they go home laughing to themselves at how successfully they had performed a different role? Did they play me yet again, this time face to face? Were they nervous too? Were they actually glad to revisit their past, maybe even to "make their peace," as officer "Grigorescu" had said?

Perhaps they just thought that I too was surprisingly nice, for a spy.

> > >

I have dinner with Andrei and ask his advice: What do I do about my meetings with these "nice guys"? He agrees with my friend Silvia's reaction: I can't do an apologia of the Securitate. It has to be something else. "Whatever else you do, you shouldn't whitewash them, justify them, or be too understanding." I think later, the point ultimately is not to whitewash or justify but to understand them *as part of a social system*. This is the privilege ethnography affords. But we can do that only now; during the Cold War, we had no access to them, and the context was too polarized. So the condition of any new understanding—and of my meetings with these men—is that the Cold War is over, at least in the form it took during the twentieth century. That, of course, changes the reality we now discern in those times.

"Shouldn't whitewash or justify them." I am in a quandary, caught between the expectations of two very different audiences: U.S. and Romanian. The former—or at least my academic readers in it—will not necessarily expect me to make a judgment against the Securitate on the basis of what I have learned from my file, though they might not take it amiss if I did. Many Romanian readers, on the other hand, will expect precisely that, as I learn from a conversation with a Romanian colleague in New York. She has read a draft of this chapter, and she wants a judgment. "It can be nuanced," she says, "but you need a position. You can't suspend judgment, or abstain." She scoffs at the clichés my Secus have fed me, which she recognizes from her own work in their archive. "You're so excited to see them that you don't subject their clichés—about the 1950s, for instance—to the same scrutiny you do in your other work." At the very least, I should have different endings for the English and Romanian versions of the book. She seems dismayed that I have given them a great opportunity: to look me straight in the eye and say, "I did you no harm." Meanwhile, former Securitate officers and their KGB stepsiblings elsewhere (Bulgaria, Macedonia) corrupt numerous economies in Eastern Europe and undermine the European Union from within. Too benevolent an attitude toward them is hazardous.

Although I understand and respect my colleague's position, I remain ambivalent. All countries have intelligence services, and no one familiar with the actions of the FBI under J. Edgar Hoover can confidently point a finger without its shaking a bit. It is true that the Securitate was much worse (a fact not well represented in this book), but it is also true that certain judgments have now become possible that were not available in the 1970s or 1980s, when scholars who hoped to return to Romania or to protect their friends there chose to hold their tongues. After 1989, condemnation of the entire communist system, and particularly its hated Securitate, was a virtual requirement: it became the main public ideology.

But nearly three decades later, the options are more open. Many Romanians are forgetting that the Securitate was so bad, and their children have no interest in the matter. I speak one evening with three friends, women my own age. We discuss surveillance. One was married to a journalist and tells about the reports he had to write whenever he met journalists from other Eastern bloc countries. But he didn't view it as inappropriate or a burden; it was just part of his job. I ask them, if we wiped out 1989 and went back to the society they lived in before then, what would they want to change about that society? They reply, "Nothing." Memories can be short, and views of the Securitate correspondingly malleable.

"Do No Harm"

The following excerpt is from a telephone wiretap, in which the Biermans and I plan the secret trip to Cluj in June 1985:

TARGET [T = RALF BIERMAN]: When will you get there?

K: Monday afternoon.

T: And that's where I should pick you up?

K: Yes, and it's fine, it's certain, you won't have any problems.

T: You're sure?

K: Yes.

T: The main thing that interests me is that everything be secure.

"My motto was, Do no harm," officer "Grigorescu" had said to me, and one if not both of the other two said something similar: "*Ce rău v-am făcut?* What harm did I do you?" Cristina at CNSAS says that *securiști* confronted with their targets would often ask this or would say "I don't think I did you any harm." So now she is asking me that question: What harm did they do me? First, I reply, they certainly changed the course of my research, poisoning the atmosphere with rumors and ultimately compelling me to end my fieldwork. When I finally realized the devastating effects my "friendship" had had on some friends and associates they recruited as informers, I felt deeply upset: harm done to them was harm to me as well.

But second and more important, I say, the way the question is posed puts the emphasis very slyly on the officer and me, rather than on the system of surveillance in which they were cogs. Even if my own *securiști* did not harm me personally, that larger system in which they participated harmed many people I cared about, not to mention the tens—even hundreds—of thousands of Romanians whose lives they ravaged over forty years. Individual officers cannot be blamed for this (other than for having joined the Securitate to begin with), only the apparatus as a whole and the Party it served. This system of repression, intended to purge the country of enemies and keep Romanians "safe," did people plenty of harm. To ask about harm *to me* is to miss the point.

Aside from the previous cases of my informers, yet another example of what the Securitate could do to people it plucked from my orbit came from my friends the Biermans. Following our visit to Leipzig in 2010, at which we had read the pages about Ralf from my file, he decided to request his own (though I tried to discourage him from doing so), suggesting it might also be useful for me. In January 2015 he received five dossiers, three of which (totaling 774 pages) contain his DUI as target "Manu," from 1985 through 1989. He shared its contents with me, giving me several sleepless nights and making me ask yet again what "harm" meant.

The first volume was entirely about his family's relation with me, the second consisted of wiretap reports that I had at least partly occasioned, and the third was opened using me as its motive. The first volume, dated 29 September 1986, starts with the proposal to open a DUI on Ralf based on preliminary surveillance of him as of 15 June 1985, eleven days after our escapade. Its justification? From the time we met in 1974, he had not informed the Securitate about our friendship, despite the renewal in 1985 of the 1971 law requiring everyone to report conversations with foreigners. The officers defend their suspicions with a verbatim transcript of my phone call to the Biermans following our trip to Cluj. I ask if everyone is OK and whether there were any repercussions from our visit (underlined by the officer). They reply no, and I continue, "I kept thinking about the telephone. Good that there was no reason." (Wrong again.) Ana then says, "The boots are ready. I can't wait to get together." The officers interpret this, using the term "conventional" in the sense of coded speech:

From this conversation emerges eloquently the care manifested by the foreigner concerning her relations among people in Romania. . . . At the same time, there also emerges the conventional character of the conversation (what kind of boots can they be talking about in June?).

Among the other documents in the file—and this seems to me crucial—is an earlier officer's report:

I mention that in the period in which Verdery Katherine visited Bierman Ralf, on the self-labeled radio station "Radio Free Europe" unsuitable commentary was made concerning the situation in our country, including some aspects at [Ralf's workplace].

This concern appears more than once. Clearly, they think he is feeding me secret information about his workplace that I am passing on to Radio Free Europe, an institution despised by the Romanian Communist Party and its repressive apparatus. From the Securitate's point of view, that is a very grave offense.

My friendship with the Biermans either brought on their surveillance (the very first page says so) or served as the pretext the Securitate seized upon to draw him into its net. It is true that, for whatever reason (his ethnicity? the flight of relatives to the West?), his telephone was bugged before they opened his DUI on my account; otherwise the officers would never have known the details of our plan to escape to Cluj on 4 June 1985. Ralf's file indicates that from the moment he and Ana had picked me up hitchhiking, the Securitate had taken extensive measures concerning them—mobilizing informers for both of them, tapping their phone, intercepting all their correspondence, following them, finding out their circle of friends. As of 29 September 1986, their home was to be searched as well as fully wired for eavesdropping on not only phone conversations but all other actions in their apartment. Officers placed Ralf's elderly mother in Vlaicu under surveillance and sought to recruit new informers from the Biermans' "entourage." By this time the pressure to inform on me was causing Ralf an ulcer. Through a clever ruse, officers finally managed in 1987 to get him to declare his friendship with me in a lengthy report and to explain why he had not done so previously. Shortly thereafter, Ralf's DUI was closed, with a proposal that he now be recruited *as an informer*. Pressure on him intensified after Ana's flight a year later: he would be groomed to spy for the Securitate *in Germany* once his emigration papers came through, and probably as a condition for getting them.[26]

There's nothing like reading Ralf's file to make me furious at these Secus. It's clear that I occasioned the extensive bugging of their apartment and phone, opening of their mail, investigations into their friends and family members, and periodic shadowing, and that he was taken from his home and held, terrified, for several hours, while his equally terrified wife awaited his return. I would call this "harm." I would definitely call it harm if I were a citizen of that country hoping to be protected rather than persecuted by my government. In 1986, the rumor reached him that "the Biermans will never again travel together outside Romania." Whereas previously Ralf, Ana, and their two children had regularly vacationed in Hungary and East Germany, visiting relatives, now each spouse would be allowed to travel with one child every other year: because of me, they had lost the Securitate's trust. This had major implications for their plans to flee all together. In consequence, Ralf and his daughter spent a year and a half living under constant surveillance in the most repressive times in Romania with no idea of when they would get out or see their family whole again. Both Ana and Ralf suffered this separation terribly.

Reviewing the havoc wreaked on my friends' lives on my account, I have to condemn the apparatus of rule that treated Romania's people in this way. Regardless of the motives and possible decency of one or another Securitate officer, they served a hateful repressive apparatus that propped up an ever more inhumane political project, run by Nicolae Ceaușescu and his mafia. Because secrecy largely protected that apparatus, we can feel angry only in retrospect: at the time, most people didn't know exactly what it was doing. Certainly the Biermans didn't, and I didn't, and people who thought they did had only the barest inkling. This is evident from others who have read their files and found the level of surveillance appalling and unexpected. So for all those years many lives were doubled by Secus listening, watching, concocting schemes, manipulating their informer networks, and interpreting data on the axiom of guilty until proven innocent (and even that, provisionally). This was possible because of secrecy oaths and work compartmentalization, which undermined the certainty that would support our outrage—outrage that the opening of the CNSAS archive enables now.

This judgment, however, ignores the complex questions about harm and responsibility that arose with my informers, who might have argued (as Mariana did outright) that I was the one doing the harm—with my ignorance and naiveté, my clumsy but useless efforts to shield my interlocutors, my propensity for excessive and premature emotional commitments. The urge to condemn collides with the intricacies of human connection and obscures their complexity. Discussing Ralf's file with him and Ana in 2016, we spoke at length about the consequences of our friendship for their life. I asked if they had ever wished we had not met. They had already asked themselves the same question and answered it with a firm no.

> > >

With these conversations, I have tried to render visible some of the mechanisms of Securitate surveillance, without revealing the actors themselves. Moreover, like Sheila Fitzpatrick in her *A Spy in the Archives*, I have shown something of how personally demanding it was to do anthropological research in the Soviet bloc during those years—and later, as well, if one exploits one's file as I have. But more important, confronting my file and my *securişti* made me realize that in many ways, I was the Securitate's dupe. I was given a research visa and allowed to come, and I was then turned into their very own "native," their Trobriand Islander, subject to scrutiny much more intense than anything I did to Romanians. They followed me out into the Romanian population, letting me find new people to talk with and then selecting from among my contacts new targets and informers for themselves. They let me do some research for them, too, discovering things they might have missed concerning what people thought about the regime. The Securitate made me its tool—perhaps another reason why they did not throw me out.

I arrived as a graduate student who needed people to share their lives with me, and I reciprocated by throwing myself into my relationships wholeheartedly. But does this sincerity justify the hardships some people endured on my account? I had very little idea at the time as to what was going on, that a web was being secretly spun around me designed to entrap those I became close to and to keep others away. "She's a spy!" Knowing I wasn't a spy and not believing I was under such scrutiny, I inadvertently delivered some of these people to the Securitate on a plate, most especially the Biermans and Mariana. Although I didn't torture or blackmail them, I did complicate their lives greatly—earning me Mariana's judgment, "What harm you did me!" Under these circumstances, it is amazing that I formed durable relationships at all, much less that these continuing friendships are among the most meaningful of my life. If anything proves that the Securitate failed in their goal of insulating Romanians from foreigners, it is that.

4

Ruminations

Evil is unspectacular and always human,
And shares our bed and eats at our own table.
—W. H. Auden, "Herman Melville"

Having voluntarily thrown myself into the pit with *securiști*, I now find that
I must try to account for them in terms different from those with which I
began, and more adequately than I was able to do in *Secrets and Truths*, before I met some of them. My intense emotional response to my officers—
the people who produced my file, created "VERA," and frightened my friends
into informing—makes that very clear. In these ruminations I bring together
the two moments of my research, the 1970s–1980s and 2008–16, to offer some
tentative thoughts about this organization that gave me so much of its time.

> > >

It took me a while—months, in fact—to gain some sense of what had tran-
spired in these meetings and why I had felt so deeply confused after the first
two. Here I thought I was going to track them down, maybe confront them
(albeit not in hostile fashion), but what has happened instead is that *they have
recruited me!*—not to inform but to see them more positively. As I think about
it I am amazed. This was why I suddenly seemed to have a less condemna-
tory view of them, felt strong remorse for revealing their names in my book,

kept remembering their warm and smiling faces. Even though the times are "postsocialist" now and these guys should be on the defensive, they most definitely are not. Shouldn't I have imagined this could happen?

Officer "Blidaru" was the most overt in his goals: he had wanted to recruit me in the 1980s to a positive vision of Romania and now to a positive vision of his organization. But the others with all their smiling were also involved in a kind of recruitment—perhaps better said, a seduction—toward a similar end. This was, after all, their metier. Moreover, they have been perfecting their new image for twenty-five years: the men I'm seeing now are doubtless quite different from when they wrote in my file. I was trying to recruit them too, of course, with my garrulousness, face sore from smiling, and constant parallels between their work and mine, as if to draw them closer. Whether I succeeded with them or not is immaterial, however: they are not writing books about former spies. But I am writing one about former securişti, I will provide an image of them, and I have scholarly authority. They have good reason to recruit me to their view.

A conversation with Virgiliu about meeting my Secus makes this plausible. He says they're now engaged in a fierce battle for their public image. Having started out as Securitate agents, they have become "information officers," a much less alarming label that makes them seem more benign. They say, "We were protecting Romania by gathering information." A number of them are hiring very expensive lawyers to fight accusations that they were Secus, so they can avoid being labeled as such and having their names published, as well as losing whatever privileges they may have acquired (such as pensions for being "revolutionaries" in 1989). Refusing to fight it, as "Blidaru" has done, is now unusual, Virgiliu says. Some officers are even planning to take their cases to the European Tribunal for Human Rights! He thinks their concern with image is mainly for themselves as individuals rather than for the institution, but they do participate in two groups, for the main branches of the former intelligence service: internal and external.[1] The historian Richard Hall also writes in his blog about the changing image of the Securitate, providing a list of some of their appearances in the online press in December 2013.[2] The battle for public image extends, of course, to me: hence their seduction, once it appears I'm not out to get them. As I discovered, their well-honed abilities as recruiters of their informers serve them well in this effort.

I imagine that this battle over image connects with the rapid entry into (if not indeed takeover of) the Romanian economy by former Securitate officers after 1989, a process whose beginnings are recorded in Marius Oprea's *Heirs of the Securitate*.[3] They were already an important presence in economic institutions beforehand, running both local and foreign-currency businesses, in part to help shore up Romania's collapsing budget. For example, after 1990 Mariana's recruiter and my case officer Ovidiu Ținca was pensioned from the Cluj Securitate; in 1995 he was taken back into its successor, the SRI, where he was made head of the intelligence services for western Transylvania. He moved west to Oradea and opened a business with electronic games, which grew nicely. Parlaying it into two casinos, he then became professor and dean of the law school (until finally thrown out in 2007).[4] He definitely landed on his feet, and he was not alone.

As elsewhere in the former communist bloc, ex-*securiști* have been at the forefront of Romania's communist-era elites in privatizing and plundering its economy. In a conversation I learn that because many *securiști* had completed studies in law (as had two of my three), it was easy for them after 1989 to be recognized as lawyers and from this vantage point to protect each other against attempts to unseat them. Their role in the previous economy, heading important enterprises both in Romania and abroad, had given them excellent contacts, which have served them well in the new one. (An extremely well-connected friend whispered to me over lunch in 2016, "They're running the country!" "They," in this case, refers not just to previous Secu officers but to their successors brought into the new intelligence services after 1989.) My meetings, then, fall into this context.

How am I to think about all this? Like any ethnographer, I begin by collecting reactions from my friends and colleagues.

The Empire of Fear

One difficulty ethnographers face is that of adopting too fully the perspectives of our primary respondents/friends, who may have strong, collectively held opinions of which they convince us.[5] One such perspective is what we might call the "empire of fear" paradigm: the view, much indebted to the Cold War, that communist regimes were based on terror and repression, of which the secret police was a central agent. Despite my dismissal of this kind of Cold Warrior talk when it came from the personnel of the U.S. Embassy, gradually I came to accept it as I discovered the extent of Securitate surveillance during the 1980s and as I absorbed the world view of those around me. Only well after the fact, as a result of my work on my file, did I perceive that this paradigm was preventing me from glimpsing the much more complicated place of the Securitate in Romanian society. Though my data on this question are very limited, I will now tentatively suggest some thoughts about how communist secret police organizations functioned in ways that Cold War stereotypes and the testimonies of dissidents have shielded from view.

The "empire of fear" paradigm and the stereotype of the fearsome, hateful Securitate were widespread in Romania during my fieldwork. It is undeniable that the Securitate stirred up fear and anxiety by various means, but my conversations indicate something more. Historian Marius Oprea, for instance, who has been carrying out exhumations of people the Securitate killed in the 1950s, tells me that some of the former officers talk with him and have won his sympathy. Many were just kids from the village trying to better themselves and having at least some remnants of decency. Often they didn't like the work they were ordered to do, especially during the 1980s. But Marius also talks about the completely arbitrary violence of the early years. During his exhumations, the dead person's relatives and other villagers speak of the fear they are re-experiencing as they do this. A peasant once told him, "Even now when I hear a car engine I'm afraid, because in those days the Securitate were the only ones with cars." As a child he would pee in his pants from fright whenever he heard a car coming. Such reflexes could live on for decades, even if the organization itself was changing.

I ask my friend Liviu what he thought of "Blidaru": "He wasn't a bad fellow. He was especially close to your pal 'Groza'—they were drinking buddies." He mentions some other *securiști* who were also decent people and with whom he, as director of an institution who was their liaison, got along very well. When I say I'm caught in the propaganda of fear from the time I worked in communist Romania, when they were represented as monsters, he replies vigorously, "Noooo!! It wasn't like that at all!"[6]

Next I visit Radu to ask his view of "Blidaru," whom he knew at university; he uses the very same language. "He wasn't a bad fellow." I tell him my dilemma of meeting these officers and finding they're nice, friendly, intelligent—to which he replies, "The biggest mistake is to extend one's view of the 1950s Securitate to the whole communist period. Many of the early ones were Jews and Hungarians, not Romanians. All kinds of terrible things happened then: arresting people, sending them to the gulag, collectivizing agriculture with the attendant violence, which destroyed the peasantry's way of life. People who experienced these things carried that image into the future. But those *securiști* were cleaned out in the 1960s and the organization was transformed into something much less fearsome." (Evidently, it is not only *securiști* who see things this way but even some Romanian academics.)

> > >

When I tell another friend, *Sandu, about my meetings and their effect on me, he replies, "They've complicated your image! The Party's personnel policies were very good, despite Ceaușescu's idiocies. They recruited the very best people from universities and factories to enter the Party and Securitate—people with education, with a broad vision. In thinking about the Securitate, you have to specify what period, and from whose point of view you're talking. At the beginning, they got people from the Siguranța [the interwar intelligence service] who were very brutal, partly because they had to prove themselves to the Party in order to be kept on. Just as with any institution, there were many kinds of Secus, some good and some bad." Perhaps, I suggest, the Siguranța people set a tone that pushed subsequent competition for career advancement in the direction of cruelty and brutalization? He thinks that's possible.

This conversation helps me think differently about the undeniable brutality of Secus in the 1940s and 1950s, which helped to establish the empire of fear paradigm. The view of Secu cruelty, well represented by my officers, was that in those days the organization was full of Hungarians, Jews, and Russians; getting rid of those people brought to the surface sweet and intelligent, nonbrutish, Romanian Secus. This kind of nationalist explanation for all manner of issues has always bothered me in my Romanian friends. It implies that Romanians are incapable of being communists, or violent, or avaricious, or cruel (as if the bulk of the Communist Party apparatus and Securitate had not been Romanian). Sandu is offering me a much better account. The new communist state, just like the one that arose after 1989, lacked the personnel to form new administrative and intelligence services from scratch. It is true that Hungarians and Jews (who had suffered discrimination in earlier years) were overrepresented in not just the Communist Party but also the new Securitate, as were the Russians who linked it to Moscow. But to train the new recruits the Party had to retain some of the personnel from the older Siguranța (as officer "Blidaru" had indicated to me), actively inviting them into the Party so as to discourage them from going over to Western intelligence services. To prove their loyalty to their new master, these older cadres overexecuted their job; killings and violence would be a sign of their reliability, and they would get results. They probably also created undesirable behavioral models, such as an appetite for cruelty and even an urge to demonstrate prepotency. A *securist* present at the death in 1951 of anticommunist partisan Teodor Susman, for example, cut off the man's penis and would twirl it around in his hand thereafter.[7]

Over time, as new cadres were formed, these older ones could be gradually dispensed with. Thus, after ten to fifteen years, the organization would be filled with new officers, who by 1964 were being trained as intelligence officers not in Moscow, as occurred in most other Eastern European countries, but in the officers' training school set up in Bucharest. Perhaps by now the "quotas" of arrests and beatings had been filled and policy could take a different turn under the new Party secretary, Nicolae Ceauşescu, using better-trained Securitate cadres. Their improved educational quality in the 1970s was part of an improvement in the educational level of *all* secret services worldwide at that time, owing to the changing nature and complexity of both information and the technology for gathering it. The uneducated brutes of before could no longer keep up and were replaced by officers with better instruments.

Thus, the early years of communist rule were indeed marked by violence and brutality, but these diminished thereafter—though their effects might permanently mark those on whose bodies the violence was imprinted.[8] This is not to deny that violence takes many forms, and the clever psychological/ emotional manipulations used by later cohorts of officers could produce extreme stress that took a huge toll, as we saw with Mariana. Moreover, the new *securişti* inherited the fearsome reputation of the older Siguranța-inflected Securitate, especially in the eyes of those who had directly suffered from it. This fear was not groundless: even though the general tendency may have been toward less violence, *securişi* hardly renounced force. Reports throughout the late 1970s and 1980s provide plenty of evidence that having people with a university degree did not keep the Securitate from exercising brutality. We see this in the fates of those who founded a free trade union in 1979, a year before Poland's Solidarity movement, as well as those who started the Braşov tractor factory strike in 1987—most of whom were badly beaten, jailed, or killed in "unfortunate" accidents—or of others who dared to raise a voice against the regime, such as the dissident engineer Gheorghe Ursu, beaten to death in 1985 while in Securitate custody. Therefore, *securişti* were able to instill fear right up to the regime's end, even if its exercise had been considerably reduced.

Visible and Invisible

An aspect of this fear was the power of the invisible, of which the Securitate were masters. I too was susceptible to it. A colleague asks me why I wanted to see my officers; I have no good answer. Why indeed? I wonder. Perhaps it has something to do with what interested officers "Dragomir" and "Blidaru": the invisible. By seeing them, I wanted them not to be able to escape again into the shadows. I wanted to reveal their secret, if only to myself. What I found, however, was that I had been captured by their gaze. The images of officers "Grigorescu" and "Dragomir" (him especially) that remain most vividly in my recollections are of their eyes, which seemed to me to suggest intelligence and warmth. (I must pull back against their charm, however, so as not to commit the fatal blunder of President George W. Bush, when he looked into ex-KGB officer Vladimir Putin's eyes and believed he was seeing into the man's soul.)

There is something about the invisibility of intelligence services, particularly those involved in repression like the Securitate, the East German Stasi, or the KGB, that creates a special kind of psychological tension—or so I found, at least. Once I realized I might actually locate them, my pursuit of these officers took on a fanatical quality: I couldn't stand the idea that *they* had been able to watch *me*—even in my underwear, through the video cameras in my hotel room—yet I couldn't see *them*. The very thought of it enraged me. Gabriel Liiceanu writes, similarly, "Reading my file, I had no representation of them. They were pure abstractions. I didn't know how old they were, if they were tall, thickset, blond, German, if they lisped, if they had nervous tics, or what families they came from. . . . Being spectral, they were like characters in a thriller, of whom the spectators see only the shoes or hat or a gloved hand with a lit cigarette. Or a silhouette from behind. Or nothing! *The occult is their ontology. And the seal of their power is: to see without being seen.*"[9] Therefore, Liiceanu has to *invent* the officer he "meets" in his file and try to imagine how the man might explain himself. Being an ethnographer rather than a philosopher, I sought them out.

In his evocative meditation on the notions of "face" and "defacement" concerning secret police officers in Poland, Saygun Gökarıksel describes the exhibitions held in central areas of many Polish cities during 2006–7, in which huge billboards were erected bearing the photographs, names, and descriptions of secret police officers from each city.[10] The intention of these exhibitions was expressed by the Institute of National Remembrance that put them up: "These are the evil perpetrators whom you have seen on the street without knowing who they really are." The idea of the face is also central to one of the most widespread practices of communist polities: the "unmasking" of spies, saboteurs, enemies of the people, and so on. That is, revealing their "faces" by removing their mask of secrecy was essential to establishing communist rule. The various projects in Eastern European countries to "unmask" the apparatus of repression after 1989 were a direct mirroring of this process.

Gökarıksel reminds us of the importance of the face in social communication and its role in political spectacle, as well as in social defacement. Indeed, in the Polish city of Katowice, the exhibition of officers' faces was destroyed and the images defaced more than once. "Located at the crossroads of visibility and invisibility, the face closely associates truth with visibility, transparency, or the exposition of the secret," he writes.[11] Moreover, both philosophy and neuroscience see the face as tied to ethical behavior: to behave ethically one must "face" the other.[12] Is this what makes hiding and secrecy the condition of the Securitate's work, which non-securiști so often see as devoid of ethics?

Gökarıksel's research calls to mind arguments concerning the nature of the state.[13] Against the standard view of the state as a reality, some argue that we should see it as a mask, whose work is masking. That is, there is no "reality" behind the mask of the state, only a performance. Or, to follow Coronil, the state is "the union of mask and what is being masked, the visible and the hidden. The state is produced by a process of masking. . . . Visibility and invisibility are two sides of the state."[14] Perhaps my experience with my Secus indicates this. Instead of revealing some new reality, these meetings have sown confusion—were somehow anticlimactic, beside the point. What mattered was the illusion securiști propagated with their supposed invisibility: that they were everywhere, supporting communist power by propagating fear. It was an illusion I too absorbed through my life in Romania, and it was the reason why meeting my officers occasioned such anxiety. (As officer "Grigorescu" had rightly said, I was very brave to seek him out.)

Although in Secrets and Truths I took the invisibility of the Securitate at face value, I am now learning that in some senses it was not invisible at all: people could see the officers responsible for their work unit, or the guys hanging out in places where potential "dissidents" might congregate. Secus were known as the "boys with the blue eyes," or as in Ana Blandiana's poem "Everything," "the boys on Victory Avenue." In her memoir she describes how easily recognizable were those in the special units on Victory Avenue, dressed the same, their hair cut the same, their shoes the same, even their stature and hair color about the same; likewise their expressionless faces, their eyes unmoving. She observes, "They didn't hide themselves, didn't operate under cover; on the contrary, they had to be seen and recognized, though without being observed, it had to be known that they existed, and their simple existence was sufficient to cause everything. . . . The Securitate had become a preventive institution. Thus was invented the most efficacious, the most poisonous and the most dissolving of fears: prophylactic fear."[15] Simply by being seen, this special cohort of securiști made people afraid, keeping alive the illusion that securiști were everywhere. This illusion prospered, however, on their invisibility, their secret activities that remained unseen. The Securitate thrived not just on invisibility but on its dialectic with the visible.

Most particularly, it thrived on the networks of relations the officers exploited and built.

An Embedded Securitate

I'm at dinner with Andrei one night in June 2014. As usual, he tells me some wonderful stories, this time about Secus. Dissident poet Mircea Dinescu, when he was being followed constantly in the late 1980s, went to a market to buy food one day. He approached the stall for tomatoes, asked for a kilogram (a "kil' "), and was told they didn't have any. He insisted, "I'm a poet, can you help me?" The seller replied, "Well, if you're a poet, you'd better have the guts of Mircea Dinescu. . . ." "But I *am* Mircea Dinescu." The fellow gets very excited and calls out to his wife, "Hey, bring a kil' of tomatoes for Mircea Dinescu!" So Dinescu walks out with his kil'. There at the door are the Secus who follow him. When they find out what he's gotten, they become very agitated (indicating that, by then, not even Secus had all the food they wanted): "These people have tomatoes!! Please, can't you get some of those for us too?" So he goes back in and talks to the seller again—"I need some tomatoes for the guys who follow me"—and he comes back with a kil' for them as well.

Andrei talks about his own experience. He was under close house arrest, with Secus at the door all the time. One of them in particular is trying to make him stop complaining and just read the books in his library and write some others. But he doesn't. So they tell him they're going to move him to another city and expect him to go quietly. He says, "I'll go quietly if you agree to leave my house alone. My wife and children live here, and I don't want them to be bothered all the time." The Secu says he'll see what he can do. Two days later he comes back and says, "OK, if you'll go quietly we'll quit watching your house." "So you see," Andrei concludes, "it was a negotiation"—adding later that this is not to imply that Secus were *always* ready to negotiate.[16] He too talks about the 1950s, when the political police was far more radical and you couldn't negotiate with them. But after 1965, when Ceauşescu became Party secretary, his tactics changed along lines already begun by his predecessor—reduced repression—and the behavior of *securişti* changed as well: now you could more often deal with them.

> > >

In late June 2014 I have a game-changing dinner with *Adrian. I tell him about my conversations with Secus and my dilemma as to how to handle them, and his reaction is surprising. Like several others, he thinks that certainly by the 1980s, fear was no longer the driving force of most people's relation to the Securitate. He describes the attempt to recruit him around 1983: at the beginning they revealed something about his personal life that startled him and made him ask himself, "What else do they know?" After that, however, their approach was mainly to try to draw him into something positive, rather than to make threats: " 'Your career will take off, you'll get trips abroad.' That sort of thing." He met with them about three times and they did not return to their opening gambit, instead trying to entice him with only material incentives.

But then he goes on: "We can't just keep emphasizing fear and terror. People *knew* who they were; neighbors, former classmates, even kin. People were mixed in with them. They needed stuff from people, and people needed stuff from them. So it was kind of a negotiated relationship." He recalls, "I had a classmate whom I ran into a few years after graduation and asked what he was doing: working for the Securitate. 'What do you do there?' I asked him, and he answered, 'Not what you'd think. In the first place, so many directors and personnel in state firms are signing contracts unfavorable to the state so as to make extra money, and we have to spend huge amounts of time trying to stop it. In addition, we get thousands of letters from people writing us to complain, denouncing others.' " He called them "volunteers": people who were not informers and had no formal relationship with the Securitate but were nonetheless writing to them with information or complaints for which they wanted resolution. "Isn't this like all those letters written to the Party," I ask, "published in newspapers, complaining about things the Party was supposed to fix? Why send them to the Securitate?" "Because they would be addressed faster and more efficiently. If you sent a complaint to the Party or police, you could end up in a court case, wasting a lot of time. With the

Securitate, the issue would be taken up more quickly." In a word, the problems of society were being socialized as the Securitate responded to people's concerns. I think of the office hours the East German Stasi held twice weekly, for the same reason.[17]

Adrian is talking about the 1980s, when the economic situation in Romania was becoming increasingly desperate and the Ceauşescu regime had gone off the rails. In that context, these "volunteers" were giving Secus information without their having to go through the whole recruitment process to get it. That is, increasing numbers of citizens had become active participants in the apparatus of repression—though I doubt they saw it that way—rather than the victims they generally say they were. Adrian had the impression that when the Secus were courting him, they weren't really pressing it, which made him think they had plenty of other options. "People had to create a horizon of normality," he said. "They couldn't keep living with such uncertainty." In this situation, they appealed to anyone who might be able to help them out: they "volunteered" to be clients in a clientelistic system. Patronage and the exchange of favors, long central characteristics of Romanian society, were now urgent practices. Many Soviet historians have studied letters, complaints, or other information addressed to the Party or security police, seeing them as appeals for central intervention when local administration malfunctions.[18] If such "volunteers" proliferated in the 1980s, perhaps that indicates the erosion of local administrative functions together with the economic crisis. Since Secus had more resources at their disposal than most, why not create or make use of relations with them? You use social relationships to solve problems however you can.

An example of this in my interviews came from Radu, discussing Officer "Blidaru." He said, "To 'Blidaru's' credit: there was a period when Romanian-Hungarian relations were terrible and it was almost impossible to get visas to go to Hungary. One of my Hungarian colleagues had a mother in Budapest who was gravely ill and he wanted to go to her; he hoped I could help. So I asked my wife, who knew 'Blidaru' better, to contact him. Within two days the visa came through." It was very important that officers' networks extended into the population, for whom they might do favors.[19] Indeed, the officers had seen it this way for some time, writing in their magazine *Securitatea* in 1968 that a reason for people to agree to become informers was so they could have someone to help them out.[20]

During my conversation with Adrian, I ask him, "But were you afraid when they tried to recruit you?" "Yes, because I had no idea how far they'd go and

I didn't know what information they had." "So the fear thing isn't just our imagination. How did your recruitment end?" "We came to an agreement that it wasn't working out. The officer said, 'You mustn't tell anyone,' and I obeyed: I told my wife and now I'm telling you, and I've told no one else!" Why did he follow the order? "In some crazy way I was glad the guy let me off, and I didn't want to repay that by going public. So I felt it as a kind of contract even though the deal wasn't clinched. After the revolution I saw him on the street; he walked past me without looking me in the eye."

He closes by observing that Romanian intellectuals, the principal keepers of the anticommunist discourse, are unwilling to try to understand *securişti* for what they were. Instead, they stick with the old image of a Securitate united and homogeneous in its exercise of terror and coercion. This under-writes the propagation of fear upon which the anticommunist intellectuals insist in their representations of the Securitate. As to why the anticommunist discourse became so hegemonic after the revolution, Adrian says, "To cover up the amount of actual continuity with the communists. I have the impres-sion that the way the Securitate is coming to be perceived in the present is part of a system of representations having important functions. The image of fear being perpetuated is in some way useful to the field of power—in the first place by reducing the evil produced under communism to the actions of a maleficent organization and a few madmen, the 'torturers.'" Since so much of politics in Romania—unlike some other Eastern European countries—after 1989 has been in the hands of communism's heirs, this is an interesting thought, one that casts my officers' "recruitment" efforts in a new light.

This conversation breaks open my relation to my subject, reminding me that if we accept only the "big picture" fed on both sides by Cold War propaganda (the fearsome image of the invisible Securitate), we will never understand that organization. Having recognized that I was pursuing them because their invis-ibility galled me, I now have to admit that it was especially *to me* that *securişti* were invisible. Many Romanians knew at least some of them and even main-tained friendly relations with them. People used them for favors, saw them in workplaces, lived in the same buildings with them, perhaps talked with them at family gatherings, negotiated with them about informing—all things I could not do, at least not knowingly. One has to think of them, then, as people doing a certain kind of job in a society in which social connections were the basic currency of life, a means both of surveillance/repression and of accomplishing things. As the difficulty of accomplishing anything increased throughout the 1980s, more and more people would have approached them for help.

This was possible precisely because *securişti* were not isolated from the general population but rather entangled with it. Relations with them were of a piece with people's efforts to form usable and positive social relations over their lifetimes, the basis of their civic culture. As in much of Eastern Europe, Romanian society under socialism functioned through thick networks of social relationships, which made inroads into the general atmosphere of suspicion by gradually building trust. Although this had been true to some degree before the communist takeover, the new regime had both diminished the possibilities for trust and greatly enhanced the suspicion. This dialectic of trust and doubt, openness and secrecy, was the medium in which Romanian citizens lived, varying in their awareness of the extent of surveillance and in their helpful connections with Securitate officers in daily life.

Thus, instead of imagining an invisible Securitate preying on a frightened populace, we should imagine a dense and varied field of relations, as Secus connect with friends, neighbors, and relatives, develop complex relations with their informers, and do favors for "volunteers" who send them information uninvited. Sometimes the informers are fearful, but sometimes they become such friends that the officer even attends their funeral. Since much of the officers' work requires them to be hidden, they perpetuate images of their invisibility and fierceness that are not wholly accurate. Thus, the Securitate was not somehow "above" society in the apparatus of the state but *inside* it, with tentacles that crept into people's social relations in generally destructive ways. A friend who is a military officer observed to me, "Their job was to control society, and networks were their means." In brief, like everyone else, they depended on sociality and the elaborate management of social relations. These thoughts suggest that we envision the Romanian communist state not (or not only) as a mask supporting a system based on terror and repression but rather more like a tributary formation rooted in the concept of "wealth in people,"[21] a form of wealth the former Securitate and its successor control in spades.

If the officers themselves are only partly hidden, however, this is less true of their auxiliaries: the informers, rendered invisible by oaths of silence— and, as with "Beniamin" and Mariana, by their dread of being discovered and ostracized, even after the end of the regime. In a society based on dense networks of social relations, it was the *informers'* invisibility that sustained the most insidious effects of officers' practices: using hidden informers to reshape people's social relations toward the organization's own ends, away from the organic ties people would otherwise have relied on. Invisibility did play a role in the Securitate's work, then, but not quite as common understandings would have it. The basis of the regime's power was less fear, secrecy, and the hidden than the colonizing of Romanians' sociality, an extraordinarily powerful resource.

> > >

I felt the power of this sociality on my own skin. Thinking over my years of association with Romania, I realized that whereas at the beginning I arrived with theories that were fashionable in the United States and used them (in a rather colonializing manner) to shape the "raw material" I collected, with each project my themes and treatment were more and more shaped by my connections in the field. My books on collectivization and property restitution came from what villagers wanted to tell me after Ceauşescu fell, not from my own theoretical interests, and my work on the Securitate—something I would never have been drawn to otherwise—from a Romanian colleague's suggestion.

This change parallels another. One of my traits as a scholar has been a tendency to go for the "big picture," sometimes at the expense of the nitty-gritty of everyday life. It has taken effort for me to move from a compelling generalization or macro model down to the particulars that sustain it (or don't). I am not unique in that, but as a trait it was both a strength and a liability in my earlier work. Over my forty years of ethnography, however, I have gradually learned that macro models are no good without data, and data come from a sustained engagement in social relations. There is an echo of this in my trajectory with these officers. I began (in *Secrets and Truths*) with claims about the place of the Securitate in Romania's system of rule and the role of secrecy and fear in it; then I tried through my file to see this in practice; and finally I determined that I should test the rule of secrecy and my own fear by trying to find some actual *securişti*. Meeting them and then talking about those meetings brought me insights I would not have had otherwise. The effort can be exhausting, however, and it required me to use my very self as an instrument for research. Because I felt in the most visceral way the huge discrepancy between my fear of the Securitate and my three encounters, I was compelled to try to understand it differently, coming to see its officers as people embedded in social relations just like everyone else.

Although ethnography is possible without trust, trusting relations enhance both the quality of the information we gain and the possibility of *using ourselves and our emotional reactions as research instruments*. The method of relying on social relations to deepen knowledge pulled me ever more closely into Romania's orbit, opening me to what people wanted to tell me about their lives. It is a deeply personal instrument, strengthened by long-term continuity that gives the method coherence. This is yet another difference between ethnography and surveillance, a matter I posed earlier. Although both create relationships that are essentially ambiguous—the interviewer strives to be likable, looks for and amplifies common ground, drops little details to suggest depth of knowledge, while the informer does much the same—Securitate surveillance does not take the extra step of interrogating its own reactions. Sometimes the ethnographer develops no more than the quasi-friendship appropriate to a professional relation, yet sometimes her friendships become genuine and profound. My mutual attachments with Mariana and "Beniamin" enabled our lengthy and illuminating discussions of their informing. My deep bond with the Biermans led to my seeing from Ralf's file just how damagingly their trajectory had met with mine. It is our constant effort to experience with our whole being while also standing back and analyzing what we feel that distinguishes the ethnographer from the world of Securitate surveillance.

The Target Function

When I read my file for the first time, what struck me was the disproportion between the means the Securitate set in motion and the derisory person that was their "target." Certainly, the employees of the Council of State Security, so as to justify their existence, had to create a permanent "work object," to invent it, to give it a consistency and a prestige that the hapless "target" most often did not have.

—Gabriel Liiceanu, *My Dear Snitch*

When things go wrong, the urge to explain has several outlets: God, or fate, or some other external power decreed the outcome; I or we were inadequate to the task; enemies sabotaged it; and so forth. The Securitate served a system based on that last option, which projects failure outward onto others rather than attributing it to limitations of the self, as the second option does. The third option is a form of explanation common to unlegitimated rule: since rulers have attained power without seeking support from the populace, they rightly fear its challenges to their social order. One result may be a continual hunt for saboteurs—or people who can be made to fill that role. Those people then become "targets"; some of them are called spies. These are the roots of my life as a "spy" in communist Romania, and they help us to answer a question I am often asked: How could someone be closely followed as a spy across fifteen years and continually allowed to return? Here is a somewhat schematic possible answer.

Targets and spies are ultimately not people with qualities and behaviors; they are *functions*.[22] As such, they embody the enemy that power fears, and they occupy the site of danger that must be contained. The target function congeals those fears and dangers in a way that justifies an apparatus of repression. Its manner of congealing them helps to brake the potentially endless proliferation of resistance and opposition that unlegitimated rule invites. Among the means by which the target function limits resistance is funneling it into a few known types: the bourgeois capitalist, the dissident, the saboteur, the "irredentist element," the spy—all types of people the communists "made up," as Ian Hacking would say.[23] The job of containing them goes to an organization within the state apparatus—in this case, the Securitate. Its job in stabilizing rule is very important; less important is whether the targets followed are actually spies and saboteurs. Simply gathering oppositional characteristics under these headings helps to contain the dangers they pose.

The target function not only generates the Securitate apparatus with its immense retinue of informers. It also enables officers in a small, relatively insignificant country to justify their existence and become "big men" by following targets from larger countries, like me. Their monopoly over the target function may give them an edge in internal power struggles with other organizations of the state.

Although the target is above all a function, those occupying this role nonetheless experience it as an acute form of surveillance—of being spied upon. These pages have shown what it was like to be spied upon in this way. "We are all under surveillance," I wrote at the beginning, but not all forms of surveillance produce the same experience. The Securitate's form of it had at least two characteristics that distinguish it from the twenty-first-century high-tech variety. First, it was labor-intensive, relying less on technology than on informers and on manipulating the target's social relations, fouling them with deceit. This form is particularly damaging to ethnography, with its reliance on trust and human connection.

Second, this form has specific effects on identity, which it both undermines by destabilizing social supports in the target's network and also fragments by multiplying pseudonyms and hypotheses of a spy's evil purposes. The person occupying the target function thinks she knows who her friends are and derives an anchoring sense from that, but in fact she is deluded. She will come, in the end, to wonder who she really is. High-tech surveillance, by contrast, does not rely on undermining people's social relationships to control them but instead simply maps those relationships to discern potentially treacherous patterns. It does not instrumentalize people's social relationships in the same way as does Securitate surveillance. We will know more about the experience of high-tech surveillance once we gain access to our National Security Administration, Facebook, and other files. Perhaps my stories here will prepare my readers somewhat for that inevitable disturbing moment.

The idea of the target function is one form of answering those who wonder why Romanian exchange programs kept letting me in if they thought I was a spy. Gabriel Liiceanu phrases the idea somewhat differently, quoting interwar Indologist Heinrich Zimmer on an ancient Hindu text about the friendship between a lion and a tomcat. The lion is bothered in his cave by a mouse, so he befriends the tomcat, who, he hopes, will kill it. The tomcat, however, doesn't kill the mouse but keeps it at bay, realizing that his own continued existence depends on having the mouse alive. Then one day the mouse really gets on the tomcat's nerves and he kills it — only to be thrown out of the lion's den as no longer necessary to keeping the peace. Zimmer comments that officers of the Gestapo and the KGB have taken this lesson to heart, always keeping a few "mice" around to ensure their importance to the dictator.[24]

Here, then, is my final identity: I am the mouse. You might object that this is too insignificant a role, but it is not: the mouse, the target function, was essential to the processes that sustained Romania's communist state. Despite the differences between high-tech surveillance and the Securitate's more labor-intensive version, both forms flourish by keeping the mouse alive. In both, a bureaucracy exists to find enemies—spies, terrorists—and to ferret out secrets. If in the Securitate's case this meant that all foreigners became spies and the atmosphere of suspicion somehow invited people to produce secrets and transgressions, does high-tech surveillance too help to produce the very threat it seeks to obliterate?

My occupancy of the target function helps to unify the proliferating selves that have emerged in this book. My doppelganger "VERA" and her pseudonymous siblings—nefariously engaged as military spy, closet Hungarian, friend of dissidents, and collector of socio-political information—come together with Kathy and Katherine Verdery, ethnographers, as well as with the strategies they adopted in their work (married woman, motorbike rider, user of pseudonyms of their own). Discovering the target function's unifying effects enables me to counteract the looming fragmentation of my officers' practice of creating multiple spying identities. Here "VERA" is a help. Unlike KATHERINE VERDERY, who found all this multiplication of identities disconcerting, "VERA"—that is, Katherine and her various doubles—realizes that these doubles echo experiences all of us have, even though we seldom have them as acutely rendered on paper as she does. "VERA" knew from the outset that Katherine was mistaken in her belief in a singular self with a stable, unique identity, and she took pleasure in how life in Romania gradually subverted Katherine's perspective.

Epilogue

12 OCTOBER 2013. I am in Vlaicu, throwing a party to mark forty years since I first arrived in this village. My guest list of twenty-three contains people—or in some cases their grown children—who helped me the most with one or another of my village-based books. Some of them I've known for decades and consider cherished friends. Meri's son Florin, my cohost for the event, has helped me find a lovely restaurant in Orăştie. We enter a large, nicely decorated hall containing a long table, weighed down with food and drink. Music plays in the background, a mix of traditional Romanian and soft pop. I have dressed up in my most smashing teal-and-brown silk jacket and, unusually, put on makeup. To get things going, I give a little speech explaining my purpose with this party and in some way mentioning each person present. I say that nowhere but in Vlaicu have I known five generations from a single family—Meri's. Her tiny great-grandson sits like a little Buddha, gazing benevolently at us with an expression I fancy I first saw on the face of Meri's mother.

Things are rather quiet for a little while, then gradually warm up. During the course of the evening I go around the table about three times, talking with everyone for a bit. At the end, Florin gives a short speech and suggests that instead of general toasts, I should go around the table one last time with

Connections: Meri (*left*) and Katherine in 2012. Photo by Nicolae Mărgineanu.

Connections: At fortieth-anniversary party in 2013. Photo by Vasile Vasiu.

champagne and toast each person. So I do, telling them how much they've helped me and thanking them. Some of them tell me how much my presence in their village has meant to them. By now I've had quite a lot to drink, and emotions are close to the surface. When I get to Uncle Petru Bota's grandsons Onu and Sivu and their wives, I'm practically crying. I have also invited "Beniamin," and we *both* cry.

What a relief, this sudden sadness, given the last several years of feeling that my Securitate file had alienated me from Romania, a place where I had enjoyed innumerable good times in years past. I am surprised to receive some presents—bouquets of flowers, a beautiful suede vest, and a classy leather jacket. It seems I'm saying goodbye to Vlaicu, after these forty years. I think about what I have gained from my long association with this country, above all an immeasurably richer appreciation of the value of human connections, which this event itself embodies. The gratifying durability of the connections in Vlaicu stands sharply opposed to my life at home, fractured by multiple moves from place to place.

Although the file has put many obstacles in the path of understanding my trajectory through those times, it has also proven unexpectedly instructive. Using it to revisit that trajectory has yielded unpleasant and contradictory reactions—bafflement, depression, rage—that I have had to tame. For my informers, I have sought to temper anger with gratitude for what they were willing to teach me, even though they found it painful; for my officers, I have tempered fear with curiosity, in order to grapple with the culture and apparatus of secrecy. But for the role of the Securitate apparatus as a whole from 1948 to 1989 and beyond, I find no reason to temper my criticism.

I do not flatter myself that I have fathomed the Securitate and its place in the Romanian communist state. Rather, I have scarcely begun to make out what lies in its shadows. Those shadows are quintessentially the stuff of state-making, at which the Securitate and its successors excel. From their work will emerge more and different selves, more doubles, more mysteries, as the vectors of state-making shift with changes in the global political economy. By using the Securitate's archive to cast some light onto those processes, I hope to have illuminated something not only of how Romanian socialism worked but of the new forms of statecraft, promising greater security through ever-heightened surveillance, that are developing worldwide.

NOTES

Prologue

1. Romania's Securitate was formed in 1948, with the help of the Soviet NKVD/KGB. It contained both foreign and domestic intelligence divisions, each of which—but especially the former—underwent massive restructuring after 1978, when the deputy head of foreign intelligence, Gen. Ion Mihai Pacepa, defected to the United States, the highest-ranking officer from the Eastern bloc ever to do so.

2. I do not know how widely it happens that intelligence organizations follow people back to their home country. Through a Freedom of Information Act (FOIA) request, I received sixteen pages from my FBI file. On one heavily redacted page there is a note: "It was ███'s opinion that several other agents of the RIS [Romania Intelligence Service] were also deployed in actions against Verdery."

3. Haggerty and Ericson refer to this same product of contemporary surveillance as a "data double." Kevin D. Haggerty and Richard V. Ericson, "The Surveillant Assemblage," *British Journal of Sociology* 51 (2000): 613.

4. This organization was formed in 1967 with a mix of government and private funding to sponsor scholarly exchanges with the Soviet bloc; it was an offshoot of a program started by the Ford Foundation in 1956 that sent scholars to the Soviet bloc on tourist visas. The idea was to have scholarly exchanges, but because of Senator McCarthy's actions, they could not be run through the government, as Fulbright grants were, without becoming so politicized as to render them useless for scholarly purposes. See David C. Engerman, *Know Your Enemy: The Rise and Fall of America's Soviet Experts* (Oxford: Oxford University Press, 2009).

5. Herta Müller, "Securitate in All but Name" (interview), *Signandsight.com*, 31 August 2009, http://www.signandsight.com/features/1910.html.

6. Gabriel Liiceanu, *Dragul meu turnător* [My dear snitch] (Bucharest: Humanitas, 2013), 196.

7. For instance, Romanian writers Stelian Tănase, in *Acasă se vorbeşte în şoaptă: Dosar şi jurnal din anii tîrzii ai dictaturii* [At home they speak in whispers: File and journal from

the late years of the dictatorship] (Bucharest: Compania, 2002); and Dorin Tudoran, in *Eu, fiul lor: Dosar de Securitate* [I, their son: Securitate file] (Iaşi: Polirom, 2010).

8. A somewhat different form in which anthropologists might occasionally catch glimpses of themselves under surveillance is the files of the FBI. In his book *Glimpses into My Own Black Box: An Exercise in Self-Deconstruction* (Madison: University of Wisconsin Press, 2010), George Stocking writes of the pages he was able to retrieve from that source.

9. In Poland, for example, where a lustration law was passed in 1997, only journalists, certified victims seeking exculpation, and researchers had access to the files: people accused of collaboration might or might not be allowed to see their files, and if so they could not make copies or notes, as is possible in Romania. In Hungary, following a period of partial access, Prime Minister Viktor Orbán proposed giving the files back to those on whom they had been kept—in other words, dismantling the secret police archive altogether. Files are particularly available in the former East Germany, for the public acted to prevent much of the destruction that occurred elsewhere (including Romania). In the Czech Republic and Slovakia, citizens have access to their files, but many more were destroyed than in Germany.

10. See, e.g., Florin Poenaru, "Contesting Illusions: History and Intellectual Class Struggles in (Post)socialist Romania" (PhD diss., Central European University, Budapest, 2013); and Lavinia Stan, ed., *Transitional Justice in Eastern Europe and the Former Soviet Union: Reckoning with the Communist Past* (London: Routledge, 2009).

11. That book differs from this one in several ways, including its more extensive scholarly apparatus, its discussions of secrecy and power and of compartmentalization in the work process, and its basis in archives and libraries rather than interviews and field research. The main substantive difference concerns its treatment of the secrecy of the secret police (see part II of this book).

12. For example, Steven Sampson and Sam Beck, among anthropologists, and a number of scholars from the Fulbright exchange. Beck, for instance, had been working on economic specializations, which included some fieldwork with Roma—a topic not welcomed by the authorities. This led to his being made *persona non grata*.

13. See, for instance, David Price, *Cold War Anthropology: The CIA, the Pentagon, and the Growth of Dual Use Anthropology* (Durham, NC: Duke University Press, 2016); Frances Stonor Saunders, *The Cultural Cold War: The CIA and the World of Arts and Letters* (New York: New Press, 1999); and Engerman, *Know Your Enemy* (e.g., 91, 242–43). The existence of CIA connections, or suspicion of them, may have been truer of grantees who went to the Soviet Union than of those who went to Eastern Europe.

14. Price, *Cold War Anthropology*, ch. 8.

15. Archive of the Consiliul Naţional pentru Studierea Arhivelor Securităţii (ACNSAS), Fond D, 12618/5, p. 23.

16. Information from Steven Sampson, email communication.

17. In his celebrated essay "On Ethnographic Authority," James Clifford writes of how we develop knowledge of other cultures, emphasizing a method that involves two or more conscious subjects negotiating a reality together. The result, he suggests, is not experience-based interpretation but a dialogic and polyphonic account. This view strikes me as wholly inadequate for the situations in which I found myself in the field.

James Clifford, "On Ethnographic Authority," in *The Predicament of Culture* (Cambridge, MA: Harvard University Press, 1988), 21–54.

18. There is ample research on the phenomenon of secrecy in sociology, political science, and especially anthropology, which contains a large body of work on secret societies in places like New Guinea and Africa. See also Graham M. Jones, "Secrecy," *Annual Review of Anthropology* 43 (2014): 53–69. Because I report on some of this work in Katherine Verdery, *Secrets and Truths: Ethnography in the Archive of the Romanian Secret Police* (Budapest: Central European University Press, 2014), my treatment of it here will be cursory.

19. István V. Király, *Fenomenologia existenţială a secretului* [The existential phenomenology of the secret] (Bucharest: Editura Paralela 45, 2001), 84.

20. Cristina Vatulescu, *Police Aesthetics: Literature, Film, and the Secret Police in Soviet Times* (Stanford, CA: Stanford University Press, 2010), 4–5.

21. Pierre Bourdieu, *On the State: Lectures at the Collège de France, 1989–1992* (Malden, MA: Polity, 2014), 3–10.

22. Quotes from Philip Abrams, "Notes on the Difficulty of Studying the State," *Journal of Historical Sociology* 1 (1988): 68, 76, 69, 82.

23. For the former, see, e.g., Paul Amar, *The Security Archipelago: Human-Security States, Sexuality Politics, and the End of Neoliberalism* (Durham, NC: Duke University Press, 2013); David Lyon, ed., *Theorizing Surveillance: The Panopticon and Beyond* (Cullompton, UK: Willan, 2006); Mark Maguire, Catarina Frois, and Nils Zurawski, eds., *The Anthropology of Security: Perspectives from the Frontline of Policing, Counter-Terrorism, and Border Control* (London: Pluto, 2014); Joseph Masco, *The Theater of Operations: National Security Affect from the Cold War to the War on Terror* (Durham, NC: Duke University Press, 2014); and Verdery, *Secrets and Truths*. For the latter, see, for instance, John Borneman, *Belonging in the Two Berlins: Kin, State, Nation* (Cambridge: Cambridge University Press, 1992); Fernando Coronil, *The Magical State: Nature, Money, and Modernity in Venezuela* (Chicago: University of Chicago Press, 1997); Philip Corrigan and Derek Sayer, *The Great Arch: English State Formation as Cultural Revolution* (Oxford: Blackwell, 1985); and Gail Kligman, *The Politics of Duplicity: Controlling Reproduction in Ceauşescu's Romania* (Berkeley: University of California Press, 1998).

24. Abrams, "Notes on the Difficulty of Studying the State," 77.

25. John Borneman, Joseph Masco, and Katherine Verdery, "Espying Spies," *Cambridge Journal of Anthropology* 33 (2015): 131.

26. See, for example, Steven C. Caton, *Yemen Chronicle: An Anthropology of War and Mediation* (New York: Hill and Wang, 2005) (for Yemen); John Borneman, *Syrian Episodes: Sons, Fathers, and an Anthropologist in Aleppo* (Princeton, NJ: Princeton University Press, 2007); John Borneman and Abdellah Hammoudi, "Fieldwork Experience, Collaboration, and Interlocution: The 'Metaphysics of Presence' in Encounters with the Syrian Mukhabarat," in *Being There: The Fieldwork Encounter and the Making of Truth*, ed. John Borneman and Abdellah Hammoudi (Berkeley: University of California Press, 2009), 237–58 (for Syria); and some of the papers in Martin Sökefeld and Sabine Strasser, eds., "Under Suspicious Eyes: Surveillance States, Security Zones and Ethnographic Fieldwork," special issue of *Zeitschrift für Ethnologie* 141 (2016) (ranging across South Asia, Africa, and elsewhere). One did not have to work in Eastern Europe to be

suspected of spying. What distinguishes my case from those others is not just being under surveillance but having the officers' notes.

27. Talal Asad, "Thinking about Terrorism and Just War," *Cambridge Review of International Affairs* 23 (2010): 7.

28. Timothy Garton Ash, *The File: A Personal History* (New York: Vintage, 1998), 42.

29. I could extend it further than I do to show some effects on Romanian identity of being raised in an atmosphere of suspicion, but that would have required a different kind of fieldwork.

30. Ian Hacking, "Making Up People," *London Review of Books* 28 (17 August 2006): 23–26.

Chapter 1. The 1970s

1. Bill Skinner saved our 1973–74 correspondence until his death in 2008. I am grateful to his widow, Susan Mann, who was kind enough to send it to me, greatly enriching my recollection of that period.

2. Franz Boas, "Scientists as Spies," *The Nation* 109, no. 2842 (1919): 797.

3. See David H. Price's excellent books on this subject, particularly *Cold War Anthropology*. Among other cases that aroused anthropologists' ire were Project Camelot in Latin America, with its counterinsurgency goals, and the Human Terrain System in the U.S. war in Afghanistan.

4. Lily Tomlin, *The Search for Signs of Intelligent Life in the Universe*, written by Jane Wagner (New Almaden, CA: Wolfe Video, 1992). Tomlin's word was not "paranoid" but "cynical."

5. "Moarte sigură cu cobră / Dar mai sigură cu Mobra."

6. This minority had been settled in Transylvania in two waves, during the twelfth and the eighteenth centuries, to guard the borders and improve agriculture. They were Romanian citizens but took their German identity very seriously.

7. In 2010 Romanian ethnographer Cosmin Budeanca carried out a few interviews in Aurel Vlaicu, asking what people thought of me, and was told, "They said she was a spy, they did. But after a while they got used to her. She stayed a long time, and they got used to her." Another response Budeanca received was more skeptical: "People said she was a spy, but if she was one they wouldn't have let her into the country. And she didn't have anything to spy on, 'cause we just talked about the collective farm. So if she has permission from Bucharest to be here, why would she be a spy? . . . What would she have wanted to do, overthrow our government?" My thanks to Dr. Budeanca for sharing his interviews with me.

8. Diana Georgescu, " 'Ceaușescu's Children': The Making and Unmaking of Romania's Last Socialist Generation (1965–2010)" (PhD diss., University of Illinois, 2014).

9. To distinguish among people with the same name, like "Maria," Romanians often add a possessive with the person's spouse or parent. "Maria lu' Relu" was thus "Maria, Aurel's wife."

10. The film was arranged for by Dr. Cristina Anisescu, of the CNSAS, as part of the institution's youth outreach activities. Made by filmmaker Nicolae Mărgineanu, it included conversations with a number of my friends and colleagues in Cluj and Vlaicu, as well as a running interview with me about my earlier years in Romania.

11. Katherine Verdery, "Homage to a Transylvanian Peasant," *East European Politics and Societies* 3 (1989): 51–82.

12. Hoping to build my story in counterpoint with others from my field site, I did not plan to have the other main figures be members of national minorities in a book about Romania. When I asked the Romanian friends who would have been the obvious possibilities, however—that is, people with whom I had an important and lengthy relationship from early in my research—they all preferred not to be made visible in this way, for a variety of reasons. I would not want Romanian readers to conclude from my frequent mention of the Biermans that I preferred them to my close Romanian friends.

13. In these documents, Directorate III, or the Third Directorate (present in the provinces as "Service 3 [or III]"), was the Securitate branch covering counterespionage for the whole country. Among its subunits were the special unit "T" for installing and using wiretaps and other technology, the special unit "S" for monitoring correspondence and handwriting, the special unit "D" for disinformation, and the special unit "F" for shadowing and investigations.

14. Examples of this from an earlier time can be found in Lynn Visson, *Wedded Strangers: The Challenges of Russian-American Marriages* (New York: Hippocrene, 1998).

15. In fact, I usually kept my three copies locked in my suitcase until I could go to Bucharest (about once a month), where I sent all three copies through the diplomatic pouch on separate days, never putting any in the Romanian mail. This does not guarantee that they were not read by U.S. government agents, as David Price points out (*Cold War Anthropology*, 246).

16. Although I do not usually correct the bits of misinformation in extracts from my file, I must disagree with this one. The "historical reality" is that a number of Hungarians lived in and around Vlaicu right up to World War I (see Katherine Verdery, *Transylvanian Villagers: Three Centuries of Political, Economic, and Ethnic Change* [Berkeley: University of California Press, 1983]), and a handful remained thereafter.

17. Herbert Reinke, "Policing Politics in Germany from Weimar to the Stasi," in *The Policing of Politics in the Twentieth Century: Historical Perspectives*, ed. Mark Mazower (Providence, RI: Berghahn, 1997), 101.

18. They included a large group project run by John Cole (Sam Beck, John Cole, David Kideckel, Marilyn McArthur, Stephen Randall, Steven Sampson), as well as Andreas Argyres, Margaret Hiebert (Beissinger), Gail Kligman, and me.

19. Cristina Anisescu, "Dinamica de structură şi rol a reţelei informative in perioada 1948–1989" [The dynamics of structure and role in the informers' network in the period 1948–1989], in *Arhivele Securităţii* I [Securitate archives], ed. Marian Stere (Bucharest: Editura Pro Historia, 2002), 29.

20. This would distinguish socialism's ethnographers from those of colonial times, who, Talal Asad suggests, were of rather limited utility to colonial authorities. Talal Asad, *Anthropology and the Colonial Encounter* (New York: Humanities Press, 1973).

21. Pronounced DAH-veed pro-DAHN. Born in 1902 in a village not far from Vlaicu, he wrote definitive works on the Romanian national movement and Transylvanian feudalism.

22. Sheila Fitzpatrick, *A Spy in the Archives: A Memoir of Cold War Russia* (New York: I. B. Tauris, 2014).

23. In my meeting with Securitate officer "Blidaru" (see chapter 3), I asked if he happened to recall the gender of the transcriber; he believed it was female.

Chapter 2. The 1980s

Epigraph: Quoted in Ira Jacknis, "Margaret Mead and Gregory Bateson in Bali," *Cultural Anthropology* 3 (1988): 172.

1. Robert Gellately, "Denunciations in Twentieth-Century Germany: Aspects of Self-Policing in the Third Reich and the German Democratic Republic," in *Accusatory Practices: Denunciation in Modern European History, 1789–1989*, ed. Sheila Fitzpatrick and Robert Gellately (Chicago: University of Chicago Press, 1997), 220.

2. Emily Gerard, *The Land beyond the Forest: Facts, Figures, and Fancies from Transylvania* (Edinburgh: W. Blackwood, 1888), 124.

3. Vatulescu, *Police Aesthetics*, 32.

4. George Ardeleanu, *N. Steinhardt și paradoxurile libertății* [N. Steinhardt and the paradoxes of liberty] (Bucharest: Humanitas, 2009), 276.

5. Tănase, *Acasă se vorbește în șoaptă*, 20, 57.

6. Herta Müller, *The Appointment: A Novel* (New York: Metropolitan, 2001), esp. 204–14.

7. "PROCES VERBAL de constatare a efectuării unor acte premergătoare . . . în vederea strîngerii datelor necesare începerii urmăririi penale."

8. Liiceanu, *Dragul meu turnător*, 340–41.

9. Katherine Verdery, *National Ideology under Socialism: Identity and Cultural Politics in Ceaușescu's Romania* (Berkeley: University of California Press, 1991).

Excursus: Reflections on Reading One's File

Epigraph: Radu Ioanid, "Anatomia delațiunii" [The anatomy of denunciation], *Observatorul Cultural* 139 (22 October 2002).

1. Gilles Perrault, *Dossier 51: An Entertainment*, trans. Douglas Parmée (London: Weidenfeld and Nicolson, 1971).

2. "Nu-mi place minciuna, prefăcătoria, falsitatea și ostentativul."

3. Müller, "Securitate in All but Name"; Andrei Șerbulescu (Belu Zilber), *Monarhia de drept dialectic* [The monarchy of dialectical law] (Bucharest: Humanitas, 1991).

4. Tudoran, *Eu, fiul lor*, 9.

5. Liiceanu, *Dragul meu turnător*, 51–52.

Chapter 3. Revelations

Epigraph: Quoted in Michael Taussig, *Defacement: Public Secrecy and the Labor of the Negative* (Stanford, CA: Stanford University Press, 1999), 2.

1. See, for example, the beginning of the Polish film *Psy* (Pigs).

2. Garton Ash, *The File*.

3. Anisescu, "Dinamica de structură și rol a rețelei," 35.

4. Monica Grigore, "Ceaușescu și redefinirea raporturilor dintre partid și Securitatea" [Ceaușescu and the redefinition of relations between the Party and Securitate], *Arhivele Securității* (2004): 412.

5. Figures courtesy of Florian Banu, April 2015.

6. Maria Łoś, "Lustration and Truth Claims: Unfinished Revolutions in Central Europe." *Law & Social Inquiry* 20 (1995): 133.

7. Gabriella Turnaturi, *Betrayals: The Unpredictability of Human Relations*, trans. Lydia G. Cochrane (Chicago: University of Chicago Press, 2007).

8. Ana Blandiana, *Fals tratat de manipulare* [False treatise on manipulation] (Bucharest: Humanitas, 2013), 18.

9. Nicolae Corbeanu, *Amintirile unui laş* [Recollections of a coward] (Bucharest: Albatros, 1998), 237.

10. Herta Müller, "Every Word Knows Something of a Vicious Circle," Nobel Prize Lecture, 7 December 2009, https://www.nobelprize.org/nobel_prizes/literature/laureates/2009/muller-lecture_en.html.

11. Mihai Albu, *Informatorul: Studiu asupra colaborării cu Securitatea* [The informer: A study of collaboration with the Securitate] (Iaşi: Polirom, 2008).

12. In previous publications I misidentified this person as her father.

13. Tănase, *Acasă se vorbeşte în şoaptă*; Liiceanu, *Dragul meu turnător*.

14. Anikó Szűcs, "Performing the Informer: State Security Files Recontextualized in the Hungarian Art World" (PhD diss., New York University, 2015), ch. 1. My thanks to Anikó Szűcs for sharing her unpublished work with me.

15. Blandiana, *Fals tratat de manipulare*, 456. On the death-wedding, see Gail Kligman, *The Wedding of the Dead: Ritual, Poetics, and Popular Culture in Transylvania* (Berkeley: University of California Press, 1988).

16. The lawyer also claimed that Pătrulescu had brain cancer and would be dead before the case came to trial. Liiceanu withdrew his suit but still does not know if Pătrulescu died. Details courtesy of Gabriel Liiceanu (email exchange, 12 November 2017).

17. Smaranda Vultur, "Daily Life and Surveillance in the 1970s and 1980s," in *Remembering Communism: Private and Public Recollections of Lived Experience in Southeast Europe*, ed. Maria Todorova, Augusta Dimou, and Stefan Troebst (Budapest: Central European University Press, 2014), 427–28.

18. Cristina Anisescu, " 'Partiturile' agenturii" [The "scores" of the informer network], in *"Partiturile" Securităţii: Directive, ordine, instrucţiuni (1947–1987)* [The Securitate's "scores": Directives, orders, and instructions, 1947–1987], ed. Cristina Anisescu, Silviu B. Moldovan, and Mirela Matiu (Bucharest: Nemira, 2007), 19n14.

19. Once I created a direct relation with each of them, no longer mediated through secrecy, I decided to preserve their anonymity as they wished. To obscure further the identities of the three officers I present, I note that during each of my visits I was "processed" by more than one Securitate officer—at least seven in Hunedoara County, at least six in Cluj, and at least three in Bucharest.

20. The officer answered with a firm no.

21. Slavenka Drakulić, *They Would Never Hurt a Fly: War Criminals on Trial in The Hague* (New York: Viking, 2004), 190.

22. I have inserted into these notes a few points from a third meeting, in April 2015.

23. Thanks to Bruce Grant for this observation.

24. Jan Willem Bos reports that in 1991, 52 percent of officers in the new SRI were former *securişti*; by 2007 that number was down to 5 percent. Finding a reliable figure

is probably impossible. Jan Willem Bos, *Suspect: Dosarul meu de la Securitate*, trans. Alexandra Livia Stoicescu (Bucharest: Editura Trei, 2013), 73.

25. We get a sense of the different rationales for different times from a conversation between Romania's Princess Ileana and foreign minister Ana Pauker during the early 1950s. The princess asked Pauker why the communists used so much violence, when it would never convince anyone. " 'It is not intended to convince,' she replied calmly, 'but to frighten. When one replants, one first destroys everything that grows, root and branch. Then one levels the earth. It is only afterwards that one can plant successfully.' " Pauker went on to observe that, unfortunately, they could not simply destroy older generations, since they needed someone to raise the children. Therefore, the older generation had to be left alive, " 'but they must be too frightened to dare to interfere with the Communist training of the children.' " Ileana, Princess of Romania, *I Live Again* (London: Victor Gollancz, 1952), 245.

26. After the regime fell, Ralf left for Germany without such conditions.

Chapter 4. Ruminations

1. The organization of the former is called the Association of Military Cadres in the Reserves and in Retirement from the Romanian Information Service, founded in 1994. Its website and magazine, *Vitralii*, are accessible online to anyone. The organization of the external service, with its magazine *Periscop*, is the Association of Military Cadres in the Reserves and in Retirement from the Service of External Information.

2. See, e.g., Richard Andrew Hall, "The Historiography of the Romanian Revolution: The Uses of Absurdity and the Triumph of Securitate Revisionism," *The Archive of the Romanian Revolution of December 1989* (blog), 31 December 2013, https://romanianrevol utionofdecember1989.com/2013/12/31/the-historiography-of-the-romanian-revolution -the-uses-of-absurdity-and-the-triumph-of-securitate-revisionism/.

3. Marius Oprea, *Moștenitorii Securității* [Heirs of the Securitate] (Bucharest: Humanitas, 2004).

4. Cătălin Manea, "Securistul Ținca" [Securitate officer Ținca], *Tunuri din Bihor*, 26 September 2007, http://tunuridinbihor.blogspot.com/2007/09/securistul-inc.html; Florin Ciucaș, "Securist cu 'diplomă': Fostul decan de la Drept, Ovidiu Ținca, catalogat securist care a făcut poliție politică" [Securist with a "diploma": Former dean of the Law School, Ovidiu Ținca, classified as a Securitate officer in the political police], *Bihoreanul tipărit*, 31 July 2014, http://www.ebihoreanul.ro/stiri/ultima-or-31-6/securist-cu-diploma -fostul-decan-ovidiu-ținca-catalogat-securist-care-a-făcut-poliție-politică-115970.html.

5. My thanks to an anonymous reader for this suggestion.

6. Col. Filip Teodorescu quotes writer Octavian Paler, who said, "Not every Securitate worker is automatically odious." Filip Teodorescu, *Un risc asumat: Timișoara decembrie 1989* [A risk assumed: Timișoara, December 1989] (Craiova, Romania: Editura Viitorul Românesc, 1992), 145.

7. Oprea, personal conversation, August 2015.

8. See, e.g., Gail Kligman and Katherine Verdery, *Peasants under Siege: The Collectivization of Romanian Agriculture, 1949–1962* (Princeton, NJ: Princeton University Press, 2011), 32.

9. Liiceanu, *Dragul meu turnător*, 213–14.

10. Saygun Gökarıksel, "Of Truths, Secrets, and Loyalties: Political Belonging and State Building in Poland after State Socialism" (PhD diss., City University of New York, 2015).

11. Gökarıksel, "Of Truths, Secrets, and Loyalties," 377–78.

12. Stephen Marche, "The Epidemic of Facelessness," *New York Times*, 15 February 2015, SR1, 6–7.

13. See, e.g., Abrams, "Notes on the Difficulty of Studying the State"; and Fernando Coronil, "State Reflections: The 2002 Coup against Hugo Chavez," in *The Revolution in Venezuela: Social and Political Change under Chávez*, ed. Thomas Ponniah and Jonathan Eastwood (Cambridge, MA: Harvard University Press, 2011), 39–67.

14. Coronil, "State Reflections," 63.

15. Blandiana, *Fals tratat de manipulare*, 60–61.

16. After 1989 he's named to a high government post, and this same *securist* comes to his office. When Andrei asks why, he replies, "I've come to follow your orders. We have to fight together against the counterrevolutionaries!"

17. Gary Bruce, *The Firm: The Inside Story of the Stasi* (New York: Oxford University Press, 2010), 49.

18. E.g., Golfo Alexopoulos, *Stalin's Outcasts: Aliens, Citizens, and the Soviet State, 1926–1936* (Ithaca: Cornell University Press, 2003). Ioana Macrea-Toma offers a fascinating analysis of informing in "The Eyes of Radio Free Europe: Regimes of Visibility in the Cold War Archives," *East Central Europe* 44 (2017): 99–127.

19. Another example of the point that there were always connections between *securişti* and others in Romania is Gheorghe Florescu's memoir, *Confessions of a Coffee-Maker*, which shows multiple large networks unfolding, connected by patronage like a big family, in which *securişti* have tight and frequent relations of protection with people who are not in their organization. By the late 1970s, he writes, the entire economy was in the Securitate's hands. Gheorghe-Ilie Florescu, *Confesiunile unui cafegiu* [Confessions of a coffee-maker] (Bucharest: Humanitas, 2008).

20. Constantin Hulubaş, "Ce motive a avut informatorul să accepte colaborarea?" [What reasons did the informer have to accept collaboration?], *Securitatea* 36 (1976): 58.

21. That is, the most powerful people are not necessarily those with extensive economic assets but those who control other people, do favors for them, and can count on various kinds of support from them in return. See Humphrey, *Karl Marx Collective: Economy, Society, and Religion in a Siberian Collective Farm* (Cambridge: Cambridge University Press, 1983); and Katherine Verdery, *The Vanishing Hectare: Property and Value in Postsocialist Transylvania* (Ithaca, NY: Cornell University Press, 2003).

22. I develop this thought from Michel Foucault's notion of the "author function," in his essay "What Is an Author?" He suggests that the "author" is not a person, a site of creativity, but rather a function: "a principle of thrift in the proliferation of meaning." He poses the problem that signification, or the making of meaning, tends toward overabundance (especially once it is conceived of as "free" from the constraints of a unitary relation between the thing signified and the signifier). The

author function helps to slow down that process by tethering meaning to "authors." Similarly, the target function helps to slow down resistance by tethering it to spies, irredentists, and saboteurs. Michel Foucault, "What Is an Author?," in *The Foucault Reader*, ed. Paul Rabinow (New York: Pantheon, 1984), 101–20.

23. Hacking, "Making Up People."

24. Liiceanu, *Dragul meu turnător*, 94–95.

BIBLIOGRAPHY

Abrams, Philip. "Notes on the Difficulty of Studying the State." *Journal of Historical Sociology* 1(1988): 58–89.

Albu, Mihai. *Informatorul: Studiu asupra colaborării cu Securitatea* [The informer: A study of collaboration with the Securitate]. Iaşi: Polirom, 2008.

Alexopoulos, Golfo. *Stalin's Outcasts: Aliens, Citizens, and the Soviet State, 1926–1936*. Ithaca: Cornell University Press, 2003.

Amar, Paul. *The Security Archipelago: Human-Security States, Sexuality Politics, and the End of Neoliberalism*. Durham, NC: Duke University Press, 2013.

Anisescu, Cristina. "Dinamica de structură şi rol a reţelei informative in perioada 1948–1989" [The dynamics of structure and role in the informers' network in the period 1948–1989]. In *Arhivele Securităţii I* [Securitate archives], edited by Marian Stere, 10–50. Bucharest: Editura Pro Historia, 2002.

———. " 'Partiturile' agenturii" [The "scores" of the informer network]. In *"Partiturile" Securităţii: Directive, ordine, instrucţiuni (1947–1987)* [The Securitate's "scores": Directives, orders, and instructions, 1947–1987], edited by Cristina Anisescu, Silviu B. Moldovan, and Mirela Matiu, 16–43. Bucharest: Nemira, 2007.

Ardeleanu, George. *N. Steinhardt şi paradoxurile libertăţii: O perspectivă monografică* [N. Steinhardt and the paradoxes of liberty: A monographic perspective]. Bucharest: Humanitas, 2009.

Asad, Talal. *Anthropology and the Colonial Encounter*. New York: Humanities Press, 1973.

———. "Thinking about Terrorism and Just War." *Cambridge Review of International Affairs* 23 (2010): 3–24.

Blandiana, Ana. *Fals tratat de manipulare* [False treatise on manipulation]. Bucharest: Humanitas, 2013.

Boas, Franz. "Scientists as Spies." *The Nation* 109, no. 2842 (1919): 797.

Borneman, John. *Belonging in the Two Berlins: Kin, State, Nation*. Cambridge: Cambridge University Press, 1992.

———. *Syrian Episodes: Sons, Fathers, and an Anthropologist in Aleppo*. Princeton, NJ: Princeton University Press, 2007.

Borneman, John, and Abdellah Hammoudi. "Fieldwork Experience, Collaboration, and Interlocution: The 'Metaphysics of Presence' in Encounters with the Syrian Mukhabarat." In *Being There: The Fieldwork Encounter and the Making of Truth*, edited by John Borneman and Abdellah Hammoudi, 237–58. Berkeley: University of California Press, 2009.

Borneman, John, Joseph Masco, and Katherine Verdery. "Espying Spies." *Cambridge Journal of Anthropology* 33 (2015): 129–35.

Bos, Jan Willem. *Suspect: Dosarul meu de la Securitate*. Translated by Alexandra Livia Stoicescu. Bucharest: Editura Trei, 2013.

Bourdieu, Pierre. *On the State: Lectures at the Collège de France, 1989–1992*. Malden, MA: Polity, 2014.

Bruce, Gary. *The Firm: The Inside Story of the Stasi*. New York: Oxford University Press, 2010.

Caton, Steven C. *Yemen Chronicle: An Anthropology of War and Mediation*. New York: Hill and Wang, 2005.

Ciucaş, Florin. "Securist cu 'diplomă': Fostul decan de la Drept, Ovidiu Ţinca, catalogat securist care a făcut poliţie politică" [Securist with a "diploma": Former dean of the Law School, Ovidiu Ţinca, classified as a Securitate officer in the political police]." *Bihoreanul tipărit*, 31 July 2014. http://www.ebihoreanul.ro/stiri/ultima-or-31 -6/securist-cu-diploma-fostul-decan-ovidiu-tinca-catalogat-securist-care-a-facut -politie-politica-115970.html.

Clifford, James. "On Ethnographic Authority." In *The Predicament of Culture*, 21–54. Cambridge, MA: Harvard University Press, 1988.

Corbeanu, Nicolae. *Amintirile unui laş* [Recollections of a coward]. Bucharest: Albatros, 1998.

Coronil, Fernando. *The Magical State: Nature, Money, and Modernity in Venezuela*. Chicago: University of Chicago Press, 1997.

———. "State Reflections: The 2002 Coup against Hugo Chavez." In *The Revolution in Venezuela: Social and Political Change under Chávez*, edited by Thomas Ponniah and Jonathan Eastwood, 39–67. Cambridge, MA: Harvard University Press, 2011.

Corrigan, Philip, and Derek Sayer. *The Great Arch: English State Formation as Cultural Revolution*. Oxford: Blackwell, 1985.

Drakulić, Slavenka. *They Would Never Hurt a Fly: War Criminals on Trial in The Hague*. New York: Viking, 2004.

Engerman, David C. *Know Your Enemy: The Rise and Fall of America's Soviet Experts*. Oxford: Oxford University Press, 2009.

Fitzpatrick, Sheila. *A Spy in the Archives: A Memoir of Cold War Russia*. New York: I. B. Tauris, 2014.

Florescu, Gheorghe-Ilie. *Confesiunile unui cafegiu* [Confessions of a coffee-maker]. Bucharest: Humanitas, 2008.

Foucault, Michel. "What Is an Author?" In *The Foucault Reader*, edited by Paul Rabinow, 101–20. New York: Pantheon, 1984.

Garton Ash, Timothy. *The File: A Personal History*. New York: Vintage, 1997.

Gellately, Robert. "Denunciations in Twentieth-Century Germany: Aspects of Self-Policing in the Third Reich and the German Democratic Republic." In *Accusatory*

Practices: Denunciation in Modern European History, 1789–1989, edited by Sheila Fitzpatrick and Robert Gellately, 185–221. Chicago: University of Chicago Press, 1997.

Georgescu, Diana. "'Ceaușescu's Children': The Making and Unmaking of Romania's Last Socialist Generation (1965–2010)." PhD diss., University of Illinois, 2014.

Gerard, Emily. *The Land beyond the Forest: Facts, Figures, and Fancies from Transylvania.* Edinburgh: W. Blackwood, 1888.

Gökarıksel, Saygun. "Of Truths, Secrets, and Loyalties: Political Belonging and State Building in Poland after State Socialism." PhD diss., City University of New York, 2015.

Grigore, Monica. "Ceaușescu și redefinirea raporturilor dintre partid și Securitatea" [Ceaușescu and the redefinition of relations between the Party and Securitate]. *Arhivele Securității* (2004): 395–420.

Hacking, Ian. "Making Up People." *London Review of Books* 28 (17 August 2006): 23–26.

Haggerty, Kevin D., and Richard V. Ericson. "The Surveillant Assemblage." *British Journal of Sociology* 51 (2000): 605–22.

Hall, Richard Andrew. "The Historiography of the Romanian Revolution: The Uses of Absurdity and the Triumph of Securitate Revisionism." *The Archive of the Romanian Revolution of December 1989* (blog), 31 December 2013, https://romanianrevolutionofdecember1989.com/2013/12/31/the-historiography-of-the-romanian-revolution-the-uses-of-absurdity-and-the-triumph-of-securitate-revisionism/.

Hulubaș, Constantin. "Ce motive a avut informatorul să accepte colaborarea?" [What reasons did the informer have to accept collaboration?]. *Securitatea* 36 (1976): 56–59.

Humphrey, Caroline. *Karl Marx Collective: Economy, Society, and Religion in a Siberian Collective Farm.* Cambridge: Cambridge University Press, 1983.

Ileana, Princess of Romania. *I Live Again.* London: Victor Gollancz, 1952.

Ioanid, Radu. "Anatomia delațiunii" [The anatomy of denunciation]. *Observatorul Cultural* 139 (22 October 2002). http://www.observatorcultural.ro/numar/nr-139/.

Jacknis, Ira. "Margaret Mead and Gregory Bateson in Bali." *Cultural Anthropology* 3 (1988): 160–77.

Jones, Graham M. "Secrecy." *Annual Review of Anthropology* 43 (2014): 53–69.

Karnoouh, Claude. "Une plongée au cœur de la police politique roumaine." *La Pensée Libre* 26 (September 2009). http://www.lapenseelibre.org/article-une-plongee-au-coeur-de-la-police.

Király, István V. *Fenomenologia existențială a secretului* [The existential phenomenology of the secret]. Bucharest: Editura Paralela 45, 2001.

Kligman, Gail. *The Politics of Duplicity: Controlling Reproduction in Ceaușescu's Romania.* Berkeley: University of California Press, 1998.

———. *The Wedding of the Dead: Ritual, Poetics, and Popular Culture in Transylvania.* Berkeley: University of California Press, 1988.

Kligman, Gail, and Katherine Verdery. *Peasants under Siege: The Collectivization of Romanian Agriculture, 1949–1962.* Princeton, NJ: Princeton University Press, 2011.

Liiceanu, Gabriel. *Dragul meu turnător* [My dear snitch]. Bucharest: Humanitas, 2013.

Łoś, Maria. "Lustration and Truth Claims: Unfinished Revolutions in Central Europe." *Law & Social Inquiry* 20 (1995): 117–61.

Lyon, David, ed. *Theorizing Surveillance: The Panopticon and Beyond*. Cullompton, UK: Willan, 2006.

Macrea-Toma, Ioana. "The Eyes of Radio Free Europe: Regimes of Visibility in the Cold War Archives." *East Central Europe* 44 (2017): 99–127.

Maguire, Mark, Catarina Frois, and Nils Zurawski, eds. *The Anthropology of Security: Perspectives from the Frontline of Policing, Counter-Terrorism, and Border Control*. London: Pluto, 2014.

Manea, Cătălin. "Securistul Ţinca" [Securitate officer Ţinca]. *Tunuri din Bihor*, 26 September 2007. http://tunuridinbihor.blogspot.com/2007/09/securistul-inc.html.

Marche, Stephen. "The Epidemic of Facelessness." *New York Times*, 15 February 2015, SR1, 6–7.

Masco, Joseph. *The Theatre of Operations: National Security Affect from the Cold War to the War on Terror*. Durham, NC: Duke University Press, 2014.

Miłosz, Czesław. *Native Realm: A Search for Self-Definition*. Garden City, NY: Doubleday, 1968.

Müller, Herta. *The Appointment: A Novel*. New York: Metropolitan, 2001.

———. "Every Word Knows Something of a Vicious Circle." Nobel Prize Lecture, 7 December 2009. https://www.nobelprize.org/nobel_prizes/literature/ laureates /2009/muller-lecture_en.html.

———. "Securitate in All but Name" (interview). *SignandSight.com*, 31 August 2009. http://www.signandsight.com/features/1910.html.

Nedelcovici, Bujor. "Amara bucurie de la capătul drumului spre adevăr" [The bitter happiness at the end of the road to truth]. *Revista 22* (15 April 2002). http:// revista22online.ro/69/.html.

Oprea, Marius. *Moştenitorii Securităţii* [Heirs of the Securitate]. Bucharest: Humanitas, 2004.

Perrault, Gilles. *Dossier 51: An Entertainment*. Translated by Douglas Parmée. London: Weidenfeld and Nicolson, 1971.

Poenaru, Florin. "Contesting Illusions: History and Intellectual Class Struggles in (Post)socialist Romania." PhD diss., Central European University, Budapest, 2013.

Price, David. *Cold War Anthropology: The CIA, the Pentagon, and the Growth of Dual Use Anthropology*. Durham, NC: Duke University Press, 2016.

Reinke, Herbert. "Policing Politics in Germany from Weimar to the Stasi." In *The Policing of Politics in the Twentieth Century: Historical Perspectives*, edited by Mark Mazower, 71–106. Providence, RI: Berghahn, 1997.

Saunders, Frances Stonor. *The Cultural Cold War: The CIA and the World of Arts and Letters*. New York: New Press, 1999.

Şerbulescu, Andrei (Belu Zilber). *Monarhia de drept dialectic* [The monarchy of dialectical law]. Bucharest: Humanitas, 1991.

Sökefeld, Martin, and Sabine Strasser, eds. "Under Suspicious Eyes: Surveillance States, Security Zones and Ethnographic Fieldwork." Special issue of *Zeitschrift für Ethnologie* 141 (2016).

Stan, Lavinia, ed. *Transitional Justice in Eastern Europe and the Former Soviet Union: Reckoning with the Communist Past*. London: Routledge, 2009.

Stocking, George. *Glimpses into My Own Black Box: An Exercise in Self-Deconstruction*. Madison: University of Wisconsin Press, 2010.

Szűcs, Anikó. "Performing the Informer: State Security Files Recontextualized in the Hungarian Art World." PhD diss., New York University, 2015.

Tănase, Stelian. *Acasă se vorbeşte în şoaptă: Dosar şi jurnal din anii tîrzii ai dictaturii* [At home they speak in whispers: File and journal from the late years of the dictatorship]. Bucharest: Compania, 2002.

Taussig, Michael. *Defacement: Public Secrecy and the Labor of the Negative*. Stanford, CA: Stanford University Press, 1999.

Teodorescu, Filip. *Un risc asumat: Timişoara decembrie 1989* [A risk assumed: Timişoara, December 1989]. Craiova, Romania: Editura Viitorul Românesc, 1992.

Tomlin, Lily. *The Search for Signs of Intelligent Life in the Universe*. Written by Jane Wagner. New Almaden, CA: Wolfe Video, 1992.

Tudoran, Dorin. *Eu, fiul lor: Dosar de Securitate* [I, their son: Securitate file]. Iaşi: Polirom, 2010.

Turnaturi, Gabriella. *Betrayals: The Unpredictability of Human Relations*. Translated by Lydia G. Cochrane. Chicago: University of Chicago Press, 2007.

Vatulescu, Cristina. *Police Aesthetics: Literature, Film, and the Secret Police in Soviet Times*. Stanford, CA: Stanford University Press, 2010.

Verdery, Katherine. "Homage to a Transylvanian Peasant." *East European Politics and Societies* 3 (1989): 51–82.

———. *National Ideology under Socialism: Identity and Cultural Politics in Ceauşescu's Romania*. Berkeley: University of California Press, 1991.

———. *Secrets and Truths: Ethnography in the Archive of the Romanian Secret Police*. Budapest: Central European University Press, 2014.

———. *Transylvanian Villagers: Three Centuries of Political, Economic, and Ethnic Change*. Berkeley: University of California Press, 1983.

———. *The Vanishing Hectare: Property and Value in Postsocialist Transylvania*. Ithaca, NY: Cornell University Press, 2003.

Visson, Lynn. *Wedded Strangers: The Challenges of Russian-American Marriages*. New York: Hippocrene, 1998.

Vultur, Smaranda. "Daily Life and Surveillance in the 1970s and 1980s." In *Remembering Communism: Private and Public Recollections of Lived Experience in Southeast Europe*, edited by Maria Todorova, Augusta Dimou, and Stefan Troebst, 417–36. Budapest: Central European University Press, 2014.

INDEX

Ceauşescu, Nicolae (*continued*)
141, 142; and "Gang of Four," 156; and
Hungarians, 156, 175; opposition to, 167;
and village demolition plan, 155
Cernea, Mihail (or Michael), 34, 45, 64
Charter 77, 167
CIA, 154, 157, 184–85, 260, 300n13; front
organizations of, 16; KV suspected as
agent of, 13, 15, 24, 36, 113, 130, 133, 136,
178, 223–24, 257; and Woodrow Wilson
Center, 172–73. *See also* embassy, of the
U.S. in Bucharest; Verdery, Katherine
CIE (Centrul de Informaţii Externe).
See Foreign Intelligence Service
(Romania)
clientelism, 287, 307n19
Cluj, 5, 13, 50, 106, 112, 145, 166, 176, 183,
184, 186; and Hungarians, 105, 113,
150–52; secret trip to, 133–36, 272–74;
and Securitate, 36, 85, 121, 153, 157, 158,
166, 171, 196, 260–61, 269, 305n19
CNSAS (National Council for the Study of
the Securitate Archives, Romania), xiv,
9–10, 14, 85, 113, 117, 131, 154–55, 170,
171–72, 186, 196, 199, 200, 212, 214, 237,
267–68, 275, 302n10. *See also* Verdery,
Katherine: documentary film about
Cold War, xi–xii, 2, 9, 15, 34, 38, 62, 63,
104, 113, 125, 151, 247, 265, 271; and anthropology, 18, 24, 81, 164; and "empire
of fear" paradigm, 279–80, 288, 289;
ideology, 62–64, 179; and production of
knowledge, 188
Cole, John, 303n18
collective farm, 47, 49, 51, 53, 65–66, 71, 92,
99, 178, 302n7
"communism," as construct, 38, 55, 57,
62–64, 104, 164, 186
compartmentalization (Securitate work
practice), 14, 29, 250, 265, 275, 300n11
Corbeanu, Nicolae, 231
Cornea, Doina, 24
counterespionage. *See* Third Directorate
Cugir, 48, 50, 51, 53–54, 79, 89, 92, 223–24
Czech Republic, 167, 300n9

data-mining, 185
Davis, Gloria, 59, 68, 89, 183
deconspire (reveal informers' names), 196,
199, 230
denigration of Romania, Securitate concern, 104, 132, 133, 224, 265, 267–68.
See also "socio-political information"
Deva, 42, 44, 45, 46, 48, 72, 83, 89, 96, 100,
113, 134, 149, 157, 224–25
Diaconescu, General Gheorghe, 111, 154, 161
Dinescu, Mircea, 285
diplomatic pouch, 35–36, 45, 60, 303n15.
See also Bucharest
Directorate 3 (or III). *See* Third Directorate
disinformation: by CIA, 173; by KV, 103,
150; by Securitate, 6, 48, 127, 159–60,
247, 269–70, 303n13
dissidents: in Eastern Europe, 24, 166–68,
172, 178, 258, 280, 282, 284–85; and KV,
xi, 5, 166, 174, 176, 260, 294
doppelganger, 4–8, 16–18, 25–28, 48, 60,
81, 191, 233, 294; as virus, 7. *See also*
identity, identities; "VERA"
Dosar de reţea (file of an informer). *See*
informers, for Securitate: files of
Dossier 51, 181
"Dragomir, S.," 166, 168–69, 171, 245,
257–63, 265, 268, 283
Drakulić, Slavenka, 255–56
dreams, 93, 96, 148, 187–88, 199, 249–50,
256–67
DUI (*Dosar de urmărire informativă*, or dossier
of informative pursual), 15, 76, 97, 98,
111, 135, 177, 216, 273–74

eavesdropping, 14, 27, 38, 43, 60, 82–83,
105–6, 108–9, 114–15, 135, 151, 157, 160,
209, 217, 257, 274. *See also* "Teo"
"element" (person being followed). *See*
"target"
embassy, of the U.S. in Bucharest, vii, 38,
45, 60, 78, 98, 112; KV connections with,
35–36, 116, 131; personnel suspected of
being CIA agents, 16, 253. *See also* diplomatic pouch

Ghani, Ashraf, 59, 165
Gheorghiu, Mihai Dinu, 159–60
Ghibernea, Dan, 87–88, 90, 127, 170, 171, 183, 284
Gierek, Edward, 141
Gökarıksel, Saygun, 283–84
Gorbachev, Mikhail, 113, 156, 175–76
gossip, 51, 61, 116, 149, 152, 160, 219, 269; as field resource, 67, 69, 178. *See also* surveillance
Graduate Center, City University of New York, 99
Greek Catholic (or Uniate) Church, 215–16
"Grigorescu, I.," 245–40, 251–57, 260, 262, 264, 270, 272, 283
Grudzinska-Gross, Irina, 185, 189
Gurasada (Transylvanian settlement), 45–46
"Gypsies" (Roma), 99, 300n12

Hacking, Ian, 29, 292
Happiness Journal (Nicolae Steinhardt), 168
harm, 6, 96, 177, 233, 238–44, 253, 271, 272–76
Hiebert (Beissinger), Margaret, 303n18
homosexual behavior, 82, 163, 214, 221–22. *See also* informers, for Securitate: recruitment of
"hostile" (Securitate label, as in "hostile manifestations"), 4, 101, 112, 153, 158, 167–68, 170, 173, 177, 213, 220
Hotel Continental (Cluj), 114–15, 127, 160, 183, 219
Hotel Lido (Bucharest), 166
hotel receptionists as informers, 42–43, 83–85, 128, 130, 209, 219
Hotel Sarmis (Deva), 42, 82–83
Hunedoara County, 64, 102, 113, 145, 176, 305n19; census of, 46; Center for Popular Creation and Folklore, 42; KV trip through, in 1973, xii, 1–2, 41–46, 64, 76
Hungary, 44, 49, 102, 142, 223, 241, 268, 287, 300n9

Iancu, "Aunt" Lina, 69–70
Iaşi, 13, 85, 117, 131, 152, 159, 167
identity, identities, xi, 5, 7, 21, 28, 61, 79, 294; of ethnographers, 15, 23–25, 26–27, 59, 69; ethno-national, 70–74, 118, 125, 158, 302n6; fragmented, 270, 293; hiding of, 18, 37, 97, 137; and informers, 196, 211; and kinship, 24, 55; of KV, 9, 35, 59–60, 62, 69, 81–82, 96–100, 131, 175, 179, 293–94; of people in this book, 25; of Securitate officers, 19, 305n19; and sex, 81–82, 84, 162–64; and surveillance, xi–xii, 5, 165, 293–94
Ileana of Romania, Princess, 306n25
inequality, social, 65–68, 70
Informer, The (Mihai Albu), 185, 233
informers, for Securitate, 22, 77, 85, 98, 195–97, 210, 236, 241; "depth," 244; doppelgangers and, 195, 211; exculpating, 93–94, 240, 243–44; files of, 93, 204, 209, 210, 212, 216–17, 234, 266; and identity, 234, 239–40; instructions to, 42–44; numbers of, in Romania, 94, 208; and pedagogical relations with officers, 89–90, 203–4, 206; and political prisoners, 215–16, 235, 240; recruitment of, 15, 19, 22, 54, 60, 78, 83–86, 92–94, 136, 163, 183, 196, 200, 202–5, 209–14, 221, 232–33, 235, 240, 242–43, 260, 266, 269, 274, 286–88; reports by, 35, 74, 85, 87–89, 92–95, 98, 100, 105, 123, 150–51, 159, 160, 162, 170, 173, 183, 198, 201–3, 208–11, 213, 214, 215–17, 219, 220, 224, 226, 227, 230, 234, 242–44, 249–50, 254, 261; and sex, 78, 85; and stomach aches, 202, 204, 206, 221, 234; and third-person pronoun, 211, 239. *See also* "Beniamin"; betrayals; deconspire; Verdery, Katherine
informers of KV: "Alex," 219–22; "Anca," 159–60, 183; "Groza," 214–17, 249, 269; "Iacob," 90–93; "Lazăr," 86–90; Mariana, 174, 206, 214, 233–41, 244, 275; "Muller," 212–14; "Silviu," 100, 198, 222–27, 230; "Viorel," 217–19

"nationalist-irredentist" (Securitate code word for Hungarians), 102, 112, 152, 174, 222, 292, 308n22

networks: of KV, 54, 81; of Securitate, 54, 174, 199, 275, 285, 287, 289, 307n19; social, 243, 289, 307n19

NKVD (Soviet Secret Police, 1934–46), 20, 299n1

N.O. (officer's note on Securitate document), xiv, 42, 67, 72, 82, 197, 217, 223

Noica, Constantin, 167

oath of secrecy/silence, 196, 201–2, 210, 211, 213–14, 218, 235, 237–38, 244, 245, 248, 255, 258, 275, 288, 289. *See also* informers, for Securitate: recruitment of; secrecy/secrets

"obiectiv" (person being followed). *See* "target"

Oprea, Marius, 279–80

Orăştie, xiv, 46, 148, 224, 295

Orbán, Viktor, 300n9

Pacepa, General Ion Mihai, 103, 104, 299n1

Paleologu, Alexandru, 166–67, 169–71

paranoia, 38, 149, 156, 186, 199, 201, 218, 266, 302n4

Patriotism, as grounds for recruiting informers, 202, 211, 213, 235, 269; and Secus, 104, 268

Pauker, Ana, 306n25

Periscop (magazine), 306n1

persona non grata, 15, 154, 176, 178, 300n12

plan for recruiting informers. *See* informers, for Securitate

pledge of secrecy. *See* oath of secrecy/silence

Pleşiţa, General Nicolae, 268

Poland, 141, 167, 211, 241, 282, 283, 300n9

police, local, 3, 127, 143, 149, 208, 286; and KV, 79, 94, 148–49, 218

Pop, Professor Mihai, 39–42, 44–46, 48–50, 65, 119, 148, 222

Popescu, Ştefan, 54, 69

"positive influence," 101, 117, 119, 175, 178, 266

"precursory acts" for penal pursuit, 170–71, 258, 261, 304n7. *See also* Verdery, Katherine: planned arrest of

Price, David H., 16, 300n13, 302n3, 303n15

Prodan, Professor David, 104–9, 119, 122–26, 167, 178, 214–15, 303n21

pseudonyms, xiii–xiv, 5, 14–15, 25–26, 85, 88, 114, 130, 166, 172, 195–96, 209, 210, 268, 293, 305n19

"Pygmalion moments," 27, 245–70

"radioactive," as quality of targets, 85, 88, 94, 95, 174

Radio Free Europe (RFE), 122, 218, 274

Randall, Stephen, 303n18

Reagan, Ronald, 113, 265

recruitment. *See* informers, for Securitate: recruitment of

redactions of documents, 12, 196, 207–8, 299n2

Reed College, 84

reflexivity, 19, 28, 227, 300n17

Romania, and file access, 9, 300n9

Romanian Communist Party, member of, 54, 64, 67, 135, 209, 218, 266

Rosaldo, Renato and Michelle, 129–30

rumors, 19, 48, 54, 61, 127, 129, 133, 143, 148–49, 152, 176, 219, 272, 275

rural areas, Securitate coverage of, 94, 127, 210

Sampson, Steven, 300n12, 303n18

second economy (black market), 116, 145–46

secrecy/secrets, xii, 3, 14, 19–23, 27–29, 164, 175, 189, 205, 218, 245, 248, 293–94, 301n18. *See also* fear; invisibility; oath of secrecy/silence; state

Secrets and Truths, 12, 22, 28, 259, 262–63, 277, 284, 290, 300n11, 301n18

Securitate (Romanian secret police), xii, 29, 104, 185, 208–9, 239, 284; actions of, concerning KV, 60–62, 72, 74, 77–78, 84, 89, 101–2, 112, 116–18, 125,

128, 140–41, 157–58, 162, 168–74; and
austerity, 143–46; and battle over image,
278–79; as co-authors of this book, 27;
education of, 17, 214, 233, 247, 281–82;
as embedded in population, 248, 250,
266, 285–89, 307n19; follow KV to U.S.,
172–73; as "information officers," 278;
and injunction to silence, 203; "making up people," 29, 131, 175–76, 245;
negotiated relations with, 285–86, 288;
after 1989 revolution, 8–9, 194, 200,
237, 262, 267, 278–79, 288, 307n19; and
reasons for seeing KV as spy, 130–31;
"recruit" KV, 277–78; and relations with
Communist Party, 54, 304n4; technical
endowment of, 137–39; workings of, 28,
156, 185. *See also* disinformation; doppelganger; eavesdropping; informers,
for Securitate; oath of secrecy/silence;
"positive influence"; shadowing; "Teo";
Verdery, Katherine
self-fashioning, 26, 81, 84, 117, 131
self-verification, 137
serfs, Romanian, 101, 122
sex, 77–78, 81–85, 130, 149, 160–63, 197,
203, 217, 222
shadowing (following a target, R. *filaj*),
8, 11, 14, 20, 78, 85, 134–35, 136–37, 157,
168–71, 181, 184, 188, 265, 275, 303n13.
See also eavesdropping; "Teo"
Siguranța, 93, 281–82
Skinner, G. William, 34, 36, 44, 45, 46, 60,
62, 64, 66, 68, 81, 88, 302n1
social media, 27, 199, 228, 293
social relationships/connections, 244, 285,
287, 288–90, 293, 297
"socio-political information," 4, 18, 68,
104, 133, 139, 146, 157, 166, 174, 176–78,
260, 265, 294
solidarity movement, 141, 167, 282
Soviet Union, 20, 73, 103, 206, 300n13
spies, spying, 5, 15, 23, 49, 60–61, 132–35,
301n26; culturally specific meanings of,
79, 103, 113, 132, 253, 260, 265; as role
with function, 132

Spy in the Archives, A (Sheila Fitzpatrick),
276, 303n22
SRI (Serviciul Român de Informație; Romanian Information Service post-1989),
12, 178, 267, 279, 299n2, 305n24
Stahl, Henri H., 118
Stasi (East German Secret Police), 27, 93,
118, 130, 181–82, 208, 283, 287, 300n9
state, 5, 21–22, 281, 284, 293, 297; apparatus of, 289, 292; and secrecy, 19–23
Steinhardt, Nicolae, 138, 167–69, 171
Stockholm syndrome, 262
Stocking, George, 300n8
stomach aches, of informers, 202, 204,
206, 221, 234
suitcases, 10, 20, 62, 89, 102, 128,
303n15
surveillance, xi–xii, 3, 11, 86, 272, 297; and
effects on ethnographer, 5, 11, 18–19, 28,
119, 127, 137, 145, 147–50, 165, 181–90,
276, 293; efforts to evade, 133–35; file
(DUI), 15, 33, 74–78, 121, 216; of foreign
scholars, 9, 155, 293; high-tech, 292–93;
of Hungarians, 156; intensified, 103, 135,
265; as labor-intensive, 292–93; of Ralf
Bierman, 273–75; by Romania's Foreign
Intelligence Service (CIE), 172–73; rules
concerning, in Romania, 54; and socializing, 92; U.S. Embassy warnings about,
38, 45, 279; village gossip as, 60–61, 160;
worldwide, xii, 297. *See also* informers,
for Securitate; Securitate
surveillance photos from KV file, 6, 20,
161, 169, 170
Szűcs, Anikó, 241–42

Tănase, Stelian, 142, 239, 299n7
tape-recording, 25, 49, 87, 129, 137–39,
147–49, 169, 184, 199–200, 235–36, 238,
248, 252, 259
Tar, Sándor, 241–42
"target" (suspected spy being followed;
also *obiectiv*), 1, 7, 14–15, 116–19; function, 291–94, 308n22; as "radioactive,"
85, 291–93

"volunteers" (spontaneous informers), 286–87, 289

Vultur, Smaranda (Romanian ethnographer), 243

Wallerstein, Immanuel, 99

"wealth in people," 289, 307n21

winter of 1984–85. *See* austerity

Wm. *See* Skinner, G. William

Writers Union, 167, 169

Zilber, Belu (Andrei Şerbulescu), 188

Zimmer, Heinrich, 293

Zub, Alexandru, 167, 170